Horoscope for the New Age

by E. Alan Meece

philosopherswheel.com

ISBN: 9781695874268

Table of Contents

Horoscope for the New Age

by E. Alan Meece

Chapter One

The New Age is Dawning

The New Age is dawning. A new consciousness is rising. New movements are coming forth to change the world. This chapter, and this book, describes how I see this new age unfolding.

We can see the New Age dawning everywhere. All over Planet Earth, people are waking up to the miracle of life, and to their potential to create beauty and joy. All around the world, people have more access to wealth and prosperity than ever before. New technology connects each of us to everyone, in every country and in every city and town on the planet. People have been freed as never before from old restrictions, and we can pursue lives that we want. More people seek a higher purpose in life than mere survival, and they have greater freedom to unfold it. We are no longer restricted to one career path chosen for us by the authorities for our entire lives but can continue to change and develop new talents. The limited goals and expectations of the past are behind us, as the people of every race, gender and creed stretch beyond the ancient barriers put upon them and claim their rights and their powers.

No longer can tyrants and bigots hold us down without suffering the consequences, at least eventually. No longer can a few rich tycoons and barons hoard the wealth of the people without feeling that their days of domination are numbered, and that they will suffer the reckoning and realization that the world belongs to all of us, not just to them. No longer can one nation or tribe claim our sole allegiance, as we realize that we are linked together as one humanity, that we are all in this life together, and that peace is our destiny.

No people in history has ever had the access that we have to all the knowledge and experiences in the world. Buried and restricted from our sight for centuries, all the great art and architecture from all of humanity's cultures and traditions has been revealed to us, and it can inspire even greater works than these. Books, movies, libraries, concerts, schools, universities, and the vast resources of the internet are all available to us. No people in history has had such ability as do we in the New Age to learn about any subject and acquire any ability. No people in history has ever possessed more tools and more media in which to express our inspiration and imagination than we have, just waiting for us to take up our brushes, pens, graphics, instruments, cameras, and high-tech multi-media, and make it real.

New experiences have awakened and inspired us. Modernist movements, counter-cultures, human potential techniques, social liberation movements, cyber worlds, fairs and festivals, new age spirituality, psychedelic agents, teachers and gurus, and spontaneous spiritual awakenings; all these and more have helped bring the New Age to life for us. It has been expressed in our music and visionary arts, including in new age and ambient sounds, in the most inspired of rock n roll music, through brilliant songwriters, and in imaginative paintings and multi-media creations few could have seen anywhere on Earth before recent times. Barriers have been broken in human relationships too, as possibilities have opened up for us to be more authentic, more alive and more intimate, and to discover what it really means to be human. We've learned how to release ourselves from the repressive programming of the past, as we discover how to truly care, value and respect ourselves and each other as the amazing miracles that we are.

The New Age worldview is spreading, despite efforts to suppress, co-opt and marginalize it. The New Paradigm is here and can no longer be denied. We are liberated from authoritarian, confining traditions and beliefs, whether they come from dogmatic religion, or from limited, outdated scientific notions. No one religion or one scientific theory or method can be held up any longer as the absolute truth, or as the only way that renders all others as heretics and superstitious fools. We all have immediate access to the truths from all lands, all times, all peoples and all sources. We are no longer slaves to what we are told to believe; we can know and discover the truth for ourselves. Nothing can be hidden away from us anymore.

Quantum physics shows us how every particle of light and every wave of energy is entangled with every other, and how we the observer are intimately connected with everything we observe. Ecology and the environmental movement have impressed upon us how all life forms are interwoven and interdependent on our whole, conscious Mother Gaia Earth Being. We know now that our every action affects everyone and everything on our planet, and that we must take care of Her if we wish to survive and prosper in the future. We know now that we can continue to grow and learn throughout our lives, and that our age in years is almost irrelevant. We know that the miracle of conscious awareness cannot be reduced to or explained by mechanical forces, and that the idolatry of falsely modeling the universe upon our own human ability to use forces of Nature to build our own machines has become apparent to us. We know now that technology and commerce cannot define and confine our life and our spirit.

In the New Age, esoteric and occult knowledge from East and West has become available to us again, and our psychic and intuitive powers are opening up. We are looking not only into the once-hidden realities of life on Earth, but into the spirit worlds beyond this life, and into the divine being within all. We are discovering our connections to eternal Infinite Spirit, even amidst the changing and eternal here and now. We are finding that the old hidden hermetic maxim deep within Western Tradition that says "as above, so below; as within, so without" applies to every aspect of our lives, as revealed in the holographic nature of reality, in fractals and epigenetic DNA replicated in every cell of our bodies, and in the rebirth of astrology and alchemy in our time. As the New Age dawns, the world is becoming more and more enchanted again, more alive with subtle, mystic, tender beauty again, and alive with wonder and joy again.

But all this is only the beginning. The New Age has only just started. Much remains to be discovered, and many problems and challenges remain. And there's many different opinions about the best ways forward. Again, this is how I see it.

In my previous book, upon which this one depends and which it extends, I asked whether we were entering hell or paradise. Was a golden age dawning, I asked, or was the world coming to an end? That book, <u>Horoscope for the New Millennium</u>, laid out in print the landscape of time, showing where we came from, where we were, and where we were going as the milestone of the Year 2000 (or Y2K as it was known) approached. Many other prophecies were being made from many sources too in those years; some reliable and some not. Many people feared for the future, just as they had done when the previous new millennium was approaching 1000 years before. I laid out the cycles and positions of the planets in order to provide some perspective and clarity from the larger view. I looked into the temporal telescope to chart the rhythms of hundreds and thousands of years of history and relayed to my readers a vision into where these rhythms and cycles might take us. I gave verifiable evidence that the planetary cycles are reliable guides to the course of events on Earth and provided the first complete account of their unfolding. What I found was conclusive evidence that indeed, a golden age was upon us, and that a new age was dawning.

At that time, in the 1990s, we had just elected the first president from "my generation," the so-called Baby Boomers; a president who intended to bring back some progress and some shared responsibility to our nation. The "cold war" between two superpowers and two alliances that had threatened the world with nuclear destruction had just come to an end, opening up the prospect of a "peace dividend." Many new nations had been formed, bringing new freedom to the world. The last president from the world war two generation had just declared a "new world order" in which the United Nations for the first time could actually enforce rules of good behavior among nations, as had been its original purpose. The high-tech inventions of personal computers, the internet and the world wide web powered an unprecedented economic prosperity in the "dot.com boom" and brought the world together in communication as never before. It seemed like commerce was shifting forever away from brick and mortar stores to an online realm. The multi-media cyber-world gave everyone for the first time the ability to publish their works and their views to the whole world and opened up whole new vistas of amazing computer art creations. The exciting possibilities of psychedelic culture, first explored in the mid-1960s, was coming back in new ways in the wonderful group dances called "raves," with their elaborate new electronic music that was sweeping through the youth cultures of the world. My prophecy of a golden age seemed plausible, back then.

But as the New Millennium actually began, the war clouds that I predicted would hover over this new dawn appeared. The United States and some of its allies went right back to unending war, this time with "terrorists" as the enemy, in the wake of airplanes crashing into the World Trade Center in New York City on 9-11-2001. With this horrendous terrorist act as a pretext, the next Baby Boomer president decided that the United States had the right and the duty to "spread democracy around the world" by invading other countries without reason, and so the USA attacked Iraq in March of 2003, in spite of the largest protests the world had ever seen. The peace dividend was squandered, and the USA national debt was forever inflated beyond redemption. In the years from 1994 to 2017, shared responsibility was often ditched again in favor of unleashing the unrestrained free market. The clouds were gathering again, and people once again feared for the future. The new golden age lost its luster. Were we entering hell, after all?

As I predicted, the economic crash and great recession in 2008-2010 resulting from these policies brought down the dot.com boom and destroyed prosperity for untold millions. Waves of revolution thereupon spread across the world starting in 2011, causing unprecedented civil wars and waves of refugees from the third world to the first, again just as I had predicted would happen in my previous book. The greatest ecological disaster ever caused by humanity broke open hundreds of oil wells to pollute the Gulf of Mexico in 2010. This amazing calamity only further warned the world that our continued use of fossil fuels for energy, our meat farming, and the tearing down of our forests was warming the globe to such an extent that the continued existence of civilization was threatened. But the warning of global warming went largely unheeded. In spite of unimpeachable evidence, the old outdated and dirty energy companies financed a campaign of denial and conspiracy theory that delayed action to solve the climate crisis, in spite of a worldwide agreement to do so in 2015. Then, as the late 2010s proceeded, a host of demagogues and tyrants regained or ascended the thrones and oval offices of many governments around the world, cutting off the revolutions for freedom that had erupted in 1989 and 2011, and using the refugees and "terrorists" as scapegoats. Meanwhile, the younger generations and many older ones seemed swept up again in the old modern and traditional skepticism, as the outdated physicalist dogmas and religious fanaticisms obscured once again the new age vision that had opened up in the decades before the New Millennium began.

And so, the question remains unanswered. Where we are going? What lies beyond that marker of time in 2012 indicated by the Mayan Calendar that became famous as "the end of the world as we know it"? Can the promise of the New Millennium ever be fulfilled? The challenge remains for the people to rise up and bring about the New Age; to create a peaceful and sustainable world with freedom and prosperity for all. The prospect remains to fully unleash human potential, and to continue rekindling and restoring the wonder and miracle of life.

What do "the stars" have to say about this prospect? Maybe this newly revised *horoscope for the new age* cannot be so glowingly optimistic as the first version from the 1990s was. Maybe my years have brought more realism into my forecasts. But the stars also indicate that an alternative course from inevitable destruction is still possible. The planets predict that the crisis of the 2020s and 2030s can be successfully overcome, despite the inevitable conflicts, and that a new progressive era will unfold in these decades as I originally predicted. We can meet the challenge of climate change; it's not too late. We can restore progress again. We can depose the tyrants and the racist reactionaries again. We can bring back shared civic responsibility and economic opportunity for all and restrain the greedy again.

No, it's not too late! We still have all the potential for greatness that we had before the New Millennium arrived. We can still transform the New Millennium into the New Age. So please read ahead and discover what a thorough, continued investigation into the rhythms and cycles of the planets can reveal about the future. Examine the evidence of my predictions and decide for yourself if astrology works and to what extent. I have laid it all out for you again, without flinching and without prejudice. The basic landscape of time is the same for all, even though there's other interpretations of it besides my own idealistic and spiritual one. You can also look ahead to Chapter 13 and see what might happen for you personally. And the more you know about the larger landscape of time that applies to everyone, the more you'll understand your own destiny too. This road map is in your hands. It's up to us to use it for the best.

Chapter 2

Discovering the Great Cycles

In this chapter and the next, I review the meanings of the planets and their cycles I refer to in the coming chapters as I make my predictions. The great cycles which I describe in this chapter provide the framework within which I make my predictions in the following chapters. If you know astrology well, you can skip to Chapter 4. If you're new to astrology or need a refresher, this chapter and the next should help you, and you can also see the glossary in the back. In any case, I need to explain here how I discovered the great cycles, and why I think they are so significant. Then I will review here the basic landscape of time that these cycles outline for us, as described in my previous book Horoscope for the New Millennium, as well as many other terms I use for making the prophecies. So let's start at the beginning.

In the Fall of 1965, I would look out my window and see a strange fuzzy light. I was not sure what it was. But I knew that I was getting more curious about life then, and that something was happening in my world. I was only a teenager, but my mind was full of questions. I had been brought up in a scientific home, and I was interested in astronomy and biology. My Mom was a biology teacher, and my Dad an engineer. They did not believe in astrology, and were both agnostic or atheist. I accepted their ideas and I thought in scientific ways. But now I started to question this worldview of mine. Was mathematics really the greatest truth in the world, as I thought? Could science explain everything? If so, how could it explain the beauty that my eyes now beheld and that so moved me?

Many people of all ages were also starting to question things they had formerly believed. Authorities were under siege, from the civil rights movement, and from demonstrations against the War in Vietnam. Students were just starting to take LSD in huge numbers and experiencing alternate states of consciousness. Soon they were having acid test dances to the Grateful Dead rock band and forming new utopian communities. Young musicians all over the world started to form bands, hoping to be rock stars like The Beatles. It was a cultural explosion that they called a youthquake, and more than that, it was a turning point in history for everyone. People of all ages had mystical experiences at this time, many of whom I got to know a few years later. Others started questioning their social roles, protesting war and injustice, discovering new meanings and throwing off old restrictions.

Nowhere was this new counter-culture bigger than in the San Francisco Bay Area where I was living. One early Summer's Day in 1966 I went to my neighborhood theater in San Jose to see a movie called The Russians Are Coming, The Russians Are Coming. It was like a break in the Cold War then raging between the USA and the Soviet Union. I walked home from the movie as if I had felt something shift in me. A few days later, I felt ecstatic over the new music that started to come over the radio. The Byrds, Petula Clark, The Association, and then soon afterward a new album by the Beatles that featured a submarine, just like in the movie, and also an amazing psychedelic song that said love is all and love is everyone. I was discovering love as the source of beauty. It flowed through me as I looked into the sky. I felt the new culture rising up, and I said to myself, "there's something in the air!" Soon I was more sensitive than I had ever been, and visions of a new life stirred inside and around me. The enchantment I was talking about in the last chapter became a part of me. Then in August, our family went on an unforgettable vacation trip to Mendocino where the movie was filmed, so we could walk in the footsteps of the Russians and the Americans as they went through their comical, frenetic adventures. Mendocino was already a favorite place for us, and from then on the images from the movie and the town stayed in my mind.

With all this going on, my worldview was changing and I was opening up to new ideas. I was fascinated with ghosts, and I started studying Zen and philosophy. I heard an old prophet on the radio, Gavin Chester Arthur, grandson of the president, talk about the LSD experiences he had with his friend Alan Watts, who was one of the philosophers I was reading, and whom my parents also knew from their days as co-founders of Pacific Radio. Gavin Arthur was also an astrologer, and his words opened my eyes. And I found out that a lot of the hippies in San Francisco called themselves star children because they followed "the stars." So a few months later, in late 1967, I started reading about it. Then right after learning the meaning of the planets and signs, I started testing it out for myself. I discovered to my complete surprise that I could predict all the positions in my horoscope before looking them up.

Not long after that, I learned that the planets Uranus, Neptune and Pluto, although far away and invisible, represented the movements and changes in society and culture. They were, said the astrologers, the carriers of the new ideas brought into our culture by a creative minority; the genius inventors and artists, the revolutionaries and the non-conformists. So, I thought, it was time for another test. Considering the amazing movements and counter-cultures that were shaking the country and the world at that time, in 1968 I predicted that at least two of those planets must then be lining up in a conjunction, since astrology says that's when they are at their most powerful. I looked it up and I saw that Uranus and Pluto were indeed making a conjunction. As they say, "the stars aligned." Then I asked myself, when would the energy of this alignment have been the greatest? I thought I knew when that was. So I looked it up, and to my shock and amazement, the exact alignment had happened exactly when I thought it did; just when I experienced my own awakening in the early Summer of 1966, when the new culture was exploding the most powerfully, and when mystic experiences were happening everywhere to people of all ages. I had verified astrology for myself to such an extent by these two tests that I could never doubt its truth again, no matter what the skeptics might say.

As I read more books and started learning to read charts for myself and other people, and to see it working in our lives, I came across The Modern Textbook of Astrology by Margaret Hone. I was struck by the statement in her book that the significance of the Neptune-Pluto conjunction in 1892 (the year she was born) would be unfolding throughout the 493 years of its full cycle.

This meant two things to me. First, I decided I needed to study history and see what happened at the times of all of these outer-planet conjunctions, not just those like the one I experienced so vividly in the sixties, but also those like this longer and more significant one from 1892. Second, I needed to consider that the movements of these outer planets mean something to us not only when they're exactly aligned, but also throughout their whole cycle of relationship through all their phases, just like phases of the Moon, and that we can still feel the conjunction of Neptune and Pluto as if it were sounding and ringing throughout the world from 1892 until this very day. The changes indicated by this conjunction, said Hone, were still developing.

Besides during the sixties, Humanity as a whole had already been through times of much greater adventure over the last two centuries. The discovery of Uranus, Neptune and Pluto by astronomers indicated the times when these new ideas and new abilities were opening up to us. When **Uranus** was discovered in 1781, the United States of America had just been formed, and it achieved its independence through victory at Yorktown that very year. This Revolution soon inspired the French to make a Revolution of their own, which spelled out for the first time ever the rights of man. Thomas Jefferson soon followed their example by proposing the Bill of Rights for the US Constitution. These events were like lightning bolts that awakened humanity and began a worldwide revolution for liberty, equality and fraternity that continues to this day. It opened up something like a Pandora's Box of new problems too.

Uranus also brought down more literal bolts of lightning at the same time by expanding our knowledge of light and electricity. Galvani galvanized the world in 1786 by discovering electric currents, which allowed Volta to make the first battery in 1799, and this soon opened up the whole world of magnetic fields to us, leading eventually to a new physics. The same scientist that found the first invisible planet Uranus soon afterward also discovered ultra-violet and infra-red rays, taking us beyond visible light. And the first radio-active element to sparkle into our awareness was quickly named after the new planet. Then Lavoisier invented chemistry in 1789, which transformed the world as we knew it into an ever-widening sea of invisible electrons and protons lighting up and radiating into our world. The Montgolfier Brothers fascinated us by inventing the hot-air balloon in 1783, and by carrying its first human passengers in 1786 in a fancy contraption decorated with the signs of the zodiac. Just as America achieved its independence in 1781, Immanuel Kant demonstrated how knowledge depends on our own categories of thought; a declaration of independence for the mind. Jacques Louis David electrified the art world in 1785 with his shocking call to action in Oath of the Horatii, beginning a new revolution in the arts that would be further expressed in the romantic turbulence of Turner and Delacroix and the prophetic poetry of William Blake, William Wordsworth and Lord Byron. Even the electricity within the body itself was revealed at this time by the mesmerizing work of Franz Mesmer, opening up the field of hypnotic healing. With the steam engine having been invented in 1769, in the 1780s it was harnessed to the industrial revolution, which mobilized productivity as never before, made Britain into the workshop of the world, and threatened to turn the whole planet into one big dehumanizing factory, and human beings into impoverished slaves to the machine.

Fortunately, the romantics saw through this destructive side of industry, and already the revolutionaries were demanding liberation for the new slaves. A new planet was on the way into our lives. Astronomers noticed that Uranus was not behaving as expected, because another planet further out was affecting its orbit. In fact, it was making a conjunction to it in about 1821. In 1846 they found it and named it **Neptune** after the god of the oceans. Indeed, new oceans were sweeping over humanity in the time of Neptune's discovery, as we started sailing over them as never before. Steamships started taking goods and people everywhere across the seas, including millions of refugees fleeing from a frightening famine in 1846. A new Revolution stirred the fires of national freedom all across Europe in 1848, and gold was discovered in California too that year, which attracted even more fleeing refugees, failed revolutionaries and fortune hunters, and helped to finance the industrial revolution as it expanded worldwide in the following years.

But the question soon became, who was entitled to possess all the gold that industry was generating? Karl Marx and Frederich Engels wrote the manifesto for the working class in 1848, providing the slaves to the industrial machine with a new path to power. From then on both the socialist movement and trade unions expanded, challenging the right of tycoons to be the sole owners of the new industries, and demanding safe working conditions and fair distribution of its profits. At the same time, benevolent heroes like Charles Dickens, Florence Nightingale and Clara Barton were calling for genuinely humane treatment for all those suffering in the factories and prisons and on the battlefields. Neptune signaled the dawn of real kindness and compassion in human society for the first time, and from then on it became the planet of the common people and their rights, and it represented the power of collective society to rein in and humanize competitive capitalism.

Meanwhile the oceanic feelings stirred by the new planet were also being formulated into new mystical religions in the mid-19th century, from the prophecy of world oneness in the Bahai Faith, to the Mormon latter day saints, to Christian Science, New Thought, Spiritualism, Theosophy, and all their New Age descendants. It was the religious dispensation for our time, just like those of Buddhism and Judaism, Christianity, and Islam in ages past. And Neptune is perhaps best expressed in romantic music and art, which has captivated the world from Beethoven and Chopin to the visual as well as the musical impressionists, and later it was further developed into the most sensitive ambient sounds.

By the 1890s, though, Neptune too was making a conjunction to a planet further out. Some astronomers were wondering if Neptune was straying from its orbit too. It turned out that it wasn't, but the quest was on anyway for Planet X. In 1930 it was found and named after the old god of the underworld, using the initials **PL** of the man who predicted its discovery. When **Pluto** was found, Humanity was entering a great economic depression. Government power was expanding, and a world war was about to complete the destruction of all the world's old empires and to threaten all life on the planet. The nature of light and electricity first unveiled in the time of Uranus' discovery had in 1927 just finished transforming the old physics into quantum mechanics, overturning the determinist science that had reigned for 250 years since Newton and transmuting the formerly-presumed particles of dead matter we thought we knew into probability waves. And since the 1890s an underworld of sensitive seekers were undermining all the old paradigms and worldviews of western civilization in a lonely and courageous quest for new life. They sought the hidden truths that could heal our alienation and unlock our full potential and power as human beings. By the late 1920s, just about when Pluto was discovered, the depth psychology of Freud and Jung, the philosophy of Bergson, Heidegger and Whitehead, the critique of Oswald Spengler, the bioenergetics of Wilhelm Reich and gestalt psychology, the modern art of Picasso and Dali, and many more had pretty much finished the demolition.

It turned out that in the early 1930s the astronomers really had not fully discovered Pluto, however. It appeared larger than it really was, because the fuzzy image they saw was really Pluto and its undiscovered Moon Charon together. An astrologer named Brunhubner already knew in 1934 that Pluto was a dual planet[1], but the scientists didn't. It was not until the time of the sixties awakening, when Pluto aligned with Uranus in the first conjunction of outer invisible planets ever known, when the counter-cultures were shaking up society, when my own worldview and that of so many others was changing, when a new generation and legions of others were questioning all the authorities, social roles and institutions of the world, and when psychic, psychedelic, esoteric and occult realms were becoming available to all people for the first time in history, that the image of Pluto seen through our telescopes began to shrink. Quantum theory was already being tapped to develop the high tech tools of modern 20th century society, but amidst all this material and commercial success from these new inventions in the 1950s and 1960s, the full implications of the theory were ignored, and the scientists and philosophers had left the old paradigms standing.

It was an illusion, however; a house of cards, because in 1964 John Bell determined that the energy packets or "particles" known to quantum theory were "entangled" no matter how far away they got and could only be known and measured when they were observed. The world is non-local, he proclaimed. Experiments proved that Bell was correct in the 1970s, and by this time Pluto had been discovered for real as well. In 1978 **Charon** was finally clearly distinguished in the astronomers' telescopes, and what's really amazing is that it was discovered to be "entangled" with Pluto in a complete gravity lock of mutual rotation, so that an observer on Pluto would see Charon in the same place in the sky all the time, and an observer on Charon would see Pluto in the same place in the sky all the time. It was only now, as Pluto was fully observed, that its meaning was clear for us. Pluto-Charon is a symbol of complete quantum entanglement, and thus of polarity, interdependence, and unity in diversity too. And so it was that only in the late 1960s and 1970s did quantum theory and the entire New Age paradigm of higher consciousness become public knowledge, upheld by many new writers, philosophers and activists who also proclaimed the re-enchantment of the world and the inter-connection of all beings, and who offered the goal of a new society based on holistic relationship, diversity, and sustainable living practices that would preserve the planet from the clutches of industrial

---

[1] Brunhubner, Fritz, Pluto, American Federation of Astrologers, 1934, 1966, page 13 and 16.

capitalism and war. The human potential movement gave us the ability to release ourselves from our limits and bring down the walls between us. We were emerging into a new life. From the mid-1960s through the 1970s, the Counter-Culture, the New Age Movement and the Green Movement were well and fully launched for the first time in the greatest mass awakening of people the world had ever seen. Pluto coming fully into human awareness in the 1970s, and its conjunction with Uranus in the sixties, was its index and symbol. And the heart-shaped glacier seen in more recent photos of Pluto, as well as its entangled nature, portrays beautifully the rediscovery of love, and sex, in the sixties and 70s.

 Uranus, Neptune and Pluto are the keys to the larger trends of destiny, and the foundation stones for the Horoscope for the New Age. **Uranus** is the carrier of individual liberty, the lightning bolt, the creators, inventors and innovators, the progressives and reformers, the eccentrics who live and think outside the box, and whatever is revolutionary and unexpected. **Neptune** is the cosmic ark of Humanity, the carrier of the zeitgeist or spirit of the age; the symbol of universal compassion for all and the collective will of the modern state and the common people; the dissolver of boundaries, the sensitive weaver of dreams, the escapist, the delusional deceiver and intoxicator, and the mind power of the spirit. **Pluto** is the destroyer of old worlds, the key to the netherworlds and the afterlife, the courage to transform ourselves, the seeker of hidden powers and vitality, the reckoning with death and the bringer of new life, the builder of the wealth and power of civilizations, and the symbol of ecology and interdependence. Together the cycles of these 3 planets tell the story of the ages, and of the movements that change the world, and they lay out the larger view of the landscape of time.

I call Uranus, Neptune and Pluto the guides to higher consciousness, and the transcendental trinity; the planetary equivalent of famous trinities in other traditions, such as Father, Son and Holy Spirit, or Brahma, Vishnu and Shiva. Fittingly indeed, the three planets are in a 1-2-3 relationship in their distance from the Sun and in the length of their orbits. Many very small minor planets have since been discovered both further in and further out from the transcendental trinity since Pluto was confirmed to be a dual binary planet in 1978. The first of the small "centaurs" named **Chiron** was located between the 5 outer planets in 1977. It has been considered almost as significant as a planet by some astrologers. It represents a key to the invisible realms, and it was given that symbol because it moves between the visible and invisible planets. It is considered a healer and a consciousness shifter, but it is only one of many such centaurs. And there are no other resonant proportions in the orbits of any of these bodies besides the big three and their close companions; just the transcendental trinity. Besides Charon and Chiron, these other "belts" of smaller objects were first mapped out in the early 1990s. In my previous book, I said that this was the moment when our "modern spirit" matured; the end of the valley of transition, about which more below.

Planetary Dynamics

Humanity had also been going through a voyage of discovery even before we knew the invisible planets. As we moved through earlier history we also ascended through the visible ones, and this was especially noticeable in The West. From ancient times mystics, poets and philosophers have used the planets to represent our personal journey from above into birth, and then back to God in contemplation. Writers such as Clare Graves and Steve McIntosh have noticed this progressive development through history and have called it Spiral Dynamics.[2] It has become well-known and popular and is used to describe which phases may predominate within a person's or a culture's behavior and ideals. But they did not use the planets to represent these phases of discovery and social evolution. They call them value memes instead, or just memes for short, and they give each one a color. A meme is an idea or an image that catches on within the culture and shapes it. Value memes dominate whole cultures and civilizations for hundreds or thousands of years. The phases have gotten shorter in time as we have progressed and added to our population.

Because their meme descriptions fit the planetary symbols so well, I call it Planetary Dynamics and have revised it to add a few more phases to their original scheme. This process is not based directly on the cycles or influence of the planets, but instead reveals how the planets and their archetypes have governed our agenda through historical phases of development *in astronomical planetary order,* up through the visible planets and beyond into the invisible ones right up to our modern spirit's maturity. Near the end of each phase, the next one began to be felt, and all previous planetary memes continue to exist in various places and revised forms. It is amazing how well the planets describe our journey. My web site http://philosopherswheel.com/planetarydynamics.html and my forthcoming book The Philosophers Wheel have more information on Planetary Dynamics.

⊕ EARTH represents the environment in which life and humans evolved. Up to 100 or 200 thousand years ago, our species was still physically developing in Africa and learning how to use stone tools. Some related human species were also around.

☽ MOON represents fluctuation and change, family ties, instinct and nurturing. Now fully human and increasingly dominant over other human species, during this phase from about 100,000 BC to about 40,000 BC we spread through the world and separated into different ethnic groups or races, developing our family values and our first culture with small artistic crafts. In Spiral Dynamics this phase is called Beige.

☿ MERCURY represents knowledge, language, travel, magic and association with relatives. In this phase from about -40,000 BC to about -9000 BC we developed our nomadic hunter-gatherer culture and used magic to command natural forces and connect with our ancestors. Verbal language was fully developed through story-telling around the campfire, and the first art in the cave paintings helped connect the people with their rituals and with the beauty and power of the animals. This era is also called the Paleolithic or Old Stone Age, and in Spiral Dynamics it is known as the Purple meme.

---

[2] Brunhubner, Fritz, Pluto, American Federation of Astrologers, 1934, 1966, page 13 and 16.

♀ VENUS represents love, the arts, feminine power and the fertility of Nature. In this phase from about -9000 BC to -2300 BC, agriculture and animal herding were invented, creating a more settled life in towns with division of labor and classes. The goddess was worshiped everywhere and sacrifices to the gods were made to insure fertility. The arts blossomed in stone circles and pyramids to connect the people with the sky and the ancestors. This era is also called the Neolithic or New Stone Age.

♂ MARS is the planet of war, conquest, energy and male dominance. Beginning with Sargon of Akkad, in this phase from -2300 BC to 300 CE city states were ruled by war lords who conquered vast territories in a series of ever more powerful empires, including those in Mesopotamia and Egypt up to Persia, Greece and Rome as well as in India and China. Male war gods and emperors were worshiped, and heroes sought fame, glory and identity. The need for weapons led to work with metals rather than with stone in what we call the Bronze and Iron Ages. This era is quite-fittingly called Red in Spiral Dynamics.

♃ JUPITER is the planet of religion and philosophy, faith and generosity, world travel and moral guidance. During the Age of Mars, such guidance was lacking among the warrior rulers, but prophets and philosophers were rising up to try, unsuccessfully, to provide it. As classical Mars civilization fell to barbarian migrations, the Church and religious empires became dominant in society from 300 CE to 1300. The Christian and Islamic Empires, among others, ruled the world, and even the Pope became an emperor. The Church and monasteries provided some order, helped the people and preserved knowledge. The Age of Faith inspired the people and their pilgrimages and was made visible in magnificent cathedrals.

♄ SATURN is the planet of the state and realism. The old empires were not really states as we came to know them, but just the boundaries of the latest conquest. But from the time of Edward I and Philip the Fair in 1300, the fast-rising dynastic secular kings and aristocrats became dominant over the churches and priests. The Pope was even exiled for a time, and soon reform movements were splitting the Church up entirely. The Kings and Queens held the allegiance of the people, and their power was on display in elegant palaces. Discredited by the Plague of 1348, religion gave ground to secular science, which (aided by Renaissance artists) framed the world in a realistic, human perspective and pronounced that seeing is believing. Explorers colonized many lands, and their need for navigation spurred revolutionary advances in astronomy and the natural science of the visible world. Both this era and the Jupiter phase were grouped together in Spiral Dynamics and given the color Blue.

♅ URANUS, as we have seen, opened up the invisible world and spurred the development of industry and democracy from the time of its discovery in 1781. The middle class and its commercial capitalism became the dominant power in the world, and its works transformed the landscape and our lives as inventions multiplied. This phase is called Orange in Spiral Dynamics, and they include in it the "Enlightenment" era of about 100 years that preceded the Age of Revolution that began in 1781. Most Spiral Dynamics writers also include the next phase under Orange as well.

NEPTUNE was discovered soon after Uranus and provided an alternative and a restraint on capitalism. As industry expanded worldwide from the time of its discovery in 1846, the new movements of socialism and labor rose increasingly to power, especially from the dawn of the 20th century through the 1970s. Humanitarian awareness grew. The gallant classical revival style of the Uranus era gave ground to emotional romantic, lush impressionist, and chaotic jazzy styles. New mystical movements appeared.

PLUTO, as we've seen, is a dual or binary planet, and fittingly it has two symbols. It is the ghostly planet of both death and rebirth, the destroyer and the builder of civilizations. It is also seen to be both a planet and not a planet. We were awakened to Pluto though Uranus' conjunction with it in the 1960s. It was the first alignment of invisible planets ever known, which is why so many of us felt it so keenly. Part of Pluto's two-sided nature has been the two phases of its discovery. In its first phase in 1930, government expanded to meet the need, but nuclear weapons and fascism became existential threats. By the time of its second phase of discovery in 1978, when its interdependent dual nature had become known, life began to be seen as an inter-related whole, and the diversity and the human potential movements expanded in the 1960s and 70s into what Spiral Dynamics (quite aptly in this case) calls the Green Meme. Some writers also include the Neptune phase under Green.

At the same time that Pluto's gravity-locked moon Charon was discovered in 1978, the minor planet CHIRON was found orbiting between the 4 giant planets and was seen as likely to fall toward the Sun after a million years or so. Since the discovery of Charon in 1978 and Chiron in 1977, we have seen not only increased green and new age consciousness, but also have regressed or fallen back toward the memes of the visible world through such backward trends as neo-liberal economics, fundamentalist fanaticism, and new imperial wars of choice. The hope is that this regression paves the way for the inclusive Integral Meme of Spiral Dynamics, which is supposed to bring all the old and new memes together in a working whole.

This "integral meme" is one of two (colored Yellow and Turquoise) which are called higher tier, which means that having progressed through all the planetary memes, we can all now access these higher ones which were available to initiates all along. Claimed by Spiral Dynamics to be arriving within human society since the early 1990s, the higher tier memes are represented in Planetary Dynamics by the several belts of minor planets that orbit beyond Jupiter and which were all first elucidated by astronomers at this very moment. Pluto-Charon was just the first and largest planet of the Kuiper Belt to be discovered, and Chiron was just the first of the "centaurs." The asteroid belt between Mars and Jupiter including Ceres was discovered in the 19th century, and small bodies orbiting with Jupiter were found in the 20th.

The Cycle of Civilization

All things move in cycles. We wake up and go to sleep every day, and we adjust to the seasons of the year. These are the basic cycles of astrology, and the primary basis of our interpretations. The daily cycle is charted by the 12 houses of the horoscope, and the year by the 12 signs of the zodiac. All the planets go through cycles, beginning in Aries, the first sign defined by the Spring Equinox, and then through all 12 signs and returning back around. The planets also move in cycles with each other, just like phases of the Moon, from their alignment in conjunction, through all the phases and back again. These phases in their cyclic relationship with each other are called aspects, and they are the most important thing in astrology.

So knowing this, and knowing already how significant the conjunctions of Uranus with Pluto in the 1960s and Neptune with Pluto in the 1890s were, I checked the dates of previous and future conjunctions to see if they are really reliable guides to the movements that change the world and the story of the ages. And indeed, they are. Even though they were not discovered yet, unbeknownst to humanity they were still indicating subconsciously what was happening in human society all through history.

Neptune's cycle with Pluto I call the cycle of civilization. It is the most important cycle. It charts the rise and fall of civilizations, including their political power, their science and their art.[3] I laid out the details of the dates and events for this cycle in my first book, Horoscope for the New Millennium, in the chapter called The Fortunes of Civilization. I recommend this book as the place to go for a full account of the foundations of my prophetic work. I give a summary here, but I must start with a discovery so amazing that it even defies belief, a finding even more powerful and significant than my initial discovery of the conjunctions of 1966 and 1892. For I discovered that in the 570s BC, not only were Neptune and Pluto in conjunction, but Uranus joined it in a triple alignment; the only one in history, and the closest such alignment in at least tens of thousands of years. What would one expect to coincide with such a rare and momentous conjunction? How about this: the greatest age of enlightenment in human history. It happened in the period that started from about 590 BC as the conjunction formed, and it developed over the next 200 years.

This "Axis Age" witnessed the breakthroughs that have shaped civilization ever since. All the world's religions were either begun or transformed. The visions of Ezekiel and of the second Isaiah, the beginning of The Bible as a written text while the Jews were held captive in Babylon, and then the rebuilding of the first temple, all happened during and right after this conjunction. Buddha gained enlightenment under the Bo Tree, and his vast movement began then in Asia and later spread around the world. Hindu philosophy was reaching its apex in the Upanishads, the foundation of Vedanta. Mahavira founded Jainism on the principle of ahimsa, or not harming life. Confucius laid out the moral tenets of Chinese civilization, and Lao Tse wrote the wisdom of Taoism that shows "the way" of balance for both rulers and the common people alike. Zoroaster, the great Persian prophet, was speaking for the ages. And during the conjunction Greece witnessed the first philosophy and science of Western Civilization, from Thales and Pythagoras and their successors who discovered the first principles of the world, leading to the sacrificial moral wisdom of Socrates and the world's first academies like the one founded by the idealist

---

[3] See **Appendix I** for historical references for events corresponding to this cycle, and to the other planetary cycles mentioned in this chapter and in Chapter 3.

philosopher Plato, and finally to the thorough investigations of Aristotle that have shaped science for thousands of years. Plus we saw the first republics in Greece and Rome, the classical age of art and drama and the building of the Parthenon in Athens in the Golden Age of Pericles, and its great architecture, sculpture and vase painting that spread all over the Eastern Mediterranean world and beyond that inspired western culture over and over again ever since. The Celts rose to power across northern and western Europe and became the source of mythic deities and enchanting tales of wisdom.

From this propitious beginning in 578 BC a whole series of conjunctions between Neptune and Pluto followed every 493 years, in 83 BC, 411 AD, 905, 1399 and 1892. Each one indicated a great new beginning in its own right. Each conjunction includes the 7 or so years immediately before and after them when the planets were close together, and their resulting momentum and meaning continues to unfold in the following decades.

In 83 BC Sulla ended the Roman Republic and provided the groundwork for the imperial caesars in the most eventful and recorded century until modern times. The result was the Age of Augustus and the Pax Romana, which was the foundation of subsequent Western and near-eastern civilization and the model for future golden ages in literature and the arts. Hinduism was newly summarized in their great spiritual book The Baghavad Gita, and spiritual ferment in the Middle East gave rise to a similar story of salvation soon to be told by Jesus and his disciples.

In 411 AD Alaric the Visigoth conquered Rome, and its catastrophic Fall opened the way to new kingdoms established by new "barbaric" leaders and conquerors, including Attila the Hun and Theodoric the Great, and the establishment of a new religious empire at Byzantium which created inspiring mosaic art and temple architecture and kept civilization alive for a thousand years, along with the foundation of Catholic Church power in Rome and monastic rites across Europe. In America the Mayans rose to their greatest golden age ever as expressed in their great temples.

In 905 new dynasties and kingdoms were rising in Europe, founded by such leaders as Alfred the Great and Hugh Capet, culminating with a new Holy Roman Empire and a new artistic revival under Otto the Great. The great monastery of Cluny was founded, which reformed the Catholic Church and provided the foundation for its power across Europe and for the style of its magnificent cathedrals. In China at the same time, the ancient Tang Dynasty collapsed, which opened the way for its greatest golden age under the Song Dynasty. The Byzantine second flowering revitalized that empire as well.

In 1399 a great contest to design the doors of the new Cathedral of Florence inaugurated a fabulous, enlivening Renaissance of classical art, music and literature, inspiring a humanistic, graceful and balanced style of painting and architecture that would last for 500 years, and opening the Age of Exploration in which Western navigators would meet and colonize the rest of the world, which in turn launched a revolution in science that revised our view of the cosmos around us.

Since the conjunction of the late 1880s and 1890s, exact in 1892, our worldview has been reshaped once again-- expanding to incomprehensible vistas complete with galaxies, black holes and a big bang starting it all. Space, time, matter and energy for us became mutually relative, and reality became based in probability waves. Quantum mechanics launched high electronic technology, but eventually also awakened us to the interdependence of consciousness and its objects. More inventions than ever before or since shifted our entire landscape and way of life during the years closely surrounding this conjunction, and they began to challenge our future survival too. Just as bold explorers soon after 1400 led to Columbus discovering a New World 90 years later, opening a new phase in civilization, so the flight experiments of the 1890s paved the way for voyages to the Moon 80 years later, opening up new worlds to Humanity. Modern art, psychology and philosophy began in the 1890s era too, breaking through all limits to expression and self-discovery, and this helped prepare the way decades later for the dawning of the New Age in the greatest spiritual awakening yet in human history. By that time the groundbreaking Art Nouveau styles of the 1890s had found an echo in sixties psychedelia. Meanwhile the arms race begun by Kaiser Wilhelm in 1892 and the ensuing world wars destroyed the dominance of imperial and colonial Europe and built the foundations of today's emerging global civilization.[4]

Reviewing the pattern then, here are the conjunctions which correspond to the crucial turning points in civilization, not only since 578 BC, but extending back to the cycles that shaped the societies of Mesopotamia, Africa, China, India, the Americas, and elsewhere since 3000 BC:

1892------- Modern art, depth psychology, atomic physics, fall of European empires, etc.

1399------- Early Renaissance, Great Schism in the Catholic Church, first explorers, Turk invasions, Aztecs rose in Meso-America, Ming Dynasty in China, etc.

905------- Viking and Magyar invasions of Europe, Cluny reforms sparked revival of Catholic Church power, early European dynasties begin, Fall of Tang Dynasty, Fall of Mayan cities, Toltec rule in central Mexico, etc.

411 A.D. Barbarian invasions in Europe, Fall of Rome, fall of Tsin in China, rise of Mayan cities, Ghana founded.

83 B.C. Sulla, Roman civil wars/conquests, the Baghavad-Gita, etc.

578 B.C. Axis Age of enlightenment, Neo Babylonia, Celtic expansion.

1073 B.C. Fall of New Kingdom in Egypt, Dorian invasions of Greece, Israel and Judea founded, fall of Shang and rise of Chou dynasty in China, etc.

1568 B.C. New Kingdom of Egypt founded, civilization of Mycenae, New Palace Minoan Crete, Shang Dynasty began in China, Aryan invasions in India and first Vedas.

2064 B.C. Middle Kingdom of Egypt founded, Fall of Ur to Semitic invasions, Old Palace Crete period began, Chinese Hsia Dynasty, Olmecs in America arose.

2560 B.C. Old Kingdom of Egypt founded, Great Pyramids built, Ur & Akkad founded. Indus Valley civilization in its mature era.

3057 B.C. Narmer founded Egypt, greatest Sumerian cities established.

---

[4] Regarding the 1890s, see Meece, <u>Horoscope for the New Millennium</u>, pp. 38-39, pp.203-206.

About one hundred years later (varies from about 50 to 150) came the Golden Age or Renaissance that arose from these new beginnings:

1990------- New Age Renaissance, worldwide web, global and green awakening, and more.

1500------- Discovery of New World; High Renaissance of Michelangelo, Da Vinci, Durer, etc.; the great Moguls of India, Suleiman the Magnificent in Turkey, Ming China, etc.

1000------- Ottonian and Byzantine Renaissance, Sung China, Tamil India, first great cathedrals.

520 A.D. Byzantine golden age, Mayan golden age, Hindu revival, Benedictine Order, Theodoric.

10 A.D. Roman golden age, Sun pyramid, Mahayana Buddhism, Christ.

470 B.C. Greek golden age, Greek and Roman Republics, Persian Empire, Buddhism, growth of Benares in India as religious center, Chinese classic age, etc.

970 B.C. Israeli golden age (David and Solomon), rise of Assyria, Korea, etc.

1470 B.C. Crete golden age (Minos), Egyptian age of Thutmose III, etc.

1960 B.C. Babylon, Rock tombs of Egypt built, etc.

2460 B.C. Ur golden age, Great Pyramid paintings.

2950 B.C. Sumerian golden age.

Phases of the Cycle

When Neptune and Pluto join together in conjunction, a "New Moon" of civilization happens. As they go through their mutual cyclic phases in the following years, civilization develops, reaches full flower and then decays. Our New Age which began in 1892 also follows these phases. Each of them is indicated by aspects or angles which Neptune makes to Pluto during their 493-year cycle, and we will cover these phases in more detail in Appendix D.

The first three phases are "waxing," when Neptune is "increasing in light," and civilization is building its creative power. The last three are "waning," when Neptune is "decreasing in light," during which civilization may decline and become fixed in its ways, but also may distribute the new culture more widely and release "seeds" that will only bloom in the next cycle.

Following the conjunction, the first phase is the waxing 60-degree sextile, when Neptune has moved about two signs ahead of Pluto. It is like a Crescent Moon phase. These are the creative golden age or renaissance periods we mentioned in the list above. It is still the phase we are in as of this writing.

At the waxing square phase, Neptune has moved three signs or 90 degrees ahead of Pluto, like in a First Quarter Moon. At this time a crisis tests the foundations of the New Civilization. such crises include the Peloponnesian War that ended the Golden Age of Greece, and the Wars of Religion that tore apart Europe after the Reformation. We can expect this phase of crisis to arrive again in the years 2065-70, which we will describe in a coming chapter.

The waxing 120-degree trine is like a Gibbous Moon. At this time civilization is confidently expanding and moving toward its climax, as when Trajan and Hadrian brought the Roman Empire to its greatest power in the brilliant conclusion of its "silver age," or when the First Crusade in 1095 mobilized the expanding Christian Medieval world. The dynamic cathedral art and sculpture of this "Romanesque" era around A.D.1100 is often compared to the Baroque style 500 years later during the era of expanding colonization. The next waxing trine is scheduled for about 2090. "Stay tuned" and read all about it later in the book.

When Neptune opposes Pluto across the heavens, so that the two planets are 180 degrees apart, it is like a Full Moon of civilization, which now attains its greatest power and expression. During the opposition a culture's ideals are most clearly and scientifically defined. Afterward, however, civilization may start to split apart or rot from within, or else encumber and rigidify itself with too many rules and structures. For example, at the time of the opposition of 323 B.C., Alexander the Great died at the height of his power. His empire soon crumbled into the fractured "Hellenistic" Age. During the opposition around 1140 the first Gothic cathedrals were built, but soon afterward the Inquisition began. In the mid-Seventeenth Century, Louis XIV, the French "Sun King," brought classical European Renaissance culture to its height, but later this "Ancient Regime" got more oppressive and corrupt, and 130 years later collapsed in war and revolution. Greek scientists like Euclid, Roman ones like Ptolemy, and the modern scientific revolution of Descartes and Newton that separated Matter from Spirit, all belong to this Full Moon/opposition phase. The next opposition is due in 2140. We can expect our high-tech, spiritual and Earth-centered Aquarian Age culture to reach full flower then. Great temples to new spiritual ideals will be built, and a new architecture will refashion our cities. But some of our worldwide institutions may get too rigid and powerful after 2140.

During the waning 120-degree trine, the beliefs and ideas of the new civilization are disseminated, distributed, and institutionalized. The dissemination of Buddhism through Ashoka's empire in India, the lightning-fast spread of Christianity through the Roman Empire before its establishment by Constantine, and the spread of "rational" Enlightenment ideas by the Eighteenth Century's "enlightened despots" illustrate this phase. This is usually a happy, light, or decadent period, so we can expect the Twenty-Third Century during the next waning trine to be relaxed and peaceful but complacent. Liberating new ideals and powers will be distributed to the people of the world.

The period leading up to and during the waning 90-degree square is like a Last Quarter Moon, representing a "last glory" of civilization. Usually a powerful leader, such as Ashurbanipal, Constantine, Charlemagne, or Napoleon, unites a great empire; but it seldom lasts for long. Hopes of a New World (as in the French Revolution) soon fade, yet seeds of new ideas are planted which will bloom in the civilization of the future. These seed times have also seen the momentous arrival of 4 Planetary Dynamics value memes that shaped civilization: the Mars meme in 2200 BC, the Jupiter meme in 300 AD, the

Saturn meme in 1300, and the Uranus meme in 1781. This turbulent, romantic, emotional period will arrive again in about A.D. 2300. Powerful seers will then help us glimpse the coming "Age of Light," due to arrive after the next conjunction of Neptune and Pluto in 2385, but they won't be able to bring it into being yet.

Instead, if the pattern holds, a period of dissolution or disintegration will ensue. This is the waning 60-degree sextile, equivalent to a Balsamic or "Dark Moon" phase. Peasant and worker revolts erupt, and barbarians like the Dorians, Celts, Huns, Vikings and Turks appear on the horizon and start crashing the gates. It's also a highly inventive period when new economic arrangements are developed. So when the next waning sextile arrives around 2338, we know something of what to expect: much revolt, migration, plague, famine, and perhaps a catastrophe or two, and perhaps, toward the very end, some developments that may indicate what's just over the horizon in the new cycle. New methods of keeping track of value could replace the monetary system. Today's "new paradigms" (the fundamental beliefs and world views now emerging) may start to unravel in a time of skepticism, controversy and fanaticism. If we are ever invaded by a race from another planet, this could be the moment. The barriers between our Earth civilization and those of other planets and planes may begin to fall at an alarming and unprecedented rate. More likely, perhaps, we'll see an increasing dispersal of some of Earth's population onto the Moon and other planets and moons.

Aspects

When these phases or aspects between any of the planets happen, important events are more likely. They are important prophetic tools, and they are mentioned often in the following pages. If you're not clear on what an aspect is, this chart should help you. The planets are pictured here located in a circle, which represents the zodiac through which the planets travel as they make their cycles and their mutual phases in relation to each other.

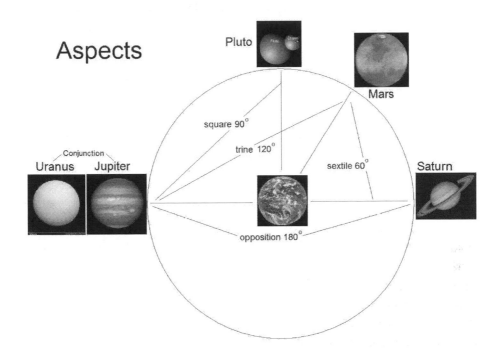

You can see in the diagram that Saturn is in opposition of 180 degrees to Jupiter and Uranus, which are in conjunction. Mars is making a 120-degree trine to Jupiter, and a 60-degree sextile to Saturn. Jupiter and Uranus are in 90-degree squares to Pluto.

In charts pictured in this book, the signs of the zodiac and the planets traveling through them are arranged counterclockwise. There are 30 degrees in every sign, 1 degree being basically the distance the Sun travels each day. Next to the symbol for a planet, there's a number often followed by a sign symbol; this indicates which degree of a sign the planet is in. If the planet is in 2 degrees Aries, for example, it is near the beginning of the sign. If it in 15 degrees Aries, it is in the middle. In 29 degrees Aries, it is near the end, and about to enter the next sign (Taurus). A good way to spot aspects is to notice which degrees the planets are in. One planet that is in nearly the same degree of any sign as another planet is making an aspect to that planet. Planets may also be in aspect when at the beginning or end of a sign, as for example Mars in 1 degree Leo in square to Jupiter in 29 degrees Libra.

In some charts, such as the national chart for the USA shown below, you'll see lines connecting the planets that are in aspect. The symbols for these aspects may also be shown (see chart below). Here you can see the Moon at 26 Aquarius in trine to Venus in 3 Cancer, the Sun in 13 Cancer in square to Saturn at 14 Libra, and Venus in 3 Cancer in conjunction with Jupiter at 5 Cancer. Within each degree there are also 60 minutes of arc, as shown. Often these degrees are referred to as rounded up, so that for example Jupiter is actually considered to be in 6 Cancer.

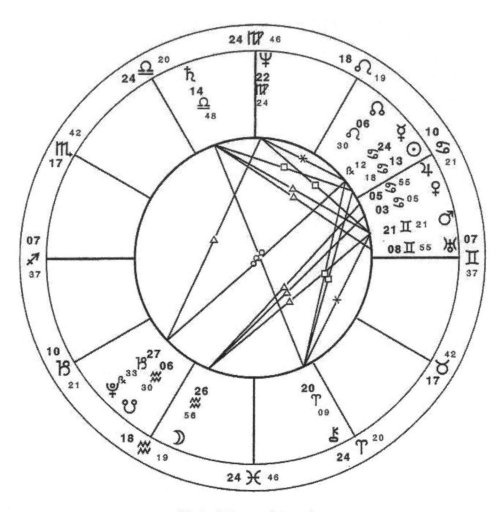

United States of America

Chart data: July 4, 1776, 04:47 P.M. Philadelphia, PA, U.S.A., 39W57, 75N10.

Aspect	Symbol	Degrees
Conjunction	☌	0
Opposition	☍	180
Square	□	90
Trine	△	120
Sextile	✳	60
Inconjunct	⚻	150
Semisquare	∠	45
Sesquiquadrate	⚼	135
Semisextile	⚺	30

The conjunction (0-degree angle) is like a New Moon. It is an alignment of planets, usually in the same sign. During important conjunctions, explosive events erupt spontaneously, and daring new initiatives are taken in fields represented by the two planets. Their energies are powerfully combined, concentrated and intensified. The aims and direction of the new cycle remain unclear, and often the most crucial changes unleashed by a conjunction remain hidden until later.

The opposition (180-degree angle, 1/2 of the circle) is like a Full Moon, and planets are usually six signs apart on opposite sides of the Earth. It brings fulfillment of what began at the conjunction, but also a schism or polarization into two opposing sides. The opposition usually indicates major events in a very powerful and obvious way. People know clearly what they're doing and why, but they may be locked in a frustrating stalemate.

The square (90-degree angle, 1/4 of the circle) is like the first or last quarter phase. Planets are at right angles to each other, usually three signs apart. Together with the conjunction and opposition, the squares are the most critical phases of the cycle. The two planets are "squaring off" with each other, producing tension, crisis, conflict and dynamic activity. People stir up trouble, and important decisions must be made. Dangerous events tend to occur. Squares and oppositions are also called "afflictions" or "hard aspects." A grand cross happens when 4 or more planets are all in square and opposition to each other, stabilizing and intensifying the indications.

The trine (120-degree angle, 1/3 of the circle) is like a gibbous phase. Here, planets are about four signs apart. Under trines events move quickly, and people are lively and confident. A flood of light and energy is released, and good fortune may result. The trine gives us a wider perspective, but it often indicates that we are being frivolous, wasteful, uncontrolled or complacent. A grand trine is 3 or more planets all in trine to each other, making those trines even more significant.

The sextile (60-degree angle, 1/6 of the circle) is like a crescent phase. In this aspect the planets are two signs apart. Like the trine, it tends to be a fortunate aspect. When it occurs, people are more creative, intelligent, and productive. It may indicate a crisis, but important events will generally move more smoothly. A grand sextile is 3 planets in sextile to each other enclosed by a trine, generally a very fortunate indicator.

Minor aspects:

The semi-square (45-degree angle, 1/8 of the circle) is one half of a square. It is an aspect of friction and dynamic, constructive activity.

The sesqui-square or sesqui-quadrate (135-degree angle, 3/8 of a circle) is a square plus one half. It also generates activity, and frequently brings upheaval. It is especially dangerous during a waning phase.

The quincunx or inconjunct (150-degree angle) may contribute to trials and tribulations that force us to make adjustments or confront uncomfortable karmic issues. In this aspect, the planets are usually five signs apart.

The semi-sextile (30-degree angle) puts planets one sign apart, and acts like a weaker sextile. It may show a phase of growth, or perhaps events that lead to larger ones at the time of the following sextile or conjunction.

When exact, an aspect's significance is peaking. Before exactitude the forces and events it indicates are building up. After exactitude, the energy is released and distributed, bringing results and consequences. The orb, or amount of inexactness, allowed for conjunctions, oppositions, trines, and squares, is ten degrees. For sextiles, allow up to six. For semi and sesqui-squares, it is two degrees, and for semi-sextiles and quincunxes, use one degree. The closer an aspect is, the more important it is and the more likely it is to correspond to a major world event. But this varies, and astrologers don't always agree on allowable orbs.

At any given moment, there is more than one cycle unfolding, and thus more than one aspect going on. In fact, a whole pattern of them is forming at all times. When a greater number than usual of important aspects are happening, it means the "cosmic weather" is more active; big events or the start of major trends can be expected!

Astrology is a very natural science. Aspects come and go in graceful waves. The closer it is, the stronger it is. The contrast between the more fortunate and the harder aspects are revealed in our everyday lives. A trine is like a waltz, which has 3 beats per measure: a very easy-going, flowing, joyful and upbeat dance. A square is like a march, which has 4 beats per measure; energetic, determined, disciplined and ready for combat. If two cars meet at an intersection, where the streets are in square (or right angles) to each other, they crash unless they take turns and obey the law. But at a sextile or trine angle you can merge into the lane. In a conjunction you are in alignment with the other cars, as long as you don't bump into them. But a car traveling in the opposite direction from you must stay on the other side of the street, or a head-on collision will occur.

The Cycle of Revolution

The mutual phases between conjunctions of Uranus and Pluto, like the conjunction we experienced in the 1960s, is called the cycle of revolution.

In ancient times, Uranus-Pluto conjunctions coincided with such sudden and explosive events as the outbreak of the Peloponnesian war, the death of Alexander the Great (after which his empire broke up), the Roman slave revolt of Spartacus, and the founding of Constantinople. Five years after the conjunction of 1090, Pope Urban suddenly and dramatically announced the First Crusade in 1095, opening an inspired age of European expansion. Soon after the conjunction of 1343-44, the Black Death of 1346-49 wiped out half of Europe's population and eroded the foundations of feudal Catholic society. The following conjunction in Leo in 1455-56 coincided with the invention of printing, which gave all future revolutionary movements their prime weapon. Two years before, in 1453, Constantinople succumbed to the same conjunction under which it had been founded, as the city fell to Turkish invaders. Scholars fleeing west then propelled the

Renaissance into high gear. During the Uranus-Pluto conjunction in Aries in 1597-98 Baroque art and music were invented, and Galileo opened the scientific revolution.

After every conjunction comes the Uranus-Pluto opposition, about halfway through the cycle. Its impact is often as great or greater than the conjunction. In fact, when Uranus stands opposite to Pluto in the heavens, the revolutionary movement reaches its peak. We are at the Full Moon of the movement, and the light of this "Full Uranus" lasts over an entire generation. This pattern took hold most noticeably from the Renaissance onward. For example, right after Uranus opposed Pluto in 1395, Henry Bolingbroke led a rebellion against King Richard II of England. A similar upheaval took place in France. Bolingbroke took power as Henry IV, but when the next conjunction came along in 1455, another rebellion broke out (the Wars of the Roses), leading to the Tudor takeover. Another great revolutionary full moon came in 1649, the year Charles I met his fate at the hands of Oliver Cromwell and the Great Rebellion. The absolute rule of the English kings was forever overthrown and gradually thereafter replaced by today's parliamentary system. Puritans and other religious dissidents gained their freedom. Simultaneously the Fronde revolt in France challenged Louis XIV, but it failed.

The Uranus-Pluto conjunction at the end of Leo in 1710-11 opened the first of three great revolutions whose impact have dominated modern history. The first revolution began with the early incendiary works of Voltaire around 1711. The authorities were so incensed at him that they locked him up in the infamous Bastille prison, thus turning him into the great hero of liberty. Freemasonry began a few years afterward, spreading revolutionary ideas through secret societies. Signs of even more disruptive upheavals came when iron smelting and the Newcomen steam pump were invented the very same year. The Industrial Revolution was on the horizon.

The goal of the Enlightenment and the first great revolution that began with the Uranus-Pluto conjunction of 1711 was individual liberty. The leaders of the movement, such as Voltaire, wanted to overthrow the Kings and replace them with governments who depended on the consent of the governed and protected human rights and liberty. Representing the rising power of the bourgeoisie and merchant classes, they also protested against tariffs and regulations that restricted free enterprise. By the 1780s, soon after Uranus was discovered, this cycle was moving toward its "Full Moon." Just as Charles I lost his head in England during the Uranus-Pluto opposition of 1649, so Louis XVI lost his head in France during the Uranus-Pluto opposition of 1793. The first great modern cycle of revolution came to its climax in the French Revolution. Aristocratic power was smashed and bourgeois power took its place. A great charter of liberties was proclaimed, inspired by the American Revolution a few years before. The French revolution set into motion that "engine of liberty" which transformed the nations and peoples of the world. Its slogan of "liberty, equality and fraternity" not only encapsulated its own aims, but the goals of all three modern revolutionary movements, each in turn. Uranus, as we saw, became the planetary emblem of this first great Revolution.

Just as Oliver Cromwell seized the reins of the Great Rebellion and became a despot, the French Revolution was seized by the "despotism of liberty" and the Reign of

Terror. Napoleon took power soon afterward. The opposition is always the climax of the revolutionary movement, but it brings conflict and schism, too. In our modern revolutionary age, old tyrants are often replaced by new ones. The new boss is the same as the old boss, as Peter Townshend would say, and the cycle turns. The old revolution becomes the new despotism, and new rebels arrive to challenge the revolutionary power of the old rebels. The commercial and business interests that rose to power in the French and Industrial Revolutions eventually became more oppressive than the aristocrats. The new capitalist industry dehumanized and practically enslaved millions of workers. Soon they were rising up in angry protests, out of which emerged the new movement of socialism to challenge the power of capitalism.

The people moved into action during the next Uranus-Pluto conjunction in 1850, at the cusp of Aries-Taurus. The next movement erupted at virtually the same moment as Neptune's discovery in 1846, and the new planet of self-surrender and compassion came to represent the second great revolution. Its goal was not liberty, but equality. The movement's leaders wanted to overthrow not only the king, but also the capitalists by taking control of the "means of production." They exalted cooperation and collective identity above the competitive spirit of the individual. The masses rose up in revolutions throughout the European continent in 1848, and in China in 1850 in the Taiping Rebellion (the most massive uprising in history). Also in 1848, Karl Marx described the aims of the new movement in The Communist Manifesto. Social realists like Engels, Courbet, Millet, and Dickens vividly portrayed the plight of poor workers, and humanitarians demanded proper treatment of the sick and downtrodden for the first time in human history.

The new socialist movement was easily crushed at first, but Marx saw that as industry and capitalism expanded from about 1850 onward, the proletariat would become stronger. Each succeeding crisis of "boom and bust" would bring the revolution closer. The second great cycle reached its climax at the opposition of Uranus and Pluto at the turn of the Twentieth Century (1901), when labor unions and socialist parties expanded as they never have before or since. A more violent labor movement (syndicalism) exploded at the same time, while the "muckrakers" launched the progressive movement in the USA. European imperialism suffered a black eye around 1901 through the Boer War, the Chinese Boxer Rebellion and elsewhere, and "anti-imperialism" became an integral part of the Communist program.

In 1902-03, Lenin's Bolsheviks split from the other Russian Communists and took over the movement. In 1905, the already-launched Russian Revolution against the Tsar went into high gear and exploded in the greatest socialist upheaval yet. In 1917, Lenin founded the Soviet Union, which institutionalized socialism. Once in power, the Communists unleashed their own "reign of terror" that was far longer and deeper than the French one. Instead of the "despotism of liberty," they created the "dictatorship of the proletariat." The turn of the Twentieth Century thus represented another generation of revolutionary change that corresponded to the "full moon" or opposition of Uranus and Pluto in 1901.

Throughout the remainder of the second revolutionary cycle, socialism and communism advanced relentlessly, and half the world came under the "red" sway. Even in "democratic" countries, socialism made gains. The communist and democratic-socialist movements succeeded in making people more equal in wealth and improved living standards, as in the New Deal under FDR during the Uranus-Pluto square of 1933. But in so doing, they reduced the individual to an anonymous cog in the industrial machine. As industry advanced it destroyed the quality of life in many ways. It also threatened all life on Earth for the first time ever. Once again a new tyrant had replaced the old; this time the tyrant was not only the greedy capitalist, but also the machine itself, and the corporate and communist states. What's more, since 1850, scientists and politicians alike had divided humanity into warring classes, races and nations.

This is the background of the third great revolution. The next conjunction arrived in 1966 in the sign Virgo. The U.S. was rocked by massive protests against the war in Vietnam, and by ethnic groups asserting their civil rights and powers. Revolutions attempted to overthrow the state in France and Czechoslovakia, and the worldwide student movement shut down universities and blocked military activities. In China, the "cultural revolution" erupted, but soon it discredited its leader Chairman Mao and his brand of communism. This, coupled with the Czech movement, would eventually inspire radical reforms in China and throughout the Communist world. The counter-culture created alternative lifestyles based on psychedelic and spiritual experiences that raised consciousness and freed boundaries between people.

What do the revolutionaries of the third movement want? Its aims can be summed up in three words: peace, ecology, brother/sisterhood. We who believe in this revolution want an end to war. We want to save the planet from destruction. We want all people to join together as brothers and sisters in one common family, a true human "fraternity." We ask you to "imagine," as John Lennon did, a world without rigid barriers of wealth, race, sex, creed or nationality. The third revolution is not only political, but cultural and spiritual. We want to discover the life and spirit within us and explore psychic and spiritual dimensions. Women's Liberation (Uranus-Pluto in Virgo, the Virgin) began transforming our culture too, as the National Organization for Women (NOW) was formed in 1966, extending the movement begun in July 1848 under the previous Uranus-Pluto conjunction at the Seneca Falls Convention. Just as they and various ethnic groups empower themselves, so all of us are throwing off outdated social and sexual roles.

The new movement has superseded the older ones, although the goals of the first two revolutions remain. Wherever human rights and liberty are denied, there is the place for the first revolution. Wherever the working class remains in poverty and subjection, there is the place for the second. To use a phrase from spiral dynamics, the third movement transcends and includes the first two, and the earlier aspirations are still part of it. But the third revolution became the new vanguard of change. Its ultimate symbol is ecology, the union of all life which enhances the quality of life of each individual. This new "Green Revolution" answers the needs of the New Age: survival of the planet, and recovery of our own humanity. Thus, green has replaced the socialist red as the new radical color. Pluto, which by the 1970s was newly discovered to be dual and interdependent, is the planet of this revolutionary cycle.

Indeed, for astrologers, Pluto remains in full planetary status. We know its powerful significance, and certainly this and my previous book would both crumble at the foundations without it. And just as the third revolution still struggles for recognition, so does its planet.

To get an idea of the powerful resonance of this Uranus and Pluto conjunction, and why we at the time felt it so keenly and saw its expression in society so vividly, check out the amazing aspect alignments during this solar eclipse a few months after the conjunction. Not only does this chart represent the energies and surrounding conflicts during which the Third Revolution of our time began, but it shows the power of eclipses, which I will explain in the next chapter. Amazingly all the planets formed into the approximate shape of a peace symbol, which became the emblem of the movement. Jupiter in the chart was actually in grand trine to Saturn and Neptune in this period, with all three planets in sensitive water signs.

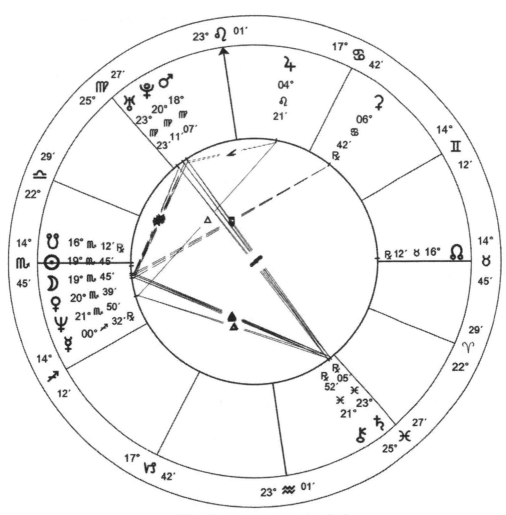

The Cosmic Peace Symbol

At the total solar eclipse of Nov.12, 1966, all the planets formed into the famous pattern of the peace symbol for the only time ever, with Jupiter stationary-retrograde and just out of orb. It thus became the signature of our destiny of peace. Chart data: November 12, 1966, 2:26 UT, San Francisco CA, 37N47, 122W25.

At this time, Bertrand Russell and Jean-Paul Sartre organized the International War Crimes Tribunal to oppose the USA-Vietnam War. A debate of extraordinary proportions swept over the USA. In this picture of the eclipse pattern below, you can also see how the 5 outer planets formed the peace symbol in Summer 1966 and early 1967.

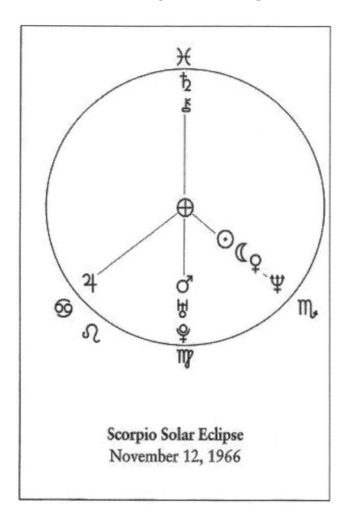

Scorpio Solar Eclipse
November 12, 1966

The third cycle of revolution reached a powerful first-quarter phase as Uranus and Pluto squared off between the years 2008 and 2016. 40 years of growing inequality, the resulting great recession, and accelerating climate change, ignited revolt around the world in 2010-2011, from Greece and Southern Europe to Ukraine, Turkey and Brazil and the Occupy Movement in the USA, among other places, but it was felt most strongly as the "Arab Spring" in the Middle East. At this writing many of these movements have been suppressed in another reactionary wave of despotism, and just as I predicted we struggle to deal with the refugees and migrations unleashed by this worldwide calamity. As the next trine of the mid-2020s approaches, however, we look forward to a time when progress will expand again, and the United States faces the return of its revolutionary and civil war eras that could split the country or launch it on a new path of renewal. The next opposition in the late 2040s will bring the third or "Green" Revolution to its fulfillment and climax, as we will see in a chapter to come.

Cultural Shifts: The Uranus-Neptune Cycle

Uranus and Neptune represent the most lofty and inspired experiences of humanity, so their conjunction is very significant. Unlike Uranus-Pluto, these conjunctions occur on a very regular cycle-every 171.4 years or so. This is almost three times more often than the conjunction between Neptune and Pluto, which has to do with the "fortunes of civilization." "Culture" generally has a more restricted meaning than "civilization," so I assume that this shorter cycle between Uranus and Neptune has to do with "culture." It mostly boils down to four things.

First, it stands for high peaks of cultural achievement in the arts and humanities. For example, the trial and death of Socrates in 399 B.C. (soon after the conjunction of 404 B.C.) inspired Plato to write his great dialogues. The column of Trajan in A.D. 111 marked the beginning of Rome's "silver age" when the Pantheon was built-- the inspired masterpiece of Roman architecture. Charlemagne restored art and culture from the clutches of the Dark Ages around the time of the conjunction of 794. Under the alignment of 1136 (also opposite Pluto), Medieval culture soared as Gothic architecture and philosophy were created. Giotto anticipated the coming Renaissance with his great paintings under the conjunction of 1307. The conjunction of 1479 just preceded the High Renaissance of DaVinci and Michelangelo. The conjunction of 1650 inspired the greatest Baroque artists like Bernini, Poussin, Hals, Rembrandt and Vermeer. The conjunction of 1821 marked the height of Romanticism, including composers such as Schubert and Beethoven, the painters Gericault, Friedrich, Delacroix and Turner, and poets like Byron and Shelley. During the conjunction of 1993, the invention of the world wide web helped launch and expand the upsurge of creativity in the cyber and electronic realms.

Second, and most clearly, Uranus and Neptune conjunctions and their cyclic phases or aspects profoundly affect the course of international affairs. These planets carry the collective soul of whole nations and peoples, and their aspects chart the relations between them. Since Neptune has to do with endings and conclusions, the few years immediately before this conjunction or early during it seem to wrap things up that have been unsettled for decades. Apparently though, shifting the international furniture around just allows new conflicts to surface that have been buried beneath the old ones. Whenever Uranus-Neptune aspects are in force, there are always major international tensions which may explode into war whenever Mars, Saturn and Pluto aspects indicate. On the other hand, under Uranus-Neptune trines and conjunctions there is also always great opportunity for international cooperation.

Here is how Uranus-Neptune has shifted world order throughout history. Southeastern Europe and the Eastern Mediterranean has been a favorite target (though not the only one) going back to the Axis Age and the Peloponnesian War. That war (which had begun under a Uranus-Pluto conjunction) ended in 404 B.C. under Uranus conjunct Neptune. The alignment of 232 B.C. happened soon after the first Punic War between Rome and Carthage was settled, and in the last years of Ashoka's rule in India, which established the first Buddhist Empire. Under the conjunction of 61 B.C., Pompey organized the Near East into Roman provinces, after which Julius Caesar, Pompey, and Crassus formed the first Roman triumvirate, leading the way to the Roman Empire. Around A.D. 112, the emperor Trajan established the Roman Empire's greatest extent of power after conquering Dacia (Romania). In 282, Diocletian restored the empire from collapse with a series of drastic reforms and reorganizations, right after his predecessor had lost Dacia again. During the conjunction of c.453 AD Attila the Hun's raids ended.

It was just a few years before the Uranus-Neptune conjunction of 623-24 (in 618) that the elegant new Tang Dynasty ended centuries of a splintered China. Charlemagne established the first Holy Roman Empire under the conjunction of 794. He was crowned Emperor by Pope Leo on Christmas day, in the year 800. The Khmer Empire in Cambodia that later built Angkor began in 802. Otto the Great restored Holy Roman Empire in 962. Two years earlier, the Sung Dynasty restored the Chinese empire. Both these events happened just a few years before the Uranus-Neptune conjunction of 965. The conjunction of 1307 happened when King Philip the Fair of France made his kingdom more powerful than the Catholic Church. The conjunction of 1479 saw the decades-long Wars of the Roses come to their climax, after which the Tudor Dynasty restored peace and order to England. Other European rulers like Ferdinand and Isabella of Spain consolidated their power around this same time.

The Uranus-Neptune conjunction of 1650 (also opposed to Pluto and Saturn) was a perfect example of one international order superseding another. The Treaty of Westphalia in 1648 ended the Thirty-Years War and the wars of religion, but competition between France and England and other great powers followed, and these wars were also fought in the American colonies. During the ensuing square (around 1700), Louis XIV tried and failed to defeat England and the Germans. During the opposition (around 1740), the French fought England and Austria over Prussia's annexation of Silesia, and during the square around 1780 they fought over the American Revolution. The conflict finally ended with the defeat of Napoleon in 1815, just before the next great Uranus-Neptune conjunction in 1821. The Vienna Conference of 1815 resolved all the disputes of the past and created a settlement that lasted for decades, but by trying to repress all succeeding revolutions and by ignoring the issue of national rights and boundaries, the treaty contained within it the seeds of all the conflicts of the following years.

New revolutions in southern Europe in 1820-21 were promptly snuffed out by the restored monarchs. But they couldn't stop the colonies of the Spanish and Portuguese kings from gaining their independence, thanks to the Monroe Doctrine and the British Navy in 1823. And when Greeks rose up for freedom from the Turkish Empire during the conjunction of 1821, it began a decline in its power which precipitated all the troubles throughout the 19th and 20th centuries in the vast Near Eastern lands it once ruled, and which have disturbed world peace over and over again ever since. During the square of the late 1860s came the German wars of unification, which ignited the Franco-German border tensions unresolved since the fall of Charlemagne. Both of these vexing problems exploded in the First World War, which closely followed a set of crises that began in Bosnia during the opposition of 1908. During the square of the early to mid-1950s, the United States confronted the Soviets during the height of the Cold War. Israelis and Arabs also clashed during the Suez crisis in 1956.

The next conjunction in 1993 resolved the Cold War conflict in 1991, and also eased Middle East tensions with a new framework for peace in 1993. The Berlin Wall fell in Nov.1989, bringing down the European Iron Curtain between Communism and The West which Churchill had declared in 1946, and then the Soviet Union dissolved in 1991. South Africa ended Apartheid, and Mandela became president in 1994. More new nations were created in the few years of the 1991 period than ever before in history, and the European Union was formed in 1993. After the USA and its allies repelled Iraq's illegal invasion of Kuwait in January 1991, with world and UN cooperation, President Bush pronounced that a New World Order had arrived. With all of these events, it truly had. Uranus conjunct Neptune proved its significance in the reshaping of world order as never before, as I predicted that it would.

Unfortunately, plenty of new conflicts surfaced beneath old ones. Just as a crisis in Bosnia in 1908 under Uranus opposite Neptune led to World War I a few years later, so the crisis there that began in 1992 under Uranus conjunct Neptune exploded just before the New Millennium, just as I predicted in my book. Ethnic conflicts became the bane of the New World Order. The still-fledgling United Nations represents the best hope to overcome them, but the next Uranus-Neptune square (in 2037) and the next opposition (in 2078-2080) will mark times when world order will be tested again, and another Balkan or Austrian conflict could threaten our new dedication to world peace once more during that upcoming opposition.

Third, in modern times the major Uranus-Neptune aspects bring revolutions, though these are less drastic than those which occur under Uranus-Pluto aspects. Significant alignments with Uranus, the solar system's lightning rod, are always bound to bring political revolutions. Uranus-Pluto conjunctions initiate revolutionary movements, but the Uranus-Neptune conjunction often brings them to fruition.

For example, the German Reformation erupted into peasant revolt in 1522 exactly as Uranus squared Neptune. The conjunction of 1650 coincided with the great rebellion of Cromwell in England. The American revolution was fought during the square of 1777-83. The conjunction of 1821 saw revolutions erupt throughout southern Europe (Greece, Romania, Italy, Spain) and the Americas (Mexico, Brazil, Chile, etc.). The following square around 1870 witnessed the famous Paris Commune celebrated by Karl Marx. Under the great opposition around 1908, successful revolutions happened in China and Mexico. During the square of the mid-1950s came the first group of revolts against Soviet communism in Eastern Europe (East Germany, Poland and Hungary). They failed, but they were signs of things to come. Successful pro-communist revolutions also broke out in Cuba, Vietnam, and Iraq that would later haunt the United States. Then in 1989 the most successful series of revolutions ever seen took down communist control in Eastern Europe and threatened the Chinese state as well. Successful revolts also happened in this same period in U.S. satellite regimes such as South Korea, the Philippines and Chile.

Fourth and finally, some Uranus-Neptune conjunctions and oppositions challenge and alter our most dearly-held beliefs and ideals, and mark the times when great religions are born. We could say that Uranus and Neptune bring spiritual or religious revolutions as well as political ones. These are called times of religious dispensation.

Uranus-Neptune and the Age of Aquarius

In a series of brilliant articles in The Encyclopedia of Astrology, Charles Jayne described a 600-year cycle of great religions, indicated by eclipse cycles.[5] Every 600 years, he said, a new religion or its founders are born, and at each of those times Uranus is either aligned with or opposing Neptune. Starting with the great triple conjunction of the Axis Age, these are the dates:

575 B.C. (conjunction): Births of Buddha and Pythagoras; careers of Lao-Tzu, Mahavira and Confucius. Babylonian captivity of the Jews. Final Upanishads written.

A.D. 25 (opposition): Beginning of mission and the crucifixion 3 years later of Jesus the Christ. Grand cross of all 4 large outer planets, closest in May and June of 25 A.D. (or C.E.).

623 (conjunction): Flight of Mohammed from Mecca in 622 C.E., the birth of Islam.

1222 (opposition): Founding of Franciscan and Dominican Orders in Catholicism; career of St. Thomas Aquinas; great Gothic cathedrals built-- the peak of the Age of Faith.

1821 (conjunction): Births of the co-founders of the Bahai Faith; Joseph Smith's visionary conversion (Mormonism); birth of Mary Baker Eddy (Christian Science, Unity, etc.), births of Thoreau and Whitman (American Transcendentalism); founding of the American Unitarian Association. This was also the time when Marx and Engels were born, suggesting that this cycle represents socialism as a religion, while the Uranus-Pluto conjunction of 1850 represents socialism as a revolutionary movement. Its career as the former may thus long outlast its history as the latter. The primary tenet of the religion of socialism can be summed up in the phrase, "we are all in this life together."

2422 (opposition): The next great religion is not due until then. It may advance the essence of the Aquarian Age, just as St. Francis did for Christianity in the Piscean Age. We can further speculate that the previous opposition of 1175 B.C. may have coincided with Moses, the conjunction of 1779 B.C. with Abraham, and the conjunction of 2980 B.C. with Krishna. The next conjunction in the series after 2421-6 will be in 3025.

The Age of Aquarius is one of the 12 phases in a great Earth cycle. Our planet's pole wobbles as it spins, and one complete wobble is about 25,680 years long. This polar shift gradually moves the star constellation that the Sun is in at the vernal equinox backwards, about one constellation every 2140 years. This is called the precession of the equinoxes, and it is the source of our idea that the New Age is dawning, because the equinox is now shifting back through the constellation Pisces and into Aquarius.

---

[5] Charles A. Jayne, "Cycles" in The Encyclopedia of Astrology, by Nicholas DeVore, Philosophical Library, 1947.

Curiously enough, some skeptics point out that the signs of the zodiac that most western astrologers use are not the same as the constellations they were apparently named after, and therefore they say that astrology is wrong. And yet this very difference is the basis for the most famous prophecy ever uttered by astrologers-- that today is the dawning of the Age of Aquarius! If astrologers didn't know about the precession cycle, why would they use it to make this prediction? Although the significance of the constellations is doubtful, the Earth cycle itself is most real. I use the recent beginning of all 3 new mutual cycles of the outer three invisible planets (and the first conjunction of visible planets Jupiter and Saturn in Aquarius in 800 years in 2020, with 3 more to come, and the first conjunction of Uranus and Neptune in Aquarius in 3600 years due in 2165) to explain the idea that the New Age is upon us, but all of our predictions take place within the story of the dawning of the 2140-year Age of Aquarius. Clearly just as Christianity expressed the meaning of the Piscean Age, since its symbol is a fish, and the zodiac symbols of Aries the Ram and Taurus the Bull correspond to the religious symbols of those ages, the New Age also represents a new religion. The sign Aquarius pictures a man pouring out water from a pitcher for his fellows. Poet Ron Lampi suggests this symbol could also be represented as a fountain.[6] And now the Man can also be feminine. Since Aquarius is the sign of knowledge, and Pisces is the sign of belief, the New Age religion will be based on knowledge of the divine rather than belief in It. Continuous creativity flowing forth from the fountain will be its blessing.

Clearly, since both Uranus-Neptune and the precession have to do with religion, the two cycles must be linked. And that's what we find. As we saw above, Uranus opposed Neptune at the time of Christ, in A.D. 25, in a cosmic crucifix. Neptune was in Capricorn and Uranus was in Cancer. In 1821, almost 1,800 years later, the two planets came into conjunction in Capricorn. In twice this time (almost 3,600 years), the conjunction or opposition always returns to virtually the same degree of the same sign. This is one reason why the religious cycle is 600 years long; it is exactly one-sixth of the time between Uranus-Neptune conjunctions in the same degree of the zodiac. Since the conjunction of 1821 happened at such a significant time, near the start of the Aquarian Age, and one-half of the 3,600-year cycle since Christ, the new religions of the Nineteenth Century (Baha'ism, Mormonism, Transcendentalism, American Unitarianism, Christian Science, New Thought, Socialism, etc.) represent the religious dispensation for our time, and the foundation of the New Age.

Two full Ages in the precession cycle also bring Uranus and Neptune into conjunction in the same place in the sky 4280 years later, as indicated by the constellations rather than the signs. The conjunction of Uranus and Neptune in the year 2165 will be the first one in the sign Aquarius since 1435 BC, and will mark 2140 years since the time of Christ at the dawn of the Piscean Age when Uranus and Neptune were in opposition in 25 AD, the exact length of a precessional Age. We can expect the New Age to come into full expression then for the first time.

---

[6] Ron Lampi, The Vision of Psyche, 2006, p.13.

There are also significant cosmic events at the turn of the third millennium that mark the oncoming New Age. For example, the galactic center is now close to right angles to the equinox, at the very moment when we are reaching out to the stars and outer space. The great 493-year Neptune-Pluto cycle in the fortunes of civilization (see above) may also be linked to the precession of the equinoxes (the 2,140-year "Ages"). A Neptune-Pluto conjunction returns to the same place in about 50,000 years, equal to two precession cycles.

Other cycles in history have been proposed which other scholars and students follow. When the "end of the Mayan Calendar" came in 2012, some predicted the end of the world we have known. I called it "a point of no return," after which we can no longer avoid facing the results of our actions and must reconstruct the world. Economic cycles and cycles of social unrest, such as those of Kondratief or Peter Turchin, might often jell with planetary cycles and confirm them to some extent. They might inform prophets like me too, adding to my insight into the future. One cycle that sometimes informs my predictions is the saeculum or generational cycle proposed by Strauss and Howe in their books Generations and The Fourth Turning.[7] In this theory there are four repeating types of generations that shape history, and the generations are shaped by history in turn. Typical child-rearing and family relationships help to shape the generations as well. When a historical catalyst happens that brings about a critical turning point, the constellation of the four generations shifts so that the next older one becomes the elders, and so on down the line. Strauss and Howe said this brings on the next in the series of four repeating "turnings," analogous to the four seasons. The reason that this cycle is attractive to astrologers like me, even though Strauss and Howe don't accept astrology, is that the saeculum cycle in modern times since about 1700 is defined as 84 years, exactly the same as the orbital cycle of Uranus. Turnings each last about 21 years, although the exact timing varies because of events. Astrologers have long known that every time Uranus returns to its original place in its horoscope, the United States goes through a crisis in which it must struggle for its very existence. These "fourth turnings" or winter-like phases of crisis happened at the first settlement at Jamestown, and from then on during King William's War, in which the Parliament replaced absolute royal rule in the mother country, and then the Revolutionary War, the Civil War, and the Great Depression/World War Two. As of this writing, we are in another fourth turning. The continued existence of the United States now hangs in the balance.

After the fourth turning, if things turn out well, a spring-like First Turning happens when society is well organized and a national consensus develops that supports the people, but conformity reigns and the spirit of life is dying. Then comes the Second Turning or Awakening, when individual rights and a new culture and spirituality blaze forth that disrupt the consensus in the long run. In the Third Turning or Unravelling, society's needs are neglected in favor of individualism, and the rising and developing new culture conflicts with the old, but individuals themselves find fulfillment. Since World War Two, in my opinion, most of our new global civilization has now attuned itself to this originally

---

[7] William Strauss and Neil Howe, The Fourth Turning: What the Cycles of History Tell Us About America's Next Rendezvous with Destiny. New York: Broadway Books, 1997.

American and Western European cycle, and this also accords best with the modern zodiac correlation. I also covered the generations in Chapter 10 of my previous book Horoscope for the New Millennium, which was released the same month as The Fourth Turning.

The Valley of Transition

I have spoken of the period from the late 18th century to the dawn of the 21st as crossing a valley of transition from one age to another. This map of the landscape of modern times is based on the cycle of civilization. Remember I wrote above of the closing square between Neptune and Pluto as a last glory of the old cycle that laid the seeds for the new world, followed by the closing sextile as a time of dissolution and disintegration as the cycle of civilization goes deeper into its "dark moon" phase. Following the conjunction of Neptune and Pluto which is like a dark new moon starting the next cycle at the valley floor, the destruction of the old world is followed by the emergence of the new in a golden age and renaissance during the opening sextile. At this writing, we are supposed to be living in this new golden age. When I wrote my previous book, it seemed like this was happening. But as of this writing it doesn't seem like we made it. This may be a reflection of the fourth turning.

We have come a long way though. It has been a long and perilous journey across the valley. Along our own yellow brick road to Oz, we met the scarecrow, who gave us a new brain: emerging in the Enlightenment and the inventive genius of the Age of Revolution (in other words, we discovered Uranus in 1781). At that time we stood atop the "Mountain," which the French Revolutionaries actually called themselves as they made leaps into the future with their activities. Then a man of tin manufactured by our new industry gave us a new heart of compassion (Neptune, discovered in 1846). Finally the once cowardly lion found his courage (Pluto, at first barely seen through a glass darkly in 1930 as the deadly powers of the atom and the dictator and existential angst, and then fully discovered in the 1960s and 1970s as the power to transform ourselves and connect with others). Along the way, right after we first saw the Oz movie itself in 1939, we defeated the wicked witches of the East and the West (the Japanese and Germans in World War II) and created the streamlined world of our 1939 world's-fair dreams. It was a real hurricane indeed. By the Year 2000 we reached what Al Gore called a "mountaintop moment," which initially seemed to fulfill Dr. King's dying promise in 1968 that we as a people would get to the Promised Land, which God had allowed him to "go up to the Mountain" to look over to the other side of the Valley of Transition and see.

We probably haven't reached the Emerald City yet. It may not even be built until 2165, or even later. But we can still laud and celebrate how much we have changed. Just consider where we started. In the mid-18th century, kings, aristocrats and emperors still ruled without restraint from one end of the Earth to the other. Manual labor was our only source of power, and the majority of people were peasants who lived lives of drudgery at the mercy of the weather and the elements. We had been through ten of these valleys before; ten Neptune-Pluto cycles of civilization. But ours was the real voyage of discovery and liberation among all these cycles, because for the first time ever the divine, invisible powers of light (Uranus), love (Neptune) and life (Pluto) were opened up to us. In the last 250 years democracy has advanced widely, although tyranny also remains. Our new technology and organizing skill have given us undreamed of physical powers and wealth, although their benefits are not shared equitably or sustainably. Once-hidden and forbidden spiritual and soul force knowledge has become available to us all, although many still deny this.

We thus have in the 21st century entered upon a new plain and plateau of progress in which we can further develop these new transcendental abilities. Considering the Pandora's Box of problems which they have also brought us, we have even greater need now to master and harness them so we can learn to live in harmony and mutual responsibility with each other and with our Earth home, as well as to continue exploring all the physical and metaphysical realms that have opened up to us. Now that we possess far more than any people ever has before of the great cultural and artistic legacy of the once-forgotten and unknown civilizations on Earth, it is up to us to be awed and inspired enough by them, and by our own recent spiritual awakenings, to rise above the merely technical and financial achievements that have obsessed us during this dangerous journey across the valley. We need now to aim instead to match and surpass our heritage by expanding our creative gifts and talents, and expressing them fully, so that our unprecedented potential for greatness is actually fulfilled.

Chapter 3

The Supporting Guideposts

While the outer three invisible planets Uranus, Neptune and Pluto chart the larger trends in civilization and culture, and represent the breakthrough ideas of the creative minority, the 7 visible planets known since ancient times give us the scoop on what's happening in the normal everyday world.

☉ **The Sun** is the center of the solar system, the basic source of our life and energy. He represents the glory attributed to the Father-God Creator or to the creative force of life. He is constant and unwavering. The Sun is our own consciousness and sense of self identity; the center of ourselves and our world and the focal point around which everything in our lives revolves. The Sun is noble, dramatic and expressive.

☽ **The Moon** represents our instincts, intuitions, emotions and feelings. Symbol of family and the Mother goddess, she nourishes life and provides for basic needs. She makes the Sun's rays more easily viewed and assimilated. More unstable than the Sun, the Moon reflects the Sun's rays and rules the fluctuating tides. She appears to wax and wane in her light. The Moon represents our personality and our changing moods. She is the symbol of the common people.

☿ **Mercury** is named after the ancient God Hermes or Thoth. He is the Magician who brings knowledge to humanity and the winged messenger who represents writing, communication, awareness of facts, and rational thought. Mercury symbolizes brethren and neighbors as well as short journeys. Quick, agile and restless, Mercury can also appear as the trickster.

♀ **Venus** is the goddess of love and the productive powers of nature who represents the sensuous allure of feminine beauty and sexuality. She represents art, but also money and values generally. She brings diplomacy, stability and peace, but also provides good strategic planning, and she balances and evaluates. Sometimes Venus-influenced people can be complacent and indulgent.

♂ **Mars** is the god of war. He stirs up trouble and rouses us to action and adventure. Mars represents conquest and the courage and strategic skill to defend against our enemies. He is a symbol of male sexual desire and has a strong sense of ego and individuality. Mars gives us the energy and dedication to fight inner battles as well as outer ones.

♃ **Jupiter** is the jolly giant among the planets. He brings us wealth, abundance, wisdom, and celebration in pageantry, ceremony and ritual. Jupiter expands our perspective and guides us so that we can understand and follow the moral laws that govern society. Jupiter represents organized religion and the priesthood as well as philosophy and the Higher Mind generally. He is the ultimate "joiner," but also sends us on long journeys and travels. The eternal optimist and enthusiast, Jupiter has the exuberant faith and confidence to dream and act big. But people ruled by Jupiter can also become restless, arrogant or over-confident.

♄ **Saturn** represents law and order. Whereas Jupiter is the Church, Saturn is the State. Saturn organizes, controls and restricts us. He sets boundaries and rules. His regal bearing is represented by the shimmering rings that crown the skies around him. Saturn is very realistic, worldly, pessimistic, practical and down-to-earth; the teacher and task-master. Saturn is ambitious and seeks status and power. He is the god of old age and Father Time, and the favorite of kings, high officials and petty bureaucrats. People ruled by Saturn are thinkers who follow well-trod procedures and formulas, and they may be dogmatic or limited in their outlook to what is traditional or strictly demonstrated by science and precedent.

Saturn is the ancient ruler of the visible world. Until Uranus was discovered in 1781, thus ending the ages-old Reign of Chronos (Father Time), Saturn was the highest authority in the world, the loftiest leadership that we could see. Questioning what the royal rulers decreed was usually not allowed, except perhaps among a few initiates and confidants and maybe the court jesters. On the other hand, under Saturn people didn't have to worry about things changing too drastically or too quickly; at least until the weather turned and the crops failed. Saturn provided a limiting, traditional and stable form and a measured, classical framework for our lives in the visible world-- what the Renaissance artists called perspective. Considered to be ruling under God and with the approval of Church authority, the King or Queen of Renaissance and Medieval times was often somewhat more considerate and amenable and less brutal than the modern dictator, who also has more tools with which to keep us in subjection at his disposal.

The Chronocraters and the Transcendental Trinity[8]

Jupiter and Saturn, the two largest planets in our solar system, and the farthest visible planets from Earth, together represent the authorities of the Establishment. Traditionally, these are the Church and the royal State, respectively; nowadays they can be political administrations and bureaucracies, corporations, businesses and academies too. Even though revolutions have been continuing for over 250 years since Saturn's reign was overthrown, established authority remains very powerful. For the ideals of the outer planets and of the New Age, those of liberty, equality and fraternity, to actually be put into practice in a lasting way, they still have to be adopted and practiced within existing, visible institutions. Revolutions and movements go through long cycles, and so does the Establishment, and this is indicated by the conjunctions and cycles of Jupiter and Saturn.

---

[8] Historical references for the events mentioned in this chapter are found in **Appendix I**

Jupiter and Saturn come together in conjunction slightly less than every 20 years. When they do, a new direction and new goals are adopted by the Established rulers and authorities. In the old days these two "chronocraters" or time-lords often indicated that a new king or a new dynasty was coming to power, either soon or right away. The king is dead; long live the king. In modern times, it is well known how this conjunction corresponded for 120 years to the deaths in office of the President of the United States elected in the zero year just before this conjunction every 20 years. This cycle can define a generation, and signifies the predominant concerns, attitudes and activities of the people and their rulers during each decade, with the opposition 10 years later marking a big climax in which huge events occur, after which the trends switch into an opposite direction. Consider the roaring 20s and the gloomy 30s, or the idealistic 60s and the uncertain 70s. Often we cast a chart for the time of this conjunction, or for the nearest new moon to it, and by referring to this chart we can divine and discern what the cycle holds over the next 20 years.

Besides their own cycle, Jupiter and Saturn also move through mutual conjunctions and cycles with the three outer planets of the Transcendental Trinity. To discern the meaning of the conjunction and the whole cycle, we also cast charts for the times of these other conjunctions among all five of the outer planets, or for the nearest new moons before the conjunctions, and also for the monthly solar-lunar phase cycle. We will summarize a bit later how we read these charts.

Conjunctions with Saturn are the most significant, as you might imagine, and often bring new and old ideas into immediate contact. **Saturn-Uranus** conjunctions can establish regimes that bring reforms or indicate reforms and new technologies coming into existence within those established and often authoritarian institutions. For example, when Napoleon invaded Eastern Europe at the battle of Austerlitz on Dec.2, 1805, Saturn and Uranus were tightly joined. His 1804 legal code was thereby extended to the continent. When Saturn joined Uranus in 1851-52, his nephew Emperor Napoleon III took over France, and his policies improved the economy and helped the poor. The conjunction of 1942 indicated how World War II required women in the USA to enter the workplace, and weapons to be modernized and made airborne. USA entry into the war eventually brought more liberty to Europe too. In 1988 major reforms within the Soviet Union were launched, leading eventually to upheaval.

On the other hand, when Saturn and Uranus are in opposition, the revolution and the establishment come into direct conflict. A wave of revolutions broke out in 1830-31, for example, putting an end to the royal restoration in Western Europe after the French Revolution. In 1875-76, an opposition between these two planetary contraries coincided with the Balkan revolutionary upheaval that eventually led to World War I. While Saturn and Uranus opposed each other between late 1917 and early 1920, revolutions broke out all over Europe after the end of that Great War, including in Russia, and in the United States rural and urban priorities clashed over labor rights, Prohibition and the League of Nations. In the mid-1960s, Saturn and Uranus (with Pluto) clashed in the United States over voting rights, the counter-culture and the war in Vietnam. There was a wave of coups in Africa too, and growing ferment in communist lands. After the Great Recession of 2008, the first black president of the USA clashed with the conservative anti-tax Tea Party Movement during Saturn's opposition to Uranus in 2008-2010, with Pluto squaring both planets in 2010. Iranians disputed their election and staged a massive rebellion from June 2009 to early 2010. As the financial crises deepened in Europe, Greeks protested and the UK prime minister resigned in May of that year, and others followed in late 2010 and early 2011. Saturn-Uranus squares (the first and last quarter phases of the cycle) are also times to watch for these kinds of conflicts to break out, especially civil wars (as in 1793 in France, 1861 in America and 1975 in Lebanon for example).

Saturn and Neptune is also an interesting cycle that brings compassionate ideals and ruling authority into contact. It has something of a gloomy and delusive cast. It can dissolve authority or put it on a new foundation of idealism or fanciful extremism. As we saw Neptune is the ruling planet of communism and socialism, and the conjunction with Saturn has marked important events in the history of that movement's power. Marx and Engels were writing their manifesto during the conjunction of 1847, for example, in which they said that the spectre of communism was haunting Europe. Famine and worker unrest there were undermining authority, and revolutions broke out early the next year. During the conjunction of 1917 communism was institutionalized in the Soviet Union. During the conjunction of 1953 Stalin, the Soviet dictator who had reigned almost from the beginning, died, and some liberalization followed. But right during the exact conjunction in 1989 the whole Soviet Empire in Eastern Europe collapsed, and the Soviet Union itself dissolved less than 2 years later. Further cycles of state socialism could emerge in the future that follow the Saturn-Neptune rhythm.

Saturn was conjunct Neptune at the top of the birth horoscopes of two presidents who were apostles and martyrs of change, and who shared a common destiny, JFK and Abraham Lincoln, as well as appearing in FDR's chart. It is notable that Saturn and Neptune were opposing each other during the height of the American Civil War in 1862-63, and during the Spanish Civil War in 1936-37; huge strikes boosted labor power in the USA too at that time. The Watergate Burglary brought scandal to the White House in 1972, as the War in Vietnam raged under this opposition. A Saturn-Neptune conjunction accompanied the Boston Tea Party in December 1773, and during the following opposition in August 1792 (when Jupiter also aligned with Neptune and with Mars, see below), the French King was overthrown, soon after which massacres of royalist prisoners began in September. But in the same month, after the new French citizen armies turned back Austrian invaders at Valmy, singing as they fought, the poet Goethe pronounced that a new era had begun in the history of the world, and the revolutionaries declared the Fall Equinox of 1792 as the beginning of Year One. The Reign of Terror followed.

Another meaning of Saturn and Neptune together is religion in politics. A notable example of this happened after the American CIA deposed the ruler of Iran and installed the Shah back in power during the conjunction in 1953. When the closing square of that cycle happened, the Ayatollah Khomeini aroused the Iranian people to throw out the Shah late in 1978 and establish a theocracy. During this same square the right-wing religious "moral majority" was on the march in the USA too. 1953 was also the height of the McCarthy hearings. I have also noticed that this cycle has been in effect during the worst floods and hurricanes, and during the biggest spikes in world temperatures resulting from global warming and climate change, including in 1998 which I predicted in my book, and so squares and other aspects between Saturn and Neptune bear watching for such events. The green revival of c.2007 also occurred under this aspect.

Pluto seems to indicate, among other things, modern war, organized on a deadly and horrific scale. If Mars is the God of War, then Pluto is the higher Lord of Mars. The obsessive-compulsive, constant *Pluto-Charon polarity* concentrates and intensifies whatever it touches. Pluto alone does not indicate war, but big wars often start when Pluto comes into hard aspect with Saturn and can be triggered by aspects from the lesser war god Mars. In fact, **Saturn and Pluto** in conjunction indicates the beginning of a modern war cycle. Wars that break out under Saturn-Pluto conjunctions, and triggered by Mars, are often related to others that happen later when Saturn and Pluto reach their opposition and square phases. It is now our job as humans to be aware of these times to see if we can prevent the wars from breaking out, and if we don't agree with them, to try to stop them once they get going. This conjunction cycle needs to be raised to a higher level if we want to survive on Planet Earth. As Martin Luther King Jr. said, **"We must learn to live together as brothers or perish together as fools."**

In 1914, Saturn conjoined Pluto and then was squared by Mars as the first World War broke out in early August. When the following Saturn-Pluto opposition happened in 1931, Japan invaded Manchuria. When the exact closing square arrived in late August and early September of 1939, as Mars squared Saturn and opposed Pluto, Hitler invaded Poland and started World War Two.

The next cycle began when Mars joined both planets in a long conjunction in late 1947 and 1948. The US-Soviet Cold War began during the Greek and Turkish civil wars and the Soviet Berlin embargo, and the Israeli war of independence against the Arabs also happened. Soon the US and Soviet superpowers aligned on opposite sides of the resulting long Arab-Israeli conflict. In 1956 during the square, an Israeli-Egyptian clash at the Gulf of Suez, and the Hungarian Revolt against the Soviets, stoked Cold War tensions. In early 1965, Saturn opposed Pluto, Uranus and Mars as the Cold War reached its hot heights in the jungles of Vietnam, when the USA invaded that artificially-divided country to defeat Soviet-backed communist rebels there, causing a huge 10-year cataclysm, and then in 1967 Israel conquered Arab lands in the 6-Day War. In October 1973, under the exact closing Saturn-Pluto square, the Yom Kippur War between Israel and Egypt almost brought the USA and the Soviet Union to blows again, and it caused the first great energy crisis due to the Arab Oil Embargo against The West.

Terrorist attacks by radical Muslims in the 1980s followed from the Arab-Israeli conflicts. In June 1982, as the three planets gathered for another long conjunction, the Israelis invaded Lebanon to suppress Muslim attacks against Israel. The USA sent a peacekeeping mission there in August, which resulted in a massacre of USA troops by Muslim terrorists in 1983, and USA hostages were taken. Then when the square arrived in

Feb. 1993, Muslim terrorists bombed the World Trade Center in New York City. On Sept.11, 2001, as Saturn opposed Pluto and Mars, in a war I predicted, they attacked there again, bringing down the two twin World Trade Center towers completely, and killing almost 3000 people. The USA thereupon attacked them and the Taliban government in Afghanistan that was harboring them, and the resulting "forever war" continues. In 2011, Saturn was in square to Pluto and opposing Uranus as revolutions and civil wars broke out in the Middle East region, which also continue. The next exact conjunction is scheduled as of this writing for 2020, and Mars will join the action then too. Stay tuned and read the chapters ahead to continue to follow the cycle!

Richard Tarnas added more to my knowledge of this cycle in his book Cosmos and Psyche.[9] He mentioned the heroic sacrifice that is often displayed in response to destructive events during these Saturn-Pluto aspects, such as those who died rescuing the victims of 9-11. This is arguably a higher expression of this often-brutal planetary combination. He also noticed that during the hard aspects between Saturn and Pluto, conservative and reactionary or tyrannical power increases, and conservative parties come to power. Although the orb he uses is wide, and the correlations are inexact, it's a pattern worth keeping in mind. It is notable already that between 2017 and 2019, as the Saturn-Pluto conjunction in the conservative sign Capricorn (Saturn's ruling sign) approached, a wave of conservative, reactionary and tyrannical rulers and trends took power around the world, including Brexit and Boris Johnson in the UK, Trump in the USA, Deterte in the Phillipines, Erdogen on Turkey, Orban in Hungary, Xi Jinping in China, Morrison in Australia, Bolsonaro in Brazil, etc. Could it be that sometimes, or someday, Pluto will transform the state and the authorities instead of intensifying their tyranny when it comes into contact with Saturn?

Uranus helps this to happen when it's around, of course. Liberals are often in power during the major Uranus aspects. When both Saturn-Pluto and Uranus aspects are happening at the same time, though, the situation is more confusing. Both revolutionary reforms and a conservative backlash and repression occur simultaneously. The mid-1960s provided an excellent example of this when Ronald Reagan got elected Governor of California in 1966 in reaction to student protests. Another was the Tea Party response in the USA to the Obama administration in 2010 and the repression after the 2011 Arab Spring revolts. In these cases Saturn and Pluto were joined by Uranus, and all 3 planets formed aspects to each other. This archetypal pattern was set in the French Revolution in 1793 by a similar T-square to the one in 2010, and it returns under hard aspects between these three planets as new bosses fight with the old bosses. The 2017-19 reactionary wave was also partly a xenophobic response to the massive refugee crisis unleashed by repression of these Arab Spring revolts in 2011, and by the huge droughts that have been caused by anthropogenic climate change worldwide since then, as I predicted.

Jupiter-Uranus conjunctions and oppositions were also extensively discussed by Tarnas.[10] Able to call forth almost superhuman confidence and faith in all of us, they

[9] Richard Tarnas, Cosmos and Psyche, Viking Penguin, 2006, p. 209ff.
[10] Richard Tarnas, Ibid., p. 291ff.

restore vitality. Uranus and Jupiter together indicate successful and liberating moments during revolutions, and extraordinary world-bridging "quantum leaps" and inventions in technology. Examples include the outbreak of the American Revolution and its first battles in 1775, and the Fall of the Bastille and the end of French feudal aristocracy during the Revolution in 1789. Nothing was more breathtaking than when the feudal lords in the new French assembly stepped up one after the other in a mania of glorious generosity to renounce their ancient privileges in August. That's when they declared the rights of man and the citizen too. The spirit of Bastille Day came to Britain during a Jupiter-Uranus conjunction in Aquarius in 1832, when massive unrest spurred passage of the Great Reform Bill. The first May Day labor demonstration and riot in Chicago in 1886 under this conjunction was remembered as a pivotal event in the labor movement that is celebrated annually in socialist countries. Another example happened during the Arab Spring when a million young activists filled Tahrir Square in Cairo Egypt for over 2 weeks in January and February 2011 and forced out their old tyrant Mubarik. Inspired by the successful rising in Tunisia that began on the exact day of the conjunction on January 4th, other such uprisings followed all over the Arab World. The Egyptian one was called the "Arab Woodstock," and that was a remarkable statement, since that culminating event of the counter-culture also happened when Jupiter was in conjunction with Uranus in August 1969. More recently, Trump's inauguration brought millions of protesters into the streets of America in the first of several annual "women's marches," as Jupiter opposed Uranus in January 2017. These were amazing moments of exhilarating liberation, but the results did not always last. Jupiter moves a lot faster than Uranus, Neptune and Pluto do, after all.

At almost the same time as Woodstock, Neil Armstrong stepped onto the Moon on July 20, 1969 and called it "one giant leap for mankind." Not only were Uranus and Jupiter in exact alignment that day, but the Moon itself was aligned with them too. This feat recalled Charles Lindbergh's solo flight across the Atlantic Ocean as Jupiter aligned with Uranus in May 1927. It was also preceded by Apollo 8's Moon orbit on Christmas Eve in 1968, when the "Woodstock conjunction" was also close, and by John Glenn's breakthrough spaceflight around the Earth in late February 1962 when the two planets were opposed soon after a great eclipse in which all the visible planets were in the inventive sign Aquarius. Another notable technological invention that broke through barriers and bridged distances was brought into being when Samuel Morse wrote "What hath God Wrought" as the first telegraph message, during the Jupiter-Uranus conjunction in May of 1844. Even quantum theory itself, which eventually became the basis of so much world-shrinking high technology, was born during a Jupiter-Uranus conjunction in 1900 in the work of Max Planck. And as Lindbergh crossed the Atlantic under that conjunction in 1927, just before Pluto was discovered, Bohr, Heisenberg and other scientists were making quantum leaps that brought the theory to a climax.

Jupiter-Neptune conjunctions are often amazing too. They are perhaps the most fortunate of all planetary alignments. For example, when Mars, Jupiter and Neptune aligned in a close conjunction (with Uranus also opposing Pluto, of course), volunteers marched in a blaze of patriotic glory from Marseilles to Paris and overthrew their King on

August 10, 1792, singing a new song as they went, and established the First Republic. This song became the French national anthem. Thomas Carlyle later wrote that a more fortunate musical composition has never been written. According to Kenneth Clark, the finest minds were enraptured, and this heroic action inspired the romantic movement.[11] Another such alignment happened when Napoleon went off to battle in his series of great victories in 1805. Many times when these three planets join forces in aspect, you can bet that a mass uprising of people is going forth to support some great cause. One example was the student-worker French uprising in 1968, when the 3 planets squared off with each other. Another was the largest protests in world history against the proposed US invasion of Iraq in February 2003, when Jupiter opposed Neptune, and Mars was in a trine to Neptune.

As that event showed, Jupiter-Neptune is also a great omen for world peace events. The first organization for peace was created in 1907 at The Hague Netherlands under this conjunction, and that was followed by the League of Nations founding in 1920, and the United Nations beginning after World War Two in 1945, both right under this conjunction. In 1971 Jupiter and Neptune were again aligned as Nixon announced US detente with China, and agreements with the Soviets were signed early the following year. In late 1984, the conjunction accompanied the start of benevolent mass movements and huge benefit concerts to help starving people in Ethiopia. Song accompanied *this* event too, including "Do They Know It's Christmas" and "We Are the World." Reforms are a frequent correlation to these aspects as well, including the New Deal in 1933 (conjunction), Civil Rights/Voting Rights Laws and Great Society proposals of 1964-65 (opposition), the Fall of the Berlin Wall in November 1989 (Jupiter exact opposition to both Neptune and Saturn), and Obamacare in 2009-2010 (conjunction).

Not as much can be said about **Jupiter-Pluto** conjunctions, since Jupiter moves so fast and Pluto moves so slow. These aspects are frequent and don't last very long. But they seem to magnify whatever is going on and add to change and mobility. Such was the case when Jupiter joined the Uranus-Pluto line-up in 1968, from the time of the Democratic National Convention to the election. It expanded the ferment of the time. Another example might be the enormous tank battles between the Nazis and the Soviets in 1943. Wars may accelerate, even toward a conclusion, under Jupiter-Pluto aspects, as in late 1918 during the Great War in Europe, or April 1975 in Vietnam. These alignments seem to inflate peoples' energies and probably contribute to extremism and reckless adventures. Financial panic might be going on, as in 1931 and 2007 under Jupiter-Pluto conjunctions. Disasters and political/religious attacks and bombings may be more likely under these aspects too. For example, the Jupiter-Pluto opposition in January and April-June of 2014, within the grand cross with Mars and Uranus, witnessed the sudden expansion of the Islamic State and the start of the Ukraine civil war.

The Other Indicators

Closer to the Earth, **Mars** is bound to get into the mix whenever there's trouble, or when action and adventure stirs the blood. I mentioned above how it contributes to the

---

[11] Kenneth Clark, <u>Civilization</u>, Harper and Row, 1969, p.296.

breakout of wars when it links up with the hard aspects of Saturn and Pluto, and to the outbreak of revolutions when it joins forces with Jupiter, Uranus and Neptune. According to a survey of *major wars* that I calculated, they are 3 times more likely to break out when Mars is in hard aspect to Saturn. They may also indicate a dangerous crisis that may or may not break out into war, depending on what we decide. For example, Mars was in opposition to Saturn during the Cuban Missile Crisis in late October 1962. Tensions between the USA and Iran ramped up when Iran shot down a US drone, as Mars opposed Saturn and Pluto in June 2019. President Trump called off a retaliatory strike that had been in process. Mars frequently also made hard aspects to Saturn, Uranus and Pluto during key events in the civil rights movement and other protests during the 1960s.

There's another major indicator of world events, however. When the Earth passes by Mars, as it looms large and red in the sky because it is close to Earth, wars and major violent events are more likely. As Mars gets closer to Earth, it appears to stand still and then turns *retrograde*. This doesn't mean Mars is actually moving backwards; it just appears that way because the Earth is passing by and moving faster. About 2 months later Mars stands still again and turns *direct*. The moments when Mars appears to stand still are called turning **stationary**, and it's a pretty big deal. It's as if the significance of Mars is being concentrated and intensified and is arousing us to action. It's kind of like the intensity of Pluto and Charon being in the same place with each other all the time. The direct station is the most powerful, and wars or violent events are likely to break out in the next few weeks after it happens. This is especially true, of course, if Mars is in aspect to Saturn when it turns stationary or when Saturn-Pluto aspects are going on, or other war indicators occur. This happened when most of the wars began that I mentioned above. I offer a list of Mars stations, aspects and events for 1760 to 2050 in Appendix F in Horoscope for the New Millennium (available as a kindle e-book), and here a list of Mars stations and aspects for 2020-2200 in **Appendix F.**

It's sometimes hard to imagine that **Venus** is the planet of beauty and love when its surface is so ugly and torrid. But from a distance, its clouds of sulphur and carbon dioxide cast a lovely yellow-orange light. The secret of Venus's power of love and peace lies not on its surface, however; we have to look a bit deeper into its "loving" relationship with the Earth. This is where Venus demonstrates her true beauty and grace.

Many people know about the divine or golden proportion, and the fibonacci series in which a number is the sum of the preceding two numbers. This series runs as follows: 1, 1, 2, 3, 5, 8, 13, 21, 34, and so on, so that for example 13 = 5 + 8, and 21 = 8 + 13. As it continues, the relationship between each number and its successor approaches the golden or divine proportion of 1.6180339887…, in which the sum is related to the larger number in the same divine proportion as the larger is to the smaller number. This proportion promotes growth and fertility in everything from the propagation of rabbits to the shape of sunflowers and pinecones, and it has been used to design temples all over the world. It is found in spiral formations from seeds to galaxies, and in proportions of the human body. The orbits of Earth and Venus are in this pleasing proportion, because 8 Earth orbits equal 13 Venus orbits.

Because of this proportion, Venus makes 5 passages close to Earth, and then returns to virtually the same place in the sky 8 years later. Lines drawn between successive positions of Earth and Venus every day will produce a pattern of 5 rose petals of 4 sizes within the circle. The rose in the center is also called a pentagram, which you can draw inside of it.

The lengths of all the lines inside a pentagram also are in divine proportion in relation to each other.

When Venus makes its passage close to Earth, Venus is moving between the Earth and the Sun. The Sun always appears to us to be going forward, so Venus seems to be moving in the opposite direction as it passes. So, when Venus approaches its closest rendezvous with Earth, it turns **stationary**, and then moves retrograde. About 3 weeks later Venus reaches a Sun-Venus conjunction, from our point of view. Then 3 weeks later, it turns stationary again, and returns to direct motion. Venus when stationary concentrates and intensifies its energy of peace and love onto the Earth. These are often times of peace agreements and diplomatic or artistic breakthroughs.

Mercury retrograde is famous, associated with miscommunications, breakdowns, mix-ups and other such misfortunes. Its retrograde motion works the same way as that of Venus, since it's also located between the Sun and the Earth. It happens 4 times a year. Mercury stations need to be watched, as they can trigger events indicated by the larger planets, especially regarding transportation and communication breakdowns or breakthroughs.

The same applies to all the other planets. If a planet is stationary, an aspect it is making can be intensified, or matters associated with it might come to the fore if other indicators agree. **Jupiter** stationary, for example, can also indicate diplomatic breakthroughs. Both Venus and Jupiter turned stationary during the Cuban Missile Crisis Oct.22-28, 1962, for example, with Jupiter stationary on the day it was resolved. That certainly helped soften the war-like indications of Mars opposing **Saturn**, which was also stationary that month.

The **horoscopes of nations** are a big deal for predicting world events, which is called mundane astrology. When a nation is founded it's like a person's birthday, and a horoscope is cast for its birth. For some nations there may be more than one national chart, since a new one is usually cast if the nation declares its independence from a colonial power or gets a new constitution, while the older one may still be important too. But for the United States, most astrologers agree on a chart for July 4, 1776 at around 5 PM. This chart for the USA is shown in Chapter 2 under Aspects and in Chapter 12 of my previous book. Readers of this book don't need to know all the details about national charts, but a few factors are good to know, and they play a role in my predictions.

A horoscope consists of 12 "**houses**," which are the 12 regions of the sky centered upon the place of birth. They represent "departments" in the affairs of a person or a nation, and they are analogous to the 12 signs. The significance of each house is mentioned in Chapter 3 of Horoscope for the New Millennium and are **listed in Appendix C**. The most important part of a national chart, however, are the **angles**. The houses and the angles are based on the *cycle of day and night* on Earth. The Ascendant (AC) is the eastern horizon where the Sun rises, and the Descendant (DC) is the western horizon where the Sun sets. The Midheaven (MC) is the zenith which the Sun reaches at Noon, and the Nadir (IC) is its place at Midnight, the start of the 24-hour day. Broadly speaking, the Ascendant represents the people, the Descendant stands for their allies and enemies, the Midheaven represents the power of the state, and the Nadir represents the land, environment and national identity. The signs and planets found on these angles of a national birth horoscope are the most significant in the life of that country.

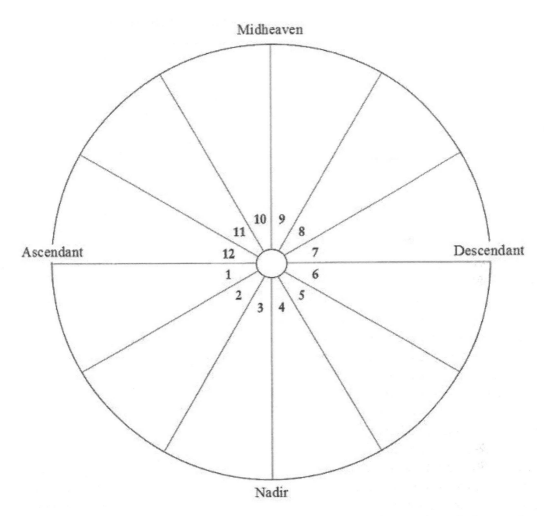

Transits are the current positions of the planets as they go through their cycles. These are very important to predictive and mundane astrology. When found on the angles of a national chart, or going through its houses, they could indicate events for the country. Even more significant is when a major aspect, such as any of the conjunctions we discussed above, happens on an angle of a nation's horoscope, or when it aligns with a planet in that horoscope, especially the nation's Sun and Moon. We look for these alignments to help us locate where the major events indicated by the major aspect will happen.

As we mentioned, we also cast horoscopes for the time when conjunctions happen. One conjunction is by far the most important. It's the first one we mentioned in the last chapter, Neptune conjunct Pluto, which inaugurates the cycle of civilization. I covered the horoscope I cast for this conjunction in Chapter 12 of Horoscope for the New Millennium, which was also the chart of a total solar eclipse (more about eclipses below). It is called the Chart of Our Age, the Horoscope of Modern Humanity, or simply, **The Horoscope of Humanity**. It is THAT significant.

Just as how I thought about myself, and then studied the meanings of the signs and planets, and successfully forecast where they would actually be in my chart before looking it up, I have done this in many lectures with the Horoscope of Modern Humanity, also with great success. I won't describe the chart again here, but you can think about the ongoing, endemic qualities of the age we live in, associate signs and aspects with them, and predict what signs and aspects are prominent in this chart, and then look up the chart in **Appendix E** or in the other book to see how closely your prediction matches the chart. I went on to describe in the book how well the chart of 1892 pictures the age we live in. The reason I mention it here, is that I also use the *progressions* of this Chart of Humanity to predict events, and I will be using it this way in this book. These **Secondary progressions**, as they are called, are found by taking one day after birth (in this case the conjunction of Neptune and Pluto in 1892, the birth of today's humanity) as representing one year of life (in this case world events). The planetary positions in this progressed chart are so significant that they can be looked upon the same way as transits. And strangely enough, these progressions often resemble the transits themselves. I will give the date and time for the Neptune-Pluto conjunction and show the progressions in **Appendix E**. Sometimes progressions to national charts, such as the one for the United States, are referred to by some astrologers as well.

Above we illustrated the profound meaning of **Venus** in its relationship to the Earth, especially when it passes Earth and turns stationary. *Venus stationary* particularly stands out in this progressed Chart of Humanity of 1892. In 1945 the progressed Venus turned stationary retrograde (SR) as World War II ended and the United Nations was founded, providing a great example of how Venus brings peace when it's stationary. But it also marked the start of the Cold War between Communism and The West, as Venus went in reverse. When it reached alignment with the Earth and Sun in 1966, the Cold War reached its hot heights in the jungles of Vietnam, and the peace movement against it revved up. The feminist movement was born too (NOW established that year). When it turned stationary again and returned to direct motion in 1989, the Berlin Wall fell and the Cold War ended. Because of this Venus position I predicted the "keystone of new values" and "greater affection among humankind" for this year in my AFA article. I also predicted that a new concern for the Earth would happen then, and in 1990 Earth Day was revived.

A chart for the **New Moon nearest in time to a conjunction** is also significant, whether it is the nearest New Moon to the conjunction of 1892 (which was also a solar eclipse), or the nearest one to any of the other conjunctions we mentioned. Seeing which signs and planets are on the angles and which houses they are in, and also which aspects are happening at the time, tells us what the conjunction indicates. There are two other celestial-earth events that are very important for astrologers to cast a chart for and interpret. The *first* is a **solar eclipse**, like the one in 1892; an exact New Moon in which the Moon blocks the Sun's light. Eclipses happen when the Sun is within about 10 degrees of the Moon Nodes, where the orbits of the Earth and the Moon intersect. Eclipses are inspiring and awesome events that people travel for miles to see. I drove up to Oregon myself in August 2017 to see the "Great American Eclipse" that swept across our country. They are awesome omens for world events too! How many minutes an eclipse lasts, usually from about 2 to 7, indicates how many years it might be significant. So naturally we want to cast a chart for the exact time of the eclipse, which can represent the ongoing affairs at the location for which we cast it. Those locations where the eclipse is *on the angles* of the chart at the time of the eclipse are targeted for the events signified by the eclipse. We also look at which houses the most powerful planetary alignments that happen during the eclipse are in, and at which locations in the world they are lined up with or squaring the angles.

A lunar eclipse can also be important. But the *second* important celestial event is the Spring **Equinox**. This has also been found to exercise great significance in the affairs of the nations and the peoples of Earth during that season and extending into the Summer. The Fall Equinox is the prime indicator for events during the Fall and Winter. Summer and Winter Solstice charts can also be cast to further indicate events during those seasons. The most powerful aspects found in these charts, especially those made by The Moon, are key indicators of the events ahead. We also pinpoint where these events might happen by seeing where the planets are found on angles. *Wherever in the world these aspects are found on the angles in an equinox, eclipse, or conjunction chart (including the 1892 conjunction Horoscope of Humanity), pinpoints where the indicated events might happen.* So, for example, if we want to predict where the people might rise in revolt during a huge Uranus aspect, we look at the locations where it appears on the angles of one of these charts. I have used these location charts for decades, but astrologer Jim Lewis developed an entire method of locational astrology based on these charts. His word astro*carto*graphy became synonymous with these location charts.

Another key idea I use to make predictions is the **cyclic Return to a critical degree of the zodiac**. If a great epoch-making event happens, when a major planet returns to the same degree during which it happened it can echo and re-stimulate the original event. For example, some astrologers note that Pluto is returning in 2022 to its place in 1776 and forecast a new American Revolution. Indeed, this might be happening as you read this, or it may have happened already. It might have been nice to know ahead of time, then! A great conjunction or solar eclipse can also create a critical degree, which can indicate new events related to the original one when planets return to it. I have even given some of these key degrees a name. 1 degree Taurus is the matter-in-motion degree, created by the enormous planetary lineup of Venus, Mars, Saturn, Uranus and Pluto in that degree in early June 1851. The stillness-of-spirit degrees of 17 Virgo/Pisces were created when Mercury, Mars, Saturn, Uranus and Pluto (with Chiron too) piled up in those exact degrees in February 1966.

When important planets return to their positions in a national horoscope, events happen to that nation that recreate in some way the nation's founding. I have noted some of these in this book, especially **Uranus Returns**. For the United States, this cycle has become legendary and can never be ignored. First of all, when Jamestown was created as the first permanent European settlement in America, the future nation could said to have been founded. Then in 1776 the United States became a nation. Every time Uranus returns to the same position it held at both of these events, a great crisis occurs which tests the foundations of the United States, which must wage a struggle for its very existence. These crises include King William's War in 1689-97, the Revolutionary War, the Civil War, and the Great Depression/World War Two. This cycle has unknowingly also become the basis of modern generation cycles such as the one elicited by the authors Strauss and Howe, which I described in the last chapter. And it is of particular concern as of this writing, because another return is just about to happen! Strauss and Howe called it "the fourth turning," and it has already begun. I will describe what this crisis will be like in Chapter 5 in this book entitled "Revving Up the Engines." Usually this crisis has meant a great war. That's because Uranus is located on the Descendant and 7th house of war and divorce in the national horoscope. Stay tuned-- and keep reading.

Another great Return in the American national horoscope is one I have discussed in articles and videos for decades, and it has proven itself over and over again. This is the war cycle indicated by **Jupiter's Return** to its place in the USA national horoscope. You might think that Jupiter is benevolent and diplomatic, but in the chart of the United States, Jupiter is also in the 7th house of war, and it has meant the "generous" self-righteous actions of Uncle Sam to impose its will on others. Besides the War of Independence itself, Jupiter has returned to its 7th house in Gemini and Cancer during almost every war it has waged. When Jupiter returned, Uncle Sam marched off to make the world safe for democracy in World War I, and to save the world from infamy and fascism in World War II. It fought to hold back "aggressors" in Vietnam in 1965, to make the world safe from oil depletion in Iraq in 1990-91, as well as to keep it safe from terror after 9-11-2001 and to beat back the Islamic State in 2014. Along with Uranus, Jupiter makes its next Return around 2025.

The **signs of the zodiac**, though less important than the planetary conjunction cycles, cannot be ignored. They represent the basic Earth yearly cycle and are significant too. *When one of the three planets of the transcendental trinity return to the place of the vernal equinox at 0 degrees Aries*, you can bet this is a very important moment. Especially when Neptune does it, as it is *also* about to do in 2025, it begins an entire 164-year cycle. Neptune inaugurated the US Civil War on the very day that it entered Aries in 1861, April 12-13, 1861.[12] As it enters other signs of the zodiac, Neptune can trigger other events, and it imparts the nature of whatever sign it's in to the zeitgeist of the times. Uranus and Pluto can also be important indicators when they begin a transit to a new sign, and as they transit through those signs, events often reflect those signs too. I covered all these transits extensively in Horoscope for the New Millennium.

Meanings of the signs:

I described the signs thoroughly in Horoscope for the New Millennium. The symbols of the signs and planets listed in this chart are important to know if you want to read horoscope charts.

---

[12] Sarah Janssen, general editor, World Almanac 2018, Infobase, p.140.

♈ **Aries**: (motto: I am) Cardinal fire sign. Represents enthusiasm, initiative, impulse, action, independence, aggression, pioneers, goals, beginnings. (Ruler: Mars.)

♉ **Taurus**: (motto: I have) Fixed earth sign. Represents peace and plenty, stability, realism, security, stagnation, sensuality, economics, arts, architecture, nature. (Ruler: Venus.)

♊ **Gemini**: (motto: I think) Mutable air sign. Represents intellect, ingenuity, novelty, progress, writing, youth, travel, networking, vehicles, speech. (Ruler: Mercury.)

♋ **Cancer**: (motto: I feel) Cardinal water sign. Represents feelings, nurturing, home, defense, patriotism, conservation, family, sensitivity, moodiness, introversion. (Ruler: Moon.)

♌ **Leo**: (motto: I will) Fixed fire sign. Represents pride, expression, nobility, leadership, gambling, speculation, games, entertainment, theater, education, youth. (Ruler: Sun.)

♍ **Virgo**: (motto: I analyze) Mutable earth sign. Represents service, criticism, health, healing, welfare, technology, science, intellectuals, labor, the armed forces, bureaucracy, medicine, anxiety, conformity, the humble classes. (Ruler: Mercury)

♎ **Libra**: (motto: I balance) Cardinal air sign. Represents diplomacy, peace, the arts, partnerships, law, politics, idealism, justice, vacillation, compromise. (Ruler: Venus.)

♏ **Scorpio**: (motto: I desire) Fixed water sign. Represents passion, transformation, turmoil, sex, death, taxes, pooled resources, corporations, economics, communion, renewal, the occult, mysteries, psychology, investigations, awakenings. (Rulers: Mars, Pluto.)

♐ **Sagittarius**: (motto: I see) Mutable fire sign. Represents exuberance, foreign affairs, travel, the outdoors, prophecy, higher mind, religion, clubs, philosophy. (Ruler: Jupiter.)

♑ **Capricorn**: (motto: I use) Cardinal earth sign. Represents ambition, government, authority, tradition, pragmatism, conservatism, endurance, integrity. (Ruler: Saturn.)

♒ **Aquarius**: (motto: I know) Fixed air sign. Represents truth, science, friendship, altruism, hope, ideals, associations, inventors, eccentricity, charisma, catastrophe. (Rulers: Uranus, Saturn.)

♓ **Pisces**: (motto: I believe) Mutable water sign. Represents compassion, imagination, faith, mysticism, intuition, escapism, dissolution, chaos, deception, delusion, martyrdom, sacrifice, religion, Christianity. (Rulers: Neptune, Jupiter.)

It's also important to notice the **elements, qualities and genders** that most of the planets are in. Below is a chart from my previous book to remind you which signs are related to which elements, qualities and genders. They will be mentioned in my predictions as well. Sometimes the **"ruling planets"** of the signs are mentioned in my books. That means that the sign is similar to and connected by nature to that planet, and that planets in or going through that sign can increase the significance of that planet, and its position.

SYMBOL	SIGN	QUALITY	ELEMENT	GENDER	RULING PLANET(S)
♈	Aries	Cardinal	Fire	Masculine	Mars ♂
♉	Taurus	Fixed	Earth	Feminine	Venus ♀
♊	Gemini	Mutable	Air	Masculine	Mercury ☿
♋	Cancer	Cardinal	Water	Feminine	Moon ☽
♌	Leo	Fixed	Fire	Masculine	Sun ☉
♍	Virgo	Mutable	Earth	Feminine	Mercury ☿
♎	Libra	Cardinal	Air	Masculine	Venus ♀
♏	Scorpio	Fixed	Water	Feminine	Mars ♂ / Pluto ♀
♐	Sagittarius	Mutable	Fire	Masculine	Jupiter ♃
♑	Capricorn	Cardinal	Earth	Feminine	Saturn ♄
♒	Aquarius	Fixed	Air	Masculine	Saturn ♄ / Uranus ♅
♓	Pisces	Mutable	Water	Feminine	Jupiter ♃ / Neptune ♆

The North Moon Node's location is marked in charts by ☊ or ♌

Why Astrology?

This morning as I write this, I recently woke up from a dream that somewhat resembled the following mythical scheme: a New Age convocation in a nearby huge park was celebrating the esoteric, spiritual powers that make our lives possible and this universe to go round and round. They were circulating a handout that explained how we can all increase the force of life within us and thereby gain creative energy and enlightenment and make peace and beauty among us. The pamphlet explained that the ancient angels who guided this solar system's development noticed that the original gas giant that originally orbited in a circular path in Pluto's special resonance out beyond Neptune was too unstable to sustain itself and disappeared, so they steered a couple of small bodies to emerge from somewhere further out on the edge of the solar system and to join forces as a binary planet, and to move into an eccentric orbit that would replace the same 1-2-3 resonance that the former gas giant was created to provide. And so Pluto is the key for us to contact that creative energy that can only be generated through the magic power of a transcendental trinity.

How-ever you conceive what created this universe and this solar system, it's evident that life as we know it could not have emerged from the stupid mechanism that outdated scientists often claim it to be. The potential for life and intelligence had to be inherent within it from the start. As Teilhard de Chardin put it, a universe capable of containing the human person, must be a continually personalizing universe.[13] Just like the Sun converts hydrogen into helium through atomic fusion, our cosmos is constantly converting matter into spirit. Alan Watts pointed out that an electric current does not flow unless its end point and destination is already in place.[14] In the context of our evolving universe, Teilhard called this the Omega Point toward which all creation is moving, and he said that this point is our destiny to transcend our material matrix and eventually depend only on God. If there is any coherence in this universe at all, he said, it must not be from below, but from above.[15] All of Being is growing up like a sunflower grows toward the Sun, aspiring toward the greater Being that attracts it, and this Omega Point is the intelligence that attracts, shapes and guides us all to fulfill our individual and group roles in the One Being's spectacular unfolding.

The most fundamental metaphysical principle, said Alan Watts, is that for every outside, there is an inside, and for every inside, there is an outside. Everything that we see exists in our eyes and our brains as we evoke it into being. In other words, we are not just separate individual egos locked inside a bag of skin, but we each depend on all that exists, and it depends on us in turn. We are connected intimately to the world around us, not only through the air we breathe, the food we eat, the water we drink, and even the very consciousness which connects us to whatever it's conscious of, but to the farthest star, the whole universe, "the works."[16] The ancient Hindus called it Brahman, the greater Self which we all are. You are That. And since John Bell's theory has proven, simultaneously with our full discovery of the gravity-entangled binary planet Pluto-Charon, that the universe is non-local, and that every quantum of energy is connected and entangled with another at the moment it is observed, we know that the Hindus were right; that everything is connected. Quantum entanglement has even been used to instantly teleport a quantum of energy from one place to another.

Evolutionary scientist Rupert Sheldrake suggested that the Sun is not just a ball of atomic fire, but that it organized itself, and thus is in some sense a living being which also organized its solar system and now communes with its fellow stars.[17] Astronomers in the

---

[13] Pierre Teilhard de Chardin, <u>The Phenomenon of Man</u>, Harper and Row, 1955, 1965, p.290. See also: p.61; https://www.organism.earth/library/document/154

[14] https://genius.com/Alan-watts-the-nature-of-consciousness-annotated See part 3
https://youtu.be/0nCzlkeYuW4?t=3452

[15] Pierre Teilhard de Chardin, <u>op.cit.</u>, pp. 287-88, p.43

[16] https://www.organism.earth/library/document/83   https://youtu.be/0CXqgLIPjwg

[17] Rupert Sheldrake, <u>The Science Delusion</u>, Coronet, 2012 (Also known as <u>Science Set Free</u>).
https://youtu.be/jShyXnyv_Q4?t=2910   https://youtu.be/VRKvvxku5So
https://www.sheldrake.org/videos/the-science-delusion
https://www.youtube.com/watch?v=VTtaAHNbsQY or https://www.youtube.com/watch?v=SFhsObpja8A
http://media.blubrry.com/science_set_free/www.sheldrake.org/files/audios/ssf_Is-the-Sun-Conscious.mp3

16th century were philosophers who wanted to demonstrate that the solar system moves in a divine order and intelligence. Later they demonstrated that the planets are kept in their orbits by the mysterious interaction called gravity. They have since attempted to define it as an exchange of virtual gravitons, or emanations of gravity waves, or as just the uneven distribution of mass, whatever *that* is, in spacetime. But at bottom it is simply a weak attraction of all objects to each other. You can just as easily describe it as the power of love and say that love moves the planets and the stars. Ultimately the universe cannot be explained as caused by something else; that's an infinite regress and reductio ad absurdum. It is its own cause. In other words, the source of the universe is the creative Being that exists right now, everywhere and eternally. The "big bang" is still going on. No-one knows what caused it; it caused itself. The greater eternal soul causes it. And now the scientists find that 96% of the universe is dark matter and dark energy that they can't explain, and that for some unknown reason its expansion since the big bang is speeding up instead of slowing down. So much for the idea that scientists have explained the universe from its first moments. The more they prove, the more remains to be proved. And every atom in our own bodies and in everything we see contains a strong force of unimaginable magnitude which holds it together, and which when released can blow up the world. Where does all this energy come from? No-one knows, and no-one can say. So amid all this uncertainty, why NOT astrology?

Astrology was given to us, according to the legend passed down to us by hermetic philosophers since the second century AD, by the wise teacher Hermes Trismegistus, who was perhaps originally the priest and scientist Imhotep who designed the stepped pyramid complex at Saqqara in about 2667 BC, and who became deified as the god Hermes or Mercury which is Greek for the Egyptian name of Thoth. He laid out the principle in the Emerald Tablet on which astrology is based: as above, so below; as within, so without. We have discovered it operating today in fractals and in holograms where one small part of a picture reflects the whole. The planets exist within us as well as outside of us and correspond to the physical and subtle-body soul centers of our being, also called chakras. Gravity, the power of love, keeps the Sun, Moon and planets in a regular "divine" order like a cosmic clock, which keeps time for us, but whose motions can be calculated out for millennia. Those motions by themselves exhibit very little freedom or creativity. But within that scheme, the planets themselves are always changing and moving, and each demonstrates its own nature and personality. The living unit we call the solar system originally developed itself with the potential for humans to emerge from it on Earth in the back of its "mind." It existed for billions of years before we arrived, but now we have given more life and consciousness to it. The meanings we now ascribe to the planets came into being as we evolved, and as we brought their potential significance into life through Planetary Dynamics. Now they offer us their wisdom in turn. They are truly our supporting guideposts, telling us when the time is ripe for every human purpose under heaven.

Chapter 4

My Prophetic Career

When I was six, I made a scrapbook called "Star Book," to record my studies of astronomy. Then later I made another scrapbook called "Star Book 1971" to record my first predictions of world events as an astrologer. I had followed that career for exactly one year, and I was already seeing myself as a budding prophet. The first thing I noticed was that Saturn, Uranus and Neptune would line up in a conjunction in the Fall of 1989. I showed it to my teacher Gary Lyte and he said, "that's pretty heavy." "Revolution will happen in 1989" I wrote in my Star Book. At this writing I have also noticed that this conjunction appears in the birth chart of a promising, dynamic young leader in the US Congress who is making waves, Ms. Alexandria Ocasio-Cortez. She could even be leading *another* Revolution as you read this.

But that sentence I wrote in my Star Book 1971 was my very first prophecy, and it came true in the greatest series of revolutions ever seen. In the Fall of 1989 most of the governments in Eastern Europe fell down like dominoes within 2 months, and the famous Berlin Wall that had divided Europe for 28 years came tumbling down too. As it happened, I said it was a great moment for Humanity. It felt great to have predicted it, and also to have written about it in greater detail before it happened in upcoming publications. My Star Book 1971 started me on a career in which I have (perhaps) made more correct predictions than just about any prophet of my time. Fascinated with how astrology seemed to reflect what was happening, especially with how the sixties seemed to come alive within the pages of the ephemeris (the book that shows the positions of the planets), in 1971 I discovered and traced the cycles of the outer planets and began writing my book, eventually entitled Horoscope for the New Millennium. At first, I called it "The Astrology of History," and then "The Horoscope of Humanity." Jupiter and Neptune were aligned in Sagittarius, sign of prophecy, for most of that year. Has my prophetic career been "brilliant" since then? You be the judge!

Many times, what I predicted might not be specific enough to satisfy determined skeptics. The symbols astrologers use often have a rather general meaning. The reader can decide how closely my predictions resembled the actual events that happened, and whether they were timed correctly enough to count as correct. As I review some of my best predictions in this chapter, you'll see that they include many of the most significant events since 1971. I got most of the important events right. I even once challenged a skeptic in the Strauss and Howe Generations forum online to name the most significant events he could think of from the past half-century, and half of those he named are events that I had predicted. When I say I predicted the most important events, and didn't just get a few of them right through hit and miss tactics, that is proven because these significant predictions are the ones I talked about before they happened in my lectures, a few of which I uploaded to youtube.

There were a whole lot of other events that I didn't predict. Many were less important events. In my book <u>Horoscope for the New Millennium</u>, for example, I wanted to say something about every year in the future from 1997 to 2050, and so I filled in the chapters with some predictions that were not very carefully thought out. Some of my predictions were more like exhortations of what I thought needed to happen, or they were a bit exaggerated or fanciful. But when I researched events listed online and in publications, I found many that corresponded to my predictions, at least to some extent. I have listed all the predictions I made in the book up to 2019, and the events corresponding to them, in **Appendix A**. It is not a scientific statistical measurement, but readers can decide how many of my predictions came true, and to what extent.

Before my book was published in 1997, I also made other predictions in magazine articles and in short previews of my book. I include some incorrect predictions too from that time, so you can see how I learned to do better as the years went by. Later on I also made predictions on my website, http://philosopherswheel.com/book.htm , and in youtube videos at https://www.youtube.com/user/eameece . I will show here some copies of the original publications where I made the predictions, or I refer to their sources. You can also see more pictures of my published predictions at my website.

A President Falls, The Wall Falls

As I review my predictions, I'm also reviewing the historical events that happened during the time I have been a prophet, from 1971 right up to the time of this writing. This provides additional historical background for the events to come. I also include here a few of the major events that I *didn't* predict. Along the way I also learned from other astrologers, or were led astray by them, so I will mention them as appropriate. I hope I have learned by now not to depend on predictions made or rumors circulated by other prophets, as I sometimes did in the past, unless they demonstrate a convincing basis for them.

The first events that I predicted correctly concerned the affairs of the President of the United States at the time of my Star Book, the ill-starred Richard M. Nixon. First, I said in my Star Book that in June of 1971, Saturn in Gemini opposing Neptune and Jupiter in Sagittarius would mean that important secrets would be revealed in the press. I was amazed when at the very moment I predicted that the *Pentagon Papers* were published in the New York Times, which revealed government secrets about US policies and cover-ups concerning the US War in Vietnam. Already I was starting to feel that I had an inside view of history before it happened, just by following astrology, and that feeling only got stronger as the years went by. That Fall I went to a lecture by famed astrologer Dane Rudhyar, at which he excitedly passed out copies of his version of the Horoscope of the United States, which showed early Libra at the Midheaven, the place in a chart which rules the executive. Uranus was about to reach it, he said, which forecast a revolutionary tumble at the top.

Meanwhile Richard Nixon decided he had to do something about these leaks to the press by breaking into the psychiatrist's office of the author of the *Pentagon Papers*, Daniel Ellsberg. To do this he formed his own secret spy agency called The Plumbers. I guess he thought this break-in strategy was useful, so his team proceeded to burglarize the Watergate

Hotel where George McGovern, who was running against him in 1972 on a platform of stopping the war, had his headquarters. When this crime was revealed in the press, Nixon instructed the FBI not to investigate it, and paid hush money to the burglars. But the truth about this cover-up came out soon anyway after he was re-elected in the famous Watergate scandal, and as I followed the aspects to his natal chart I was able to predict what would happen to him, and when. I wrote this in an article I submitted to the magazine *Astrology, Your Daily Horoscope*. I was paid for the article, but I don't know if they actually published any part of it. This is what I wrote in the article concerning the president:

> On June 20 there was a total eclipse of the Sun in 28 degrees Gemini, the exact place of Pluto in President Nixon's house of career, the symbol of his often unbridled use of power. Thus impeachment seemed a certainty, especially since Mars and Saturn joined there in April in the same degree! During President Kennedy's term there was an eclipse in 27 degrees Cancer in HIS house of career in 1963, in exact conjunction with his natal Saturn. We all know what happened to him that year, and so we ought to know what is ahead for Nixon.

In a short preview of my book which I wrote and copied for my friends in 1974, I gave another prediction about the Revolutions that would end the Cold War in 1989, but I also was too pessimistic about what the exact conjunction between Uranus and Neptune in 1993 foretold. Later on I determined that this conjunction reshapes world order, and that although aspects between these two visionary planets may increase international tensions, they don't just indicate when wars break out, because the conjunction and trine aspects, at least, are often signs of international cooperation.

> The year 1989 will be an incredible shocker for timid souls. The world government will be attempted, accompanied by frantic swells of enthusiasm(Jupiter singleton). The key events of this year will(for the first time since the 60's)shift all events to a world stage stormed by mass movements of epic proportions. The ruckus leads to rare concentrations of energy in Feb.1990. But they will not go uncontested. The critical year will be 1993, the year of the Neptune-Uranus conjunction. The war that breaks out this year could very well be W.W.III, but careful efforts may avoid a nuclear catastrophe. The world will nevertheless be engulfed in war for at least the next 10 years. Yet it will resemble the Napoleonic Wars rather than the World Wars I & II, this being a romantic period of high ideals.

In 1973 I read an article in *American Astrology* that correctly forecast a Middle East War in the Fall of 1973. The author noticed that Mars stationary and Saturn's hard aspects to Pluto frequently indicated war. I added Mars-Saturn aspects to those, and from this I developed my technique for predicting wars. In this case, the Yom Kippur War began exactly as the planets timed it.

In July through November 1976 my first articles were published in the *American Federation of Astrologers Bulletin*. The articles concerned the "progressions" from the Horoscope of Humanity or Chart of Our Age, based on the idea that *each day* following the solar eclipse on April 26, 1892, just a few days preceding Neptune's rare conjunction to Pluto, would *represent the following years* in order. In the October article I published my predictions based on these progressions. It was full of fanciful forecasts by an as-yet inexperienced astrologer, but it contained some good predictions anyway.

I had hoped that after the sixties our society would keep moving forward in the ways that I wanted. I noted the conservative reaction that happened, represented by Sun's sextile to Saturn in 1974, but I thought Sun square Uranus in 1981 would bring the revolution back. Instead, the New Deal and Great Society era tumbled in a counter-revolution called "neo-liberalism" (free market economics) led by Ronald Reagan, who I mentioned as having also helped lead the right-wing reaction of the early 70s. Many other astrologers were predicting great upheaval in the late 1970s, including my teacher Gary Lyte, and I went along with the crowd.

So I got that one wrong, but the predictions in this article got better for the years after 1981. As I mentioned, Venus stationary in 1989 allowed me to forecast in this article a "glorious" moment of "greater affection" and "new values" and a "new desire to cherish our earth home" that came true in the revolutions of 1989 ending the Cold War and the revival of Earth Day. I also correctly forecast that national or racial feelings would happen, which they did in the following years. The solar opposition to Mars for 1991, which I dated in the article as 1992, correctly presaged the Gulf War conflict that fulfilled my prediction for this opposition of a conquest and great accomplishment. Not only did President Bush's victory with UN support create a "New World Order," as he called it, but soon afterward in the same year the Soviet Union fell and multitudes of new nations were created. It was not the new world government that some prophets had been bandying about, and which I appropriated into some of my writings. But it was a more momentous change than anyone besides a few prophets like me saw coming.

I thought the "new system" would be toppled by a spiritual revolution when Mercury turned retrograde in square to Neptune in 1999. Then for Jupiter turning stationary-retrograde in 2001-2002 I forecast a new world religion and a religious war, with space voyages involved in the conflict. I thought world peace would follow. In my book I also said this progressed Mercury square Neptune in 1998 would bring disinformation and scandal too, which it did in the huge Lewinsky Affair that threatened Clinton's presidency.[18] We certainly got the religious war, but what was toppled was not the New World System, but the World Trade Center brought down by Muslim jihadists (holy warriors), followed by the attack on Afghanistan (whose religious government had harbored the terrorists) by the USA and its allies. And it was not space travelers, but air travelers that brought down the Twin Towers of the trade center.

---

[18] Sarah Janssen, ed., World Almanac 2018, Infobase, p.449. I predicted "more scandals" on page 251.

AMERICAN FEDERATION

OF ASTROLOGERS INC.

BULLETIN

VOLUME 38
NUMBER 11

TODAY'S ASTROLOGER

TABLE OF CONTENTS

If I had brought my prediction a little further down to Earth, I would have hit this exactly right, but as it was it was pretty good indeed, and a lot closer to what actually happened than what almost any other prophet had foreseen. World peace did not follow though, because the war continued and was expanded into Iraq. But the years following the Sept.11 attacks were relatively relaxed and peaceful at home anyway, as I foresaw, and I also said that "difficulties would begin to reappear toward the end of the decade." Boy, did they ever. In 2010 I predicted that the progressed Sun entering Virgo would see prosperity fade and the "euphoria" end, as more practical concerns would take precedence. The Great Recession that began with the crash of 2008 certainly more than fulfilled that expectation. And I also mentioned "shades of 1848," which certainly is what showed up once the Arab Spring chain of revolutions got going in January 2011.

In October 1986 I began writing for *Welcome to Planet Earth* magazine, and in my first article (below) I predicted "world unity" 5 years later in 1991, emerging from conflicts. I gave hints and indications of what turned out to be the end of the Cold War in 1989-1991, uniting east and west, and the war in the Persian Gulf which gave rise to the "New World Order," which at the time was hoped would establish a new Pax Americana. And our "imperial age" is indeed in some sense a new Rome.

Earlier in the article I laid out the evidence that the Neptune-Pluto conjunction of 1892 and other transits foretold a new golden age coming soon. As I mentioned in Chapter 2, our current golden age may not seem so golden to us now, but things appear better when one considers how far we've come in the valley of transition.

PLANET EARTH
Welcome To

Prospects For a ★ Golden Age

by E. Alan Meece

From all this evidence, we have every right to believe that our own time of transition and upheaval which began in the world wars will soon lead to a golden age. In fact, we have not long to wait. Already it has been 95 years since the conjunction, which means the next renaissance is only five years away!

We will see great works of art and stupendous discoveries in science. Movements of spiritual and cultural renewal will sweep the globe. World unity may emerge from conflicts recalling Roman days, bringing a peace surpassing the Pax Romana. Just as the Renaissance was the revival of Greek ideals and culture, so our age will in some sense see a new Rome and the return of Christ.

In my next article in *Welcome to Planet Earth* for April 1987 about that valley of transition, I was even more specific about the prospect of bringing down the Iron Curtain, and I had revised my view about what the Uranus-Neptune conjunction in 1993 would mean towards a more favorable outlook.

> Meanwhile, in this time of trickle-down economics and politics-by-terror and proxy, it may seem as if we are descending again. Maybe our vision of the "mountain top" ahead is only an illusion. Time will tell. It is up to us now to make it real. If we can *throw out* of power in the U.S. those who would take us back down to the valley again, we can reconcile our differences with our fellow revolutionaries on the other side of the globe and bring down the Iron Curtain. *Their* leadership seems more ready to do this than ever before. They have even met their own Imperial Waterloo in Afghanistan. The next move is up to *us*. **As Uranus and Neptune come to their triple conjunction in 1993, the competing revolutionary forces have the chance to come together, to rejoin our ideals with our national power, and to move the world toward that Global Consciousness and Peace which we need and deserve.**
>
> From "Crossing the Valley of Transition," Welcome to Planet Earth magazine, April (Taurus) 1987, page 9. Prediction that we would "bring down the Iron Curtain" and move the world toward peace (end of the Cold War).

Editor Mark Lerner had been predicting a new Russian Revolution for some time for circa 1990, and in a Sept. 1989 article I got even more specific about this prediction, writing about the "nationalism within the Soviet Empire" exploding, which referred to the Revolutions of 1989 that happened a couple of months later, and which few pundits had predicted. And I also predicted an upsurge of green activism, which turned out to be the revival of Earth Day in April 1990.

the next few months will be a crucial turning point. The Fall Equinox and New Moon charts of September 1989 are the most impressive and potent I have seen since the '60s."

The super-potent Jupiter of 1989 will soon turn stationary in that same degree of 10 Cancer. An upsurge of Green activism to go with the Black would be most appropriate now. The nationalism within the Soviet Empire could explode and bring about the "Russian Revolution" Mark Lerner has predicted.

In my 3rd article in *Welcome to Planet Earth* called "American Arrogance" in August 1987, I warned about Jupiter's return to its 7th house position in Gemini/Cancer in the USA horoscope, which often corresponds to when the USA goes to war or takes action that leads to future wars. I had also published an earlier version of this article in the AFA Bulletin in 1977. Jupiter's return was due in 1989 and 1990, and this time, as we all soon found out, it signified our invasions of Panama and the Persian Gulf.

American Arrogance: Jupiter in Taurus and Gemini

"Considering how eager our current administration is to get America involved in the Middle East and Central America, the odds for going to war are good in the months ahead."

In the same September 1989 article in which I wrote about the Russian Empire about to explode, I also predicted the Panama invasion, which happened on the exact day

Jupiter returned to its position of 6 degrees Cancer in the USA horoscope,[19] and I also mentioned the involvement in the Middle East that was to follow in 1990.

Jupiter is still in a very dangerous position. We could yet see another intervention—perhaps in the Middle East, Panama or Colombia.

In the "American Arrogance Rides Again" article that followed, I described post-mortem the Panama invasion of December 1989. Indeed "the cycle was not over yet," since soon the USA intervened in the Middle East too in the Persian Gulf, as I predicted "we could yet see." I didn't get the location right yet, but this war was predicted in greater detail in a later article called "Mars and the Middle East" (see below). Then the USA invaded the region again after the Sept.11, 2001 attacks. In 2013-14 America went there yet again, first by forcing Syria's dictator Assad to remove his chemical weapons by threatening an attack in the Summer of 2013, and then to Iraq in the Spring of 2014 to help in the 3-year struggle to repel conquests by the terrorist Islamic State. In the next chapter I discuss what might happen when the cycle comes around again in 2025. Meanwhile, as I predicted in this Dec. 1989 article, the Revolution of 1989 continued into February 1990. Drastic reforms and further revolts came to the Soviet Union then, and anti-apartheid leader Nelson Mandela was freed from prison in South Africa. Here's a couple more excerpts from the "American Arrogance Rides Again" article from Dec. 1989.

---

[19] USA invaded Panama on Dec.20, 1989 to overthrow the government of Manual Noriega. World Almanac 2018, p.447.

So American Arrogance rides again!

"Perhaps we have restored democracy in Panama and jailed another drug lord. But how long can our tattered Constitution survive the constant usurpation of the power to make war and conduct foreign policy by the President?"

How many more turns of the Jupiter cycle will it take until we learn our lesson? Where to next—Nicaragua? El Salvador? The Philippines? Lebanon? The drug war? (Indeed—the current Jupiter cycle isn't quite over yet!)

The next return of Jupiter to late Taurus, Gemini, and early Cancer will come in the epochal and symbolic year of 2001. Perhaps the alternate beat will become louder that year, since dangerous aspects like Saturn in Gemini opposite Pluto in Sagittarius will be in effect..... Then comes 2013; and then 2025—certain to be a big year, with Uranus also returning to *its* U.S. horoscope position, as it did in the Civil War and World War II. Perhaps conflict will arise then with an emerging world federation, or else another civil war. Perhaps by then we will outgrow our arrogant innocence ....

The times of change are just beginning, and February could be another incredible month of revolution.

On August 2, 1990, Iraq under Saddam Hussein attacked and conquered the small oil-rich emirate of Kuwait to the south and claimed it as an Iraqi province, thus provoking an international crisis.[20] The USA sent troops to Saudi Arabia right away to forestall any further advance by Iraq. Below in my "Mars and the Middle East" article of Sept. (Libra) 1990, I predicted that the war could break out in January 1991, which it did. Presidents George Bush and Saddam Hussein both made their aggressive "moves" then, including Bush's decision to repel the Iraqi invasion of Kuwait, and Saddam's subsequent missile attacks on Israel. As I have stated in the last chapter, after Mars turns stationary, wars or major aggressive events often follow within a few weeks. The Mars trine to Saturn not only made this Gulf War a "cakewalk" for the "new world order" coalition, but was an appropriate signal for it, since the same trine appears in the horoscope charts of both Bush and Saddam, and in the national horoscopes of both the USA *and* Iraq. In the months following the war, the economy sank into a deep recession.

> **It seems clear that the current crisis may be only the beginning. How it will play out is anyone's guess. But if it's not settled now, it may well explode again in October or at the beginning of the new year. That's because Mars is about to turn stationary (retrograde Oct. 20 and direct on Jan. 1). When it turns stationary-direct on Jan. 1, it will be in Taurus again, trine Saturn. George Bush, Saddam or another Mid-East power (perhaps Israel) may make another move then, and decisive effects on the economy may be felt at this time, too. Remember, Taurus and the other fixed signs rule financial affairs, which means that the current crisis will definitely hurt the economy if it is not resolved soon.**

---

[20] <u>World Almanac 2018</u>, p.447

Before the 1991-92 recession took hold, I wrote in June (Cancer) 1990 that it could spell the end of George Bush 41's term. I predicted this because of the 30-year Saturn cycle, which I noticed had brought a progressive era every 30 years, including in the 1900s (Progressive Era), 1930s (the New Deal) and 1960s (civil rights and the Great Society). Below is an excerpt from this *Welcome to Planet Earth* article entitled "Time for Reform: The Thirty-Year Saturn Cycle" (page 9).

I am not the only one to notice such a 30-year cycle. Arthur Schlesinger, famous American historian and former advisor to President Kennedy, also described it recently, saying it portended a reform era soon (and he is not an astrologer). Like many of us, he saw the parallels between the campaigns of 1960 and 1988. Both featured a liberal Democrat from Massachusetts and his running mate from Texas opposing a sitting Republican Vice-President. But the result didn't turn out as he or I expected. The parallel to 1988 may actually turn out to be not 1960, but 1928. George **Herbert** Walker Bush succeeded a popular 8-year Republican administration in 1988; **Herbert** Hoover did the same in 1928. By 1930 the nation was in the grip of a great depression; today many observers expect the same in 1990. Could this mean that in 1988 the reform era was still two years away, and that it could still begin in 1990, even though a conservative Republican is now in the White House? Could the American economy turn sour, causing President Bush to lose his current popularity and to be voted out of office in 1992 in favor of a Democratic New York governor, as happened 60 years earlier?

It could happen, if the 30-year cycle is really significant.

Then in January (Aquarius) 1992 in *Welcome to Planet Earth* I studied the candidates in the "Election '92" article (page 9), and I made some spot-on predictions about what would happen.

> **"If the economy *does* skid and the Democrats prevail in 1992, Clinton is the most likely winner and would probably be re-elected, but he would leave most of our problems unresolved."**

As I mentioned before, ethnic conflicts became the bane of the New World Order, and the first breakdown was in the Balkans. I could see it coming because of the great international cycle that Uranus and Neptune had laid out for us starting with the revolution against Turkish rule in Greece in 1821. In an early draft of my first book, written in about 1987, I predicted the war that broke out in the Balkans in the early 1990s to break up Yugoslavia. I had to change the wording from "could it be" to "was it" on my copy at the bottom of this page, since the prediction came true before I could publish my book.

The Greek revolt against Turkish rule was very bloody. There were such atrocities
that the Turkish sultan vowed all Greeks would die. He almost kept his promise on the
island of Chios in April 1822, when violent Mars was not only stationary, but in sesqui-
square(135° away from) the conjunction, and also occupied over 2/3 of the sky by itself-
a truly powerful "singleton"! The massacre of Chios was the worst bloodletting between
Napoleon and World War One; *was* it ~~could~~ a sign of things to come under the next
Neptune-*Uranus* conjunction in 1993?

At the bottom I had scribbled: (more Middle East massacres returned under the same Uranus-Neptune conjunction in the early1990s). "Bastille Degree" above refers to Saturn's location in 24 Pisces on July 14, 1789 when the Bastille fell. Metternich was the powerful minister for the restored Austrian Empire. See also <u>Horoscope for the New Millennium,</u> page 183 in the Llewellyn edition.

In *Welcome to Planet Earth* in Feb 1992, on pp. 11 and 12, I wrote about the upcoming great solar eclipse in Cancer on June 30, 1992. I had also passed out copies of the eclipse chart at our *Welcome to Planet Earth* writers' meeting in 1990, warning of this "dangerous eclipse." Mars was due to turn stationary a few months after the eclipse, first retrograde on Nov.28, 1992, and then direct *exactly in the eclipse degree* of 9 Cancer on

February 15, 1993 while making hard aspects to Pluto and Saturn. I predicted troubles, famine and power struggles in Africa, mentioning Kenya and Ethiopia. I was not far off, since the USA decided to invade nearby Somalia in January 1993 to deal with famine and civil war. Later on, the USA suffered the deadly "blackhawk down" affair there. In the article "The Dangerous Eclipse" I wrote:

Power struggles may erupt in Kenya or Ethiopia, and the danger of famine looms again in these areas.

I also speculated that Korea might see a battle over unification, which didn't happen, and that the USA, Russia and Israel might be involved in the conflicts I was forecasting. These are the usual suspects, after all, and the eclipse seemed to target their national charts, but the location on the angles of the eclipse and key planets indicated the area near Ethiopia was the scene of the troubles to come. But I didn't check the national chart for Somalia, born July 1 1960,[21] which put the Sun just one degree away from the eclipse and Mars station degree. If I had known that, I could have pinpointed the location of the trouble much more accurately.

Not only was the USA involved in Somalia, however, but it too suffered an attack within its own borders, when Muslim terrorists bombed the World Trade Center in New York right after Mars turned stationary-direct in February 1993. At the same time, the crisis at Waco Texas began too, which led to the government exploding the Branch Davidian cult's compound on April 19. Two years later to the day, Tim McVeigh bombed the Oklahoma Federal building "in retaliation for Waco" just a few weeks after the next time Mars turned stationary on March 24, 1995. 168 people died in the attack.[22] These were indeed signs of things to come, just as I had written back in 1987 about the Uranus-Neptune conjunction then going on.

More ethnic troubles in the former Yugoslavia followed from that conjunction. In the article "Wars and World Changes" in March 1998, I explained how Uranus and Neptune, the carriers of international affairs, opposed each other in 1908 during the Bosnian Crisis that led to World War I in 1914. Six years after Uranus and Neptune joined in conjunction in 1993, I expected another international engagement in that area in 1999. That's what happened in Kosovo.

---

[21] Sarah Janssen, editor, <u>World Almanac 2018</u>, Infobase, p.834.
[22] <u>Ibid.</u>, p.447,448.

A pattern at work that bears watching. Six years after Uranus and Neptune conjoined in 1821, when a bloody revolt by the Greeks for independence from Turkey erupted, Britain, France and Russia joined forces against the cruel Turks. Six years after Uranus and Neptune opposed in 1908, the year of another great Bosnian Crisis, the same three powers joined to battle the Austrians and Germans (World War I), who were trying to keep the Serbs from taking over Bosnia.

Bosnia and Greece, of course, are neighbors on the explosive Balkan Peninsula. In 1999, it will again be six years after the latest line-up of Uranus and Neptune in 1993, which followed by only one year the latest eruption in Bosnia in the Spring of 1992. The clear implication is that the troubles there may not be over, and that Russia and the Western powers may feel the need to intervene there again—perhaps as allies. Already President Clinton has broken his promise to bring U.S. troops home in mid-1998, announcing that they will remain longer.

WTPE MARCH/APRIL '98

I predicted the war in the Serbia-Kosovo area, and the exact timing, in an article I wrote in March. The war broke out on March 24 after the Mars retrograde station on the 18th, and ended on June 3, one day before the exact Mars direct station in Libra on June 4.[23]

More dangerous indications lie ahead. After Mars turns stationary and retrograde on March 18, it opposes Saturn on April 19, while Saturn continues to square Neptune as well. A major military confrontation, perhaps involving religious terrorists (Neptune), could break out. Since this T-Square happens in early fixed signs, the Balkans look like the most likely trouble spot. In fact, during the previous New Moon on April 16, Mars is exactly on the Descendant (house of war) in the Serbia and Kosovo areas. In June, Mars is stationary in Libra, which may settle this dispute or unleash others.

---

[23]World Almanac 2018, p.795.

Meanwhile, I called the 1996 USA presidential election right. My powers as a prophet of presidential elections seemed to be growing. I had called 1988 wrong, but I had seen that George Bush might win anyway because he had the best chart to get elected and be president. It was always easier for me to predict the Democrats would win, because that's where my bias lay. I also would not get it right for the next election in the year 2000. Another astrologer who wrote for *Welcome to Planet Earth* did though, not only picking the winner, but forecasting all the errors and tampering that went on. It was clear after 2000 that I needed to research presidential elections more clearly. Had I done so before 1988, I could have called that election pretty easily, and the one in 2000 too. You'll see the results of my research in a later chapter.

> **"I predict something quite different, and seemingly just as outlandish, as a victory by Dan Quayle in 1996. I predict that President Clinton will be re-elected and the Democrats will take back the Congress."**

From Now On, It's In the Book

As Uranus and Neptune aligned in the sky late in 1993, I finally finished my over 1000-page tome entitled <u>The Horoscope of Humanity</u>. I explored and wrote about as much history as I could, hoping to better prepare myself for making predictions up to the year 2050. The prophecies I made for 2049 and 2050 seemed to bring me back full circle to where I started, in many ways. But when in 1996 Llewellyn Publications finally called me and indicated interest in my book, they recommended that I do a shorter version and entitle my book after the coming New Millennium that was then creating such a fuss and inspiring other prophetic books. So, I quickly put together the 400-page version and called it <u>Horoscope for the New Millennium</u>.[24] They asked me to finish the re-editing quickly because of the demand, and so some hasty errors were made. But on January 9th 1997 it was published on the exact day when Jupiter and Neptune joined in conjunction late in Capricorn, near the location of my own Jupiter (which is the planet that rules publishing), just as Jupiter and Neptune had aligned when I started my work way back in 1971. Now I wonder what Saturn, Pluto and Mercury have in store when they line up exactly with my Jupiter on Jan.12, 2020.

So, from now on my predictions up to this writing are plainly visible in the pages of my book. In **Appendix A** I provide a complete list of all the predictions, and what actually happened on Earth and in "the stars" at the time predicted, so here I only need to highlight the main events. I'll also give some notes on the predictions I wrote on my

---

[24]E. Alan Meece, <u>Horoscope for the New Millennium</u>, Llewellyn Publications, St. Paul MN, 1997.

website and recorded in my internet videos, as I took advantage of the cyberworld and world wide web that rapidly unfolded from the 1993 conjunction onward.

Soon after Bill Clinton was to be inaugurated in 1997, Mars turned stationary-direct in the critical 17th degree of Virgo on April 27, so on page 250 I wrote that I expected a "Marseillaise spirit," since the French uprising that overthrew the king and was inspired by the song happened after Mars also had turned stationary direct in that exact degree. It was also the degree of the sixties too, of course, where Uranus and Pluto had joined. Jupiter was lined up with Uranus and Neptune in a liberating conjunction too in early 1997. For Clinton himself, it mostly just meant he was to undergo more scandals, including those I predicted for 1998 (including what became the Lewinsky Affair). But there were indeed major uprisings, including in Zaire on May 18 that led to changing its name to Congo,[25] plus big strikes in Western Europe on May 15, and a socialist victory in France on June 2. It was a pretty big deal. And I mentioned in my talks that as more revolutions were breaking out in Southeastern Europe under these planetary alignments in January and February 1997, CBS News Anchor Dan Rather had pronounced them the next Velvet Revolution succeeding the big one in the Fall of 1989.[26] I had also predicted controversial health and medical breakthroughs, including a cure for AIDS, in the Spring of 1997, and I came real close with that one, since the first major AIDs vaccine was announced in May, which has since put a big dent in that horrible plague. What's more, Dolly the Sheep on February 3rd[27] and 2 monkeys on March 2 had been cloned; stirring the alarm and controversy I predicted. Finally, on June 20, lawsuits against the tobacco industry were settled. More health breakthroughs came in 1998, as I also predicted on page 251.

Later in 1997 sad news came to us. I forecast that transportation accidents would dominate the news in late August and early September (p.251). On August 31 our "English Rose" Princess Diana and her new boyfriend died in a car crash while being pursued by paparazzi photographers. Elton John quickly put out a new version of his "Candle in the Wind" song and it became an all-time best-seller. Tears and flowers flooded her final route home on Sept.6. Two days later on Sept.8 a ferry in Haiti crashed and killed hundreds of people.[28] I had also predicted global cooperation on major problems for October 1997, and this was apparently happening too, because on December 11 the breakthrough agreement on climate change called the Kyoto Treaty was announced.

For Spring 1998 I forecast controversial aggressive moves by the president, and religious violence in August. These two predictions were combined in a notorious incident in August, when to respond to deadly Al Qaeda attacks on US embassies in Kenya and Tanzania, Clinton made wild bombing attacks on Sudan and Afghanistan.[29] He was accused of making these attacks to distract attention from his scandal in what was famously called "wagging the dog." Late in 1997 fires engulfed Asia,[30] and in 1998 hurricanes and

---

[25] World Almanac 2018, p.765.
[26] Ibid., p.831.
[27] Ibid., p.670.
[28] Ibid., p.319.
[29] World Almanac 2018, p.448.
[30] Ibid., p.324.

floods ravaged the world in what Worldwatch Institute called a record disaster year. It was by far the warmest year of the entire Second Millennium, and an "El Nino" year of warmer oceans. And I had called it in my book, pronouncing that 1998 would see unusually severe weather and panic over global warming. Saturn in earth-sign Taurus squaring watery Neptune was the special planetary sign, among others, of this spot-on prediction. The irony was that for years afterward, because 1998 was such an amazing spike in the global temperature, those who denied global warming used it to claim that global cooling had begun, just because global temperatures went down after this unusual year, proving that they had no awareness whatever of the notion of trends. It wasn't long in the new century before many more years broke the 1998 global heat record. But hooked on free-market ideology that prevents any government action, and drunk on their own fossil fuel profits, the deniers still closed their eyes and kept the USA from making much progress on reversing climate change. Our descendants could well suffer for years because of their blind resistance.

On August 1999, the "eclipse of the century" occurred, as described on pp.252-254. We sometimes called it "the doomsday eclipse" because Nostradamus had referred to it as foretelling a world-threatening event that included "terror from the sky." The eclipse opposed catastrophic Uranus in Aquarius, and squared Mars and Saturn as they opposed each other in a grand cross of dangerous planets. It was a foreboding sign, and we didn't reckon just how foreboding it might turn out to be. I had as far back as my article on the progressed 1892 chart in the AFA Bulletin indicated that it portended earthquakes in the Balkans, and indeed one happened in the path of the eclipse in Turkey on August 17, killing 35,000, and another big one in Greece on Sept.7, and elsewhere too.[31] I forecast upheavals in the Balkans, Mexico and Russia, and as the eclipse happened the revolts in Dagestan and Chechnya were breaking out.[32] On Sept.9 the rebels bombed an apartment in Moscow, and on October 22, the new Prime Minister Vladimir Putin (in office since August 9th), attacked Chechnya and restored Russian rule by January and February. In July on the eve of the eclipse the Serbs rose up in a huge movement to topple their war-criminal ruler Milosevic, and they held the first of many huge rallies on August 9th. Other events that I predicted for the eclipse came true too (see Appendix A), and further conflicts continued for a few years in these places as I predicted. It seemed, however, that we had eluded terror from the sky and the end of the world, at least for the moment.

In my book on page 254 I had pronounced that the Year 2000 would be the mountain top on the far side of the Valley of Transition, the one Dr. Martin Luther King had predicted. As I recorded on my website, it seemed Al Gore had announced it, calling it a "mountain top moment" because the "dot com boom" had created the greatest prosperity on record. But it was a short moment, because the dot come bust began in March. In this *Welcome to Planet Earth* article, in which I reviewed the aftermath of the eclipse of the

[31] Ibid., p.323.
[32] Ibid., p.827.

century, I forecast the fall of Milosevic, which happened finally in October 2000,[33] and cautioned investors to be careful until after June.

It turned out that terror rained down from the sky after all. Al Qaeda began planning its attack on America in August 1999. An eclipse, remember, can be significant in the amount of years that it lasts in minutes. As I had forecast for years in all my lectures and in my book, the USA was attacked and went to war soon after Saturn in Gemini opposed Pluto and Mars in Sagittarius *The Archer* in July and August 2001, with Mars

Wars and rumors of wars are also happening in India/Pakistan, Africa and China/Taiwan, too. In October, the Pakistani military overthrew the civilian government because they are dissatisfied with its conduct of the war against India in Kashmir. Concerns are being heard over the fact that one of these two new nuclear rivals is now run by soldiers. Demonstrations are increasing in Serbia; if not now, then in a few months, I think Milosevic will be ousted. Also watch the increasing turmoil in Indonesia and Iran; more turbulent change or evolution is likely in these places in the next few months.

I also predicted a stock market downturn after the eclipse, and this has materialized. A correction began in August-September, and the market lost 250 more points on October 15. I think things will improve again soon, but I'd be careful at least until after June 2000. So far we have escaped the great crash and the draconian government responses to it that the eclipse and grand cross in fixed financial signs indicated might happen, however.

WTPE NOV./DEC. '99 ◆ 7

turning stationary then. It took just a bit longer than I expected. I had announced to everyone that an attack was coming in July or August, and by early September I thought maybe we had dodged the bullet. But then it came on September 11, as the Twin Towers (Saturn in Gemini the Twins) were toppled by the flying arrows of Pluto-Mars in Sagittarius (the jet planes crashing into the Towers). Since Jupiter had returned to its place in the House of War in the US Horoscope, off again into battle we went on Oct.7, first by providing air support to the Northern Alliance, which on November 9th and 13th defeated the Taliban Muslim fundamentalist government that had harbored the terrorists.[34] But on Dec.16th Al Qaeda leader Osama bin Laden escaped from the caves of Tora Bora to a hideout in Pakistan.

---

[33] Ibid., p.831.
[34] World Almanac 2018, p.745.

I wrote that if we were lucky, the outlook for peace might improve after October 2002. But we weren't lucky, because the president was George W. Bush. Although Saddam Hussein had no connection to the attack on America on Sept.11, he was alleged by Bush to still have nuclear or chemical weapons. He didn't, but the Project for a New American Century which Bush had empowered proposed that if a new Pearl Harbor occurred, war could be waged to spread freedom around the world and assure dominance of the USA over oil resources. The new Pearl Harbor had occurred on Sept.11, and I wrote that if we weren't lucky, the "war would flare up again" in late February 2003. Many people, though, were repelled by this deliberate and unnecessary attack that was being planned, showing that the peace movement which the sixties had spawned was still growing. On February 15, 2003, as Jupiter opposed Neptune and Mars opposed Saturn, the largest demonstrations the world had ever seen protested the proposed US invasion of Iraq, much as I had predicted. This outburst of people power probably delayed the invasion, but as Saturn continued its return to a close opposition to Pluto, Bush and his "coalition of the willing" attacked Iraq with a "shock and awe" bombing campaign on March 19, 2003, followed by an invasion that Bush said the Iraqis would welcome with flowers and open arms. They didn't welcome it; in my lectures and on internet forums I predicted the war would be a quagmire because Uranus was entering Pisces in 2003. Indeed, it went on for another 8 years. Below is what I wrote in my book about this period. Latin America escaped the USA's wrath, but the USA indeed faced a holy war against the Muslim jihadists, and the "star wars" technology turned out to be the fancy drones that the US employed against the terrorists all over the world.

STAR WARS OR HOLY WARS

Whoever is elected in 2000 will also face foreign challenges immediately, since it looks like Uncle Sam will be gearing up for war in the fall of 2000. What a way to start a Millennium! Conflicts that exploded in 1999, such as those in Russia, Iran, Mexico, or the Balkans will probably come to a head in 2001. Continuing ethnic strife in Europe seems likely. Intensive diplomatic efforts and minor interventions will try to head off trouble, especially in mid-September or early October 2000-but then comes the combative Saturn-Pluto opposition in the summer of 2001, joined by a stationary Mars in July. These planets will oppose each other across the Ascendant and Descendant of the U.S. chart. Uncle Sam will be feeling righteous again in a big way, eager to show other nations the truth. Religious issues and trade embargoes will be involved, and the U.S. may try to impose its will on its Latin neighbors. A nuclear accident can't be ruled out either during this period. It might sound strange, but it's not impossible that ETs may be contacted or involved somehow in the events of these years! We may also see the first use of "star wars" technology, or else electronic communications may be used in historic new ways to defuse the conflict.

Turning points in the confrontations come near November 2 and December 22, 2001. After the December date, the U.S. could suffer losses in a serious naval engagement. An eclipse aligned with Saturn and Pluto in May and June 2002 indicates another decisive moment. Danger to the president is shown, too. After October 2002, the outlook for peace starts to improve. If we are even more lucky, we will escape further conflict until the decade ends. If we are even more lucky, we will enter "the millennium of peace." Many agreements (especially in the Mid-East or Balkans) may come in December. On the other hand, if there is no agreement, then late February 2003 could see another flare-up, as Mars joins Pluto and opposes Saturn.

I made a more positive and amazing prediction for late 2002 through the Spring of 2003, when I wrote that electronic media would be used to give everyone access to work and education (top of p.267). I had thought Uranus in Aquarius would come through with some electronic innovations, and I knew Saturn in trine to it at this time from media-savvy Gemini would get them going. This was when social media began, first with Friendster in 2002, then with My Space and itunes in 2003, and finally facebook by 2004 as the trine returned again. This certainly has changed our world, and at the same time my predictions for this moment of health improvements (Medicare drug program), and constructive changes to the defeated nation (Iraqi Parliament established), came true as well.

I thought the solar eclipse of March 29, 2006 would make Al Gore "a marked man" and put him in danger, since it was near his solar degree, but actually it put the spotlight on him as he released his best-selling and award-winning film "An Inconvenient Truth: A Global Warning." Just as the Katrina hurricane wiped out portions of New Orleans and Mississippi at the end of August 2005, leaving over 1000 dead, Saturn was beginning to oppose Neptune again, its first hard aspect since 1998.[35] It was not Gore, but his opponent President Bush who got in trouble over his poor response to the hurricane. I didn't predict such a disaster in the book, but Gore's film, which *did* mention it, aroused a lot of concern over global warming and the severe weather that it was causing. As Saturn closed in on its opposition to Neptune in 2006 and 2007, and as Uranus reached the critical "stillness of spirit degree" at 17 Pisces at the same time, my prediction in the book at the bottom of page 270 that in 2007 oil and ecology issues would come to the fore was certainly fulfilled. Green trends mushroomed, and in December automobile fuel standards were raised.

Crash, Crisis, Recovery

As Saturn reached Leo in 2006, I expected the economy to be bouncing along fine again after the dot com bust, and so it was (p.268). But in 2006 I wrote on my website that this "jobless recovery" would not last for long, and that serious economic disruption was due as the years 2009 and 2010 approached. On August 9, 2002 on The Fourth Turning Forum, I wrote: "great crash sometime during or after Fall 2008. Economic transformation

---

[35] World Almanac 2018 p.321; see Saturn opp. Neptune 2005-2007 in Appendix I.

and recovery later in the 2010s decade."[36] The collapse of the Lehman Brothers investment firm on September 15, 2008, followed by the collapse of the AIG global insurance company, precipitated the biggest financial and economic tumble since the stock market crash in late October 1929, which had caused the Great Depression in the 1930s. In my book on page 273, I declared "The year 2009 marks the start of an important and painful period." On pages 274-75, I slated the next great depression (later called the "Great Recession") to begin in 2010. But in my videos, I said a big change was coming when Pluto entered Capricorn in 2008. I pointed out that Saturn, Uranus and Pluto (with Jupiter too) would form a huge T-square in cardinal signs in 2010, which was almost the same as the one in 1931.[37] Notice that these squares were forming, and sometimes within orb, during the previous 2 years. 1931 minus 2 years was 1929, the year of the great crash, and 2010 minus 2 years was 2008, the year of the next great crash. It was a perfect parallel. The T-square also reappeared at times during 2011.

I was expecting another kind of interesting change too around 2010, because Neptune and Pluto were also reaching the same positions they were in when Martin Luther initiated the Protestant Reformation in 1517 (page 273). In March 2010 the culture warrior Pope Benedict XVI (formerly Cardinal Ratzinger), who later blamed sexual abuse of boys by Catholic priests on the swinging sixties, himself was accused of not acting to dismiss abusive priests. In 2013 he became the first Pope to voluntarily resign since 1294, citing age and fatigue, and was replaced by Pope Francis, a liberal reformer who diffused the Church's involvement in the culture wars against homosexuals, and championed the causes of helping the poor and acting on climate change. How far his reforms might go is still in question as of this writing.

I wrote on page 273 that Pluto entering Capricorn on Nov.6, 2008 would set off powerful changes. When it entered Capricorn in 1517, I pointed out, Luther had nailed his 95 Theses to the wall of Wittenberg Cathedral, thus setting off the Reformation, and when it next entered Capricorn in 1762 Rousseau had published The Social Contract which said "man is born free, but he is everywhere in chains," thus setting off the democratic revolt in France, America and around the world. In the Fall of 2008, a 94-year old French World War Two hero named Stephane Hessel gave a lecture which quickly became a short book that immediately sold 3 million copies. It was called "Time for Outrage" and it helped spark protests in Spain and Greece, and the Arab Spring revolts in 2011, and inspired the Occupy Wall Street movement starting on Sept.17, 2011.[38] This fulfilled my prediction that we would see another Luther or Rousseau at this time. Also, reform-minded Barack Obama was elected USA president just 2 days before Pluto entered Capricorn, with ringing declarations that change had come to America. Below are some relevant excerpts from pages 273-75 of Horoscope for the New Millennium about the 2008-2012 period.

---

[36] See http://generationaldynamics.com/tftarchive/5751-See-What-Tunisia-Started-00015.htm (scroll down to post
   #373)
[37] See "Predictions that Came True in 2008-2012" https://youtu.be/oKmyB1q3H68
[38] See: https://en.wikipedia.org/wiki/Time_for_Outrage! Available on amazon and kindle:
   https://www.amazon.com/Time-Outrage-Indignez-vous-St%C3%A9phane-Hessel-ebook/dp/B00500OG28

DODGING AN APOCALYPSE: A TITANIC T-SQUARE

When Jupiter and Uranus enter Aries in the spring of 2010, people will be much less restrained in expressing their frustration. "Peasants" and other poor people will rise up worldwide (Mars in Virgo opposite Neptune in June), and governments will be besieged with demands for change. This will make the year 2010 the climax of this twenty-year period, as Jupiter (with Uranus) opposes Saturn. What makes this year so critical is that Pluto also moves into a tense T-square with all three planets as they enter cardinal signs. 2010 looks like a year of sudden, cataclysmic changes and drastic, forced new beginnings.

This titanic, historic T-square involves the same four planets as the T-square which coincided with the Great Depression. The solar eclipse in July could trigger a major, worldwide financial collapse. Pluto in Capricorn suggests not only that many corporations will go bankrupt, but that the economic troubles will bring down many governments with dizzying speed as revolutions sweep the globe. But as we mentioned in Chapter 13, in 2010 the lunar cycles in the progressed Horoscope of Modern Humanity indicate that the common people may be in retreat. This could mean people will be easy prey to xenophobia and fear of "radicals," as in the 1920s, '50s, and '80s. This was just how Hitler eventually rose to power during the previous Great Depression.....

The crisis of 2010 will result from the various religious conflicts around the world, magnified by serious shortages and famines; and above all, I believe, by ecological disasters. Global warming and climate change will begin to seriously affect agriculture in many places. By 2011-2012, when Neptune crosses into the chaotic waters of Pisces, all these catastrophes will begin producing huge folk movements, revolutions, and an unprecedented stream of refugees (as Neptune in Pisces has usually indicated in the past). It is interesting that James Burke (who doesn't believe in astrology) predicted in his prophetic TV program "After the Warming" that the year 2010 would see massive waves of refugees across the borders between the First and Third Worlds, leading to many massacres. This refugee crisis will be a great moral challenge to our lingering racism.

There is no doubt in my mind that the years 2010 and 2011 will be the most difficult of any we face in the next half-century. If we survive them in reasonably good shape we will have dodged the worst bullet in our future.....

In early 2011, there could be further scandalous breakdowns of financial institutions, and some governments which collapsed during the peak of the crisis may be forcefully re-imposed. If so, mass panic could cause still more refugees and cast a pall of disillusion over the next few years. Escapist spiritual movements and conservative politicians would benefit from this turn of events.

On Oct 27, 1998 at the San Francisco National Council for Geocosmic Research, I gave a lecture covering my predictions for the period of 2008-2012, and later uploaded portions of it to my you tube channel.[39] I mentioned in the video that Pluto entering Capricorn in 2008 would set off great changes like those Luther and Rousseau started. I pointed out the parallel between 1931 and 2010, and I said that what happened when Neptune entered Virgo in 1929 and Pisces in 1848 provided clues to what would happen in the 2008-2012 period. In 1848, after a great plague, a series of revolutions occurred in which government fell like dominoes, followed by huge migrations. I predicted that the time around 2010 "of ecological disasters, of famines, of depression, of migration, of collapse of cultures, of reformation in the church; all of that, look forward to that... and uh.... don't make any unwise investments!"

In my lecture on April 30, 2000 to the South Bay Astrological Society I mentioned that the next president would launch a war to promote a "just cause" in the Summer of 2001, and that in 2010 global corporations would fall.[40] I predicted upheavals around the world for 2010-11 that we could not ignore because of all the migrations they would produce, and said people would be asking "should one group of people create an economic system to benefit themselves at the expense of the rest of us" and also mentioned the World Trade Organization (the WTO) and its global trade policies that favor corporations. This "one group of people" would later be called "the 1%" at the Occupy Wall Street rallies and in Bernie Sanders' campaigns for president, so I posted a picture of the rally to accompany my prediction. Astrologer Graeme Jones pointed out that when Pluto entered Capricorn in 2008 many people would no longer have the money to protect themselves from the pain of the losses that would be occurring. A recovery would follow after the breakdown, I promised, in which the new green economy would blossom, and when we would adjust our trade policies to help the workers. It's interesting how the trade issue helped get President Trump elected in 2016, and how he tried to accomplish this adjustment in the late 2010s with his tariffs and trade wars.

On page 95 of Horoscope for the New Millennium I was reviewing the twelve 14-15-year phases in the cycle beginning with Uranus and Neptune conjoining in 1993, and this is what I wrote for the 2nd and 3rd phases starting in 2008:

> **Second House phase** (2008-2022): This period will see environmental catastrophes such as floods, famine, disease, and mass migrations from the Third World. Economic and political structures will have to adjust to the new global realities. Many governments could be toppled (Pluto enters Capricorn, 2008; Uranus-Pluto- Saturn T-square in 2010). People may be disillusioned, causing them to re-

---

[39] See you tube video https://youtu.be/oKmyB1q3H68
[40] See you tube video https://youtu.be/WAoeW5fXJYU

treat again into conservatism. Later in the Second House phase an environmental "post-industrial" revolution will get going. High-tech, green-conscious, and New Age businesses will prosper.

Third House phase (2022-2037): Extreme political activity and reorganization will bring justice to the people and the possible breakup of the United States. A horde of new inventions, ideas, controversies, and pioneers will appear. More spectacular breakthroughs will be made in travel and communications, plus links to the solar system and beyond. Humanity will recover its youthful, expressive confidence and boldly burst forth into the new era.

Bosses were about to fall as Pluto entered Capricorn in November 2008 and began to be squared by Uranus. Because of the ongoing reign of Reaganomics, in which government is seen as a problem, not much can be done in the USA until Reaganomics is removed. But the new president Barack Obama managed to reform health insurance anyway with his Affordable Care Act (also called Obamacare). In my book I predicted that from May 2009 through January 2010 there'd be some benevolent idealism toward healing humanity and solving problems (p.273). Soon after taking office he held meeting in March, but the bill was soon stalled. No-one could say whether Obamacare would pass, but I saw that Jupiter was in a long, close reform conjunction with Neptune in Aquarius, joined by the "wounded healer" minor planet Chiron, and so in a radio interview with Tony McGettigan I predicted that it would.[41] After being watered down, it took until January of 2010 to get it through on a narrow partisan vote. The final bill disappointed many folks (as I predicted), but Obama was able to say, "this is what change looks like." Also in July and December 2009 the Dodd-Frank reform law was introduced to fix the causes of the crash, and (again after being watered down) it became law in July 2010.

Uranus-Pluto aspects can be liberal or revolutionary, but remember that if Saturn-Pluto hard aspects are also going on a conservative reaction can happen simultaneously. I wrote on page 275 that the common people may be in retreat due to xenophobia and fear of radicals. Obamacare was just too much for the free-market reactionaries who had claimed America as their own since 1980. *Any* reform would have been too much! Right after it was passed in January 2010 the Tea Party was formed to oppose it, claiming it would add to taxes and the debt. And soon afterward they cried that they were "Taxed Enough Already" (TEA). First, they elected Republican Scott Brown to Ted Kennedy's old senate seat to oppose the reform on Jan.19th, 2010, and then they managed to sweep Republicans into power in the House of Representatives and most statehouses in November. Because Republicans were then able to redraw (and gerrymander) the election districts for the next decade, Obama's new USA reform era was stopped almost as soon as it had begun.

But huge fireworks of change erupted elsewhere, with reform movements motivated by the economic crisis, as I predicted on page 277. The crash in the USA had spread to Europe in 2009, and its financial system could not handle it. In Fall 2009 through Summer 2010 the debt crisis swelled there. Instead of a stimulus like Obama had provided

---

41 Tony's website http://www.ncrising.com/ may have this interview posted.

for the USA, which eventually revived the economy there, the European rulers insisted on austerity. The people revolted. Riots broke out in Greece in May 2010, and British Prime Minister Gordon Brown resigned. Meanwhile the ecological disasters I had predicted at the top of page 276 for mid-2010 multiplied. As the T-square tightened, an oil spill in the Gulf of Mexico on April 20th became the worst environmental disaster in USA history. On July 30 Pakistan was inundated with its worst-ever flood, and in August huge fires and drought ravaged Russia.[42] All over the world global temperatures rose, food prices soared, droughts spread and crops failed, especially in Syria.[43] Governments everywhere then began to "collapse with dizzying speed," as I predicted on pp.274-75. Iran and several other Asian countries were already in an uproar since mid-2009. In late 2010 and throughout 2011 governments fell in Ireland, Greece, Italy, Portugal, Spain, Slovakia and Belgium.

On January 4, 2011, Jupiter aligned exactly with Uranus right on the solar degree of Tunisia's national chart during a total solar eclipse. That was a real cosmic lightning bolt if ever there was one, and my astrologer friend Tony McGettigan and I looked at this chart in the months preceding and knew that a huge uprising was in the works. Richard Tarnas had already just written about Jupiter-Uranus conjunctions and oppositions as signatures of social and political awakenings and rebellions.[44] Just days after this eclipse a revolution toppled Tunisia's dictator, and democracy was established there. Young people all over the Arab world were thereupon inspired to topple their dictators too. The so-called Arab Spring had sprung. Two weeks later Tahrir Square in downtown Cairo Egypt was filled with young rebels, and by February they had topped their dictator Mubarak. More revolts engulfed Bahrain, Yemen, Iran, Libya, and finally Syria in March. But only Tunisia's new democracy survived in the long run. Western allies helped rebels in oil-rich Libya defend against and murder their strongman Qaddafi, long an enemy of the USA, but chaos and anarchy ensued. The rebels in Syria had hoped for Western aid too, but none was forthcoming. Instead their dictator Assad launched wholesale terror and genocide on his people, killing hundreds of thousands. Later he got his allies from Russia and Iran to help him kill thousands more.

On my website I pronounced the refugee crisis resulting from all these catastrophes as the most likely event to result from Neptune entering Pisces in 2011-2012. I am still amazed at how fully what I called in my book this "unprecedented stream of refugees" fulfilled my prediction (p.276). Millions fled Syria's monster tyrant to surrounding countries, and then flooded across the Mediterranean Sea into Europe. Millions more soon joined the exodus as crops and governments failed in Africa, and as wars still raged in Southern Asia. Muslims escaped from slaughter in Burma into Bangladesh, and other refugees escaped to Australia and New Zealand. As tyranny, crime and drought scarred the land in Central America, the southern borders of the USA were soon besieged as well. It was getting hard to tell which was rising faster, the human tide of refugees or the related rising ocean tides and sea levels.

---

[42] World Almanac 2018: Gulf oil spill p.326, Russia fires p.324, Pakistan flood p.322.
[43] https://www.npr.org/2013/09/08/220438728/how-could-a-drought-spark-a-civil-war
[44] Richard Tarnas, Cosmos and Psyche, Viking/Penguin, 2006, p 300ff.

Sometimes this global refugee crisis seemed to shock the world into compassion, and even encouraged the global awareness I had predicted for this time in my 1998 lecture, such as when an image of a young child refugee dying on a beach in Turkey touched peoples' hearts across the whole world. Some nations welcomed the newcomers. But more often people were alarmed and afraid of the migrants, and crime and terrorist attacks magnified the concern. This reaction and repression after 2011 was similar to what happened after the upsurge of nationalism in 1848, when the new realist politicians that took over after the revolutions overturned and suppressed it for the next decade. In the same way after 2012, far-right nativist and racist politics grew, and the once open borders of countries within the European Union started closing. People in the 2010s were reacting in fear to the onset of the inevitable new global civilization, and they found refuge in hate and nationalism that snuffed out the new global awareness. The surge of migrants into Britain disrupted the nation's repose and nostalgia so thoroughly that they voted to leave the European Union on June 23, 2016.[45] But this "Brexit" vote only caused continuing crisis. In June 2015 real estate tycoon, swindler and celebrity TV star Donald Trump announced he was running for president in order to stop the Mexican and Central American immigrants from "bringing drugs, crime and rape" into the USA.[46] I'd say he wanted to try and build a wall in the middle of the Rio Grande river just like the British were trying to build one in the English Channel. After he won the election, he immediately issued a ban against people from some Muslim countries traveling into the USA. I had written that in 2007, as Saturn opposed Neptune, that "xenophobia would grow over world trade or immigration, and that the president may rally paranoia against Iran and other enemies," and that "a demagogue would foment fear of foreigners so that Republicans would win the November election of 2008." I was too early in my predictions. But a Saturn-Neptune square came around in 2016 and 2017 and fulfilled the earlier prophecies at a later time in the 2010s, for which I had also predicted a right-wing reaction.

The Revolution under Uranus square Pluto continued on into 2013, however, igniting upheavals in Turkey, Russia, Ukraine and Brazil. But I saw a big, hopeful sign that a better and more peaceful world might now emerge from the chaos. On July 17, 2013 Jupiter, Saturn and Neptune formed one of the grandest and closest grand trines ever, and its significance could be seen from June through mid-August. I wrote about possible new constitutions on page 279, and I predicted diplomatic breakthroughs in forums[47] and in my video on predictions for 2013 and beyond.[48] In Iran the people had been pushing for more freedom since 2009, and in June 2013 this resulted in the election of a moderate new president Hassan Rouhani, who promised to make a deal to end Iran's nuclear program and get sanctions against his country lifted. As the grand trine matured, negotiations promptly began with Iran, and the deal was finally completed on July 14, 2015.[49] Negotiations also

[45] https://en.wikipedia.org/wiki/Brexit
[46] World Almanac 2018, p.499.
[47] See http://generationaldynamics.com/tftarchive/5751-See-What-Tunisia-Started-00014.htm (scroll down to post #343) and http://generationaldynamics.com/tftarchive/5751-See-What-Tunisia-Started-00015.htm (scroll down to post #356)
[48] See you tube video https://youtu.be/cyVolXreDXY at 15:29
[49] World Almanac 2018, p.672-673.

began in the Summer of 2013 in Afghanistan to end the war there. Obama began offering aid to the Syria rebels at this time, hoping to force Assad to negotiate, and he also offered a nuclear deal with Russia. Meanwhile at the same time Pope Francis convinced Cuba's new leader Raul Castro to open relations with the USA, and on July 20th diplomatic relations were restored just as Venus turned stationary.[50] The largest demonstrations yet in Egypt overthrew the elected but authoritarian Muslim president Morsi on July 3, 2013, and a new constitution was proclaimed.[51] From this point on, as I predicted, the Great Recession eased and the economy slowly recovered, as Jupiter got stronger in the sky.

The results of the grand trine were mixed, however, and ultimate outcomes are still unclear. Overthrow of Morsi provoked protest demonstrations in turn, but they were bloodily suppressed by the new tyrant General Sisi, who soon won the presidency. Things returned to how they had been under Mubarak, or even worse. Afghanistan negotiations are still unresolved, and Russia refused the deal with Obama and later broke the terms of older missile treaties. President Trump largely closed off the opening to Cuba and pulled out of the Iran nuclear deal in 2017. Aid to Syrian rebels proved too little too late. And a foreboding grand cross followed the grand trine when Uranus and Pluto with Jupiter and Mars in January 2014, and again in April and May as Mars turned stationary. I predicted this would bring war, violence and reckless rebellion, and it was clear to many that Jupiter would add religious fanaticism to the mix. Sure enough, former Al Qaeda fighters rose up as the Islamic State and quickly seized territory in Eastern Syria and Western Iraq and proceeded to impose terror and death on the people there in early 2014. Among other things, I mentioned tremendous turmoil in the Middle East, furious conflicts over religion there, and kidnappings and murder in God's name for 2015-16 on page 280, and as the war against the tyrannical and horrific Islamic State continued, it was all certainly happening. By 2017 the IS was rolled back by Iraqi forces, Iranian militias, and USA air power and special forces. In January 2014 civil war also broke out in eastern Ukraine against the new liberal pro-Western government, and President Putin sent in invaders to aid the pro-Russian rebels in April and May. The war there simmers on.

An international agreement on reducing climate change was reached in Paris in December 2015, but Trump pulled out of that deal too in 2017, along with the Oct 5, 2015 Trans-Pacific Partnership trade agreement. Meanwhile as Mars joined the Uranus-Pluto square again in the Spring of 2015, I predicted more Mid-East troubles, and the civil war that resulted from the Arab Spring revolt in Yemen escalated on March 19 into a horrific proxy war between Iran and Saudi Arabia, with the Saudis getting USA support.[52]

As the decade ended, it seemed humanity was in a race between the continuing uprisings of the people and the increasing tyranny and reaction against them by their governments. President Trump inspired waves of resistance and a Democratic midterm

---

[50] Obama and Castro thanked Pope Francis and the Vatican, which they said were instrumental in promoting their dialogue, and the government of Canada, where secret talks that began in June 2013 were held. https://www.washingtonpost.com/world/national-security/report-cuba-frees-american-alan-gross-after-5-years-detention-on-spy-charges/2014/12/17/a2840518-85f5-11e4-a702-fa31ff4ae98e_story.html ; World Almanac 2018, p.674.

[51] World Almanac 2018, p.772.

[52] World Almanac 2018, p.852.

election victory in November 2018, while loud protests engulfed France and India. The epidemic of gun violence that has grown ever since the massacre from the tower at the University of Texas on August 1, 1966 has now reached the point where hundreds of mass shootings happen every year. It's impossible to find a reliable astrological cycle to explain them all. Student victims at Marjory Stoneman Douglas High School in Parkland Florida were so aroused that on March 24, 2018 they organized one of the largest nationwide mass demonstrations ever held and mobilized young voters. One of their leaders Cameron Kasky spoke like someone who had read my prophecies, saying he looked ahead ten years and saw light and a system we could be proud of.[53] Gun control has once again become a fundamental issue challenging the people of the USA to either divide up and stand still or unite and move forward. In 2019 people were rising up in Venezuela, Sudan, Hong Kong, Chile, Lebanon, Iraq and elsewhere as Jupiter squared Neptune. Young as well as older people everywhere were striking and protesting against the growing impacts of climate change worldwide, as fires, floods, droughts and storms continued to hurt and kill thousands, and as scientists warned that the time for effective action was growing short.

But as Saturn and Pluto moved through conservative Capricorn in 2019 and approached their conjunction due in early 2020, the powers-that-be resisted. On page 282 I mentioned oppression and crackdowns in the 2019 period. Sure enough, an epidemic of deadly, tyrannical and reactionary rulers took power or fought off revolts and oppressed the people in the late 2010s: Assad in Syria, Sisi in Egypt, Salman in Saudi Arabia, Netanyahu in Israel, Erdogen in Turkey, Putin in Russia, Orban in Hungary, Duda in Poland, Xi Jinping in China and Hong Kong, Duterte in The Philippines, Maduro in Venezuela, Mnangagwa of Zimbabwe, Modi in India, Trump and McConnell in the USA, Bolsonaro in Brazil, Morrison in Australia, Boris Johnson in the UK, the banana republic leaders in Central America, and others, including those who have been in power for years now; it was a long list. As the next Jupiter-Saturn conjunction on Dec. 21, 2020 approached, a new era in government affairs and in states around the world beckoned. But this would not be an era racked by competing national alliances, as in years past, but a developing conflict between the aspirations of concerned and progressive people against their reactionary rulers. Even as the planetary champions of the people Jupiter and Neptune were squaring off from their most powerful signs with Mars making it a Marseillaise T-square in September, as Neptune reached the critical sixties' stillness of spirit degree of 17 Pisces, and as the cosmic plumber and transformer Pluto itself was undermining the tyrants' rule in its approaching conjunction with Saturn, the people were already rising up in 2019. The tyrants are supported by the fears of the haters and motivated by their own lust for power. They need to be overthrown; the whole lot of them. Only if the people have won in the next few years against their rulers could progress resume and the New Age dawn in the next decade, during which the planets would move on into hopeful Aquarius.

---

[53] See you tube video: https://youtu.be/rgc2il-20g8

Chapter 5

Revving Up the Engines: 2020-2030

As we gaze into our crystal ball, our prophetic vision needs to be 20/20 to see beyond 2020. Yet it's clear that a crucial turning point in American history lies just past that imposing marker of time. As a new score of years opens, Americans may be counting their blessings that they don't live in the Middle East, Russia or Africa, where rumblings of war will be getting louder. Yet in a few years these troubles will help trigger troubles in America too, and meanwhile Americans with investments abroad will be counting their losses.

Jupiter and Saturn will make a conjunction, on December 21, 2020, as they do every 20 years. Such conjunctions are also called Great Conjunctions or Great Mutations. The fact that this conjunction will be closely preceded by a total solar eclipse on December 14th, is all the indication we need that the 2020s will be a decade to remember. The conjunction of 2020 is especially significant because it is the first one of its kind in *Aquarius* in over 700 years. This is a magnificent shift, a great mutation indeed, and a sign of the New Age. For the last 200 years, and consistently since 1841-42, Jupiter and Saturn have aligned in earth signs: Capricorn, Taurus and Virgo. They have also made trine aspects to each other in these earth signs. At the same time, the equivalent and very-similar conjunction among the longer cycles on the transcendent level, Uranus and Neptune, have *also* been making conjunctions and trines in earth signs for even longer. From 2020 onward, both of these planetary alignments will be happening in air signs, Aquarius, Gemini and Libra.

It would be hard to overstate what this shift from earth to air means for all of our affairs. The epoch of earth signs has been an amazing double-phenomenon this time around. We have abundantly fulfilled the directive the planets gave us by mastering technology and commerce and learning to make any product to satisfy our physical and emotional needs. The industrial revolution has benefited all the pursuits which earth signs are noted for: practical concerns, making money, establishing material security, planning out our entire lives, analyzing all things, and swarming over and conquering Planet Earth and submitting it to our material desires. It is amazing what we have been able to do, and how much power we have amassed. It was almost like a genie was released from the bottle, and he turned out to be Santa Claus on Christmas. But in 2020, a great shift is at hand. From now on the conjunctions and trines of Jupiter and Saturn, and also of Uranus and Neptune, will happen air signs. We are moving to a more refined plane now. It has been called the transition from the industrial to the information age, and it has already been underway. We will be making unprecedented and powerful connections with each other and across the planet, as our social and technological networks of communication and transportation expand as never before. Our Neptune-Pluto conjunctions in the air-sign Gemini in the last thousand years have already instigated *this* particular change, and now it will be even greater. It goes beyond a new age of information in our economic system, though. Physical security and material gain will no longer be our top priority. The currencies and pastimes of the next 200 years will be based on new ideas instead. We'll be more idealistic and optimistic; more interested in justice and reform for its own sake. We'll be ready to associate and organize in groups for a common purpose. Every ancient assumption will be "up in the air," as our visionary curiosity threatens every established authority.

The chart for the eclipse on Dec. 14th shows Mars in Aries in trine to the solar eclipse itself, revealing a confident people ready for action.[54] The people's aggressive optimism will only increase once Neptune, the planetary Ark of Humanity, also enters Aries at mid-decade. What's more, Pluto will also align with the Jupiter-Saturn conjunction, and in 2022 the "cosmic plumber" will also return to its original position in the U.S. horoscope for the first time ever. Destiny has its target set on the USA, and the America which emerges from this chapter will be greatly transformed and almost unrecognizable from the America which preceded it.

Not only will Pluto be making its karmic return in America's chart in the 2020s, so will Uranus-- and Neptune will be *opposing* its natal position too. This triple whammy indicates that a great American crisis, another "hinge of history" comparable to the Revolution, the Civil War, and World War II, is due in the middle 2020s. The United States will pursue another "struggle for its very existence," as astrologers have called these crisis times. With Neptune returning to the Nadir of America's chart (also called the "house of home"), where it last stood in 1860, the Civil War seems the best analogy for what we can expect, as I originally said in my 1997 book. But history never quite repeats itself: this time, the bone of contention and the contenders themselves will be different. The result could be the same, however: the breakup of the United States.

People will begin to wonder why the "last remaining superpower" should stay standing. If the Soviet Union could split up, why not the United States? Has the nation become too big and cumbersome to meet America's needs? Many immigrants have poured into our nation since the 1970s. Ethnic groups have grown in population in certain regions. If this "multi-cultural" nation is no longer a "melting pot," the people may be boiling mad at each other from separate pots, especially now that Trump has already stirred the pot. Decades-old conservative and libertarian arguments about the "intrusive power of the federal government" will feed into the impulse to destroy it.

Furthermore, the cultural wars between religious-right traditionalists and secular feminists may not be over. The need to develop alternative energy pits regional interests against each other too. Militias may form to fight against gun control. Meanwhile, in 2020 our democracy is stalemated by the divided passions of the people. Congress has been handicapped by extremist party politics (mostly on the right), by filibusters, and by gerrymandering by which legislators draw up their own districts to preserve their power.

---

[54] Charts for 1966 through 2048 were cast using the Swiss Ephemeris from astrodienst. All eclipses were cast for New or Full Moon times. Charts for 2060-2100 were cast on solar fire using the Michelsen Ephemeris times.

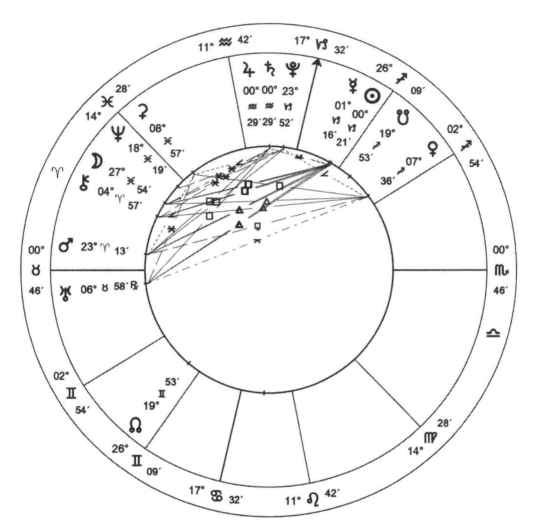

This is the chart for the exact time of Jupiter's conjunction to Saturn in Aquarius. The theme of change is emphasized again by Mars and Uranus rising, and Pluto on the Midheaven. Chart data: December 21, 2020, 6:21 PM UT, Washington DC, 38N54, 77W02

Voting districts started to look like moldy Swiss cheese, and the system smelled rotten. The people are already asking at this writing whether the politicians should choose their voters, or voters choose their politicians. The system has become ever-more rigged in recent years. Wealthy interests still buy politicians to such an extent that people think our government doesn't represent them but is beholden instead to the almighty dollar. And our whole society favors the rich and the corporations, who accumulate ever more wealth and power at the expense of everyone else, and who gamble with our economy with free money handed out to them by their friends in the Treasury and the Federal Reserve. It looks more like a casino that favors the house while it bankrupts its addicted customers. Many may wonder whether we should scrap the current system altogether and start over.

New proposals to do this will be circulated intensely in the 2020s. Campaign finance reform, free media for candidates, and public financing will all be proposed to get money out of politics. Proportional representation, open primaries and ranked-choice voting could break the duopoly of the two political parties. A parliamentary system instead of electing a "virtual king" every 4 years, ending the electoral college, and reforms to rein in the national debt and lower taxes; all these and more will be considered. Most threatening of all to the old order will be the urge to secede by red or blue states (Republican or Democratic voting states, respectively; whichever faction is out of power after the 2020 or 2024 elections). If all reforms are frustrated, this could be the only remedy.

As of this writing, indications are that, at least by mid-decade, the red states will be the ones left out. That would fit the pattern of the *earlier* civil war. It might be Texas that leads the way, whose governor had called for secession in the 2000s. On the other hand, a blue state like Hawaii may also trigger moves by other states, and the West Coast could unite as Pacifica. Some people might wonder what statehood for Puerto Rico would mean for the balance of red and blue power. And the District of Columbia itself is still not represented in Congress.

Meanwhile, unlike during the Civil War, America will still find itself the leader of the world. Many Americans by now will want to resign the position, which could suit other nations just fine. Self-reliance and self-determination are popular buzzwords when Neptune is in individualistic sign Aries, as it will be starting in the mid-2020s. America First has already become a popular slogan. At the same time, the power of the UN might be growing in this period. How much sovereign power should America give away could be an issue. It could be a choice between America First or Earth First.

So, in spite of its domestic conflicts, foreign affairs won't leave Americans alone in the 2020s. The war(s) likely to break out at the end of 2020 will certainly demand attention. The Fall Equinox chart puts Mars right near the Descendant (house of war) in Washington DC. The USA powers-that-be might take an aggressive stance toward some troublemakers and ambitious tyrants, but because it is consumed at home, it will not be able to put any swords behind its words. The chart indicates that Russia and West Africa (e.g. Ghana, Libya) will be targeted for these troubles. Then, a month after Mars in Aries turns direct in November, in square to Jupiter, Saturn *and* Pluto, a powerful solar eclipse on December 14 looms over the world. The month following the eclipse will be very dangerous. The chart shows that the Middle East (probably Syria and Kurdistan), Russia, India, China, Korea and Japan may be affected. Just like the phrase in the Bible, wars and rumors of wars could erupt in diverse places.

As I see it though, the emerging global conflict in many places will not be between alliances of nations, such as those that represented the "free world" and "communist world" in the Cold War. No, the primary emerging battle is between the tyrants of the 2010s and the rising power of the people in each country; an alliance of the people against an alliance of tyrants everywhere. Which one will win depends on how dedicated the people are to the cause, and how well they can link up and support each other. This kind of world war has already been brewing in the New World Order since 1989.

In spite of this looming international crisis, which could drag on for years, the first half of the decade will be relatively comfortable in many places. The economy, though unstable, will recover after 2020, spurred on by the new "green post-industrial revolution." As Mars turns stationary-direct in our progressed chart of modern humanity in 2022 at 7 degrees Aquarius, our "post-modern" aversion to "progress" will end. Since the 1960s, in spite of advances in technology, many people have wanted to slow down progress to make sure we were going in the right direction. Environmental damage and depersonalization have concerned us. Politics has been stalemated too, as people have become skeptical about a political system that seems more like a shouting match than a forward march. Now, knowing again where we want to go, progress will be off and running again full-blast. The pace of inventions will skyrocket, and aggressive demands for social change will be loud, unceasing and effective in the 2020s. In the 1860s, the last time Neptune entered Aries, railroads were built to span the continent. In this heady decade of the 2020s, we may construct some new pathways to the planets, as the new space race between America and other nations will spur expansion into the solar system (this prediction from my 1997 book is already starting). Lightning-fast, giant electronic networks will be constructed for both people and ideas. The millennial generation, who since the 2000s had their noses stuck almost 24/7 in their smart phones, are tech-obsessed, and as they mature in the 2020s, they will drive a technological boom. It may seem like we have entered a virtual world. Massive building projects will transform the landscape, and new tech solutions will be advanced for every problem. The people will be organized in efficient new institutions and companies. Before long we'll wonder if we're all turning into robots.

Because of the positive mood, a springtime of action reborn, I think we will emerge from this "hinge of history" in the 2020s in good shape, despite many severe bumps and bruises along the way. By mid-decade the three outer planets will be forming a very-exact, harmonious double-sextile, featuring a trine between revolutionary planets Uranus in Gemini and Pluto in Aquarius, with Neptune in Aries in the middle. It's a powerful sign of confident, can-do attitudes returning that will launch North America and the world into the new Aquarian Age. This double sextile shows we will connect with each other better socially and combine our energies in powerful networks and organizations. A similar pattern happened during World War II but was absent from the skies over the Civil War. Therefore, a fratricide on the scale of the civil war is unlikely this time. All of this suggests a fortunate outcome. The many aggressive pioneers of the 2020s won't be building empires of blood and iron like those of the 1860s, but arteries and capillaries through which the world's people can circulate in a global "empire" of mutual commerce and understanding. The 2020s will also present our best chance to begin building a post-industrial economy that supports instead of destroys the Earth and offers equal opportunity to all its people. The world as well as America will attack every issue and address every concern. We will be ready to rumble, and oppressive powers will take a tumble. Nothing will be too small to tackle.

Jupiter and Saturn's conjunction in the 12th house in the USA during the Dec.14 eclipse is another clear signal that in the 2020s established institutions could bite the dust or be consigned to the dustbin of history. So is Uranus' square to the conjunction. The secret plutocratic potentates may be knocked off their silver thrones. And whereas after past Jupiter-Saturn conjunctions we saw the deaths of presidents in office, this time the office or the power of the presidency *itself* could be threatened. It could go the way of royal English colonial rule-- one Pluto cycle before.

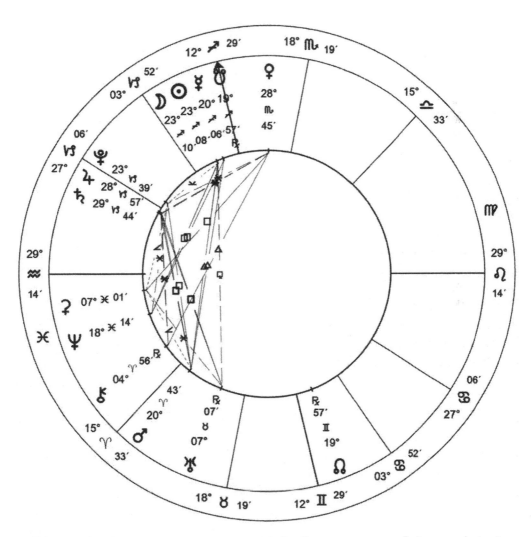

This total eclipse happens one week before Jupiter and Saturn join in conjunction in Aquarius on Dec.21, the first such conjunction in over 600 years. The following 20 years are a true "Aquarian Age" in which we get back into high gear and witness the transformation of America. Chart data: Dec.14, 2020, 4:17 PM UT, Washington DC.

We can't rule out some reforms in the mental health field either, given this position of Jupiter and Saturn. By the Spring of 2022, some mental hospitals may be transformed into spiritual renewal centers, as "cuckoo nests" become places to "fly high." The continuing need for spiritual awakening will not be totally forgotten either amid the mad rush into progress. *Real* social change always requires some self-examination on the part of the people. And the progressed chart of humanity, as well as the signs occupied by Uranus and Neptune, indicates that artists and architects will be ambitious too in the early 2020s. Their soaring visions could eventually be made into imposing realities. The new renaissance may still be around to complement the renewal of material progress.

Passions Rise, Laggards Fall

In the early 2020s Jupiter and Saturn will again be where they were in the early 1960s. Rebellious spirits will be back too. We may take up where we left off. As I predicted in Horoscope for the New Millennium, disillusion during the crisis of 2010 *did* empower Republicans, but they will be ousted again sometime in the early 2020s. An age of aggressive pioneers is no time for stick-in-the-mud conservatives-- they'll be pushed aside in nothing flat. Just as the Republicans quickly emerged in the Civil War era as the most powerful American political party, so another new party (or several of them) may become powerful as America threatens to split apart *again*. Since the Republicans were *born* in the *first* civil war, they could *die* in *this* similar crisis. Meet the old boss; used to be the new boss.

In fact, the entire two-party system will be in peril. Most people in the USA as of this writing are already fed up with the political duopoly of Democrats and Republicans. The number of independent voters is expanding, especially among young people; and this will continue. If a Democrat such as Joe Biden or Bernie Sanders is elected in Nov. 2020, and the Democrats win the Senate too, they may finally have some power to initiate a new era of change. But the Democrats will not have won the White House if anyone besides Sanders or Biden is nominated. The question is always whether a candidate can communicate and connect with the people. It always depends on the candidates' natal horoscopes who it is that ends up in the Big House, and when. But if Democrats win the White House in 2020, they may well lose it in 2024, unless someone with a very high horoscope score is nominated (see Chapter 12). It's hard to conceive that the Grand Old Party would benefit in such a progressive decade as the 2020s. On the other hand, if Donald Trump or Mike Pence is re-elected in 2020, the Republicans will be able to tamp down some of the growing Democratic strength in Congress for at least a couple of years. I will review the election patterns in Chapter 12.

Already in April 2020 passions could be high and a few violent outbreaks could happen. By the Spring of 2021 the people will be pushing for reform and demanding the truth. No more secrets will be allowed! The fever rises higher in the Spring of 2022 when universities could be hotbeds of dissent.

Advances in new energy technology will inspire calls to action. Petroleum was discovered exactly one Neptune cycle before; could we find another new energy source now that doesn't pollute our environment, and could it get government support? The Spring of 2022 will indeed be a very fertile time for reforms that restore Mother Earth, as indicated by the "reform" conjunction of **Jupiter and Neptune in Pisces**. New ecology and energy programs will rev up in the Fall of 2022 because Uranus in green Taurus is rising in the Fall Equinox chart. The new congress could devote a lot of its energy to this issue in early 2023. Such innovations and reforms will mushroom even more once Jupiter reaches Taurus and joins inventive Uranus there starting in May 2023 and aligns with it in the Fall of 2023 and Spring of 2024. By then, a green energy boom could get going that eventually eases the public economic fears from the previous few years.

Although the economy will not crash and burn as people in years now past *feared might happen* in the early 2020s, that won't stop the peoples' concerns from burning through the blocks to further reform. The fires of change will grow steadily and get ever hotter as the decade goes on. Since Uranus is in Taurus, taxes could be up for debate again. Fears of another recession, especially around Nov. 2021, will spur congressional action. Since the Social Security System was founded one cycle of Uranus before, and since 2022 and especially 2023 are years of reform, it may be time to make it more solvent for the future. Support for reforms will be given abroad too by the USA in the Spring of 2022, hoping to rein in the wars in the world. Southeast Asia (e.g. Thailand), South America (Colombia), or Central Africa (C.A.R.) could benefit from these efforts. Overall, 2022 and 2023 look to be very constructive years.

It's a decisive and historic year too. As October 2022 ends, just as the ghosts and goblins come out on Halloween, ghosts from times past may come out to haunt us too. That's when Mars turns stationary in 25 degrees Gemini, very close to its position in America's horoscope. Just then, Neptune is opposing its original position in that horoscope, and in *square* to Mars. This indicates that 2022 is a tremendous milestone for America's collective soul. Neptune means "dreams," so American dreams will re-awaken in 2022, and that could inspire the midterm elections. Historically, 6th-year midterms are a disaster for the party holding the White House for 2 terms, and this time if it happens it would be a tsunami, and a real chance to regenerate the USA. Saturn, now squaring rebellious Uranus, is stationary in late October 2022, *and* in the very same degree where it was on the day JFK was assassinated. With Mars stationary signaling action and even violence now, could the planets be trying to tell us something? Is it that the business that was cut short when JFK died finally needs some attention now? It really seems so when we consider that Mars will also finally be turning stationary and going direct again in the progressed chart of humanity in 2022. That's a huge deal, and therefore this will be a key moment. You could say this is the exact month when the engines of history rev up and click back into high gear. We see that the Uranus-Neptune-Pluto double-sextile formation is beginning to form in 2022 too, so that all three planets of the transcendental trinity are moving harmoniously together. That means that many people will be working together. That could eventually be a huge breakthrough for our polarized nation, even though now it basically means that the progressive side will be winning.

Exactly 60 years before, JFK faced down the Soviets over missiles in Cuba, in what the psychics had predicted would be an "end of the world" moment that year. Since a solar eclipse happens on Oct. 25, 2022, just days before Mars turns stationary, the earth will shake (maybe literally too). It does remind me a little bit of the 1999 Nostradamus eclipse. Mars on the 9th house cusp in the eclipse chart shows that the troubles abroad could force the USA into desperate diplomatic action. As with the crisis in October 1962, a beneficial breakthrough for peace is likely, by late November this time.

Neptune opposing its position in the US chart and squaring Mars indicates scandals ongoing in the US administration and in foreign relations. The people will be outraged; their moral sensibilities severely offended. Remember **Pluto** is also returning to *its* place in 27 Capricorn in the US chart now. This indicates a challenge to the American *corporate* establishment too, as well as to the government, and public demands to take progressive action will be sounded loudly. This time they will be heard, and new reforms will begin in 2023. Economic kingpins keep coming up with ways to keep themselves from falling over by rigging the political system to stall progress and to concentrate ever-more economic power. They have already erected huge obstacles. But this time they will largely fail, and congress will act to take down the walls, perhaps even packing the Supreme Court. That means the US corporate structure will not emerge from the 2020s without some major restructuring. Banks and corporations will be especially prone to huge scandals around 2022, which will rattle the markets and the public. They will have to come clean, or they will have their clocks cleaned. It could be more than a "slap of the wrist" this time. The aggressive corporate American tiger must learn to "share the wealth" and be responsive to the public interest, or else have its sharp teeth trimmed in the years after 2022.

The Deluge Arrives

Meanwhile, as Uncle Sam continues to "generously" help rescue other peoples in trouble, Americans may question how much trouble this is making for themselves. As Saturn enters watery Pisces in March 2023, as it did in the mid-1960s, many governments of the world may start to find themselves in over their heads. By July and August the tide will rise literally too, as the results of climate change start to drench the people as never before.

Generosity of another kind could erupt in 2022-23. People will be more willing to share the good life. As Jupiter joins Neptune in Pisces in 2022, and then joins Uranus in Taurus in 2023-24, just when similar indications occur in the progressed chart of humanity, our enthusiasm for change could reflect itself in a renaissance of the arts and culture. The flood of feeling will overflow onto canvases and into architecture and multi-media venues. This period could literally sparkle with great artistic ideas that fascinate the people. Meanwhile, 20th century hedonism will make a comeback too and temporarily overwhelm the austerity of the 21st. Young people will burst into prominence again, and a galaxy of new show-business stars will sparkle and shine in the early 2020s, especially in the Autumn of 2022. Virtual reality will yield to virtual fantasy.

The flood waters of change become a deluge in 2024, as Saturn wades deeper into the waters of Pisces. We know how revolutionary an alignment of Jupiter with Uranus can be too. Uprisings and revolts for nationalism and democracy and against climate change and corruption around the world will shake authorities in April 2024, especially in the USA, China and the Middle East, where the solar eclipse on April 8 highlights the conjunction of Jupiter and Uranus in these places. People everywhere will be well informed about the inequality and injustice of society, and they'll be soaked with ideas on how to cure it. As economic fears and corporate scandals continue to reverberate through the land, the liberating energy of the people will be aroused as never before by compassion for the oppressed and by expectations of a brighter tomorrow.

Revolutions and uprisings in one place continue to trigger troubles in other places. As global humanity becomes one, connected into one global mind, so also social and political movements become one. Mars will turn stationary again in domestic-oriented Cancer in February 2025, so disputes among US ethnic groups could be aroused again, as well as the peace and environmental movements. Accidents, spills or weather disasters could add to the urgency of climate change at this time. With Uranus and Jupiter in Taurus, the sign of Earth Day, breakthroughs in new energy technology will be challenging the old ways as never before, and April 2024 will see massive movements to support new green industries and lifestyles. Many old fossil fuel companies could bite the dust this year, or face severe resistance and boycotts, despite their success in buying and deceiving many people.

By election day 2024, the American people and their government will have begun some significant reforms. But the people will remain severely divided, and we won't agree on where to go from there. Many will say change hasn't gone far enough, while others will say it has already gone too far. Although it depends on who the candidates are, both now in 2024 as well as before in 2020, indications are that the people may reject the party in power in November 2024. But who will replace them? We know that the two major parties have already been very unpopular for decades. By the 2024 election, an independent or third-party candidate has a better chance than ever before. The movements among the people, both right and left, will be pushing beyond the bounds of the old political duopoly. It may be hard to keep the election entirely free of cheating and disruption too, given the level of turmoil and travail abroad in the land. People are *very* dissatisfied with the powers that be and fed up with how stubbornly and ruthlessly the elites resist *any* perceived threat to their status. In the 2020s, both Uranus and Pluto will be returning to their positions when the USA was founded in 1776. They will *also* be in trine angle to each other, with Neptune between them. This astounding planetary event means that a revolution is coming to the USA.

The time of decision is at hand, and destiny calls. Whoever assumes office in January 2025 will be overwhelmed by a veritable tidal wave of troubles, as Saturn, the planetary ship of state, sails through the muddy waters of Pisces. It will take extra skill for leaders to navigate these waters. By taking office in the year that Uranus enters Gemini, and when Neptune crosses into Aries for the first time in 164 years, everything the new president does could set off national and international fireworks. Changes that are started in 2025 will be unstoppable, and the consequences will reverberate for years. When all is said and done, this president may not emerge from this 4-year term with full powers intact, as changes to the system are likely.

One can scarcely imagine a more significant conjunction for America than **Saturn lining up with Neptune** at the start of Aries. But there it is, through most of 2025 *and* early 2026. Just like during the Boston Tea Party (when Saturn was also in conjunction with Neptune), and the Battle of Gettysburg (when Saturn was opposite Neptune), people will be ready to sacrifice their "full measure of devotion" to the causes they believe in. The periodic "great crisis for survival of the Unites States of America" will have returned. This time, the crisis will lift the nation out of its Piscean chaotic muddle and into a forceful new beginning in Aries. It shall be a spring-like spirit of active determination. New leaders will emerge among the people, and many folks will feel the call, ready in 2025-26 to become part of something larger than themselves, and at the same time become the kind of self-empowered and resourceful people who can make new visions into realities.

If the new president and congress keep the 2020s progressive ball rolling in early 2025, the reactionaries will erupt. Gun control could be rolled out by a liberal government, which will spur the gun lobby and their followers to scream that Uncle Sam is taking their guns away, and they may take up their arms in reply. Reactionaries may still be around to declare that welfare cheats are stealing their tax money. Climate change rolls forward, but that doesn't mean conservatives will roll over and give up all their money rolls and submit to the new rules. The right-wing Rebellion will be up and running as early as March, and the president will feel the heat and will need to take action to deal with it.

But the left-wing will be aroused even more, especially if the new president and the government stall and dither around. Progressive peoples' demands will swell in June 2025, and crest on July 7, 2025 when Saturn and Neptune at the cusp of Aries turn stationary. As fate would have it, this is the exact moment of America's Jupiter Return to 6 degrees Cancer, and also of Uranus' first entry into Gemini. This will be the moment of decision, and a permanent parting of the ways for the old America and the new. In early August 2025, Mars opposes the conjunction of Saturn-Neptune. The progressives will assert themselves (Mars and Neptune), and meet resistance (Saturn) from the right-wing rebels.

People-power actions could take us far, but firepower could bring us blood. The people will decide the shape of this battle. A progressive president would have willing recruits for the fight against a Right-wing Rebellion. I would expect this rebellion's fires to burn out within a couple of years. The "great war" that usually highlights the great crisis every 80-plus years could be no more than this.

On the other hand, the USA might also find itself further embroiled in the ongoing troubles in Asia too, concerned over terrorist threats. The Jupiter US war cycle returns in the mid-2020s, and this time it means possible war abroad *and* a war at home at the same time. Uncle Sam could have both his hands full. One key date to watch as such a foreign battle gets going is October 2024, when Jupiter is stationary right at America's Mars degree in 22 Gemini, and then when Mars itself turns stationary in December. In March, June or September 2025, more key commitments abroad could be made by a new president. The wars begun at the end of 2020 in Asian lands will now reach a critical point. What's more, the foreign crisis may be connected to the domestic one in several ways. New revolutions abroad could threaten the perceived interests of the United States. Also, if the USA falls apart in these years, then it may have to deal with interventions by other powers taking one side or another. That would be a new experience for Uncle Sam. Anti-war movements could also play a key role in the fortunes of American leaders.

When outer planets enter a new sign of the zodiac, it can signal the start of an important new phase. When this sign is Aries, a whole new cycle among peoples and nations is launched by key events. Neptune is the most important planet in world affairs. Also important is the chart for when it enters Aries to stay, rather than just temporarily testing the waters. **On January 26, 2026, Neptune enters Aries to stay.** Remember that the previous time Neptune entered Aries, on April 13, 1861, the Civil War began in the USA. The following year on Sept.22, just 3 weeks after Mars stood stationary in Aries, was Lincoln's key victory at Antietam, and simultaneously a new aggressive leader took over Germany.[55] The immediate result were wars of unification and aggression in both places, as well as the new ideals which Abraham Lincoln enunciated at Gettysburg. What began in 1861-62 with Lincoln in the USA and Bismarck in Germany have dominated to a great extent the years that will end in 2026.

Now in 2026, a new Neptune cycle begins that lasts for the next 165 years. This time, the signs generally look very positive. This is good news to Earth and its people who, in the times of this writing, have become very pessimistic about the future. The keynote of the new cycle appears to be "visionary pioneering," rather than the aggression or "blood and iron" (Bismarck's slogan in Germany,[56] and two closely-related attributes to his own sun sign Aries, which Neptune entered in 1861), which characterized the previous period starting in 1861. The chart for the new Neptune cycle that begins on January 26, 2026[57] shows no less than five planets in Aquarius at or near the Midheaven in the USA, suggesting that the American people will be more idealistic and progressive in their attitudes from this date onward. The Sun is located at 7 degrees Aquarius, e*xactly* where Mars is turning stationary-direct in these years in the progressed Chart of Modern Humanity. The revival of action shines through! Mars is transiting the same sign in *this* chart for Neptune in Aries too, closely conjunct Pluto in Aquarius. Non-stop, fearless activism begins as Neptune enters Aries; no more Piscean muddling around! Meanwhile, Uranus rising in earthy Taurus in this chart for the new Neptune cycle reveals that

---

[55] Civil War began: Sarah Janssen, ed., <u>World Almanac 2018</u>, Infobase, p.140. Antietam: Thomas A. Bailey, <u>The American Pageant</u>, D.C. Heath and Co., 1956, p.432. Bismarck: Gordon A. Craig, <u>Europe 1815-1914</u>, Dryden Press, 1972, p.207.

[56] William Langer, ed., Richard Pipes, <u>Western Civilization from the Struggle for Empire to Europe in the Modern World</u>, Harper and Row, 1968, p.397-398.

[57] Neptune ingress time obtained from Swiss Ephemeris: https://www.astro.com/swisseph/ae/neptune1600.pdf Charts from Astrodienst used by permission.

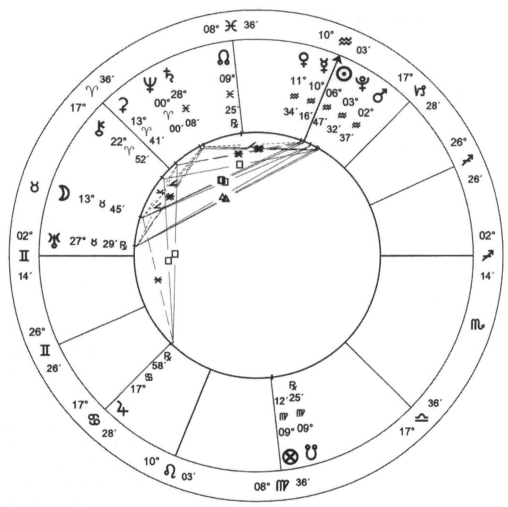

Neptune in Aries ingress
This is the chart for the moment (or ingress) when Neptune enters Aries on January 26, 2026 which is also the start of a new 164-year cycle of Neptune through the signs. Note that the Sun is in the degree of 7°Aquarius where Mars turns stationary-direct in 2022 in the progressed Horoscope of Humanity for the current civilization cycle. Chart data: January 26, 2026, 5:34 PM UT, Washington DC, 38N54, 77W02.

"Nature's Green Revolution" is at work, further emphasized by the Moon in Taurus and expansive Jupiter in sensitive, conservationist Cancer.

The chart for the exact moment Neptune enters Aries on January 26, 2026 announces that America is in the spotlight for the next 165 years. So many key planets are located on the key Midheaven and Ascendant points in Washington DC, that the USA could feel like it's melting from all the pressure. But the revved-up energy will disprove many peoples' predictions that America is on the verge of decline and fall. As I keep pointing out, since America is the new Rome, that won't happen until at least 2385. This Aries ingress in 2026 is indeed a positive forecast for the USA, after the previous 45 years of backward movement. Western Europe and the UK will especially benefit from their relationship to America during this cycle, as will the whole world. That's because the new global awareness, represented by Neptune, will be given state sanction in the USA and everywhere during this new 165-year cycle by Saturn's conjunction with Neptune in 2026. This could result in the formation of many new global institutions in the 165 years to come. China will also benefit from opening up its entertainment and communications during this new cycle, and from allowing more freedom of speech. Saturn's conjunction also indicates that new Neptunian ideals will need to be practical and workable, and that they will take time to fully unfold.

Further optimistic signs of the times include the fact that in 2026 we are still early in the mutual cycles of all 3 outer planets. If we take the longer-term view, this suggests that awakening and rebirth is still unfolding. Uranus at its original place in the American horoscope every four score and four years signals ominously that the periodic great US upheaval is at hand; but now, for the first time ever, it coincides with the 59-year "progressive Saturn cycle" too. Saturn has come around to Pisces and Aries during some of the most progressive times in history: 1789 (French Revolution), 1848 (revolutionary wave in Europe), 1907 (during the progressive movement) and 1965-66 (the sixties revolution). This combination means that, this time around, the Great American Crisis should result in some substantial advances in social justice, even more than it generally does. The resistance might not be able to stop it. The conservatives and cynics of the past will be proven wrong. The revolutionary movement should get quite a boost in February 2026, as the people rise up and launch the new march forward.

Many prophecies about American society and government grab our attention, as we look at this amazing and important chart for the next 165 years. Neptune's new beginning in Aries will inspire some promising changes that disturb the status quo. 5 planets in Aquarius at the top of the chart, the place that rules the president, suggest that the presidency itself might change. Many have suggested that the United States could shift to a parliamentary system. Since Aquarius in astrology rules congress, it suggests that the United States could join the rest of the democratic world and invest its executive power in a prime minister, either immediately in 2026, or sometime in the following 165 years. Alternatively, this could indicate that the president leads the congress to enact legislation to advance social justice and environmental progress. In any case, a progressive agenda is now in the driver's seat within the zeitgeist of Humanity (the spirit of the times), and in its legislative bodies. In other words, from 2026 on, the world moves forward. The gears have shifted; the rocket is lifting off. The United States will be in the vanguard of change again for the first time since that 1892 progressed Mars turned retrograde with JFK's assassination in 1963. The US will push for change abroad again too, as JFK did then. Since Pluto is now in Aquarius, sign of the legislature, the new congress will be doing a lot of the pushing over the next decade and a half.

The Battle for America

The battles will be joined by 2026, especially after the total solar eclipse on August 12. First, the USA Congress will get moving in a big way in the Spring. Things will move forward with breakneck speed. Battles will be swift and decisive if a civil war is going on. Expect an exuberant and eventful Summer in 2026! The people will be ready to push the envelope, both in society at large and in their own lives. Meanwhile, some diplomatic breakthroughs are possible in August 2026, not only in America and central Europe, but in some poor countries in north-central Africa too. But new battles could erupt in these places in the Spring of 2027 as Mars turns stationary right on the degree of the big eclipse in August 2026. The African cradle of Humanity will be rocking and coming to life.

Expect the people of the USA to be aroused to a fever pitch in early 2027. Not only will the Great Crisis be reaching its climax in early 2027, but attention could be diverted from all the troubles by fantastic sports events. New stars and heroes could burst across the entertainment landscape, and the arts will show greater imagination, almost as if another Manet has come back to record another picnic in the grass (the sensational first spark of modern art in 1863, soon after the last time Neptune entered Aries[58]). Youth will be in high spirits, as riots in the streets and at sports events grab headlines. Computer hackers could be in the news too, as the civil wars become cyber wars, and as high-tech saboteurs wreak havoc with the Establishment in both the Spring and Summer. By August 2027, expect the French to be asserting their rights and their passion for justice.

The engines of progress rev up big time in 2027. But activists will also face more resistance. The reactionaries will want to rev up their own engines too and send them into reverse. The big eclipse on August 2, 2027 will happen just days after Uranus returns exactly to its USA horoscope position for the first time on July 26. We know what a big deal that Return is; it's the linchpin of American history. Crucial battles are due. It could be the Gettysburg of the new civil war; the Do or Die Day. Big mobilizations will occur in July and August, linked up with worldwide protests and demonstrations. But then they will run into brick walls. The Establishment will fight back, and the reactionary rebels will gain ground, threatening to turn off the engines of progress. The president will probably be reasserting authority too. In late December, repressions could get very ugly. Reactionary organizations and groups might seem to be winning, as Mars in Capricorn squares Saturn in Aries.

The possibility that the USA might split up will likely loom largest in late 2027. The future of the nation is at stake. Many questions could suddenly arise as the time of destiny arrives. Can the right-wing rebels be defeated? If the corporate Establishment still rules, can they be reined in? How would assets and responsibilities be divided if the United States is no longer united? Who will have the nuclear powers? Will the United Nations have to be given more power, and do most nations want this? Can the UN bring peace and resolve conflicts? Can it stop aggression? Will the United States be able or willing to be a great power now? And for how long? Will the USA help bring peace to the world? If not,

---

[58] Gardner, De La Croix and Tansey, <u>Art Through the Ages</u>, Harcourt, Brace and World, 1970, p.666-667.

who or what would take its place? In the USA the world's indispensable nation? Will anyone mind the store? Can humpty-dumpty America be put back together again?

It looks like some conflict resolutions could suddenly start happening after the eclipse on Jan.26, 2028 and through the Spring. This eclipse date is very significant, since it's on the same date that Neptune entered Aries two years before which started this new progressive 165-year cycle. And that's the very degree where Mars got progress going again in the progressed chart of Humanity. It also aligns with Pluto exactly, which should really give things a push. Pluto is good at that. So once again, the forces of progress look to be on a roll in 2028. Congress will assert its power, just as benevolent Jupiter soars to prominence and opposes compassionate Neptune. Some agreements may now slow down the bloodshed and the conflict. I think the sunlight of new beginnings will be seen on the horizon in early 2028, breaking through the stormy clouds.

Decisions made in Jan-Feb 2028 should make it clear who is going to take more power, and which way possible agreements will go. It is a chance for heretofore backward nations like Russia and some Middle Eastern and South Asian countries to make some progressive reforms too, which could shape the relations between these nations and the United States and United Nations for years to come. But trade wars are still on the table in some of these places in May 2028, especially Pakistan and Afghanistan. Fruitful agreements may result, but further confrontations could follow anyway. The appetite for turmoil is hard to satisfy when Neptune is in Aries. The storm clouds will not have quite gone away yet in 2028.

Economics will probably cloud everyone's mind in America too in May 2028. Another key turning point will be at hand as Uranus returns to its American horoscope position in 9 Gemini for the final time. Deal makers will replace war makers, hoping to make change by putting more change back in peoples' pockets. At stake may be health care reform and labor relations, and victims of war and poverty will get some much-desired attention. Jupiter will give them a prominent place at the cosmic table by going singleton and turning stationary in Virgo in May. But the reactionary rebels may not like these trends and might use some last-ditch tactics to keep their class conflict going.

Saturn and Pluto square off in June and November 2028, and finally in March and April 2029. Warlike Mars joins in the fray too by making hard aspects to them in May and Sept. 2028. People may wonder about now if we haven't had enough "fray." They will be demanding peace and progress, so these may be among the final battles. Because things have been shaky for so long now, the end of the 2020s look to be shaky times financially everywhere. States may turn their sights on controlling the bankers and speculators instead of their own people (Saturn in Taurus square Pluto, etc.). What a capital idea.

The partial eclipse of January 14, 2029 happens in the powerful degree of 25 Capricorn and on Washington's Midheaven degree. This time, the executive could be a council of leaders, who may be Aquarians in spirit with a mandate to restore peace and order and to institute justice and equality for all. And they would be actual Aquarians too since that sign rules groups and legislators in general. They could be New Age pioneers for America in any case.

Confrontation will continue, but progressives are likely to have the upper hand in the battle now, as they do whenever the 3 outer planets form their liberating double-sextile. And in February 2029 mighty Mars will make this into a great grand trine with revolutionary Uranus and Pluto, turning stationary in Libra and opposing Neptune. We know that Mars stationary in Libra can show either dynamic breakthroughs for peace or signify another war, depending on the cosmic situation. People's activism can be mightily aroused by Mars opposing Neptune too, and that will apply all the more as Mars turns stationary in Virgo in May. But Saturn will still be squaring off with potent, explosive Pluto that Spring, so peace will be just out of reach. It seems that during this great crisis, and especially whenever Mars in Libra sets the tone, many people will want to restore peace and fairness, but they will be upset over and over again by their opponents.

This revolutionary grand trine of Mars, Uranus and Pluto in early 2029 certainly means progress can no longer be stopped. The tide is shifting toward victory now, and the administration is opening the floodgates. As in August 2027, so again in early 2029, Mars in Libra opposite Neptune (now joined by Jupiter, as often happens at revolutionary moments) will rev up the masses. They will attack injustice and oppression at every turn, in America and all around the world. Whenever such aspects happen, the people in their magnificence can't be denied. The people will write new pages of history in 2029. Then as Jupiter and Saturn first reach opposition late in 2029, the full moon of society will have arrived. This means climactic public events are due, just as it did when Arab youth awakened the world to a new but violent "Spring" in 2011. Recent other such Jupiter-Saturn opposition climaxes include the velvet revolution and nationalist revolutions in late 1989 to 1991, and the Earth Day and nationwide campus revolts in April-May 1970[59]-- and go all the way back to the French Revolution's Marseillaise rising in 1792. Considering the harm that happened both to Cambodia, and to the Earth itself, after 1970, the protests of that climactic year would seem to have been especially prescient. What people protest or awaken us to in 2029 and 2030 may be equally so. It will be time to truly conceive the basis for a more workable government and corporate system in the United States, with resources made both sustainable and available for all; and if this is done, it will be shared and copied elsewhere in the next decade, and perhaps for years to come.

As the wars and revolutions of the 2020s reach their stirring and violent conclusion in 2029, the grand trine in air signs may indicate spectacular air battles, vast computer hack attacks, drone wars and unusually clever maneuvering by brilliant tacticians. But the eclipse in June 2029 proclaims a degree of peace will finally be at hand, as Jupiter in peaceful Libra turns stationary and the Saturn-Pluto square ends. New United Nations agreements and accommodations among Americans will bring the Crisis to a close. Final decisions will be made in the following months, and the people will begin to relax-- at least a little bit. The people will want greater peace and order now. They will get their way, to some extent. The next decade will be somewhat calmer; meaning at least some notches below total frenzy.

---

[59] Tarnas, Cosmos and Psyche, p.180. World Almanac 2018, p.444.
   https://en.wikipedia.org/wiki/Student_strike_of_1970

Chapter 6

Consolidating Chaos in a Revised World Order: 2030-2040

In the years 2029, 2030 and 2031, the people of Planet Earth will see many of the military and economic disputes from the past ten years settled, and the results will give us a revised world order. In spite of these settlements, the rebellious, chaotic, *ram*-bunctious mood of people everywhere will peak in 2030-31, and it will not fully end until Neptune leaves Aries "the Ram" a decade later in 2039 and enters calmer Taurus instead.

People will make some bold and strange experiments early in 2030 to help people bring some order to the prevailing chaos. Innovative mind-expanding drugs or mental health techniques could be developed to help people cope and unwind. Meanwhile the after-effects of the time of crisis will demand attention. The year could be tinged with scandals involving the military and the health of combatants in recent conflicts, especially in the USA. Secrets about these issues could be exposed by the press and social networks in June 2030, when Saturn enters Gemini, and in November when Jupiter moves into Sagittarius. Some reader may recall that the Pentagon Papers were published in 1971 when Saturn also entered Gemini opposite Jupiter in Sagittarius, leading to the Watergate Scandal; this exposure of secrets in the press was my first successful prediction as an astrologer. Financial worries and money scandals could break out early 2031 too. Meanwhile, travelers should take care in June 2030, November 2030 and October 2031, as severe accidents are forecast, leading to more revelations of misdeeds. More transportation woes and air/space disasters will be in the news in June 2032. Some of these incidents in the early 2030s may be due to problems with new technologies. If you aren't a diplomat, be careful traveling from June of 2030 through June 2032, at least.

Although the conflicts are subsiding in 2030, frustrated warriors will strike out again in early November, as Uranus crosses the "battle of Gettysburg" degree of 22 Gemini, in square to militant Mars in Virgo, sign of dedicated service. Leaders will rise to the occasion at the end of 2030, eloquently echoing Lincoln's call to the people in 1863 to give their last full measure of devotion and service to the cause of justice and progress, and to defeat the reactionary forces of obstruction. This call will echo throughout the world, impelling great diplomatic breakthroughs and openings between nations and peoples. As Mars comes around to Libra and opposes Neptune in late 2030, the people will rise up once more to demand that this revised world order come to fruition, and that all avenues of information be opened and all secrets revealed.

The new openness will encourage many people to speak up for more liberty in 2031, as Jupiter opposes Uranus all year. Mars stationary in Scorpio might cause some rebels to go to extremes during the Summer. In spite of this spasm, political reforms could lift up many nations in the Fall of 2031, especially after the eclipse of Nov.14. Central Asia (perhaps India, Kazakhstan) could benefit from these reforms, and so could Iran. Restless winds will be blowing in late 2031, bringing some fresh ideas in communications, trade and education. Congress will pass some constructive proposals regarding health and education in June 2032. This time health reform will include mental health, as leaders begin to realize that a healthy body requires a healthy mind. I guess you could say that the mental health of politicians is improving too, if they have finally realized *that* little idea.

Mars will echo its original position in the Chart of Modern Humanity (25 Capricorn) during this Nov.14, 2031 eclipse, and will also re-stimulate the eclipse of January 2029 in the same degree. Mars and the other planets here paint a picture of an American executive power working to reshape and revise the world order, and this may bring back some order to America itself too. Americans will resolve disputes and make trade agreements. The USA will be working out its relationship to the UN and other powers, and some boundaries could shift between nations. The world political map may look a bit different after 2031 from what it did in 2028, as people and their leaders seek a revised world order that works better to resolve global issues and facilitate better cooperation and communication between peoples. The map of the United States might shift too. If a new "Confederacy" has emerged from the 2020s, after the two sides of America (perhaps the red and the blue) have earlier agreed to separate, they might come together again now as a "Confederation of Independent States of America," in which states or regions have more power. 2031 will seem like a climatic year, as the people speak up and shift the direction of events toward a new era in which the chaotic conditions of the previous decade are consolidated into a revised world order.

With Saturn and Uranus moving together in air sign Gemini, like they did in World War Two, 2031 will see our ability to fly make spectacular leaps forward. Breakthroughs in space travel seem likely. Technology will leap forward in this tech-obsessed age. Intellectuals will be flying high too, as all the scandals and political adjustments make for engaging battles of ideas. The universities and the press will be hotbeds of heated discussion, and witty pundits will pour each other over hot coals. Barriers and taboos will be breached; everything will be out in the open. America may have trouble adjusting to the loss of some of its world leadership and internal unity in the last 10 years, causing much of this anxious punditry. Americans may still be asked to render service to heal all the turmoil, disease and weather problems in the world in the Fall of 2031. The American military might no longer be top dog, but it will still be called upon to act as head nurse.

Later in 2032, the two planets arousing all this discordant discussion (Saturn and Uranus) move into Cancer. This usually signals some shortages in goods and energy production, and lack of competent executive leadership too. In fact, a shake-up may occur among executive powers in America in the Fall of 2032, leading to a change in the party in power in November, and anxious adjustments in congress. And what's more, in this new "reconstruction period" after the recent troubles, Americans will have to restrain themselves to avoid another "age of hate" like the 1860s[60] or the McCarthy era. The climate is suffering badly enough from all of the carbon dioxide that we will have dumped

---

[60]Thomas A Bailey, The American Pageant, p.481-482.

into the air; spewing out hot ethnic passions and patriotic nationalist fevers on top of that will pollute our civic discourse even more. Calls for retribution or reparations might flare up and cause riots, especially by the Fall of 2033.

Some "reconstruction" efforts may be forced on some recalcitrant American Rebels. Meanwhile, America's rivals may feel the heat of economic sanctions or trade wars, as the shortages and energy conflicts spark another economic recession from the Fall of 2032 through mid-2034. Economic protests will be heard in the streets. Many nations, not least the (formerly?) United States of America, will have to reorganize themselves now in the wake of all the upheaval unleashed in the 2020s, and to restore some semblance of order out of the reigning chaos. All these changes in many lands may heighten ethnic tensions too. In February 2033 though, the planets give us a hopeful sign. Jupiter crosses potent Pluto, now at the power point in the middle of Aquarius. Reform fever may rise just as fast as the storm clouds and sea levels are rising around the world. The new Congress of the USA and many legislatures worldwide will act on some of these economic and environmental issues. FDR might be proud of this 100-year mini-echo in February 2033 of his famous 100 days. He might be less impressed if he saw all the retributions and hatreds of these times, though.

Un-Pacific Chinese Seas

The nation most ripe for change in these years is probably China. In 2033 one full cycle of Uranus and one-half of Pluto's will have passed since the People's Republic was founded in 1949. The Chinese will decide if its outmoded communist system can continue, given the economic stresses of the times. In any case, it will be modified. The year 2034 looks to be a revolutionary year, since Pluto will return to its position of 1789 (when the French Revolution happened) and make a sesqui-square to Uranus in May. The solar eclipse and Spring Equinox charts of March 20, 2034 look ominous for the powers-that-be in Beijing. A change at the top is possible, not only in China but in Western Europe too where the people will be rising up for better leadership. China will be in the throes of revolution through the Spring. But to really kill the ancient imperial Chinese Dragon and nurture a new serpent power of freedom and democracy for the people there will probably take further uprisings down the road.

In the Spring 2035 an aroused public may be feeling generous. The giant, inflatable balloon of the planet Jupiter joins oceanic Neptune that year, and in Aries it shows swelling enthusiasm for human rights and independence. Generous Jupiter-Neptune conjunctions are always indicators reform and diplomacy. So, with the help of the UN, rebellious conflicts that still may be raging and getting hot in April 2035 could be resolved in a very constructive and respectful way for the people. As their economy revives, Americans will feel more confident and optimistic in 2035 too. Generous social programs could alleviate the pain caused by recent shortages. Worldwide diplomatic breakthroughs may be achieved now, with American help.

So, by 2035 our old helpful Uncle Sam may be back on the world stage, and he (or one of his "children," after the possible break-up in 2025-26) will be feeling his oats again.

The war cycle is coming around. As Jupiter moves into Taurus in May of 2035, Americans may find themselves over-extending and making dangerous commitments again in order to defend "just causes" abroad. By October 2035, as Saturn in Leo opposes Pluto in Aquarius, the crisis will become acute, as war threatens with China that could affect Australia and nearby regions. The Pacific Ocean will get very un-pacific, as warlike Mars turns stationary in 17 degrees of water-sign Pisces, and warnings of "another Vietnam" or "another Korea" echo through America. China will have been defending its water rights since Spring 2033, and she was already trying to draw a line in the seas back in the 2010s. Now America wants to make the world safe for shipping. Waterways, ocean rights, or freedom of the seas may be disputed among China and its neighbors in 2035. Battleships will butt heads, and terrorist attacks and accidents on shipping may be expected. Environmental concerns could be provoked by a gigantic conflict over liquid fuels or by oily dangers to the seas.

These crises continue into 2036, which looks to be an historic year, thanks to two key eclipses and a notable planetary pile-up (multiple conjunction/opposition). This will also be the first year of Uranus' next square to Neptune, so some sort of new imperialism or another cold war (probably an economic one) could be in the stars. It's a good bet that shortages in energy and resources over the last few years could provoke a few nations to make moves on their neighbors, especially with Saturn opposing Pluto. The eclipse of February 2036 with Mars and Jupiter in Taurus shows that territorial ambitions may break out in West Africa (e.g. Ghana), and India and Pakistan are likely to start fighting each other again. Italy may need to make some political adjustments to stay economically viable. Restive nations in need of treasure may make happy hunting grounds for leaders who want to take advantage of other peoples' troubles or arouse religious hatreds.

When I reviewed the great cycles that draw the landscape of our times in an earlier chapter, I mentioned two key "planetary pile-ups" in which Uranus, Saturn and Pluto joined with other planets to set the tone of the following years. In May-June 1851 it was called "matter in motion," as 5 planets lined up on the cusp of assertive Aries and materialistic Taurus-- signaling that the industrial revolution was shifting into high gear and that "realistic" politics that culminated in Bismarck's Reich were being launched. Later, these events led to the rise of Hitler, who's natal Sun was in the same degree where the planets had lined up in 1851. That degree of 0 Taurus figured in the major events of the next 100 years-- at least. In February 1966, 5 planets joined in a conjunction/opposition in 17 degrees Virgo and Pisces, signaling a change from matter-in-motion toward "stillness of spirit." It was time to get off the rat race and slow down the "industrial progress" that was hurting the environment and disturbing the peace, and to recover the inner space of our spiritual lives. 17 degrees of Virgo and Pisces became key positions that figured in future events. Now, nine months after Mars turns stationary in that same "stillness of spirit" degree of 17 Pisces in October 2035, a partial eclipse happens on July 23, 2036, whose chart looks a lot like that "stillness of spirit" figure of 1966; I call it "spirit in motion," combining the two previous pile-ups. This third "pile-up" is not quite as powerful as the first two; only four planets are involved, centering around Saturn in Leo's opposition to

Pluto in Aquarius. Still, this figure signals that the "progress" which has revved up again since 2022 now is happening in a more spiritual or sustainable way. Just like in February 1966, as Mars, Mercury and Saturn line up again and oppose Pluto, they form an inspiring trine angle with spiritual Neptune, now in activist Aries and exalted overhead in the USA. Plus, tightly-aspected planets in mobile Gemini add further "motion." 20-21 degrees Leo-Aquarius, highlighted by the planets in this eclipse, could become key degrees that bring spirit-in-motion back into action in the years after 2036.

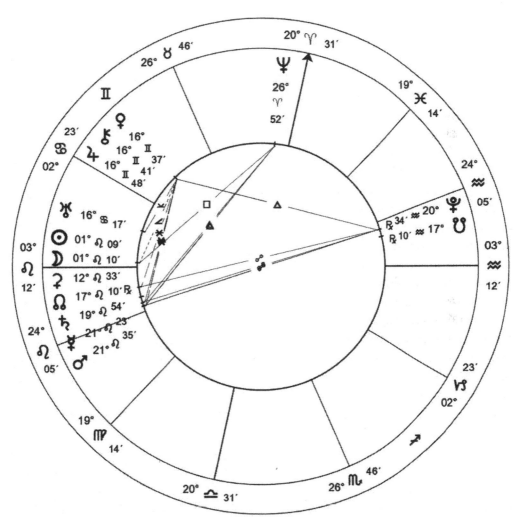

A new energy policy and American actions abroad are possible meanings of this powerful "spirit in motion" solar eclipse. Iraq and Africa may be stimulated. Chart data: July 23, 2036, 10:17 AM UT, Washington DC.

We can make this *spirit in motion* "progressive" chiefly by continuing to make our world more fuel efficient, thus showing respect for our spiritual Earth Mother as well as independence from the mother of civilizations in Mesopotamia and the Middle East. With both Jupiter and Saturn in the same places as when Jimmy Carter (whose Neptune is aligned exactly with this conjunction) made his energy proposals fifty-nine years before, as well as one Saturn cycle since Al Gore (also born with Mars-Saturn in Leo near this same degree) called attention to global warming in "An Inconvenient Truth" in 2006, 2036 will be a year to reorganize our transportation system, promote energy conservation and develop new fuels, thus putting our society in motion again in a more "spiritual" and Earth-friendly way. And people will feel the urgency of acting. Under Pluto in Aquarius, congress will lead the way with a generous and inventive program that takes on and transforms the big energy companies.

Congress will be eager to export this program abroad too. Americans are likely to be involved in some of the conflicts of these times, since Jupiter is now in Gemini. They may think that exporting their ideas on energy and resources could solve problems elsewhere, although others may resist American advice and meddling. Since the USA war cycle has come around again in 2036-37, North Americans will be tempted to use force to impose their "new ideas" on recalcitrant peoples and solve their conflicts for them. If we're lucky though, this could lead to new accords like those at Camp David in 1978.

This *spirit in motion* cosmic figure puts the Iraqi people and their leaders in motion towards rapidly transforming their government and their national identity. In October 2036, Uranus in Cancer will re-stimulate nationalist passions from the 1990s in Europe too, as well as in Iraq. New ethnic and nationalist movements could erupt in the Russian sphere of influence. Saturn's return to Leo shines the spotlight on India and Pakistan too, as we mentioned, and also on Israel and its neighbors. The troubling affairs that erupted in western Africa in late 2035 or early 2036 might continue. Since Uranus is square Neptune in the late 2030s, international affairs will be unsettled. Conflicts in these places in 2036-38 could be the first serious challenge to the Revised World Order, leading to further changes in the diplomatic arrangements among peoples. Troubles will continue to pile up in April 2037, when Mars piles on to Pluto and opposes Saturn. Power struggles in these places could continue at full tilt.

Bringing It All Back Home

Saturn in Leo generally indicates some recovery of confidence in the economy, as well as greater optimism among individuals and companies. But Saturn soon moves on into Virgo on July 7, 2037, where it usually forecasts a bust (as it did in 2007-2008). People should invest cautiously in this period and be wary of speculative financial schemes that promise what they can't deliver. National debts can't pile up forever without consequences, and they may be coming home to roost now. The USA and other nations will be over-reaching too in their attempts to help or meddle with other nations. Generous programs to boost energy production conceived in 2036 may face opposition at home and abroad as Saturn returns to Virgo in 2037. The people may want to trim back their taxes or reduce budget deficits. If spirit in motion is to be put on a more stable footing after 2037, public support for sustainable energy worldwide will *itself* need to be more financially "sustainable" too.

Several critics back in 1997 who reviewed <u>Horoscope for the New Millennium</u> (which this book updates) claimed that the entire book predicted little more than a "return to the counter-culture of the 1960s." They obviously didn't read the section of the book which covered *these* years, which forecast "greater interest in family values." Despite Uncle Sam's involvement in the uneasy diplomatic climate, Americans will be riding a wave of domesticity in 2037, which may be a peak year of a new "baby boom." This is because Jupiter joins Uranus in domestic Cancer in 2037 and is ignited by an eclipse there on July 13. Children will be important to people in these times of "spirit in motion," as parents try to keep up with their spirited new idealistic offspring, and as they demand reforms in education that stimulate their creative curiosity.

Richard Tarnas in his book <u>Cosmos and Psyche</u> showed how reactionary trends in politics and heroic efforts to maintain security happen near the times when Saturn and Pluto are aligned.[61] So we can expect a conservative climate in some quarters in the mid-2030s, as families protect themselves from high taxes and debts and defend traditional culture. Battles among groups and nations over scarce land and resources could erupt. The late 2030s could be a new gilded age, or a new age of anxiety, with many middle-aged people obsessed with money and power, anxious to conform and keep up with their neighbors in the rat race. The "men in gray flannel suits" of the 1950s could return. [62]

With these two planets in Aquarius and Leo, and Neptune still in fiery Aries, the fires of reform will still be ablaze. Many people will demand that the state and society support their growing families and provide energy security. People will want to keep the home fires burning. And Tarnas also celebrated the liberating, innovative events that happen whenever Jupiter joins Uranus, as it will in 2037. So, we can expect new programs and inventions that help the spirited children-in-motion of 2037.

At the end of 2037, Saturn turns stationary in a familiar degree, 17 Virgo, while Mars turns stationary in Taurus in trine to Saturn. On Jan.5, 2038, an eclipse in Capricorn makes this a grand trine. This figure brings back memories of when I predicted the Persian Gulf War in January 1991. This time, similar conflicts over energy and resources that began in October 2035 could erupt in Africa (e.g. Nigeria, Angola), Central and Southeast Asia (e.g. Burma), or other places. But settlements will soon follow, as business and government act cooperatively to preserve and distribute resources fairly. It will be another chance to help humanity achieve true "energy self-reliance" and make green ideals more workable.

The powerful Spring Equinox chart for 2038 only confirms these indications, as Jupiter joins Uranus in Cancer exactly at the Nadir, thus "bringing it all back home" in Washington. It will be a new thrust of environmentalism, as the Green Revolution of the late 2040s and Neptune's entry into earth-sign Taurus in 2038-2039 beckon on the horizon. We will now accelerate the nutritional and agricultural reforms so essential to the health and freedom of people and planet alike. There could also be rising nativist or racial

---

[61]   Richard Tarnas, <u>Cosmos and Psyche</u>, Penguin Viking, 2006, page 226 ff.
[62]   William L. O'Neill, <u>American Society Since 1945</u>, New York Times Company Quadrangle Book, 1969, p.11,13.

passions, fears of foreign conspiracies, and demands by traditionalist culture warriors to preserve family values, property rights and fiscal restraint.

If their best side comes out, North Americans will lead the worldwide environmentalist movement that Spring, knowing that they can't preserve America without preserving the Earth-- and asking other peoples to do it too. As Jupiter returns to Leo in the Summer of 2038, and Neptune first crosses the old 0-Taurus "matter in motion" industrial age/Middle East trigger point, another crisis in the Middle East over declining oil revenues could force the issue. The Fall charts of 2038 show intense diplomatic activity by the Americans to resolve this and other crises.

Three days after the Spring Equinox of 2039, Neptune enters Taurus to stay. This will indicate a calmer, more cautious and pragmatic attitude among the people. Radical movements will occur later on, as Uranus opposes Pluto in the late 2040s, but they will be firmly grounded. The greater stability of a Neptune-in-Taurus era will provide the foundation and framework in which valuable changes in society and consciousness can be made later on. Earth-sign Taurus will provide fertile ground in which justice and compassion can grow. But in 2039 and the early 2040s people will want change to be slower, and in some places this might mean political conservatism or the entrenchment of big money authority. In other places, like France and California, the slower pace could mean another "Belle Epoque" in which delicate, refined art and decadent pleasures flourish.

This slower trend will start in 2038, as Neptune tests the ground of Taurus (just as Taurus' ruling planet Venus connects to Neptune in the Progressed Chart of Humanity), and in some ways it will last for up to two decades, as people escape from the fast pace of city life and the omnipresent technology that prevailed during the Aries age of progress, seeking instead a more pastoral and personal lifestyle. In other words, the revved-up engines of the 2020s will be cooled down, as chaos consolidates into order. This may not all be by choice, though. We may be forced to slow down by a mild recession from 2038 to 2040, which usually happens around the times that Neptune enters an earth sign like Taurus or as a new Jupiter-Saturn conjunction happens. By then the international trade troubles and increasing ecological disasters since the early 2030s will slow the economy. Many people will be anxious, stingy and possessive. A moderate financial panic will cause economic (Taurus) dissolution (Neptune), as old corporations melt into new ones.

As Neptune moves through Taurus during the next 13 years, prosperity will improve. As it does, conservation and conservatism may come together at last, and *economy will melt into ecology*. A magnificent yod figure announces Neptune's grand entrance into Taurus in March 2039. The yod aspect, which resembles the symbol of Neptune itself, is an ancient sign of protection, and it calls on us now to adjust our personal interests so that they are in harmony with a new global society preoccupied with protecting the planet. It's a chance to reshape our lives and our society so that we can all experience our connection to the Earth Goddess in the New Age.

Some reforms may happen in this Spring of 2039. As new corporations and combinations form, people will need to protect themselves from them. Some rich Western governments, led by Germany, may act now to protect the people from predatory corporations and soothe the recession-rattled nerves of anxious citizens. But such reforms won't go far enough in 2039, which will allow rapacious business interests to grab still more wealth. Taurus can be greedy, after all; the last time Neptune was in Taurus was when big monopolies began.[63]

Earth-reform diplomacy will be active in the Summer and Fall of 2039. As Uranus continues through land-centered sign Cancer, and Neptune enters Taurus (trine Jupiter), international agreements can be made to improve the health of the land. Peaceful Venus in Leo brings peace to the land by turning stationary at the heart of a powerful yod figure in July 2039. But in the Fall Mars gets into the act by getting stuck in Cancer for many months and forming another yod at the Fall Equinox, and this one pinpoints Israel and other Mid-East nations as sources of trouble. With Neptune again crossing the 0 Taurus Middle East trigger point for the final time in March 2039, more problems there are possible. It is already long past time for the people in the Middle East region to see the contrast between their heritage as the first civilization, and their plight as among the last peoples to achieve real and stable democracy. But in 2039, as the oil they depend on runs out, some Middle Eastern governments won't be able any longer to buy the loyalty of their people. This trust will blow away as fast as the shifting Arab desert sands. Mars stationary in Cancer will also probably aggravate ethnic tensions there in late 2039 and early 2040. Israel and its Arab neighbors in the Fall of 2039 will need to engage in active and intense diplomacy to adjust to their diminishing resources and head off conflicts over oil in the region.

American meddling there earlier in 2039 may just make things worse at first. Alliances could shift temporarily in 2039 and 2040, as Uranus continues to square Neptune. Tensions arise between nations when this epic square happens. It could even amount to a new "cold war," as a few new border walls and "iron curtains" go up. But more hopeful signs appear soon. When Jupiter and Saturn reach Libra, as they do in December 2039, it's a sign that powers in the world are willing to deal. New breakthroughs for human rights and justice could unfold in 2040, if five planets in Libra in September and October is any indication. Remember also that the Sun will progress into Libra in the chart of humanity in 2041, joining Saturn there already. Some nations will reaffirm their commitment to fairness and justice for all in the Fall of 2040, especially in the Middle East. And the United States constitution and bill of rights, whose symbol is Saturn in Libra, still inspires those who seek justice worldwide. That includes the people of North America itself, where justice will still be needed too. As we enter the next chapter, economic interdependence will be growing among all people in the world. In 2040, butterflies of bounty will be emerging from the chrysalis of conflict. A Libra-like cooperation will be dawning, and chaos will be crystalizing into stability under Neptune in Taurus.

---

[63] Carman, Syrett, Wishy, A History of the American People Volume II, Alfred A. Knopf, 1967, p.99 (Rockefeller, 1974), p.103 Carnegie, 1870s), p.109 (J.P.Morgan, 1880s). Neptune in Taurus, c.1874-1887.

Chapter 7

The Earth-Spirit Awakening, 2040-2060

In many ways, the 21st century will be more peaceful than the twentieth, despite the looming threats to the environment, and the ongoing challenge of living and adjusting to a new global society. Wars in the 21st century will be less destructive than those of the 20th, and we will learn to resolve our conflicts more peacefully. The Global Mind continues to take hold in this century, as we sense ever-more keenly our connection to all people, the planet and the cosmos. Outdated ideologies still deceive the people, but their power will diminish. The pace of innovation continues, but the results will be far less destructive and more sustainable. We may not be able to live carelessly and wastefully the way we used to, but we can still unfold our human potential in the things that really count. In the 2040s, we will have the chance to change our lives and our society dramatically, yet still have relative peace and stability most of the time.

The planets mark the decade of the 2040s as significant, like the 2020s, 1980s and 1960s were, because the Jupiter-Saturn conjunction on Oct 31, 2040 is followed only five days later by a partial solar eclipse. The chart for this eclipse shows both the conjunction and the eclipse itself in the 8th House in Washington DC, with Pluto rising. This confirms that the 2040s will be a time, much like the 1880s and 1890s, of dissolving economic combinations and mushrooming new ones. The eclipse opposing Neptune in Taurus (economic dissolution) confirms this. Corporations and capital will dissolve and then quickly concentrate and grow again in the early 2040s. The power of money will expand. But unlike the 1880s, which saw the rise of "national socialism" with protective tariffs and monopolies to protect new industries within nations,[64] the new corporate combinations will be international. Jupiter and Saturn in diplomatic Libra along with Neptune in the money sign Taurus show how "dollar diplomacy" will facilitate global commerce, as nations become ever more interdependent.

Many diplomatic moves to resolve economic disputes should work out well in late 2040 and 2041, even though the secret dealings by these diplomats and politicians are un-popular because they are beholden to corporate interests. Secret international alliances like those created by Prince Bismarck in the 1880s could reappear,[65] including corporate ones, and they could make people nervous when they are exposed later on, creating economic

---

[64] Langer, ed., Pipes, <u>Western Civilization from the Struggle for Empire to Europe in the Modern World</u>, Harper and Row, 1968, p.437-440.

[65] Craig, <u>Europe, 1815-1914</u>, Dryden Press, 1972, p.256-258. These alliances came about after the Balkan Wars of 1875-77. Dual Alliance with Austria in Oct. 1879, Three Emperors League renewed in June 1881 with Austria and Russia, and Triple Alliance with Austria and Italy in May 1882. Bismarck hoped his unprecedented peacetime alliance system would safeguard the international order. It had some strong astrological support, with Uranus in trine to Neptune going on, and in June 1881 the beneficent Jupiter-Neptune conjunction was exact on the day of the treaty, and the two planets were aligned with Saturn and trine to Uranus as well. In the long run though, it didn't work.

tensions between peoples and nations. Some of these combinations and economic alliances could be insidious. As this oligarchy mushrooms, a lot of authority may become concentrated into a few wealthy hands. Some people may say that they themselves "aren't made of money," but power often is. Power corrupts, and concentrated corporate power corrupts concentratedly. The people and their politicians will have to watch carefully that organizations set up to regulate global commerce aren't taken over by the very corporate elites they are supposed to govern, as happens so often in our times.

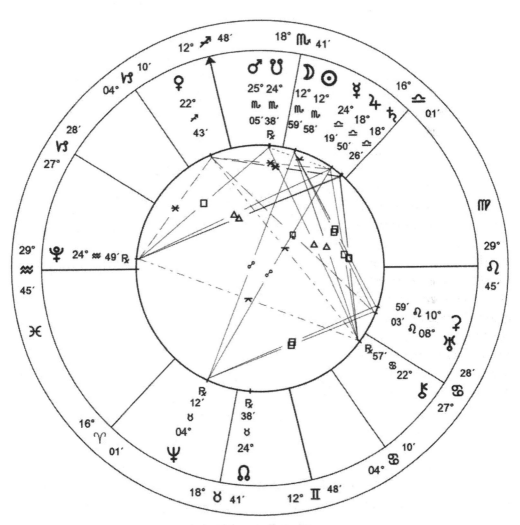

2040 Partial Eclipse

This solar eclipse follows the Jupiter-Saturn conjunction by just 5 days. Economic diplomacy and restructuring will highlight the 20-year period starting in 2040. Chart data: November 4, 2040, 6:55 PM UT, Washington DC, 38N54, 77W02. The kindle version of this book shows the conjunction chart instead.

Conservative rulers will be in power in many countries in the early 2040s, according to the 30 and 60-year pattern of more conservative decades. I don't see a major political turn to the radical right-wing in 2040 though, like what happened in 2010, 1980 and 1920. If American leaders are conservative in the 2040s, it will be in the style of the Libran President Eisenhower in the 1950s, instead of Reaganomics in the 1980s, as they preserve recent gains in social justice. But they will see to it that things run more smoothly for business than during the chaotic 2020s and 2030s. The boats and luxury yachts of the rich won't be rocked too violently-- at least not yet. Balance and order will be in vogue, but not reactionary plunder. You could call it an orderly idealism. Just as Benjamin Disraeli did the last time Neptune was in Taurus in the 1870s, the **benevolent conservatives of the 2040s** may sponsor programs to protect the people, even as they also enrich themselves.

The global corporate aristocrats may be surprised by the end of the decade though, when the Green Revolution comes. They may be knocked off their gilded thrones, and their companies will die if they don't transform. The eclipse on Nov.4, 2040 forecasts this by squaring Uranus, with the eclipse in the 8th house of death and rebirth. The chart for the actual conjunction on Oct 31 doesn't provide any more solace to the powers-that-be, because in that chart Jupiter-Saturn is on the cusp of the 12th house. That means American institutions will face still more bad karma and dissolution throughout the 2040s, and the Green Revolution will destroy enterprises that are not compatible with the planet. Bad behavior doesn't always pay well, or at least not if the people rise up in an Earth-Spirit Awakening. Although peoples' yearning for quiet, order and prosperity in the early 2040s may allow some power grabs by the elite to go unnoticed, many power structures will start to dissolve once Pluto enters Pisces in 2043.

Reorganizing the World Economy

The French go through another revolution whenever Uranus returns to Leo, re-stimulating their original upheaval of 1789-94. The early 2040s should be no exception. It doesn't take all that much to arouse the French into something of a frenzy. This time, like the last occasion in 1958, Uranus will be in square to Neptune.[66] But instead of the failures of their colonial empire causing the upheaval, as in the 1950s, in the 2040s it will be troubles in Europe itself that cause the change (as in the 1870s). The Germans will cement their position as the leaders of Europe with their constructive economic efforts in 2039, but this will encourage the French to reorganize their government, and out of this heroic task will come new ambition by the French to go beyond Europe and restructure the whole world too. The French and Germans may compete for leadership in late 2041 and early 2042, when stationary Mars joins Uranus in Leo and makes many dangerous aspects. The French people and their leaders will be ready for action. Being bold and assertive could pay off for them then, as they spearhead a movement toward a new world economy.

The last time Uranus was in Leo, France led the way in organizing the European Common Market.[67] It became the cornerstone of the European Union. The French will

---

[66] Stewart Easton, World Since 1918, Barnes and Noble, 1966, p.264.
[67] Langer, ed., op.cit, p.831-833.

become leading economic diplomats again now, commanding attention with their brilliant ideas on reorganizing global commerce. In 2041 a World Common Market will be on the table, and perhaps even a new common world currency. This is an essential step toward true world interdependence, and all countries will have to adjust. Many agreements could be made in October 2041 that advance everyone's interests, enhance economic stability and boost confidence. India will be a key player in this process too in the early 2040s, as it will increasingly be throughout the 21st century. But I am amazed at how many countries will be involved, according to their national horoscopes. Nations will be encouraged to do more to advance world prosperity, with public support. But after 2041 the road to world commerce will be fraught with more difficulty.

The signs are unmistakable that big changes to our economic systems will happen in the 2040s. Eight planets in fixed signs, including all the outer ones, shows how important and drastic the restructuring of economic institutions could get in 2041-42. Advanced technology, global trade, and environmental needs will dictate that all people update their organizations so that everyone benefits. Many competing interests will be balanced and reconciled in the Libra manner. But if the wealthy get most of the benefits from the new arrangements, poorer people and poorer nations will soon revolt. Trade agreements are bad when they lower environmental standards or allow companies to exploit and abuse cheap labor. No deal is better than a bad deal. Nations will do better this time, particularly in the light of climate change and pressure from the people. Under Neptune in Taurus, economy and ecology will merge in many minds.

Trade wars could break out if the agreements fail to address these concerns. The issues will be hammered out in tough negotiations as Saturn, Uranus and Neptune form a close, potent T-square in fixed, economic signs in 2042 and 2043. The planets suggest government schemes to manage the economy will be proposed. Strict controls could be decreed, especially as Mars turns stationary direct in Leo in the Spring of 2042. Disputes over the plans could erupt as the whole process climaxes during the stressful, very-exact T-square in May 2043, when Mars, Venus and Mercury join Neptune in Taurus, and all 4 planets square off with Saturn and Uranus-- all in fixed signs that rule the economy and concentration of power. That sounds almost like cosmic dynamite. In some countries, financial combines could take control. In others, the governments could impose new taxes and price controls designed to encourage economic and ecological "virtue," as if Robespierre had been raised from the dead and returned to power and were now making deals with Al Gore. Banks and insurance companies could feel the heat. Tariff walls may be raised up again between countries too. But some of these measures will be resisted in the Spring and Fall of 2044 (Jan, April or Nov.), as disagreements over these economic policies become power struggles between nations.

Sparks will fly in Eastern Europe, starting in the Spring of 2042 when countries like Romania, Serbia and Poland will insist on a greater role in European affairs. Remember the planets now in T-square are the same ones that aligned together when many of these nations gained their freedom from the Soviet Empire in 1989. Impatient with their economic progress, they will protest in 2042-43 (it looks like they may already cause this kind of trouble in the 2020s). If the worst happens and democracy fails, the region could even be plunged into civil war again. Then when Mars turns stationary-direct in Virgo in April 2044, worker or religious groups could agitate against tight controls. The yellow jackets of 2018 could be back and stinging like a bee.[68] The greedy gilded barons need have no fear though-- just yet. But they will be feeling the pressure, especially from poorer nations who demand that the rich help them integrate into the new world economy in the 2040s. Africans, for example, will be driving a hard bargain on the world stage in the Spring of 2043. Much of the world's wealth will need to be redistributed if a genuine world integration is ever to be achieved. The wealthy and powerful elite will not have an easy ride in the 2040s, despite many successes.

The people will tire of drastic economic changes if they are imposed too forcefully. They might even throw them out again once the planets move into mutable signs. It might seem like another French Reign of Terror is relaxing all around the world after 2043. I don't think actions by the powerful players will go as far as a "terror." But the tone of events will change anyway as Pluto enters Pisces. Peoples' faith (Pisces) may be destroyed in their leaders (Pluto), if the potent, plutocratic potentates push too far, thus discrediting themselves in outrageous scandals. Disillusioned (Pisces) with charismatic leaders trying to reorganize the whole world forcefully and quickly, people under Pluto in Pisces and Neptune in Taurus after 2043-44 will be have less faith in their leaders and big institutions. Smaller, unregulated communities will increasingly pop up that resonate with the world consciousness and act accordingly (think globally, act locally), rather than leaders trying to organize it from above by force.

Meanwhile, some of the economic measures will be relaxed when Jupiter joins Pluto in Pisces in 2045, as embargoes and sanctions fall, conflicts are resolved and liquid fuels flow again. This may unleash a new liberated spirit among the people in February 2045, especially in Western Europe and the USA, as Jupiter opposes Uranus. Americans will sponsor a new liberating, dollar-flow diplomacy in 2045. Rigid, dogmatic leaders will be resisted, and some may fall from power. By the time most planets have shifted into mutable signs in October 2045, the new leaders will be less interested in imposing their will on others and will instead respect the rights of the various peoples within the developing global market. Relaxed controls will spur innovation throughout 2045. Respecting peoples' rights can help the economy even more than controlling them. They will also be responding to environmental concerns, as the Green Revolution makes its debut in the Spring of 2045. As climate disasters keep happening in these lands, more sustainable and climate-friendly ways to use the land and to travel and communicate will be much in demand, and innovations will mushroom in these fields. Transportation breakthroughs by Americans may inspire the people too. It will feel like a great liberation is blooming among the people, as they get ready to throw off the ways of life that threaten our survival.

---

[68] https://en.wikipedia.org/wiki/Yellow_vests_movement

The New Belle Epoque

The bold actions of statesmen and corporate big shots in the early 2040s will be inspiring to many folks, but by 2045 the people will be losing faith in these leaders and will look for other things to venerate and admire. Increasingly after 2045, people will recognize the divinity of Nature, and admire that instead. Pluto in Pisces after 2043 indicates heightened romantic sensitivity too. Adventure and eco-tourism will expand in the Summer of 2045, further stimulated by the exciting breakthroughs in travel technology, as well as by new cultural thaws between peoples. Pluto in Pisces will, in turn, stimulate Earth spirituality, as represented by Neptune (ruler of Pisces) in earth sign Taurus. Neo-pagan nature religions will revive. As sensitive people lose themselves in Nature, some will return from their journey with sensuous, beautiful paintings, new music and new cyber multi-media forms. The artists of the 2040s will be the Monets and Titians of their time, creating a new kind of impressionism expressed in uniquely-delicate light and color. The belle epoque will live again,[69] as people revel in this beautiful new world and celebrate the wonder of ordinary life. Cafes will be full of observant, creative folks trying to capture subtle passing moods and make portraits of fascinating, strange and unconventional characters. The streets will blossom with organic architecture and landscapes.

Under Uranus in Leo from 2039 to 2046, the arts may become more eloquent, grander and more competently-expressed than one might expect in our utilitarian age. Sometimes the results will be strikingly realistic. Other new artists will make use of earlier modern styles, from the post-impressionists like Van Gogh to art nouveau, surrealism and pop art. They would also do well to further develop the earlier counter-cultural styles, like psychedelia from the 1960s, the cyber and rave experiments of the 1990s and the enhanced sensibility of the early 2020s. Much more potential exists in these styles than have yet been explored. By 2046, many startling new art forms will be appearing, and Humanity will see amazing works of profound power and beauty in July 2047.

Younger folks will be more influential in the 2040s than usual, as some teen-age and twenty-something rebels once again will escape from the prosperous, middle-class society to a reborn beatnik world from 2042 to 2044. Media pundits might be concerned about some of their "immoral" antics. These trends in the arts and youth culture will probably reach their height after the eclipse of February 2045, with the youth of France, Western Europe and even middle America leading the way.

Then, just in time, from 2046 until 2052, as the Green Revolution reaches full flower, Uranus goes into Virgo. This means that the "back to nature movement" will return to life from the 1770s, when Neptune was in Virgo and Uranus in Taurus, the exact reverse sign positions from now in the late 2040s. Uranus in Virgo indicates that the cult of free love, pleasure and sensibility will return too, just like happened in the first pop culture after the French Revolution in the 1790s,[70] or the utopian and hyper-sensitive cults of the decadent 1880s and 90s,[71] or the counter-culture of the mid-1960s. Meanwhile the new

---

[69] Langer, ed. op.cit, pp.560-585: excellent picture of La Belle Epoque in France as portrayed by its great artists.
[70] Furet and Richet, French Revolution, pp.322-329, 337-340, 352.
[71] Gardner, De La Croix and Tansey, Art Through the Ages, 1970, p.679-681.

organic art will bloom and overgrow society everywhere, and crafts will be in vogue. Once again flower power will find its hour. The younger people in the *later* 2040s will be more ambitious than those earlier in the decade, as they remake society to conform to the emerging Earth-Spirit sensibility. This new youth culture (with many older folks joining in), and the new art styles, will begin to bloom profusely in 2045 and 2046 from the seeds of the more blatant, wild expressions that developed under Uranus in Leo in the early 2040s.

Even as many people go on dreaming (Neptune) of making money (Taurus) in the 2040s, with the lucky ones secluding themselves in huge gaudy and ostentatious luxury estates, many materialist illusions will be dissolving into spiritual and ecological realities. It will be getting harder to get rich and hoard resources in a world where population, resources and mass markets start to decline. People will have to find new dreams-- and some folks will find them. Inner soul development will be one path. To help people along the route to inner riches, spiritual techniques and psychedelic (soul-revealing) methods will resurface in a big way in the mid-2040s (especially in Spring 2046). By the late 2040s, science too will shift according to the new philosophy that Earth is alive with Spirit. Technology will also advance us further toward natural living under Uranus in Virgo, and agricultural methods will advance. New farming techniques will increase productivity (the old definition of the "green revolution" of the 1960s under Uranus in Virgo, sign of the harvest) as well as preserve the land, the climate and the biosphere. Whether chemistry will be employed again in this new green revolution, releasing more "GMOs" into our environment, will be up to the people to decide.

In many ways the mid-2040s will revisit the 1960s, as Uranus returns to Virgo. Racism is not an easy disease to cure; in fact, it requires constant treatment. Uranus in "medical sign" Virgo will be there to provide a new diagnosis by 2046. As Martin Luther King Jr. said, the arc of history is long, but it bends toward justice. The increased population of non-white groups will cross a critical mass in America in the 2040s, and they'll be seeking greater power and wealth in society. By now Saturn has returned to Libra (sign of justice) in the progressed chart of humanity, and as the progressed Sun joins it there in 2044, more progress toward justice will happen. Even back in 2039, Uranus the liberator will have returned to Leo, just where it was when Rosa Parks refused to go to the back of the bus in 1955.[72] Activist-planet Mars will join it there during notable eclipses and equinoxes in October 2041, March 2042 and October 2043, when major movements might break out. The renewed civil rights thrust will reach full steam in October 2045, when those who feel discriminated against will flood the streets and finally achieve some reforms. Riots are possible then too. Then the women will rise for greater equality again in 2047, since by then the outer planets will have all returned to yin or feminine signs, just as in 1966 when the National Organization for Women (NOW) was founded. In another sense, our whole culture will be "feminized" in the 2040s, as many people learn more about how to nurture one another and the Earth. We'll be less interested in climbing the ladder of status and power than we were early in the decade.

---

[72] Howard Zinn, A People's History of the United States, Harper Collins, 1980,1990, p.442.

A Green Revolution Unfolds

The great solar eclipse of August 12, 2045 marks the moment when the Green Revolution really sprouts, as the Uranus-Pluto opposition approaches, and the chart for this potent eclipse targets America. Neptune in Taurus indicates that ecology will be the core issue of these times. The weather will get so bad that denying that humans are causing global warming won't be possible anymore, and its effects on our health and safety will be abundantly clear and no longer tolerable. Much will have been done to restore our environment by now, but it won't be enough so long as billions of humans populate the planet and consume its resources. Technological solutions, developed so profusely during the "green post-industrial revolution" of the 2010s and 2020s, will not have brought all the needed changes yet; the full reckoning comes in the late 2040s, and the resulting change will go a lot further. Products that harm our bodies and minds and pollute the Earth will be outlawed. Corporations that don't operate in the interests of the people and their planet will be shut down. Not only will there be alternatives to fossil fuels, but fossil fuels will no longer be an alternative. Homes and businesses throughout the world will be made resource-efficient. Forests and oceans will be restored to absorb carbon. Humanity will commit to bringing forth a sustainable, fulfilling and socially-just human presence on this planet in *all* our activities, as the Pachamama Alliance puts it. Only a Green Revolution anchored in the hearts and minds of the people can overcome resistance by the greedy to these long-overdue developments.

The Green Revolution is a new Awakening. It is also called a "second turning" in the Strauss and Howe "saeculum cycle" (see Chapter 2), which according to them is due to start in the late 2040s. But some of their readers think this Awakening will reverse the trends of the previous second turning that began in the mid-1960s. Some even suggest that this new awakening will be more puritanical and intellectual. As I mentioned, in modern times this "generational cycle" corresponds to Uranus' revolution around the zodiac every 84 years. I myself first proposed that there is also a double rhythm, because Neptune makes a cycle of 165 years around the Sun, almost twice as long as Uranus' cycle of 84 years. This means Neptune is in opposite signs from one Awakening to the next. So, in the sixties Neptune was in Scorpio, and in the 2040s Neptune will be in the opposite sign Taurus.

Indeed, the new Awakening will be different from the last in some ways. Since Scorpio, sign of elimination, tends to destroy things, and Taurus is the sign of construction, the new revolutionaries will be more patient and pragmatic and will seek more-lasting solutions. The new activists will be better organized, more focused, and much clearer about what they want. But the new awakeners will be just as sensual-- and sexual-- as the earlier ones, and just as eager to escape from the rat race. So those who hope that this will be an awakening of conventional morality may be disappointed. Liberation once begun, seldom if ever reverses itself in the next go-round.[73] Instead, historically, the next Awakening *always* takes up just where the previous one left off.

The most salient fact about *this* new Awakening, is that it will do more than just continue the previous one; it will *fulfill* it. Uranus opposing Pluto in 2046-48 will be the

---

[73] "social freedoms once gained tend to persist" William L. O'Neill, Coming Apart, New York Times Books, p.425.

full moon phase of the Green-Peace Movement that began at the Uranus-Pluto conjunction, which was the new moon or new beginning phase of the cycle. This Movement began in 1966, and it remains unfinished as of this writing. Remember Uranus also opposed Pluto in 1901 when the Russian Revolution opened, and when workers' movements, unions and parties climaxed, thus fulfilling the socialist cycle begun at their conjunction in 1848-1850 when Marx wrote the Communist Manifesto. Remember too that in 1792-93, Uranus opposed Pluto as the French Revolution fulfilled the Democratic Movement, which had begun at their conjunction in 1711 when Voltaire was hold up in the Bastille. This will be the first time ever that *both* the conjunction *and* the fulfilling opposition in the *same* Uranus-Pluto revolution cycle will coincide with, and thus unleash, *two successive* second-turning Awakenings in the 84-year saeculum cycle. There can be no doubt, then: the Green Revolution and Earth-Spirit Awakening of the 2040s will bring to a climax what Strauss and Howe call the "Consciousness Revolution" that began in the 1960s.

The new Awakening will be both personal and political, like the last one in the nineteen-sixties. We will be challenged to observe personal and inner ecology as well as the outward biological kind. I mentioned the revival of the spiritual quest and the new sensuous and organic renaissance in the arts, already well under way in the early 2040s. Remember that Pluto is in mystical Pisces too after 2043. In fact, the trend away from spirituality and counter-culture toward technology and science that dominated the start of the New Millennium means that another strong spiritual revival will be sorely needed now, and so it is destined to happen.

Lots of new unconventional religious and spiritual groups will appear during the Green Revolution. People will "drop out" again from the frazzled pressures of modern life to pursue them, and will react against the decades-long obsession with high tech. We will break through the "matrix" (as the famous movie described it) of "virtual reality" and artificial living to bring back Nature and genuine human feeling into our lives. Seekers will again populate the landscape, alive with adventure and brimming with wanderlust. Psychic exploration will cross the frontiers between life and afterlife as the New Age Movement comes into vogue again. Esoteric science will promote vivid awareness of ourselves as incarnations of the Earth Spirit, and holograms of the cosmos. The truth is that each of us *is* the Earth and solar system in miniature; in fact, the very backbone within each of our bodies is our own miniature world axis. As we learn this, the hermetic motto will resound through the land: as above, so below; as within, so without. Global consciousness of Gaia, the one Spirit of Mother Earth, will be truly born again within us all, and as it grows in the coming years and decades, all nations will come to recognize that we are one people on one planet.

As economy melts into ecology, our diet and agriculture will come into organic harmony with the health of the people and the planet alike, as what's good for one complements the other. We will feel keenly the need to heal not only the planet, but also our families and communities. Our work will become more personally fulfilling as it contributes to the common good; jobs that alienate and separate us from the land and the people they serve will be obsolete. Small business, coops and non-profits will grow and expand, and more companies will be run by their employees. Neptune in Taurus, sign of the architect and builder, will influence us to redesign our cities so they satisfy our need to belong and be in contact with one another, and people of all classes will learn to live together. Transit and bike lanes will replace cars in green city centers, and co-housing programs will proliferate. Education will be reformed so that students interact creatively with fellow students, the community and the environment. Economies will be based increasingly on local currencies and community banks and will favor locally-produced foods and goods. Global and corporate commerce will continue and grow, but fair-trade agreements will complete the world common market begun earlier in the decade. The Green Revolution will transform many of us in ways we could have barely imagined back in the 2010s, although in fact these trends were already under way back then-- and in fact date back to the start of the cycle in 1966 that will now fulfill itself.

Some of the initiative in the Revolution may belong to enlightened executives, like latter-day Elon Musks and updated Thomas Edisons. We saw that already the new Eisenhower conservatives of the early 2040s will take measures to protect the planet, even as they enrich themselves. The August 2045 eclipse puts Uranus right on the Midheaven, the astrological symbol of the state, in the USA, and then the February 2046 eclipse puts Neptune there. This indicates that in 2045 and 2046 American leaders will begin enacting some of these proposals, and many government contracts will be awarded to Earth-friendly businesses. Egypt and Central Africa will make notable green progress too. The eclipse of August 2, 2046 indicates that the people of Iraq will take action toward putting their government on the path to green democracy.

Of course, some rich reactionaries will oppose everything these revolutionary bureaucrats do, but this time they will only succeed in slowing things down a bit, at least for now. States and their governments will be moving Humanity forward despite their obstructions. In 2047 Saturn, the planetary "ship of state," now in Capricorn the sign of the government, makes a graceful and potent trine angle to Uranus in Virgo that lasts off and on for over two years. Jupiter in Taurus makes this an earth-friendly earth-sign grand trine in May. The solar system will blaze forth on Earth in green colors. Some businesses may resist the increasing regulation and taxes needed to pay for the Green Revolution, but others will cooperate and join with the trailblazing green pioneers, despite the ever-present hue and cry of the reactionaries. In reality, the green reforms will be largely business-friendly as well as earth-friendly for those companies and non-profits who help to fertilize the growth of new ideas.

Uranus in Virgo also promises that another Lyndon Johnson will arrive to build another "great society." Another war on poverty can be anticipated, gaining full momentum starting in June 2047 when Jupiter joins Neptune in another "reform conjunction" like the one that coincided with the New Deal. Indeed, *if* the revolutionary full moon (Uranus opposite Pluto, fulfilling the cycle) is destined to fulfill Dr. Martin Luther King Jr.'s original dream of shared economic power in the USA, conceived at the "new moon" of 1966, then effective "economic empowerment" measures can be expected.[74] This could

---

[74] https://www.latimes.com/nation/la-na-mlk-chicago-20160118-story.html

happen in some African countries too, who might reap some benefits from this revolution, which began long ago in February 1966 when many upheavals shook the continent under the potent planetary "stillness of spirit" alignment. Africa may be the scene where the democratic revolution completes itself, either now or later on. In the Middle East and Central Europe too, many nations will be ready now to ride the revolutionary wave, including the ongoing movement in Iran.

The difference from the 1960s is that now the Great Society will be extended to people worldwide. Global actions will have become more accepted and routine by 2047, in spite of the reactionary trends against this in the 2010s. By 2047 we will know that poverty and environmental progress are incompatible, and that controlling growth in population requires economic development. Rich nations will help the poor ones make their farms and industries both productive and sustainable. East African nations like Sudan could benefit. On July 22, 2047 a partial eclipse signals important international agreements and compassionate reforms, as stationary Venus exactly squares both Jupiter and Neptune in exact conjunction in Taurus. Since Venus turns stationary at this moment in the exact solar degree in the charts for India and Pakistan, the timing looks good for an agreement between these two nations. The planets in July 2047 will be extending beautiful vibrations of creativity and generosity to all people, through the arts and in glorious gatherings as well as financially. This is truly to be an amazing moment for humanity, perhaps unique in all of history. Love will be in the air most strongly on the northwest coast of America, as it leads the way again in a new summer of love with new artistic and benevolent movements that inspire and uplift the world. Those who say that a Haight-Ashbury, a Pepperland or a Woodstock can never happen again will be proven wrong. Despite the obstacles and high prices during other more-restricted and less-inspired times like the 2010s, they really were the harbingers of life in the future. The walls between us will fall, and greener and more gregarious worlds will grow in their place.

Next year things start moving even faster and get more aggressive. 2048 will be the next 1968. Activist Mars in expansive Sagittarius will square off spectacularly with Uranus and Pluto for much of the year, highlighted in a super-potent Spring Equinox chart. As in the days of romantic artists like Lord Byron, who gave his life for Greek freedom, Mars in Sagittarius and Pluto in Pisces will bring out the lust for adventure and revolution among the new romantics of 2048. These cosmic lightning bolts will spur vast new international networks to seek out new ways to explore the Earth and the Heavens. Empowered by their discoveries, liberated green pioneers will find new mountains to climb. Adventure sports and eco-tours revive again, and spiritual pilgrimages and progressive evangelistic crusades will convulse the planet as never before. The liberating energy of the people will be at a fever pitch in this Spring of 2048, as we rise up to extend this new Green Revolution to all corners of the globe. Though powerful interests will try to stem the tide, politicians will be forced to respond to it.

On June 30, 2048, Uranus makes its final opposition to Pluto in the current series in the 2040s, preceded by a full moon and lunar eclipse on June 26. This is a powerful, eloquent statement that the climax and "full moon" of the Third Revolutionary Cycle is at hand. It so happens that June 30 was *also* the exact date in 1966 when Uranus and Pluto joined to *begin* this third revolutionary cycle that will now be reaching its climax. Now, as then, Mars will square off with both Uranus and Pluto and thus reenact its strong T-square at the 2048 Spring Equinox. Green revolutions will bloom. Mars also turns stationary on

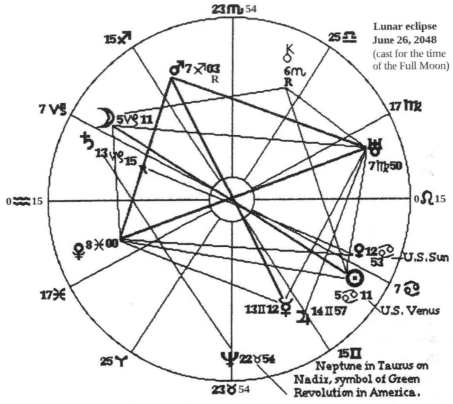

Final opposition of Uranus-Pluto, June 30, 2048. The Green Revolution will be extended to all corners of the globe. Note Venus conj. USA Sun, and Sun conj. USA Venus. Neptune in Venus' sign Taurus at the Nadir highlights the environmental emphasis. Chart data: June 26, 2048, 2:07 AM, UT, DC USA

July 10th, just days after Uranus and Pluto oppose each other, with all of these aspects nearly exact at 8 degrees. This couldn't be more amazing or more significant for Humanity and Planet Earth; it will be a peak experience and self-actualizing moment as the liberating green movement ripens. The planets are making powerful angles to each other all over the chart, distributing the planetary energy everywhere throughout the world, and the key planets all in mutable signs means they are dispersing the beneficent discoveries of the Green Revolution to many and diverse places. It also activates the 1892 conjunction in 8 degrees Gemini that signifies this great age of civilization we live in, bringing its vast transformational potentials into reality again by squaring and opposing it exactly. This planetary moment will impact us all personally, as well as in world affairs, since we will feel the energy of the larger group uplifting us from within. The new global Earth consciousness will come to its highest focus and intensity.

This time around, Mars squares the revolutionary planets from Sagittarius, instead of from the opposite sign Gemini as in 1966. This means we will act on principle, instead of youthful impulse as in the sixties. It further emphasizes the global and long-term perspective of the times. On the other hand, Jupiter makes it a grand cross from Gemini too, with Mercury joining in. So that means the American war cycle is back, as usual whenever Jupiter returns to Gemini and Cancer. Uncle Sam will seek to push the agenda of the American Green Revolution further than some nations or powers want it to go. It depends on who pulls Uncle Sam's strings in 2048, though. Some American corporate leaders might also want "him" to defend their interests against frenzied mobs of revolutionaries around the world. Since Israel may be a target of some of these mobs, US conflicts in the Middle East are likely. So, the latest American Arrogance would have several flavors. Violence by radicals may get out of control all over the world in 2048, especially in the Summer, so moneyed interests *everywhere* will be threatened and will ask or protection from rich governments. The Green Revolution could still turn bloody red.

We mentioned Lyndon Johnson earlier, which reminds us that another Vietnam-like quagmire cannot be ruled out during this return of the American war cycle, particularly since these times are so reminiscent of the 1960s, and since US and other national leaders will be so ambitious again under Saturn in Capricorn. This also indicates that economic recession could motivate many people to rise up in revolution in 2048. Rich people resisting the Green Revolution all over Planet Earth may be interested in the wrong kind of "green."

As we know from the square during the Arab Spring in 2011, these explosive Uranus-Pluto alignments can bring whole waves of revolution, with huge ripples to nearby countries in a rapidly-spreading contagion. History has seen this over and over again under Uranus-Pluto, in the 1960s, the turn of the 20th century, in Europe in 1848, the French Revolution in 1792-93, and so on. So where will the tidal waves wash up in the revolutionary year of 2048? The people of Kenya, Malawi and other East African nations should get their political surf boards ready. The rich and powerful had better batten down the hatches in the Middle East, and in China the draconian Dragon could finally be slain. Less drastic tsunamis of change will strike in Southeast Asia, where green and financial reforms could proceed quickly. The European Union's international organizations could be restructured too.

The cosmic fireworks are also likely to explode into contentious moral, philosophical and theological debates. Certainly, religious conservatives will be unhappy that the traditional family, whose purpose is to raise children, will be attacked as harmful to population control by the feminist Green Revolution. Abortion and birth control issues will rage again, and the churches as well as the activists will feel the heat. In the greater civilization cycle, this Uranus-Pluto opposition corresponds to the times when Henry VIII founded the Church of England in order to divorce his wife. This same opposition also appears in Jesus' horoscope, if he was born between 6 and 4 BC, with the planets in the same signs as now, but reversed. The Catholic Church which he founded will be pressured to make reforms in 2048; it will one day have to end celibacy and gender discrimination if it hopes to avoid sex scandals and survive in the future. Those who defend family values most stridently are frequently the most liable to violate them.

The Green Revolution could always go haywire, as revolutions often do. They unleash chaos and instability in society, and people will have to adjust to lifestyle changes if family values decline afterward, as they did after the 1960s. Disrespect for authority and resulting crime sprees may increase in the Green Revolution and its aftermath. New government bosses might also use the new green values to impose tyranny, and new bureaucracies could hamper business activities. On the other hand, it's true that economic libertarian ideas have often flourished alongside the green movement since the current revolutionary cycle began in the 1960s. If libertarian economics *is* allowed to triumph and run amok again in the middle of the 21st century, then another Reagan, Trump or Bush could arise promising that benefits will trickle down from unleashed and deregulated "job creators." My forecast, however, is that we will know better by then *not* to go down this shortsighted neo-liberal path, and instead take the more sustainable road. Government of, by and for the people helps to create a just society for all. We should not be fooled again by extremist free-market ideas. Appropriate taxes and regulations will likely be needed for some time to come as long as powerful business interests continue to use their advantages in society to prey on workers, consumers and our economic and ecological environments. Trickle-down just creates a flood of poverty, injustice and inequality for all, and is most especially bad for green values since these depend on the government to enforce regulations on polluters. The climate changers must be chased from the new Green Earth Temples during this Jesus-like planetary figure.

Our new Earth-Spirit Awakening should help us to avoid most of these revolutionary and reactionary pitfalls. Still, although the great opposition of Uranus to Pluto means the revolution has reached its climax, more struggles will lie ahead. The rough edges will need to be smoothed out and further resistance overcome, just as in previous movements. In the short term, chaotic conditions and threats to financial interests from riots and revolutions could destabilize the economy somewhat in the late 2040s. Since some older economic institutions will have been destroyed or dissolved over the previous decade, with debt piling up from extravagant programs, some financial panics may happen. Recession could deepen by 2049-2050, as Jupiter opposes Saturn in Capricorn and shifts the direction of events. Financial and ethnic disputes will rumble once more through India and Pakistan. The end of the decade might see a mild bear market or a stock market correction. Neptune's continued transit through money-sign Taurus should keep things relatively stable and prosperous most of the time, so I expect these dislocations to be minor through the early 2050s. But this recession could tamp down the revolutionary spirit as the decade ends, just as it reaches its climax, and authorities will succeed in bringing some order back again.

Meanwhile, the decade of the 2040s is capped off by one of the most remarkable and beneficial cosmic configurations one could imagine. Saturn, Uranus and Neptune, the same three planets that joined together in conjunction in the Fall of 1989, ushering in the greatest victory for freedom so far in human history that broke down the wall between the two cold-war worlds, will now come together in grand trine in November 2049 during a solar eclipse, signaling another great victory for humanity. In earth signs, they represent the triumph of ecological and Earth values. This may also be a great advance toward true liberal democracy for all peoples. The world may now adopt a binding agreement to respect a charter of liberties and sustainable living practices.

Venus and Mars will bring another great issue to the fore at this time. Venus, "the bringer of peace," is opposite Neptune during this grand trine, putting it at the apex of a "peace symbol" formation. The fondest ideal of the revolutionary cycle, as declared by John Lennon and the other leaders of the movement in the sixties, was *peace*. If the cycle, now at its climax, truly moves us forward, then we will reject war and be repelled by the pain, suffering and death it brings. From now on, perhaps we will no longer enter into it lightly. The great grand trine of Saturn, Uranus and Neptune could therefore signify a world peace commitment among nations.

Mars the God of War is still up there in the sky, however. It will square Saturn during this trine-- reminding us that if we really want to beat our swords into plowshares, and learn the ways of war no more, we will need somehow to be able to defend and enforce our agreements, and act to bring sustainable prosperity and progress to all. Naive hopes that peace can happen without such enforcement may be disappointed if wars break out at this very moment. On the other hand, realistic diplomacy can work when Mars is in Libra, as it will be in November 2049.

Earlier in the year, other hopeful signs in the heavens will appear. Venus stationary in the "stillness of spirit" degree of 17 Pisces in April 2049 could mark the beginning of Uncle Sam's return from foreign adventures, thus keeping it from falling into another quagmire just after the USA war cycle returns, and thereby fulfilling the revolutionary cycle's peace ideal. Tough negotiations may bring this about under Mars in Libra and the green grand trine of Saturn, Uranus and Neptune in earth signs in November 2049. Meanwhile, just before then, in late September, the peace movement will have been enhanced by 3 planets joining Uranus as it completes a great cycle, returning to the very degree where it joined with Pluto in the great revolutionary conjunction, at the other "stillness of spirit" degree of 17 Virgo from 1966. "Strange vibrations" of ecstatic, psychedelic light and color will climax a decade in which the sensuous arts of radiant light began to permeate our lives again. And this cyclic flashback to the 1960s also reminds us that the "Great Society" goals of that time remain unfinished. In 2047-49, the foundations of such a society will be built over the whole world. Remember, the Revolution of modern times is not over until *all three* of its cycles are fulfilled: **liberty, equality *and* ecology**. The Green Revolution of the 2040s offers us the chance to further advance all three goals by establishing liberty and a decent quality of life for everyone on a restored Earth, all made possible by the revival of spiritual *fraternity* among the people. Mars turning stationary-direct in 17 Aquarius in September 2050 could be the sign of renewed progress toward these noble dreams as the decade ends.

Saturn will be touring through this sign of progress and reform too as the decade of the 2050s begins, allowing legislators the world over to make these "great green society" ideas into working realities. The golden sunlight of the green revolution will continue to glow in the new decade, as a summertime of awakening new life and spirit continues to blossom. All depends on whether the seeds planted by the Green Revolution put forth roses or only thorns. If the rosy scenario triumphs, then the climate will be optimal for a luxuriant growth of an interconnected world green economy, nurtured by the people and their continuing new reforms.

Youthful Spirits and Burgeoning Networks: the 2050s

The spirit of liberation will be spurred again in the Fall of 2051 as Jupiter joins Uranus in conjunction at the end of verdant Virgo, just like it did in 1968-69. These liberating and inventive planets will be watered and nourished by live-giving, expansive Neptune, now in trine aspect to both of them in 2051, and to Uranus alone for the next several years. As the planetary ocean-liner of Humanity, Neptune, enters brilliant Gemini in 2051 and 2052, space-age transportation and communication breakthroughs will spread new green technology over the whole Earth into the rich soil of the recent Green Revolution and open up new business opportunities. God and Earth only knows how many new companies could be founded under **Neptune in Gemini** in the 2050s and early 60s. The new green energy systems will make our cars, boats, planes and trains fully efficient and pollution free, and barriers will fall between nations and even planets.

Uranus in Libra and Neptune in Gemini will be waltzing together joyfully in their terrific trine in the early 2050s, with most of their exact trine angles being made in these two air signs, showing the ongoing mutation to the air element since the Aquarian conjunction of Jupiter and Saturn in 2020. Air signs open up ideas, travel, communications and relationships, indicating that vast networks will be burgeoning forth and abundant breakthroughs happening in these fields. Gemini and Libra being signs of knowledge and information, curious young minds of all ages will be opening up in the 2050s to a veritable flood of ideas that challenge the old ways. Schools will continue to transform in the next decade and beyond, as links between students and the community grow further and learning becomes a life-long creative adventure instead of preparation for tests. Where the forties brought back sensuality, the fifties will inspire the intellect. Literature of all kinds will bloom, and discoveries about the universe will blossom. The 2050s will also be a time when people rediscover face-to-face relationships, as innovative social activities and connections break through alienation and bring us together as never before. Meanwhile the liberating energies of the people will continue to flood the halls of lawmakers worldwide in 2051-52, spurring further reforms to spread the wealth and heal the Earth. Climate change will be Mother Nature's continuing alert signal to the pressing need for these inventions and reforms over the next few decades.

Further confrontation and a possible new war cycle may start in the Summer of 2053 thanks to Saturn's next conjunction to Pluto. In Pisces, these planets could indicate more disputes over critical waterways and religious disputes in the Middle East. Uranus in trine to Neptune, especially in air signs, often brings forth alliances, which can make either peace or war easier. New alliances between nations in the Middle East in the 2050s and elsewhere could create new rivalries, and they will challenge the new councils formed 2049-50 to resolve the disagreements, but major wars seem unlikely in this new Green era. Meanwhile confusion and muddle will reign in many governments under Saturn-Pluto in Pisces in Summer 2053 and through 2054, including in America. Some rulers and regimes could fall then, such as in the Middle East and China. Further votes of no confidence could follow from peoples' movements in many of these places in the Fall of 2054, as Jupiter opposing Neptune is highlighted by the Equinox that season.

The rising spirits among the younger generation will push these new revolutionary movements forward, their missionary zeal bringing down walls and pushing open doors for the people. The progressed horoscope of Humanity confirms this springing forth of young blood, with a Full Moon in Aries and Sun trine to Mars in 2055. You might have heard about the roaring twenties, but these could be **the feverish fifties**. Not only will intellectual and political debates be a favorite sport, but athletes will break physical barriers too, and games of speed, skill and balance will be all the rage. Everywhere spirits will be high, new crusades and challenges proclaimed, and historic new exploits accomplished throughout the decade. Youthful conflicts with authority will be a theme of this continued Awakening in the mid-2050s, as spirits boil over into some riots and rebellions.

By then too, under Uranus in Libra, young women will be asserting their rights again, and sexual and gender barriers will be breached once more. The sexual revolution never ended with the end of the 1970s. Under a powerful Uranus in Libra, it's coming back around. The revival of modern art from the 2040s will make further strides too in the 2050s, as new expressive and lively styles proliferate. And under Uranus in Libra and Pluto in Pisces, although youthful spirits will be restless, and debates often keen, the urge to make peace will continue to keep things relatively mellow so things don't get out of hand. Lots of things are always liable to happen in this big world, and 2057 could be a controversial year with many uprisings, but overall I think the 2050s will be a relaxed and easy-going time in most places, with not too many great events happening. Communications will continue to advance, and more social barriers will fall. Peace and Liberation through spiritual understanding, respectful conversation and harmonious reconciliation will continue to grow and be a theme of society in the wake of the Green Revolution. The activists against acrimony may have to fight with tortured traditionalists in the later 2050s, as repressive Saturn in Aries opposes liberating Uranus in Libra. But Pluto reaching the critical stillness of spirit degree of 17 Pisces in 2057, opposite its place at the start of the mid-sixties revolution, could indicate a milestone in many social liberation movements.

Some newly liberated peoples and groups and their enemies will be eager to defend their territories in the Spring of 2057. Mars in Cancer stationary, squaring off with Saturn in Aries and Uranus in Libra in March, could bring back more ethnic tensions and disputes over land and the environment. More governments and regimes could fall in late 2056 and early 2057 in America, China and Southeast Asia. Accidents or violence by impetuous youth in the Spring of 2057 or in the Fall of that year could also spur new laws and inventions to protect the people in the following months. As Jupiter squares Neptune during a powerful solar eclipse at the end of 2057, financial scandals involving international communication networks could result. Young people will be rising up again then, challenging restrictive authorities and making revolution. Religious fanaticism could lead to some problems too at that time. More free trade agreements may also happen under these outer planets in mutable signs Gemini and Pisces, perhaps after some conflicts in September 2057.

In early Spring 2058 as Saturn moves into Taurus with 6 planets in Pisces, the people may become calmer and more constructive, and cooler heads will prevail. Some restrictions could be lifted and new channels opened in February, and conservation projects will further restore the Earth in the Spring. As the 2050s end, many will find occasions to celebrate exuberantly the good life that has been re-created by all the advances and reforms of the Earth-Spirit Awakening. People in some nations will feel a surge of optimism in the Spring of 2059, with lots of good vibrations in the air, and the mood of optimism extends into 2061. More liberations and inventions will uplift the people as Jupiter opposes Uranus in Spring 2059. Travel and communication breakthroughs will be spectacular in 2059 and 2060, for example, and the next decade will see even more progress in these fields. The world will be connected as never before, as new information networks are founded that are more user-friendly and more dedicated to peace and security. A breakthrough in healthcare is certainly possible in North America too in Spring 2059.

We may feel so good that we don't notice that insecurities are bubbling beneath the surface. The reforms and revolutions of this long period of Awakening could leave many people unsettled and looking for traditional moorings again. Ominous signs appear among the outer planets as Uranus moves into Scorpio. A new tax revolt or moralistic reaction might loom on the horizon. But at the same time, as radicals in some places claim that not enough has been done, a few more governments could be in danger of being toppled in late 2059, propelled by financial worries. South African and Korean regimes appear vulnerable. As the decade closes, the expansive, complacent and generous mood among the people and their leaders blends with growing worldwide uncertainty in a strange mixture, as we head into the next period of increased unraveling, adjustment and insecurity. Some darker moods will return. The Americans will increasingly be looking abroad again as the 2060s approach, acting to spread their generous compassion to help resolve these doubts and disputes, or to engage in treacherous secret dealings to expand their own influence. You could call these times at the beginning of the 2060s a veritable smorgasbord of attitudes and feelings. In any case, rising stormy seas seem certain to lie ahead for the ships of state on Spaceship Earth, even as progress continues.

Chapter 8

Forecast: Windy and Wet, 2060-2080

Jupiter and Saturn will come together for the Establishment's next rendezvous on April 7, 2060. In 1936, not long before these two great chronocrators came together in 1940 in about the same place in the sky as they will join in 2060, Franklin D Roosevelt, although not an astrologer, spoke of "a mysterious cycle in human events." He said that *his* generation had a "rendezvous with destiny" to challenge the power of economic privilege and thus preserve democracy as an example for the world.[75] For the generations living in the 2060s, much will have been done to lay the foundations of greater freedom and prosperity for all, and more will soon be accomplished, but the tides of torment will continue to rock those foundations.

Having crossed into the air element for good in the great mutation conjunction of 2020, Jupiter and Saturn will now meet in the flexible and mobile air-sign Gemini for the first time in about 700 years. Being the sign of knowledge and communication, this tells us that the new "information age" will first come into full maturity in this period. The exploding computer and telecommunication networks of the 21st century will be fully integrated into the workings of society. The ongoing challenge will be adjusting human society and the living environment to this explosion of technology without losing our human abilities and freedoms. Over coming decades and centuries we will learn to manage and adjust to the dangerous forces that these technical abilities have left in their wake: climate change and pollution, regressions into tyranny, alienation from our feelings and our bodies, loneliness, vast movements of peoples, ownership and control of the tools of prosperity by a few, and the challenges of a developing global society. Meanwhile, new ideas will be blowing like the wind into all corners of the world in the 2060s and 70s. Inventors and entrepreneurs will open up many new information superhighways. Education reform will be on everyone's mind, and writers everywhere will offer solutions to our problems. New paradigms of how society and the universe work will proliferate.

In the Earth-Spirit Awakening, Pluto powered its way through the sign Pisces and was stimulated by opposition to Uranus. Stabilized by Uranus and Neptune in earth signs, the late 2040s Awakening re-opened our spiritual aspirations and brought us into harmony with Nature again. From this point on, just as after previous "full moon" Uranus-Pluto oppositions, the new Revolution will continue to reverberate and break out again and again in the following decades, just as did the recurring revolutions of the early 19th century. In

---

[75] https://en.wikiquote.org/wiki/Franklin_D._Roosevelt#Speech_to_the_Democratic_National_Convention_(1936)
   https://youtu.be/C3H9Skx7G64?t=1539

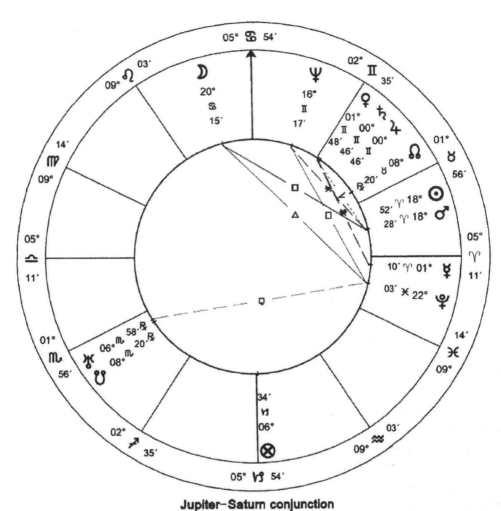

Jupiter–Saturn conjunction
April 7, 2060, 10:26 PM, UT, Washington DC, 38N54, 77W02

the 2050s we were able to stretch our wings in celebration of this new liberation. Now as we sail further along with Pluto as it plunges even deeper into the Piscean ocean, tides will rise and storms will gather. The waters of Pisces will swell even more as Neptune, God of the Seas, makes a momentous square to Pluto in the early and middle 2060s. Powerful, disruptive Uranus in the stormy water-sign Scorpio, Pluto's ruling sign, will further magnify the perils of Pluto's Piscean voyage. The moorings of society will loosen, and things will get much wetter and windier. Just as during the original romantic age in the early 19th century, this new romanticism will revel in a boundless and restless sea, but it will also recoil before the greater chaos and catastrophe of the times.

Although we will have created the new energy systems we need to stem and reverse climate change by now, much more global warming will already be baked in from the greenhouse gases we already emitted decades earlier before resistance to reform was broken. We will have to apply all of our new technological abilities and computations to the task of mitigating, reversing and protecting ourselves from these watery disasters, as floods swell and storms intensify in the early and middle 2060s under Neptune square Pluto. Weather challenges will be at their greatest when Jupiter or Saturn join this great square, as in June and July 2061 or October 2063. People will need to move *en masse* to new locations in the 2060s to escape the floods and the winds, and world organizations will have to be better coordinated to handle the adjustments.

Surging Tides Batter the Foundations

Neptune square Pluto is the moment in the 500-year cycle of civilization known as the testing of foundations. Our new global society, with its renewed commitment to Earth and Spirit, will need to revise and rebuild itself many times in the next few years to meet the challenge. Old and new institutions alike could decay, dissolve and reform themselves, especially our schools, churches and health centers. On the brighter side, Venus' conjunction with Jupiter and Saturn as they join on April 7, 2060 suggests that expanding our social life and the arts will also be high on the agenda in the early 2060s. Reinventing human relationships in the information age will be a major project, and the object of many new-age therapy techniques.

The next solar eclipse on April 30, 2060 highlights **Uranus in Scorpio** and evokes shades of the 1890s and 1970s. It targets North America, and possibly China, Eastern Europe and southern Africa. During the last such civilization foundation-testing time, the wars of religion between Catholics and Protestants happened, and the last visit of Uranus to Scorpio witnessed the Jonestown Massacre.[76] So new fanatic cults may rise and fall in the early 2060s as uncertain times magnify escapist urges. On the more positive side, as 1970s and 80s-type influences come back around in the early and mid-2060s, new age movements will be in vogue again too, and spiritual pioneers will once again make breakthroughs in our understanding of human potential and of the psychic and spiritual realms beyond this world. Conflicts could be mitigated by mass prayers and meditations, as we the people remember that "we are the world." As this is a Gemini era of abundance in literature, many new e-books and videos on these new age subjects could appear, and new prophets and religious groups will rise up to peer past the confusion and the disillusion of this time to offer real spiritual cures that meet the need for wisdom, just like what happened in the 1890s and 1970s. Wonderful mythic and heroic imaginative tales could proliferate that take us far beyond Lord of the Rings and Harry Potter, and teach timeless truths.

Uranus in Scorpio also indicates real-life troubles too, especially for the authorities. In the Fall of 2060, Saturn approaches its next square to Pluto, and lines up with Neptune in a conjunction. This is a further sign of fanaticism and international conflict. Dictators will often clash with peoples' movements in such times. The period 2059-61 will see revolutions occurring in diverse places, because Uranus will be in sesqui-square to both its transcendental partner planets. But Saturn-Pluto aspects, as Richard Tarnas pointed out, indicate accretions of conservative power, so we could see eruptions of reaction as well as revolution. Saturn-Neptune alignments also mark key moments in history too, so there wlll

---

[76]World Almanac 2018, p.782. https://www.history.com/topics/crime/jonestown

be a lot to contend with as the 2060s get going. The United States has often been at war during these times, as well as having endured challenges to its own internal freedoms. We can't take for granted that there won't be further resistance to democratic progress in the future, at home and abroad, as the 2010s already taught us. Peoples' government is still a new experience among many nations of the world, and still will be in 2060. Tyrannical and conservative takeovers could occur in the early 2060s, along with progressive revolutionary ones.

Since this era is also a cyclic recurrence of 2001, utopian religious and technologically-advanced terrorists could be threatening us again too, probably from the air. I don't say that an attack will be made on America as serious as that of Sept.11, 2001, but it could be major. Add a Saturn-Neptune alignment to the square to Pluto by these two planets, and you have an ominous sign for 2061 just sixty years after 9-11. And such terror threats would be an excuse to take away personal freedoms too. Meanwhile, various weather and climate events are always likely to be triggers of the troubles in this era, as seas continue to be very stormy in more ways than one. Winds of air, winds of war, and winds of change will all be blowing. In the Fall of 2060, India and Bangladesh are especially vulnerable. Floods in these countries could lead to internal strife or clashes with world authorities and neighbors. If diplomatic efforts work out though, these countries could receive lots of heroic assistance.

With Jupiter returning to Gemini and Cancer in 2060-61, North Americans (and the USA, if still "united") will be eager after such an attack to enter the fray and protect "democracy" again, as well as its own interests. It could be feeling the urge to expand too. So, interventions by Uncle Sam are likely. As Jupiter and Saturn join together in Gemini in April 2060, North Americans will have the urge to help neighboring countries in the Western Hemisphere. In the Spring of 2061 though, the Saturn-Neptune conjunction gets its closest to squaring Pluto, and Mars turns stationary, indicating the time when conflicts may happen within greater America, or when it could be attacked. Fortunately, Mars is stationary in the sign Libra, which can be a sign of peace as well as war, so American interventions could have a peaceful outcome.

As further troubles or conflicts erupt in the Balkans and the Middle East in Summer of 2061, and in the Middle East areas again in September (Iran vs. Israel for example), things may get even rougher. Western allies may need to take action at these times to resolve and stem violence in these and other places. Things will come to a head in February 2062 (Mars conjunct Pluto and square Saturn-Neptune). An American executive may then cooperate with other peoples to help make peace possible through key world economic reforms. People who are treated fairly don't fight, thinks Uncle Sam. But if that doesn't work, then when warlike Mars turns stationary together with Uranus in April 2063, North Americans may take more decisive actions (especially in June) toward other nations. Ambitious Middle Eastern leaders, as well as American ones, will need to have their expansiveness checked in the early 2060s. Powerful potentates can act like hungry wolves if they are not restrained, as the people might learn in these turbulent times.

Lots of cosmic planetary energies gather in early 2064, and they all focus on puny but potent Pluto as it navigates the stormy waters of Pisces. Not only will the square to Pluto by oceanic Neptune, ruling planet of Pisces, now be making a perfect storm, but Saturn and Uranus will align with Pluto in a great grand trine in water signs too. By June 2064, Pluto in Pisces will stand out from all the other planets by occupying half the sky by itself, in what we call a singleton or handle planet. This will happen to Pluto often in the 2060s. This indicates that storms and floods both literal and figurative will batter the world in 2064, so humanity had better batten down the hatches! Rescue teams will have their hands full all over the place in the soggy sixties.

No need to localize *this* cosmic figure too much; the whole world will be affected. But Iran will take center stage again, prodded by these events to further transform its Islamic theocracy and religious traditions. We know that Uranus returning to its place of Revolution in 1776 means a great struggle for the United States of America to remake itself, but Iran will undergo its own Uranus Return in the early 2060s, climaxing early in 2064 and in May of 2065. The people will make their passions felt there, and they will continue to work out the new post-carbon basis for their economy and how they relate with neighboring nations. Perhaps in part because these changes in Iran could disrupt oil exports, as well as because of all the floods and storms in the world, shortages of resources can be expected in many countries under Saturn in Cancer in 2063-64. Creative and talented people working together around the globe will reorganize and reconstruct a battered world to fill the need. If they are wise, parsimonious financial institutions will loosen their fists and make new, innovative investments to adjust to the stormy times. This collective activity could help restore the shaky economy later in 2064.

Many barriers will fall between peoples as we work to come to grips with these disasters. We can expect many passionate crusades as well as scientific and charitable expeditions on behalf of suffering citizens of the world. Of course, we'll also have to watch out for charlatans and cultists taking advantage of peoples' needs for solace and salvation. Pisces and Neptune can be signs of deception as well as charity. More religious and moral battles may break out. We can expect various kinds of emotional addictions to grip the public, as the watery grand trine of Saturn in Cancer, Uranus in Scorpio and Pluto in Pisces in 2063-64 brings back some similarities to the roaring nineteen-twenties, including a recovering economy. The people will partake of manifold forbidden and escapist pleasures, just as if they were all drunken sailors. Crime syndicates will take advantage of the opportunity.

Meanwhile the yellow press will have much to sensationalize and magnify out of all proportion, including lusty scandals, as Neptune finishes up its voyage through literary Gemini. Sexual barriers will fall away in many places, while prudish moral majorities will try to raise up prohibitions again. Conspiracy theories will abound too. Radicals and revolutionaries will be peddling lots of utopian solutions and fomenting strikes and riots, especially in North America in early 2064, as Mars joins with the unusually potent Pluto in the raging waters of Pisces and then travels through fiery Aries.

Shades of the 1890s resound in all these ways, as the square of Neptune and Pluto brings back many of the trends from the time of their conjunction way back then. But if Humanity can get a handle on things and protect itself from the battering waves, this could actually be an adventurous, joyful, stimulating, constructive, innovative and fulfilling time for many people. Important accomplishments will reassure the public, and feelings of liberation will ripple through the world in October and November 2064, as electric Uranus trines transformative Pluto, and Jupiter trines Neptune. It could be a most memorable year. Just as the catastrophic war of 1812 was succeeded by the era of good feelings, so relief and revival of spirits could follow the challenges of the early 2060s, as Uranus enters exuberant and fiery Sagittarius in 2065 just as it did in 1814.

The Sizzling Sixties

The chart for the Fall Equinox of 2065 indicates that the powerful alignments going on among the outer transcendental planets will be very significant in the Americas that season. Although I don't see new military engagements for Uncle Sam in 2065, he may still need to support neighboring nations as they struggle with climate disasters and internal disruptions. It could be the time of some transformative and charitable meddling by the executive branch. I hope it works out well. It could be a new alliance for progress, and other more-secret alliances could be formed too. No doubt more literal kinds of storms will also continue at this time in America, and they will soon be joined by destructive fires. Many fiery conflagrations can be expected everywhere and at any time as part of the warming world of the 21st century, but historically Uranus crossing into fire signs like Sagittarius and aligned with Jupiter may signal the worst fire years. So it will be in 2066, especially in June as Pluto also enters fiery Aries. Jupiter and Uranus in conjunction together will stand out as singletons then, and for much of the year in 2066. Fire crews will have their hands full. The soggy sixties could start to sizzle instead.

Of course, this is not the only kind of event that an overwhelmingly powerful Jupiter conjunction with a Uranus singleton in Sagittarius will signal. And what a powerful and loud alarm it will be. The people will swell with enthusiasm in the Fall of 2066 in Washington, as they bring proposals to provide generous relief to suffering citizens. Powered by commentators and pundits who bring out startling revelations of wrong-doing, reformers will ferret out corruption in the halls of power and oppressive labor practices. Meanwhile, New Age missionaries will continue to share their liberating visions. Breakthroughs in space travel and transportation can be expected too, since they occur regularly under this conjunction, and they could inspire the people just the way Lucky Lindbergh did in 1927 at a similar time in cyclic planetary history. Uplifted by such exploits as this, the stormy floods and passionate moods of the people during the early 2060s will expand into a new confidence at mid-decade and the following few years.

In our times, whenever Jupiter and Uranus make a conjunction, Neptune simultaneously enters, or has recently entered, the next sign of the zodiac circle. This means that every time Neptune, the Planetary Ark of Humanity, marks and suffuses the Earth Spirit with the essence of a new sign, with all its lessons and gifts for us, it comes to us as a new awakening and liberation. And as Neptune enters conservationist Cancer in 2066, the ongoing need to restore the planet from the challenges wrought by climate change will stir our thoughts and actions even more than usual. Neptune in Cancer will encourage restoration work by adventurous repair crews and eco-tourism groups across the world. Many latter-day Teddy Roosevelts could even appear to lead us through these new progressive projects. New worlds will open up for many people as Pluto navigates the border of Pisces and crosses into Aries. Empowered by Jupiter and Uranus in conjunction in Sagittarius of 2066, Pluto will stimulate our willingness to emerge from chaos and push forward assertively into the future. This could be said to be a return of the Earth-Spirit Awakening. People could also be reminded of the early years of the 20th century in the progressive era.

And under Neptune in Cancer, a new interest in and enthusiasm for history could help us stay connected to the historical cycles of the times and inspire us to emulate our collective past achievements and adventures. We don't always have to narrowly focus on our current troubles and desires, or those of our own generation. We can recall the enormous energy locked within our worldwide heritage and our collective memory of other sizzling, progressive and creative times like these in 2066, whether they happened in 1966, or in 1906, or in other such times. Each of us can do this *whenever* we feel the urge.

But just like in those other times, other less-progressive trends will be stirring as well. Neptune in Cancer, we know, has stimulated ancestral, patriotic and nationalist sentiments in the past. Along with the more expansive moods, some people may be consumed with nativist passions and fears of radicals later in 2066. Saturn in Virgo could magnify this trend in 2066-2067, as a tax revolt gets going. Saturn in this sign and the following sign Libra has corresponded to red (anti-communist) scares and tax revolts. Entrepreneurs might react now against increasing state controls and regulations that have been set up to meet the climate crisis over the past few decades. It could be a **green scare** this time, instead of a red scare. In January and in November of 2067, these emotions could express themselves openly in demonstrations and riots, as well as aroused by outspoken leaders, but the more compassionate and pro-environmental sentiments of the times will be out in force too as Jupiter opposes Neptune through most of the year. October 2067 will be a peak of peoples' activism, as Mars squares these two planets. Arising from this movement, I see the altruistic reformers getting the upper hand in the Spring of 2068.

But later in that year, Saturn comes around to its next opposition to Pluto. This indicates even more intense confrontation between progressive reformers and conservative reactionaries. The tax revolt will surge again in the Spring of 2069, as entrepreneurs in Middle America protest against government controls. This movement could launch a more cautious and conservative decade in North America, if the 30-year Saturn cycle holds. It could also arise through battles over labor rights and health care, as well as fear of foreigners. Saturn's next square to Neptune makes this a potent, fearsome T-square with Pluto throughout 2069. Ethnic and national rivalries aroused by Cancerian nativist attitudes could lead to international complications, as Saturn's opposition to Pluto congeals in 2069. Pakistan and the Northwest African coast could be involved as well as the USA.

Who occupies the center stage of action could continue to shift back and forth in the late 2060s during this cosmic T-square. While some nativist, reactionary demagogues have their way with the public in the Spring of 2069, by Fall the winds of change will blow again and the liberals may get the upper hand. More physical windy storms and wet floods are also indicated by this T-square in 2069, and people will be reminded again that mitigation and restoration are still necessary to meet them. Although Saturn's tattered and torn 30-year cycle, and its current tangle with Pluto, portends more cynicism and cautious conservatism in the 2070s than in recent decades, the other planets may have other ideas-- just as they did in the late 2040s. Powerful Pluto in Aries will keep many activists pushing forward in the next two decades, and another revolutionary outbreak is due soon, thanks to Uranus squaring it in 2072-74. This could rough up the conservatives' hopes for protection of their wealth and privileges in the USA in the 2070s. America's penchant for intervention in the affairs of other countries will be stimulated too by another returning Jupiter war cycle in the early 2070s. The planets just keep turning, burning and churning, and as around and around we go, where it all ends the pundits just never seem to know.

The new Pluto in Aries pioneers will continue to shape new ways of managing our threatened lands and endangered species. Great conservation projects by activists and officials alike are in store after the great eclipse and equinox of Sept.22-23, 2071. The Green Revolution of environmental consciousness that was born in the 1960s as Uranus conjoined Pluto and was fulfilled during its opposition during the Earth-Spirit Awakening in the 2040s, will now reach its climactic closing square of the cycle. Therefore, from 2072 to 2075, the sixties revolution will be heard from again, as counter-cultural radicals seek to remake society in accordance with green values. But in the midst of a somewhat more conservative decade in the USA, they will encounter the usual resistance. The other 2 revolutionary movements often come up during Uranus-Pluto aspects as well. If there are places where democracy or equality are still denied, the people may rise up to demand it in 2072-75.

American Milestones, North and South

Both reformers and xenophobes may be rattling some sabers and swords in North America in 2070 and 2071, but not taking much action yet. More radical steps will be taken in the Spring of 2072, when Uncle Sam may get involved in revolutionary troubles abroad again. This of course usually comes as Jupiter Returns to Gemini and Cancer, bringing its intervention cycle around again. Burma may be one place that needs attention from Western and Eastern allies. But the States of North America will have stirred things up so much in the rest of the Americas in recent years that the natives will be restless there too. Brazil and all Latin American countries will experience their Uranus Return in 2072-73. Remember how important the USA's Uranus Return is, when it returns to its natal place from 1776 at 9 Gemini. In this case, during this Uranus Return in Latin America, its square to Pluto makes it doubly significant. The square is a powerful aspect within the Uranus-Pluto Cycle of Revolution. Its significance cannot be denied, since it last occurred during those big Middle Eastern upheavals called the Arab Spring in 2011-2014, which at that time also found echoes in Brazil and elsewhere. And this Uranus square Pluto aspect in 2072 will happen in the same signs of the zodiac as in 2011 (Aries and Capricorn). You may also remember that back in the early 1820s Simon Bolivar and other liberators set Latin America free from Spain and Portugal and created new nations when Uranus and Neptune joined together in Capricorn. They were *also* was in square to Pluto *then*. This happened right after Spain's king was briefly overthrown in 1820. Once the king recovered his throne though, thanks to armed action by his fellow monarchs, they wanted to put his colonies back under the Spanish crown too. But Uncle Sam protected these new Latin American nations by audaciously proclaiming the Monroe Doctrine-- and got a large amount of help from the British Navy. With Uranus returning to the *same degree* of 2 Capricorn in February and March of 2072, just where it was in 1821-22, the destiny of Latin America may be challenged again by new upheavals within their countries, and by Uncle Sam from without, eager to provide "protection" once again.

America at the same time will still be getting *really, really* wet, as oceanic Neptune crosses over the USA natal Sun position in 13 Cancer from July 4 1776, and Mars will just happen to get stuck in the waters *right there* at 13 Cancer too, turning stationary-direct on February 19th of 2072 on the very day of a New Moon. America's impulses, both protective and xenophobic, will be aroused again as another president much like Monroe leaps into action with another Doctrine. You may remember too that Neptune last crossed this degree of 13 Cancer just when Uranus was making its *previous* Return to Latin America in 1906 and 1907. As I mentioned before, another Teddy Roosevelt may be on the scene in 2072 too. In 1906 the original TR intervened so often in Latin American countries in the Caribbean Sea that it became known as a Yankee Lake, and he justified his actions with his "corollary" to the Monroe Doctrine. Teddy will apparently be back in 2072, in one way or another, to make the same claim.

How benevolent this intervention will be remains to be seen, of course. With or without US help, or in spite of its hindrance, regimes may be toppled and new freedoms gained in Latin American nations. A good sign will be Jupiter's conjunction to Neptune in Cancer in June 2073. This conjunction is always generous and peaceful, so the best opportunity to make this Latin American cycle positive will happen then. New international missions and organizations could be founded. Warning should be given to financial speculators, however, that Neptune's last Return to the natal Sun of the United States coincided with a brief but powerful financial panic in 1907. If investments in real estate in these troubled Latin lands go sour amidst all this turmoil and change, some big shot American tycoons could be devastated. Prices could tumble in North America then too. Another Uranus-Pluto square is not such a good time for financial stakeholders in the USA, as demonstrated by the previous such square that began in about 2008 when the Great Recession hit, and by the same square that began in about 1929 when the Great Depression struck. Investors should be careful in these years. Companies in Latin America could be nationalized, which might make some North American investors shirtless and unhappy. And money laundering to hide their troubles from the law won't keep them clean either.

The people could sweep Washington up into a tide of reform in 2072, as indicated by the stationary Mars and Neptune together at the USA Midheaven during the New Moon in February, and again by the powerful, benevolent conjunction of Jupiter to Neptune in late 2072 through mid-2073. Major financial and environmental reforms could follow in the USA and in Brazil too, as the wet weather continues in the sky and rains down on the fortunes of the money speculators. This being the climax of the greenpeace revolutionary cycle, these environmental reforms could be major, and will encourage more liberating green lifestyle changes among the people. The entire American continent will experience the Green Revolution again in the early 2070s, as all its nations seek to work together to create a sustainable and financially-workable way of life for the people. And as Neptune crosses the USA's natal Sun in Cancer, changes could reach deep into family life too, transforming our approach to our communities and the land. Politicians could be asked to get their heads together and work across borders in the Americas through the new organizations founded under Jupiter conjunct Neptune in June 2073. The winds and tides of change will be blowing and rising through all the nations of the hemisphere and beyond.

Patriotic support for Uncle Sam's army could arouse the people too at the very same time, possibly enhanced by trumped-up fears of radicals and refugees from the Latin American troubles. This could upset some American powers and interests in August 2073, because an eclipse will strike the Midheaven then in Washington DC. Meanwhile, by the Spring of 2073 the authorities in the old nations of Iran and Iraq could be suppressing uprisings there, and America might feel the need to interfere in those places too, or protect itself from them, perhaps in August after the eclipse. Some progress might have happened in Iraq in April 2073. But things could get more unruly there as Uranus and Pluto make their final square in October 2074, causing more crackdowns. Freedom has a long way to go before it fully arrives in this forsaken Iraqi land, the cradle of civilization that has been rocked by war and oppression for millennia. So further upheaval can often be expected there in the 21st century. And the great opposition of Uranus and Neptune due in 2079-2080 will be approaching in the middle 2070s, and that's a warning of new rumbles brewing in the Balkans too. Nations could be stimulated to form new alliances to deal with these tensions, although this time I hope we aren't going to let the Balkan countries suck us all into a great war like they did during the *last* such Uranus opposition to Neptune in 1908-1914.

With Pluto in Aries, trine to Saturn in Sagittarius, 2074 could be another year in which enterprising and ambitious pioneers make breakthroughs in exploring new lands. New ways to travel could be opened, and a new planet may be reached. Saturn in this sign often corresponds to these exciting breakthrough moments, such as the first transcontinental railroad, Lindbergh's flight, and the first space satellite.[77] Ever since the 2020s, and even further in the 2050s, we will have been making much progress in bridging distances. So just like in 1969, when a man landed on the Moon, another time of turmoil and revolution could be capped by one of these moments in 2074.

---

[77] World Almanac 2018, May 10, 1869 p.438, May 20, 1927 p.440, Oct.4, 1957 p.666.

But Pluto in Aries also indicates that violence may also be an issue for the people in the 2070s, as it was in the nineteen-sixties. I especially remember that on August 1, 1966 a man climbed to the top of a tower at the University of Texas at Austin and shot 18 people to death and injured 31, and that this was during the powerful Uranus-Pluto conjunction that opened the cycle now climaxing as Uranus and Pluto square off again for the final time on October 24, 2074. Since these planets fall on angles (the Nadir and Descendant) in Austin Texas during the New Moon of Oct.20, I wonder if we could be confronted yet again with the reality that mass shootings are the inevitable result of poor gun control in the USA. This is an issue that could come to a climax now, as the revolutionary cycle which has brought it to the fore comes to its final closing square-- the last quarter of its cycle. The unique American obsession with the "right to bear arms" needs to be curbed and well regulated, and its overpopulation of guns removed, if its society is ever to be truly safe, just and civilized. It looks like it will probably take at least until this time for Americans to finally come to grips sincerely with this problem. I always have to wonder, with Bob Dylan, about how many deaths it will take until we realize that too many people have died from this debacle.

The Spring Equinox of 2075 will put more explorers and adventurers into the spotlight in North America. Strong, innovative leaders will also grab headlines that season; and well-organized rebels will make hay in places such as Iraq, Latin America or Southeast Asia. When Uranus-Pluto aspects reach their end though, as they are doing in the mid-2070s, things can go haywire. The people will have to watch that tyrants don't take over their movements. Rebels must choose their leaders wisely, or some wonderful advances may be lost. We know the story of the new boss being just like the old boss. Ambitions for power will be rising, and they could be troublesome once Saturn gets into Capricorn in 2077. Horrific regimes took power in the wake of the squares between Uranus and Pluto in 1933 (The Nazis) and 2014 (The Islamic State and the Assad genocide). Such drastic backsliding may not happen this time, since consciousness will be expanding and winds of change blowing. Indeed, another great stimulus from Uranus will already be happening in 2076 as it approaches its opposition to Neptune, and as it aligns exactly with a total eclipse in January of that year. Leaders in America will take action for peace at that time. A powerful new progressive leader could be crowned then, in Egypt or elsewhere in the Middle East. There'll be a mixed bag of tyrants and true leaders in power after the big rebel square of the early 2070s.

Turning A Corner Into Tomorrow

The turbulence in this wet and windy time will not let up. As Uranus finishes up its square to potent Pluto, it will hand off the currents of change to Neptune, as it comes closer to opposing this watery Ark of mass humanity. Our visions will be awakened and our hearts touched in ways we can scarcely imagine now as Uranus opposite Neptune combine their energies. They bring out the most creative impulses and take us to imaginative places. This alignment always signals international tension though, and things have already been tense between peoples in the 2070s. New leaders in many nations will be ready for enterprising and heroic action now, as Saturn reaches ambitious Capricorn in 2077, along with Uranus already there, and these power brokers might challenge the diplomatic arrangements of the Revised World Order made in the 2030s, perhaps causing a new Cold War. It could be a time when assertive and impetuous leaders come to power in many fields, with audacious plans and ambitious dreams; it could be a time of building new structures and laying out plans for new cities and even whole new countries.

I mentioned that a new Teddy Roosevelt may be on the scene; Uranus in Capricorn opposed Neptune in Cancer in his time too. With Neptune in the sign of preservation and personal priorities, TR and his successor Bill Taft were breaking up monopoly trusts and boosting conservation. The late 2070s and early 2080s will see many competent organizers moving giant enterprises forward, but they will face millions of motivated citizens opposing the prerogatives of eminent domain and preaching the rights of Nature. They will require that the great building plans being put into action are beautiful too, and that large new projects and enterprises do not neglect human rights and organic values.

By the Spring of 2077, Saturn in ambitious Capricorn reaches its next square to Pluto-- the potent dwarf planet that will already be plundering through the impetuous warrior sign of Aries. Sparks will fly at the Spring Equinox as Mars joins with Pluto there. The charts of the time indicate that Syria, Iraq, Afghanistan and even Vietnam and other South-east Asian nations may be involved in some border disputes in July and December 2077, and that Americans may get into the fray. Bigoted nationalists may be screaming for protection from invaders or clamoring for conquests. People should take heed and try to head off some of these potential wars of 2077; they could trigger difficult and long-lasting troubles and unleash cruelty and suffering if not kept in bounds. Meanwhile conservative leaders now in power in many places will do their best to quell any rebellions. Civil wars could break out between these rebels and the ambitious tyrants. The markets may decline and the economy could be unstable under Saturn in Capricorn, so investors should be careful about speculating in foreign lands that are going through turmoil.

These turbulent events are just the prelude even greater ones as this wet and windy chapter ends and the new one begins. Humanity could turn a corner into a new era if it takes the opportunity that the planets will provide. Tyrants who may have taken power between 2074 and 2077 should not rest too easy on their thrones, for as Uranus and Neptune first reach their very-significant opposition to each other on March 7, 2078, the momentum will shift back to liberal and revolutionary forces, and Saturn will join Uranus to make this a threesome of planets to challenge the potentates. At the same time, in the progressed chart of Humanity, Sun conjunct Uranus in 2078 also indicates a revolutionary year. In many ways this era will be similar to the times when the Berlin Wall came down and many new nations were born from 1989 to 1991. Pent-up longings for freedom will express themselves again this time in many and diverse places.

I see several windy and wet waves of revolt breaking out in 2078-79. The perfect storm of the last 20 years will be reaching its height. Iraq looks like the first target, as its decade long period of change reaches a potential climax. The people and their leaders will be ready for bold action as Mars turns stationary in potent Scorpio and goes retrograde on

March 21, while sitting right on the Ascendant in the Spring Equinox chart for Iraq. Meanwhile Uranus will be shaking up Iraqi power players by sitting at the Midheaven in this chart. This looks like a turning point in Iraqi history, when it may move beyond its tyrannical traditions and establish freedom for its people.

India also will experience a crescendo of change and revolution starting with the total eclipse on May 11, 2078. Meanwhile California, center of New Age Awareness, will lead America toward higher consciousness throughout 2078. Look for a possible East-West "convergence" of idealism and New Age religion, as waves of awareness spread from New Delhi and San Francisco across the world after the grand eclipse on May 11, 2078, bringing much-needed peace to the inner lives of the people and guiding activists everywhere. It could be a time when the New Age comes further into fruition.

When Mars turns stationary again in Libra and turns direct on June 7th of 2078, the cosmic tides will be rising even higher as it makes a bold T-square with Uranus and Neptune; with Saturn along for the ride. The New Moon of June 10th indicates a progressive shake-up in Germany, the center of the European nations and of the European Union if it still exists by then, as I expect it will. A change in leadership could revitalize democracy within the Union. Further south, Nigeria could experience movements that push it forward, and perhaps Africa along with it. In Southeast Asia, a climax of change is due that could arouse civil strife. And with Mars in Libra stationary at Midheaven in Washington in this June 2078 chart, leaders of America will take bold action to put affairs in order throughout the Western Hemisphere. The planets will be targeting the Pluto plutocracy in the USA horoscope, likely bringing change to oligarchy and corporate structures. During the famous May Day solar eclipse in 2079, Saturn and Uranus will sit astride the Washington DC Midheaven, meaning the whole American economy could be reshaped, with powerful private and public potentates plummeting to the ground.

This new period of reform and revolution throughout the world will come to a head by February and March 2079. In rapid succession, Uranus opposes Neptune again, Saturn opposes Neptune, and finally Saturn aligns with Uranus just before both cross over into the idealistic and dynamic new age sign of Aquarius. (Note though that May 2078 or February 2079 could also be the time of a California earthquake, or others elsewhere.) The tide of transformation will come to a climax in India during these powerful alignments in February 2079. I expect to see the revolutionary wave mounting and moving forward swiftly in many other places too in February through May of 2079, and reaching other peaks in August and September, as the people rise up again in North and South America, in Israel and its neighbors, and elsewhere.

Meanwhile, the new Cold War of international tensions and adjustments may not be quite over, nor will be some of the hot wars that will have begun in 2077. The upsurge of New Age consciousness of world peace circa May 2078 will relieve tensions, however, and American leaders will be doing some tough diplomatic work as Mars turns stationary Libra in June of 2078 and squares off with the revolutionary planets Saturn, Uranus and Neptune. Mars in Libra in 2078 is a hopeful sign of action for peace, and it will be needed not only in the Western Hemisphere but in the other trouble spots as well, including during another difficult moment in December 2079. The wars of this period will also topple governments, which may open opportunities for more progressive regimes to take power.

The same 3 planets Saturn, Uranus and Neptune which all aligned in 1989 signified the end of the original "Cold War" between the allies of the United States and the Soviet Empire, just as I predicted. With Neptune now opposing Saturn and Uranus, the new Cold War will reach a critical moment in 2079. But as we look up into the sky at the end of the year, we see Jupiter getting ready to join the planetary party as it moves into Aquarius. This may be the most momentous alignment of the century, which we will cover in more detail shortly. Sparks of liberation will fly, especially in India and Bangladesh, and California too, as Jupiter joins Uranus in January 2080 and opposes Neptune. It is a clear sign everywhere that the changes happening in these scary but hopeful times will prepare the way for the next chapter in our story-- and another new start in the affairs of state with the next Jupiter-Saturn conjunction in Aquarius in March 2080.

In spite of the wet and windy turbulence, this should be largely a positive time. Resolution of the cold and hot wars of the 2070s should happen soon, and peoples' movements will offer hope. The skies will be clearing after the long storm, and the Sun will break through so that the final push for progress in the 21st Century can proceed. This breakthrough is also signified by Neptune now moving out of watery Cancer and into sunny, fiery Leo. If all goes well enough, the Establishment, having received an amazing revolutionary make-over, and having re-oriented itself within the international order, will by the early 2080s be cleaned up and all set to function at a higher level of wisdom, harmony and competence than ever before, perhaps soon ready to become the Next World Order of the dawning Age of Aquarius.

Chapter 9

The Transformation of Progress: 2080-2100

As 2079 becomes 2080, the next chapter in the dawn of the New Age opens immediately with the most powerful and significant planetary alignment of the 21st century. So, I need to discuss the whole figure and its context.

Jupiter conjunct Uranus is liberating and innovative. This time, on Jan.31, 2080, this conjunction will occur at 2 degrees-plus of the brilliant and transforming sign of the New Age itself: Aquarius. On that day Saturn will be only 5 degrees away at 7 Aquarius-- the very same degree where Mars turning direct in the progressed chart of humanity revived progress in 2022. And visionary Neptune, the planetary ark of humanity, gets in the act too by opposing all these planets from the bright, confident sign of Leo. The next conjunction of Jupiter and Saturn follows on the Ides of March 2080. This means that all four of the largest planets in the solar system will be closely aligned as 2080 begins. Then we can look forward to an expansive and confident mood, as Neptune makes its "baroque" trine to Pluto in the 2080s and 90s.

Previous times when Jupiter, Saturn and Uranus were close together happened in the midst of titanic international conflagrations. Gigantic wars tore through the landscape at these times, reshaping the human agenda and accelerating Western progress. The wars had already begun before this alignment, but they reached a pivotal moment at these times and marshaled huge forces. In 1444 for example, southeastern Europe united in the Crusade of Varna to try and hold off the vast Ottoman campaign to conquer the Byzantine Empire.[78] But that Empire fell in 1453, thereby stimulating the voyages to the New World and forcing artists to flee westward, thus revving up the Renaissance. The 100 Years War was also reaching its end at this time, transforming France into a centralized state.[79] The 3 planets lined up again in 1623 shortly after the huge and deadly 30 Years War began, which ravaged Europe and ended the wars of religion.[80] In 1762 they aligned again when the titanic Seven Years War reached its climax, setting the stage for the American and French Revolutions which were also partly inspired by the rise of the Enlightened Despots in Europe that followed the war.[81] In May 1941, the 3 planets aligned just before Hitler launched his brutal and colossal attack on Russia during World War Two in June. FDR, having made America "the arsenal of democracy" with the Lend-Lease Law in March to shore up beleaguered Britain, immediately extended it to Russia, thus launching its role as leader of the free world after its victory.[82]

---

[78] https://en.wikipedia.org/wiki/Crusade_of_Varna
[79] Stewart Easton, A Brief History of the Western World, Barnes & Noble, 1966, p.171-174
[80] Ibid., p.227-229.
[81] Ibid., p.273-275.
[82] Thomas A Bailey, The American Pageant, D.C. Heath & Co., 1956, p.873-875.

Therefore, we should expect the wars launched in 2077, although probably smaller in scale than these previous ones, to have set in motion huge progressive forces that arouse and liberate humanity. Pacific Asian nations may engage in some further aggressive actions that we hope will soon be resolved, while the nations that were formed after the Soviet breakup in 1991 put their state affairs on a new more efficient and humane footing. The United States will assist many nations to recover from their strife, while it and all other peoples simultaneously cooperate in developing international protocols for a New Age of liberation and global cooperation. This time the outcome of the struggles will be a great leap forward based on Aquarian altruistic and noble principles. When Saturn, Uranus and Neptune were in a similar turbulent line-up in the same signs back in 1917, Woodrow Wilson tried to "make the world safe for democracy" through a victory in a "great war" in Europe, and sternly commanded everyone and all the resources of his country to be focused on this visionary goal.[83] Then while Jupiter, Saturn and Uranus were all in conjunction in 1941, in trine to Neptune, Franklin D. Roosevelt pushed the goal further. The results of both of these world wars were the first experiments in uniting all nations together to build global peace. This time we should expect humanity and its leaders to erect nothing less than the foundations of the New Age of "harmony and understanding." Hey, maybe they'll even sing "this is the dawning of the Age of Aquarius" at the opening ceremonies of their convocations in early 2080. It could be like a Woodstock for World Leaders, with some tangible working results too in the affairs of nations.

Now as Jupiter, Saturn and Uranus align in Aquarius 2080, and stimulated by Neptune in opposition in Leo, American leaders and others around the world will be working boldly together as never before to bring about ambitious plans for this new age of world civilization under a unified system. But unlike those 2 previous times, the United States itself will not enter any wars in this period in order to expand its own power, because the Jupiter war cycle will not be in play. Instead it will carry out a constructive, reconstructive and assisting role. This lofty world project will involve much travail and probably more struggle, but the record shows how much can be accomplished during and after these titanic times. Happening in Aquarius, the triple conjunction reveals that great progress will take place at this moment.

Since 4 of the 5 outer planets will be in fixed signs, we can be sure that these leaders will not be hesitant to use government power to accomplish these goals. We are reminded of similar eras when the outer planets were in fixed signs, including the French Revolution in the 1790s, the Wilson administration during the First World War and the establishment of the Soviet Union in the 1910s, and the opening years of the Earth-Spirit

---

[83] Ibid., p.727-728, 735-738.

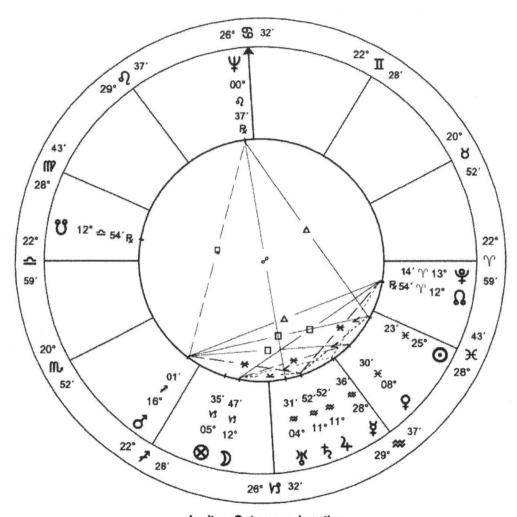

Jupiter–Saturn conjunction
March 15, 2080, 1:28 AM, UT, Washington DC

Awakening in the early 2040s. We can be sure that nations will command their economic powers and resources to meet the goals of idealistic, ambitious leaders in the late 2070s and early 2080s, and this may result in tax increases and more government programs and regulations. In some countries, dissenters may not be easily tolerated. This will be even more true in nations that are at war. The end result may be more freedom and justice for all, but for some people at the time it may seem like there is less freedom. That could certainly apply to wealthy people, whose riches may be expropriated in some poorer countries, such as Bangladesh and others we've mentioned in Asia and America in the last chapter.

If the United States, assuming it is still united, still carries on one of its seemingly never-ending political campaigns for president in 2080, the primary contest will happen in the midst of this great alignment. Since the Jupiter-Saturn conjunction is happening then, it will likely mean a new direction and a new political program in 2081. The frenetic, stringent reforms and foreign troubles going on will elicit a lot of controversy among the candidates. Although a change in the party in power is possible, the New Moon before the election of November 2080 indicates it will probably retain control, if the popular vote results prevail. Depending on who is chosen, or possibly re-elected, the leader will inherit the mantle of power created by all these audacious transformations toward a global society. Just how "global" the United States wants to be could be a major issue. In any case, it will probably be the same party as before that will lead the country through this great turning point in history toward reform and world cooperation.

The Jupiter-Saturn conjunction in 2080, with Uranus and Neptune in the background, will set the agenda for the world's powers for the following 20 years, and will indicate which nations will be most involved in the fray. Vietnam and other Southeast Asian nations will continue the process of transforming themselves into states that serve rather than dominate their people. Democratic reforms there are likely, since Uranus in Aquarius sits atop the Midheaven there in the chart for the conjunction. You can see from the chart here cast for America that Neptune is riding high as a singleton at the Midheaven there, showing that its leaders will be among the world's most dreamy and idealistic. Of course, it may also reveal some scandals or unsavory dealings in high places. I have to admit, heavy planets in the 4th house opposite Neptune could inspire some false prophets to preach protection of property against imaginary new-world-order government conspiracies, as well as to oppose the very-real globalization going on. In any case it's safe to say that according to this chart for the conjunction of Jupiter and Saturn, Neptune in Leo will rule the American nation in the 2080s, and this means that powerful and extravagant impulses will stir the people.

Aquarian Progress, Leo Frolic

This conjunction opens the next in the series of "progressive decades" that have included the 1780s, 1840s, 1900s, 1960s and 2020s, if the pattern holds. Coming on the heels of the revolutions, wars and international crises of the 2070s, it may be the most progressive decade of all. New institutions will continue to emerge on the world stage to buttress the Revised World Order against the turmoil of the times. A restructured and more powerful United Nations will likely be developed in this era. With the titanic 2080 conjunction of Jupiter-Saturn-Uranus in the 4th house in the conjunction chart for the USA, protecting our Earth home will be uppermost in the minds of reformers and concerned citizens again, as climate woes continue. Rapid, although now largely peaceful, social upheavals in many societies could help usher in a *Green Great Aquarian-Age Society* worldwide.

The election could elevate another eloquent Wilson or Kennedy-like figure to inspire us all to move forward toward the 22nd Century. It may prove a difficult bridge to cross over in the next 20 years, but at least we'll know where we need to go. Like JFK invited us to do under a similar conjunction in late Capricorn in 1961, this new leader will say "let us begin" the journey. Pluto in Aries will still be beckoning many activist and inventive pioneers to push forward aggressively across these "new frontiers." And since Aquarius is also a sign of technology, the new leader, like JFK before him (or her), will inspire plans to conquer disease, colonize other planets, and perhaps even connect with alien ET societies from the galactic federation, which we may meet as Neptune and Pluto form their expansive trine in adventurous fire signs later in the decade. This last prediction may be fanciful, but it's not impossible. At least there will now be greater interest in UFOs among a strong and growing network of star-gazing new agers. Electronic technology innovations will continue to take us to new places and bring groups of citizens together.

Neptune in Leo will rule the peoples' cultures too. During its vibrant trine to potent, transformative Pluto in the later 2080s, psychedelic, visionary high-tech space art will expand into a vibrant and dynamic baroque style that infuses the people with life and movement at the cellular level. Tremendous spiritual technology and spectacular biological discoveries will advance human potential. Meanwhile, under Neptune in Leo, social mores and inhibitions will crumble during a "roaring" decade that could make the 1920s look like a Buddhist tea ceremony. Cautionary warnings will be issued against too much intoxication with drugs and drink as the moralists sally forth again to sway us all back to sobriety. A reborn Broadway will stage spectacular lyric dramas in the 2080s that would make Wagner and Shakespeare green with envy, and the tedium of daily living will melt away in a fantastic carnival of fun and games, promoted and highlighted by a new "lost" generation of adventurous, reckless and cynical escapists. Their extreme sporting exploits will amaze devoted fans, and huge numbers of athletic records will fall.

In the Fall of 2080, as the chart indicates, the new American, Aquarian Alpha-Wave leaders will be swiftly organizing the country to accomplish great things. It will be the chance for these newest prophetic idealists to do what their predecessors the Baby Boomers could not do when it was *their* time to shine around the year 2000. A charismatic American president or prime minister will inspire the people with stunning charm and persuasiveness to carry out elaborate plans. Executive orders will come in a rush, and new missions will be launched in many fields throughout North America and the world. Congress will be a beehive of activity, and all American nations will organize and work together to accomplish great things. Over the next year vast infrastructure projects will begin, corporations will form, and institutions will be established to help the country and the world take unified action.

Meanwhile new support will be given to armed forces still in the field resolving the remaining conflicts from the era, and amazing diplomatic breakthroughs will be made. One of the final oppositions in the long series of this era between Uranus and Neptune will happen on September 4th, 2081, just one day after a total solar eclipse. It highlights these efforts to deal with the tensions that have disturbed the world over the last 5 years and will help bring peace, prosperity and justice to Africa (especially Nigeria), France and Central Europe, Pacific Islands, and even to the southern and plains states of North America. Another fabulous sign to watch for is when the *final* opposition in the era between Uranus and Neptune in December 2081 puts Uranus at 7 degrees Aquarius, right where Mars turned direct in 2022 in the progressed chart of humanity-- and thus restarted progress.

Now it will be expanding and reaching its fulfillment, as Uranus, ruler of Aquarius, reaches this degree. It will be a great season of achievement. Everyone should look forward to this time and prepare to help make it a shining moment for the world. And naturally, Americans should remember in 2080 to choose a capable, progressive and idealistic leader who can fulfill this Aquarian Age promise from the stars.

Sport, youthful exuberance and romance will be rising to a peak in the Spring of 2082, as Neptune in Leo and Pluto in Aries heighten the fires of frolic and frivolity, and really get the party going. The theater world will be buzzing, and the affairs of celebrities galore will be on full glamorous display. It will be fun just to be alive in 2082. But although the fun continues, things will get a bit more sober later in the year after the total eclipse of August 24. The plays on Broadway will get a bit more serious in the Fall, perhaps even deserving of serious critical praise, and the sporting world may be subject to scandal or injury then, so risky adventures should be avoided then. People will also be having more serious fun demonstrating for freedom in the Middle East. Remember, it's a big world, so lots of different things may be going on in different places. Although it may be unlikely at this time, governments can always be toppled whenever Uranus opposes Neptune, and the Fall Equinox chart of 2083 spotlights Israel, Egypt and East Africa as possible targets. Saturn in Pisces in 2082 and 2083 suggests greater confusion in the halls of power as the leaders start to get in over their heads, drowning in the flood of public demands for change that will be swelling in 2083 and 2084. Human rights and mental as well as physical health care programs could benefit from the peoples' activism. More literal floods are likely too, stimulating more mitigating measures and humanitarian crusades to help those affected. Around October 1st, 2082 Mars turns stationary conjunct Saturn in Pisces, so I would watch out for some dangerous international arguments over health care, water, or religion. India and Pakistan could be involved. Uncle Sam's direct, well-armed and UN-approved intervention may not be far behind, as the American war cycle returns in the Spring or late Fall of 2084, when the world will be alarmed over economic and ecological crises and calling for America's help. The disturbance will stimulate humanity's leaders to finish work on the Revised World Order and the restructured United Nations.

I see a crescendo of vibrant, humanitarian activism and spiritual healing energy breaking out around the world in the Fall of 2085, as Saturn enters activist Aries and Jupiter aligns with humanitarian Neptune. This conjunction is always a most fortunate and generous sign, and it can signify movements that uplift and arouse the people. Under such conjunctions in the 20th century, both the League of Nations (1920) and the United Nations (1945) were formed, and the United States entered detente with the Communist Powers (1971). Live Aid brought humanitarian relief to Africa soon after this conjunction in 1984, and we could see another such world performance in June 2086. Many other creative people and their leaders, including Americans, will bring peaceful healing to the world in the Fall of 2085, and throughout the momentous and most-interesting year of 2086. The long-suffering people of Iraq could benefit hugely, and this may help them to avoid trouble this year.

Saturn aligns with potent Pluto in warlike Aries at the same time, however, which means some violent outbreaks could also occur in 2085-86. Many rifts between peoples could come to Africa's Rift Valley and to Egypt, along with the other usual trouble spots in the Middle East. This time, however, we have a most-unusual combination, as the intense activism and potentially-violent power-plays of a Saturn-Pluto conjunction in Aries happens simultaneously with the humanitarian Jupiter-Neptune conjunction in Leo, with a fruitful trine aspect between them. And this double conjunction/trine figure will last for almost a year. It shows that any conflict in 2085-86 will direct catalyze for the United Nations to further reform itself into an effective governing world body dedicated to protecting international peace and human rights. It could be a crucial step toward the Next World Order to come during the Aquarian conjunction that beckons us from the future in 2165. These events will climax in June 2086, and the United States will continue to lead these activist efforts in the Fall. The institutions established at this time will be crucial to surviving the chaotic times that follow, and they will be needed if Humanity is to flourish in the New Age.

Escape from Chaos: The End of "Progress"

Indeed, the mood changes and chaos increases as Uranus leaves idealistic, stern Aquarius and moves on into moody, muddy, escapist Pisces in 2087. Any war that is not settled by 2086 could become a long quagmire for the nations involved. Developing good treaties in 2086 will be crucial. We don't want another Versailles Treaty, *do we* (as happened when Uranus entered Pisces in 1919)? Or another US-Iraq War (as when Uranus entered Pisces in 2003)? It's best for all the soldiers to come home now and *stay* home in 2087. Meanwhile Washington could still be busy keeping the peace and revising the world order in late 2088 and early 2089, and we can hope that it will use ballots and not bullets to do this.

Still more stimulus to look homeward and down to earth will come as another round of severe El Nino weather disasters hits in 2087 and 2088. Just as Saturn in earth-sign Taurus (opposite Neptune) stimulated the founding of Earth Day in 1970, and just as Saturn's next visit to that sign (square Neptune) during the big El Nino in 1998 stimulated global warming concerns under, so Saturn in Taurus (square Neptune) in 2087 and 2088 will be another reminder that we must pay attention to our great Mother planet. The plight of flooded Bangladesh will alarm the world again in the Spring of 2088, and it won't be alone. The watery Uranus in Pisces vibe will engulf the world in the late 2080s. Don't forget; not only does Uranus leave airy Aquarius and wade into the muddy waters of Pisces in 2087, the progressed chart of Humanity shows Mars leaving progressive Aquarius too after 187 years there and entering Pisces in 2089, signifying the "end of progress." Technology and politics will suddenly become less attractive. People will want to escape from the lofty goals of the new United Nations and bring things back to "normalcy," as President Harding called his Uranus-in-Piscean escapist regime in 1920. Disillusion with the new world arrangements could hit us like a pricked balloon if they don't bring peace and prosperity immediately. This spreading chaos and escapist cynicism also means that national leaders could be more corrupt and careless starting in 2087, and scandals over resources could erupt. Under the Pisces vibration, new religions and cults will also arise offering salvation and transformation for disturbed peoples. Many people will lose faith in world politics in the late 2080s, especially in the Fall of 2088, and when human arrangements seem futile, people seek the guidance from a higher power.

But many creative and adventurous souls will love this time anyway. Animal spirits will still be high, whether directed toward pleasure, plunder or politics. The expansive eighties will continue in the arts and pop culture, as baroque-like expressive confidence breaks through narrow-minded attitudes, especially in the Fall of 2087. Rowdy romance and tawdry indulgence will reach new heights, and this will break out still further in late 2088 and early 2089. Surrealist psychedelia will light up the skies and reach deep into our hearts. We've been preoccupied with technological prowess and with social or political reform over the previous two centuries, but this new era could really lift us onto a higher level of feeling and stir passions for more soulful pursuits. Progress conceived in purely material and technological forms is what will come to an end in the late 2080s. I think it's safe to say that the delusive goal of transhumanism, in which we are supposed to become immortal cyborgs and robots, will now be placed into the dust bin of history as *anti*-humanism. Progress in becoming human and living together well will take top priority from now on.

Despite the initial mood of escapism in 2087-89 among the new lost generation, many other adventurous souls will come forward to offer inspiring travel itineraries through inner and outer space and virtual realms. Barriers between peoples will be breached too, and world culture will advance. The basis of lasting world peace will be laid-- not only politically this time, but in our deepest minds and hearts. It's almost as if another John Lennon will arrive. Under Pisces, the dreamers (along with the cynics) will replace the institution builders on the world stage. But they will be no less activist in their own way, spreading their visions far and wide among the people. Progress will not just seem to end but will transform itself into opening our abilities to imagine and dream. Then they can be applied to the continuing process of reform and invention.

Times of chaos and change lead some to cling to old certainties. Pessimism and fear could make a comeback in a few places like the western states of America. Other escapists might focus on protecting their property rights in the Fall of 2088, because some of the builders of new institutions in the 2080s will have built their tax bills too high. Some people will be defending their individual and ethnic rights in the ever-more globalized world that Fall. Religious cults could be on the march and inflicting harm. Environmental and climate concerns will soar too, as the physical weather gets just as stormy and tawdry as the cultural weather in 2089. A minor civil war or revolution could erupt that year as a result of some of these stresses. After all, years that end in 89 have a certain tradition to uphold, right?

The great planetary figure of this time will be forward looking and expansive, however. As we reach the year 2090, Pluto in Aries will be in trine to Neptune in Leo. This aspect marks a "baroque" phase in human civilization when people look over the far horizons. Society and culture become more dynamic and ambitious and venture beyond limits toward new achievements and conquests. And we will need that dynamism in the late 2080s and early 2090s, because with these two primary planets in fire signs, there will be more literal fires to deal with, as climate change challenges continue. Great leaders and pioneers will beckon hearts and minds worldwide with their fiery passion and missionary zeal to handle the challenge and reach beyond what we thought was possible. Writers and artists will help us see beyond the difficult times that seem to be ahead toward great achievements that will happen in the new century. Blueprints for shiny, spectacular constructions will be proposed, perhaps at world's fairs like the ones in 1939 when the streamlined world of 1960 was revealed.[84] Artists and musicians will put our whole culture in motion, revising all the styles of the past so that they express confident, dynamic expansion and adventure. Combine this visionary, missionary, crusading zeal indicated by this dynamic fire-sign trine, with the Piscean influences, and religious or spiritual passion is suggested too, thus giving the visionary plans of circa 2090 a more prophetic and spiritual turn. The New Age Religions, and those of the Old Age too, will be on the march, offering prophetic new answers to the chaos of the times. Besides stirring words and speeches, those multi-media arts and music we mentioned above will be wonderful tools to express the new age vision, if artists take advantage of them.

Early in 2090, and again later in the year, Jupiter in exuberant, visionary sign Sagittarius makes a fiery, expansive grand trine with Neptune and Pluto. The visionary missionaries will sweep the people up into a whirlpool of wishful wisdom, as great new possibilities seem to open up for the century ahead. This grand heavenly trine should help cheer the people up, resolve differences, and allow us to enjoy the liberation achieved from the previous year's revolutions. Jupiter opposing Saturn, combined with all the expansive trines going on in the heavens, should bring all the excitement of the times to a rip-roaring climax. Various exploits in the sky and space could make it seem like Lucky Lindbergh and Neil Armstrong have made return flights to our world too. New celebratory traditions could be launched. New prosperity could have been built on reckless speculation too in the preceding years.

The artistic and hedonistic revels of the 2080s will continue into the early 2090s, now with a strong pinch of the dreamy, cynical and escapist flavor of Pisces added to the mix. A new sub-generation of decadent but energetic and dreamy dropouts will cluster in coffee houses, sipping acid-laden kool-aid and wallowing in the prevalent disillusion of the era. New forms of surrealistic and mystical abstract art will emerge, much like the styles of the 1920s. A solar eclipse in August 2091 indicates the Summer and Fall of that year will seem like a last respite of a latter-day belle epoque, as Brazil and the Indian sub-continent help set the world ablaze and on the move with exuberant arts and merry-making. More sporting exploits in the USA will dominate the cultural news in the Fall of 2092.

In May and June 2090, however, the three planets that joined together in 2080 to launch the foundations of the Aquarian world order will swerve into a very-exact T-square. This moment will be brief but spectacular. Uranus in Pisces will be caught in the middle of

---

[84] https://en.wikipedia.org/wiki/Futurama_(New_York_World%27s_Fair)

this Jupiter-Saturn full moon opposition. Squaring off in mutable signs, these 3 planets indicate a time of chaos and more chaos. We will be made aware again of how often things can spin out of human control. In addition to the usual weather challenges, the crisis of mid-2090 looks like some kind of massive cyber or social media failure or transportation nightmare. Conflicts may break out between ethnic and religious groups. Money issues will be up for fierce debate in the United States, which could suffer a financial crash. Issues and controversies will be starkly laid bare that will be at issue for decades to come. They could flare up again in the Spring of 2091 too.

Back to Reality

If the cyber crisis and financial crash of 2090 deepens into a depression in late 2092 and 2093, as Neptune enters Virgo like it did in 1929, then the revels of the previous years will soon peter out and the pleasures will evaporate. The mystic carnivals and electronic psychic theaters will be shut down by 2094, and all the cynics will smell the coffee and discover what *real* pessimism tastes like. As what William Strauss and Neil Howe called "the fourth turning" cycle returns once again in 2092-93, the issues will be stark for cynics and idealists alike. Financial speculators will lose their shirts in the 2090 and 2093 crashes. Many shortages of goods and some confused leadership will add to peoples' sufferings in 2092-93. Neptune in Virgo requires a more sober and altruistic attitude, and the needs of the common people can no longer be sacrificed to the enjoyments of the wealthy. From 2093 onward and into the first decade of the next century, the people will not be encouraged to have so much fun but invited to serve the people and learn how to help others instead. The lesson of Neptune in Virgo is to look beyond narrow self-interest, work in cooperation with authorities and teachers, and to rein in our collective ego. Serious issues will now require dedicated attention. The task of the next 12 years or more will be to work together to create equal opportunity and economic security for the poor and working people. Just as Neptune moves into the world-server and worker-bee sign Virgo, Jupiter and Uranus in conjunction in Pisces will awaken our compassion for those in need. We will rise up during this often-distressed 14-year Virgo era to serve Humanity.

Will 70 years of frequent revolutions and revelations since the last fourth turning in the 2020s be enough to equip us for this new crisis era? Will we have repaired the damage done by our industrial way of life so our future on Earth is sustainable and prosperous? Or have the richest and greediest folks deceived us into allowing them to hog all our resources and plunder our planet? Will we have given enough support to the innovators who are reshaping our technology so that it never again pollutes our environment or collapses our climate? Can we make peace and equality the new normal? Can the high arts of beauty and human community be restored to primacy in our building schemes? The 2090s and 2100s could well function like a doorway through which we pass into a wiser and brighter way of life, or into a declining world full of troubles and conflicts amid closing opportunities, diminishing resources and narrowing horizons. We will have many chances in the 21st century, as we have seen, to respond to the outer planets' promptings to fulfill our highest intentions. We will now reap the results of our actions. The expansive trine of the 2080s and 2090s indicates we can now move forward toward a climax of achievement. Progress may be transformed and raised to higher levels in these times, but we can't really afford it to end altogether. I hope we shift our thoughts and actions toward making a better world possible and use our crisis as a springboard to better behavior. Because if we do, the next century promises to be a time of abundant wonders and riches.

But notice that the runaway explosion in technical wizardry that characterized the 20th and 21st centuries will have less appeal in the 22nd. If we haven't invented what we need by now, it might never happen. In the next century, our social and spiritual development will take precedence. In the 2090s we will be moving into a more dynamic and expansive era in the following years. Cultures and civilizations will meet, and crusades will be launched to spread transforming ideas and spiritual values that will help us build inspiring, gigantic new social and physical structures. Suffering peoples in many places will look beyond technology or politics to religion for salvation and new values.

Will this new dynamic spirit of revelation bring peace, or a sword? The planets that signify war and conflict will not disappear from the sky, and they crop up in some important charts that describe the coming events in the new century ahead, as well as in the difficult year 2093. It will be up to us whether they've become indicators of courageous and ambitious activity instead of violence. The chart for Neptune's crossover into Virgo suggests that these courageous activities and potential wars will be a regular feature of the next 14 years. Despite the pall of some economic breakdowns and strife, however, Neptune and Pluto in trine continue to arouse us to move forward, and Jupiter and Uranus in conjunction at the same time will awaken us in 2093 to take compassionate and effective action. This time Australia may provide great examples of awakening among the people, and exciting new leadership.

As economic challenges threaten many peoples in this new crisis era, mass movements in Germany and the Balkans will call for relief. Religious and political awakenings will mushroom among the peoples of Iraq and the Muslim world after the total eclipse of January 16, 2094, and they may even decide on a new Great Satan. Another eclipse in June 2095 puts more fuel on these fires, as enthusiastic labor revolts break out in America, and mass movements erupt in Germany and Central Europe. This time, Mars in Sagittarius (both stationary and in singleton) calls forth the most expansive and adventurous spirit of these times and dominates the year. Rebels will be romantic and exuberant. As this super-prominent Mars squares off with Jupiter and Neptune in a titanic T-Square during the June 2095 eclipse, it will make the European movement seem like a reborn Marseillaise March for liberty, equality and fraternity. At the same time Uranus moves on from pitiful Pisces into impetuous, activist Aries too. Everyone from visionaries to crusading evangelists in many lands will be out in force in 2095. Preachers and pundits will loudly proclaim the paths to true moral progress. An attitude of adventure will be brought to bear on our ecological troubles too, including a troublesome new rash of great wildfires, and the great Green Revolutionary spirit of 2048 will be further extended to more corners of the globe.

As these mass movements and conflagrations sweep the globe, Uncle Sam along with Western Europe will be eager to enter the international fray in the Fall of 2095 to protect vital interests and shape the times in their own image. The suffering, submerging Indian subcontinent may have severe conflicts, and they may call on The West to help settle them, perhaps to their regret. Any military action that happens in the Fall of 2095 will be swift and effective though, and it will be carried out with enthusiasm (Mars, Saturn and Pluto close grand trine in fire signs, Fall 2095). There will be no quagmire this time. It's possible, however, that any such actions could leave the world *un*-settled. Problems will remain, because poverty, disease and climate impacts will probably get worse. That's because Saturn aligns with Neptune in Virgo in a very powerful conjunction in 2096, which means that not only will we be required by Neptune to sober up and serve suffering humanity, but now Saturn will ask us to focus all of our anxious efforts on it, and support massive collective (and probably unpopular) actions by bureaucrats to provide needed remedies. The momentum of all that ebullient Sagittarian energy in 2095 will now be focused on this monumental task the following year. Much may be accomplished by our institutions and by volunteer efforts alike. The powerful solar eclipse on May 22, 2096 gets Americans into the act, and if the world's powers that uphold poverty and pollution do not relinquish their reign, or if further unrest gets out of hand, Uncle Sam will have no hesitation in brandishing his sword, diplomatic or otherwise, especially if he gets full support from the reformed and revitalized United Nations. In this case, Mars and Jupiter will activate the aggressive Mars in the USA horoscope by aligning together right on top of it, and in the 7th house of war during the eclipse as well as in the horoscope too; a pretty clear indication! Of course, under Saturn in Virgo the usual xenophobic fear of feckless foreigners could endanger or distort American actions. But I think the idealistic influence of Neptune is more likely to raise Saturn to its higher standard this time.

Another distinct trend begins as Pluto enters Taurus in 2096, deepening the realism of the times already indicated by Saturn and Neptune in Virgo. These three planets in earth signs will definitely focus our attention on real problems. They could also signify a new *realpolitik*, if Uncle Sam or other powers such as India and Pakistan decide to be ruthless in some of their actions. This tough realistic diplomacy could be a trend that crops up again in the Spring of 2098. If, however, nations acting together can smooth over unrest and conflict, and bring relief and recovery to struggling people, then productive activity will pick up steam in 2096 and 2097-- as it often does when major planets travel through resourceful Taurus.

The most widely-admired leaders of 2096 and 2097 may not only be the visionaries and crusaders, but also the enterprising tycoons who can team up with world-trotting bureaucrats and politicians to get the global economy humming again. This recovery could mark the start of ambitious, expansive building and organizing plans for the 22nd Century. They may even celebrate their glittering schemes with another crystal palace, like the one at first world's fair in 1851. Preachers may have brought salvation to worried souls in the 2090s, but later in the decade it will also come from the down-to-earth work of the organizers and builders. Neptune, still barely in trine to Pluto, but with both planets now in earth signs, will put firmer practical and realistic foundations underneath expanding world civilization, and what is built will express the beauty and value of the Earth. New sensual and realistic art styles will put the dynamic neo-baroque-style of the times into stronger expression, as a reborn art nouveau architecture turns new buildings into sculptures. Giant earthworks may be constructed. By the Fall of 2097, it looks like a confident, activist, cheery optimism will return to the people and their leaders, as the economy continues to pick up steam and new enterprises are launched.

September 2098 through June 2099 promises to be a time with plenty to celebrate, as this expanding energy stirs among the people of America to assist all the ongoing service and renewal projects around the world. Mars, Jupiter and Neptune lining up in Virgo in the early Fall of 2098, much the way they did as the New Deal of the 1930s was launched, will stimulate some advances in social legislation for justice, health and welfare, and diplomatic breakthroughs may occur as well. Things will be looking up as diligent work for humanity moves forward, with people in all sectors of society working together. Fall of 2098 and Spring of 2099 will be times when vibrant volunteers, bubbling bureaucrats and cheerful corporate captains share the spotlight. Transformed progress will move ahead, steady as she goes, toward the new century in the Spring of 2099.

The next chapter in the life of established society will soon open with Jupiter joining Saturn in Libra for their every-20-year get together in September 2100. Remarkable alignments in Libra precede this planetary event at the Fall Equinox of 2099, as the two majestic chronocraters are joined there by 3 other planets, and Mars and Pluto make a potent conjunction in Taurus. American leaders will be busy laying the diplomatic groundwork for the working revised world order in the years to come. Just how ruthless they might be will be up for grabs, though, as Mars accents the *realpolitik* tendencies of Pluto in Taurus, and with Saturn in Scorpio on tap to oppose Pluto in 2101. Some leaders may then use the opportunity provided by the peoples' new faith in public and corporate organizations to advance their ambitions for power. New alliances may be lining up for some kind of threatened contest to come. But better heads will still likely prevail during the Spring of 2100, as forces of progress and optimism burst forth to launch us into the new era. As we continue to travel through this dangerous portal of transformation in the next century, the great challenge remains to come out on the other side as a sustainable and prosperous world built on Aquarian New Age foundations. The testing is not over, either for America or the world. The new century will open in much the same way as many previous chapters in our story opened. We will meet a time of decision; a true rendezvous with destiny.

Chapter 10

Century 22: Through the Doorway

In our prophetic view of time through the lens of astrology, we've arrived at Century 22. We will go through the doorway to doom or paradise. Which shall it be?

It will be up to Humanity, of course. The generations of that time will decide. My forecast for this century and beyond is not quite as rosy as it was in my first book. I have revised my views because of more careful reading of the signs, and also because things did not go as well as I had hoped in the years since my book was published. We can't provide all the details of what will happen in Century 22 anyway; the charts of billions of individuals and hundreds of nations must be looked at individually to discern how they each may behave in what at this writing is still a century or so in the future. I also can't say just exactly how all these people and nations in their freedom will respond to events, or what they will decide to do. But the main trends and events can be surmised from the principal planetary patterns and cycles, and their context. Here's some of them; and for the rest, successor astrologers can fill in the details as the time approaches. I hope they do.

The planets do provide a decisive doorway moment. The next conjunction in Libra on Sept.18, 2100 of the two great chronocraters of established civilization, Jupiter and Saturn, says it will be challenged and stimulated by the creative outsiders-- as vividly portrayed by Uranus in Aries closely opposing them.

Remember in 2080 these 3 planets were all aligned in Aquarius, and then in 2090 they orbited to an exact T-square in mutable signs. I interpreted that to mean that civilization was reorganized to meet the challenges of a worldwide order, and then was tested by sudden chaos in such potential events as a cyber crisis, economic crash or other conflicts. Now as these 3 planets combine again, climaxing this rare series of planetary events, the question is whether a new society can be built that allows the maximum of peace and beauty, but also at the same time welcomes pioneering innovation by creative, assertive individuals. Will it be able to contain and channel this genius, or will constant rebellion tear it apart? Can civilization itself become a reliable vehicle for change, and can it prepare itself to be the sponsor of worldwide projects, movements and crusades for New Age ideals of beauty, transformation and community? Will the new vision of the transformation of progress developed in the 2090s hamper our technical and scientific abilities, or will it be truly holistic and include all wisdom? Looking back at other middle or climax centuries like this one in the cycle of civilization, I see the need to make sure our full medical knowledge and wellness therapies are kept up to date and available to all.

One sign of what's to come in this initial 20-year period of the new century is given by Neptune, which has returned during the 2100 conjunction to the exact degree of the original Green Revolution in the 1960s, as sponsored by Uranus and Pluto in their alignment in 1966. Returning to where Uranus and Pluto joined together at 17 Virgo, just before they make their next alignment in Taurus in 2103, Neptune promises that the visions of that time will be available to guide the builders of this new society toward a purpose of unfolding human potential. The ideals of peace, ecology and brother-sisterhood and of spirit revival from the sixties revolution can be re-ignited without all the chaotic eruptions that attended the initial outbreak, if we choose. We will sorely need this spiritual and aesthetic green outlook to keep us from backsliding into behavior that damages the climate. Prophets will point us to the right doorway and help society to steer the ship of state toward the harbor of the New Age. On top of this, Uranus and Pluto are already getting into position to push Humanity further toward a still-greener world during their next conjunction in 2103-05. As Century 22 gets under way during the great Jupiter-Saturn conjunction in 2100, North Americans will be the diplomats and deal makers, Japanese the bold leaders, and Iraqis and Iranians will be making big changes and leading others in their region.

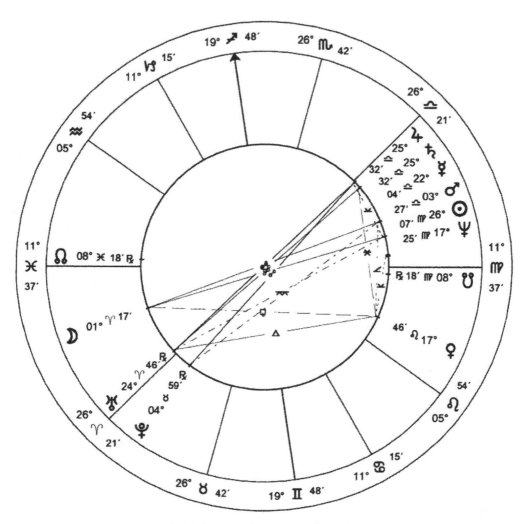

2100 Jupiter-Saturn conjunction
Sept.18, 10:32 PM UT, Washington DC

But some contrary signs indicate that the 22nd century might open just the way the 21st and 20th centuries both began, with a war or a new arms race. Saturn and Pluto oppose each other late in the year 2100 and during 2101, just like they did before 9-11, 2001. It appears that unless we can redefine for ourselves the archetypal meanings of such planets as Mars, Saturn and Pluto, the 22nd Century may not be all peace and light. Certainly, it appears that struggles for power will continue, which is what Saturn and Pluto together indicate. Without a lot of changes in society and culture, which we hope will have been launched in 2080, the kinds of conflicts we still endure as of this writing may not go away. Specifically, in 2100, diplomatic alliances may have been formed during the alignments in Libra that year, especially by Americans, that could come to blows as the 22nd Century begins. It is likely that courage will be summoned among the people to meet some emergency event as the century opens. Conservative administrations may take control. Realistic politicians will be eager to restore a balance of power, and the Balkan Peninsula may be the scene of troubles again. With Neptune in 17 Virgo continuing to remind people of the ideals of the peace movement, we can hope that leaders will be guided to seek resolution without destruction.

Uranus and Pluto in conjunction opens this "baroque" phase in the cycle of civilization soon after 2100, lifting humanity toward the "Full Neptune" at the climax of the cycle as Neptune opposes Pluto about 40 years later. We can expect this revolutionary conjunction in 2103 and 2104 to be less disruptive to the established order than the previous 3 that inaugurated the three cycles of modern revolution, namely the democratic, socialist and greenpeace movements. Instead this conjunction will rev up the engines of civilization to fully build the new world that has been emerging through the past 2 centuries. In the sign Taurus at this baroque period in the great cycle of civilization, the new movement will arouse artists and architects to initiate grand projects that take shape in new realistic, natural and sensuous styles, and will encourage private and public leaders to establish ambitious enterprises. Huge resources shall be summoned for these tasks. We can expect this new phase in civilization to further, rather than reject, the Green Revolution of 1966 and 2048, and to put it on firmer and even more workable foundations. Though all the arrangements and decisions will not be made without some struggles, the aspects look favorable for constructive activities that bring beauty and prosperity to the world during this new revolutionary cycle.

Happening in the very birth degree of modern Humanity, by which I mean the solar eclipse degree of April 26, 1892, and itself joined by Venus during a New Moon at the same time, this Uranus-Pluto alignment in Taurus on April 25, 2104 will indicate Humanity will be geared for practical and lasting results in a sustainable relationship with Mother Earth, and in societies which foster spiritual and creative fulfillment for their people. Nations that have not aligned themselves yet with the Green ideals and with realistic foundations for world peace and sustainability may find their leadership challenged in this conjunction period around 2103-05. People of the Indian subcontinent and Central Asia will rise up to get their nations on board. Americans will act to lead the world toward an age of peace and freedom in accordance with the original ideals of the American Republic, as indicated by Neptune's Return right during this conjunction to its original position at 23 Virgo in the 9th House in the United States Horoscope of July 4 1776. The sesqui-square of the conjunction with Neptune adds a compassionate and spiritual focus to these ideals. North Americans in January 2105 will express this compassionate outreach by forming private and public revolutionary alliances.

These activities will work out for the best if Americans have also become a model for the change it seeks in the world, in their personal and public lives. Neptune's Return to its original USA position in 2103-04 indicates that American society will be challenged as never before to update itself. The survival of the nation may be at stake again over the next decade. The Uranus-Pluto conjunction of 2104 indicates that the economic challenges that began in 2093 will still require more stimulus to lift the American nations out of their economic funk, and to provide all the people of all ethnic backgrounds with what they need to prosper. An even Greener and more ambitious New Deal will be put into force once again to accomplish this renewal of justice and prosperity for all during these new revolutionary years. This time they will be aided by brilliant entrepreneurs from the private sector, as Taurus the sign of independent money indicates. So I expect the stimulus to be successful, and that the economy will roar back to life after 2105.

Weather challenges will happen in 2106 to put this new resolve and this new green economy to the test, as more floods and storms require still further Green reforms, innovations and mitigations by private and public organizations. As Saturn squares Neptune again, the storms may be severe enough to threaten many places in the world. Then, as Neptune crosses into Libra, America will meet its next great foreign challenge in late 2106 and 2107. It doesn't look like a world war is in the offing, as with the last such great challenge in the 1940s. The new FDR will instead be able to lead the world toward the society that the original one envisioned, and he won't have to die before he gets to see it. Neither will the next Martin Luther King. But it does indicate that Americans will also be pulling out some of those war talons in their old great seal and may get involved in some conflicts.

2106-09 will be great years for Americans and other visionary leaders to arouse the world to action in a grand alliance toward liberal green ideals. The planets that got together in 2080, and squared off in May of 2090, will form a grand air-sign alliance in the sky in the Fall of 2109 to help the liberal world rally its resources. The greatest opponent to the liberal alliance may be Iran, which along with its Muslim allies might compete in a new cold war amidst hot desert tempers and temperatures with The West for what kind of vision the new world will be built upon. So, the USA and Iran may be at odds, and the winner may decide the fate of the world. I expect the climax of these challenges and conflicts will come for America when Saturn squares off with Pluto in early 2010, and then as Uranus returns to its original Gemini position in the United States horoscope on July 4, 2011; and that a great moment of peace and reconciliation will come to the USA and its allies in October 2111, as Jupiter and Neptune come together in Libra while in trine to Uranus in Gemini. A new time of consensus and constructive activity will then commence in what

Strauss and Howe called a first turning; a springtime for the nations of the world. In the 2110s the people will be engaged in breaking down barriers and building new alliances across the world to find common ground with each other. Building projects should get underway in a time of renewed prosperity and peace. Beautiful music should be back in vogue. There may even be some trends toward a complacent conformity, but that mood won't prevail for long.

The Crusading Spirit

The tides will swing briefly toward even more caution and conservatism as Uranus moves into Cancer in 2117, and Saturn joins Pluto in Taurus in 2118. But the Jupiter war cycle returns again in 2119, and this time Jupiter in Gemini is joined by Saturn in their next conjunction, which is squared by Mars. Neptune moves on into Scorpio the same year. The 1892 progressed chart of the age gives similar warlike indications for this time. Americans and others around the world may be ready to launch a great crusade. In 2219 it could look like another holy war as The West confronts Islam again. What happens may depend on how backward the Muslim nations still are at this time. In 2120 Southeast Asia may get into the act.

Neptune in Scorpio always indicates an exciting and stormy time. Back in the Middle Ages, the Second Crusade was launched under this transit, while in the Baroque era British rebels set out to establish the first parliamentary republic in England and to colonize America under it. It was just one cycle later that the volunteers marched from Marseilles to create the first French Republic, and from there promised to help any nation seeking to recover its liberty. The powerful citizen armies soon provided Napoleon with everything he needed to spread his empire and his legal codes all over Europe, and he even ventured out to conquer the pyramids. The last time Neptune was in Scorpio from 1957 to 1970 the space race put a man on the Moon, and Europe began its process of unification. Martin Luther King had a dream and climbed the mountaintop, and a movement to bring peace and spiritual enlightenment to a greener world was launched.

So, with these precedents, what can we expect of this latest Neptune in Scorpio crusade? With Jupiter joining Saturn in Gemini as it begins, we will certainly see a drive to spread knowledge and information to those in need, and for fabulous transportation and communication networks to be supported by the Establishment. With Uranus still in Cancer, at first we can expect some strife among neighboring nations, and some desire for protection from foreign enemies. But Scorpio tends toward a spirit of greater unity, even through force of arms if necessary. When the new crusading, transformational spirit is launched in the Fall of 2120, as Mars joins Jupiter and Uranus, we may see swarms of missionaries seeking to make their nations and their world safe for a new order, and a more sustainable system of world commerce will be established. Exploring human potential and opening up to spiritual realities will be in vogue again as Neptune goes deeper into Scorpio later in the decade, with people eagerly spreading enlightenment to more places. This will help create the unity that Neptune in Scorpio seeks. More pioneers will venture into outer space, and dreamers of justice and freedom will seek to make them real everywhere. As

Uranus bursts out into fiery Leo in 2123 and squares off with Neptune in Scorpio, the crusade will ramp up and confront some who resist, and once Pluto enters Gemini in 2127 and Uranus squares it, all caution may be thrown to the winds and troubles will multiply for the new green world, including mutinies and rebellions. As the 2130s get going though, more and more crusaders' dreams will become realized, and some large-scale, heroic efforts will be made. It will be time to make the whole world anew. As Civilization will now be reaching toward the full moon of the cycle, and the fullest expression of our New Age will start to unfold. This is the time to bring all of the ideas and all of the causes and projects of this entire age of civilization to perfection. At this point in the Medieval cycle of civilization, it was said there was so much happening it would make your head spin.[85] I think what is being done in the 2130s and 40s will surely turn some heads too.

Coming to Fruition

In the later 2130s, people will be feeling more exuberant and relaxed under Neptune in Sagittarius and Uranus in Libra. The liberated energies of a transformed world will be released as people expand and deepen personal and spiritual relationships and break down old barriers and taboos. As Neptune moves further into Sagittarius and approaches its "full moon" opposition to Pluto in 2137 through 2141, people will feel keenly the sensibilities of life. Non-conformity will be back in vogue, and people will be eager to take adventurous voyages and explore beyond safe horizons. It will seem like no frontier will be too far away to breach, including the heroic journey to enlightenment and expanding awareness of the spirit world-- the true next frontier. Others will take the crusading spirit into its older direction of religious evangelism, and a new generation of fanatics may be abroad across the land.

With Neptune in Sagittarius wider perspective, bold curiosity and a golden sense of order and balance will gradually replace the crusading spirit. Post-modern art will reach fulfillment, and the aims of New Age creators and builders will take clear shape and form. The foundations for many New Age temples and the plans for beautiful green cities will be laid out. Just as Neptune opposes Pluto the chronocraters will conjoin in Aquarius in January 2040, giving a mighty accent to the sparkling novelty of mushrooming inventions and innovations. It will seem like the old age of progress has come back for a while, and established leaders will be very keen to pour out knowledge to the people and reform education for everyone. This conjunction of Jupiter and Saturn along with Mercury in 17 degrees Aquarius, just where the 1892 progressed Mars turned stationary-retrograde in 1963, along with the momentous climax of the civilization cycle as Neptune opposes Pluto, will be strong signs that the dawning New Age is coming to fruition.

What may be a still greater milestone lies ahead in 2165. Perhaps it may even be famous among the people by then. Uranus and Neptune together is always a great white hope, like a beacon of light beaming brightly in the distance, the shining city on the hill. Before we get there though, we'll have a time of steady progress and heroic, hard work as we unfold all the plans and projects unleashed in 2140, followed by another time of restless

---

[85] Kenneth Clark, Civilization, Harper and Row, 1969, p.44

upheaval and change in the mid-2150s. As in 2154-55 Uranus reaches it first opposition to Pluto since the Green Revolution over a century before, the people will rise up again to challenge authorities and repressions in a blizzard of progressive proposals promised by a horde of new prophets. It seems as if humanity always needs a revolution every once in a while, since power gets corrupted and complacent. So, reformers will revel in revealing all the rough spots in the world order, eager to expose all its shortcomings and making needed changes in the halls and boardrooms of power. Many ideas will be bruited about which will be useful blueprints to act upon once we reach that city on the hill in 2165. North Americans will be ready to rise to the occasion in 2155, as Pluto is joined by Jupiter in Gemini as it opposes Uranus. If any arrogant leaders are still around in America in this dawning New Age, they might well succeed again in sending their boys into battle somewhere in the world. But we can hope that with Pluto in Gemini and Uranus in Sagittarius, this could be mostly a battle of ideas this time.

I see the next Jupiter-Saturn conjunction in 2159 in Scorpio, which will be in trine to its planetary ruler Pluto in Cancer, as deepening the foundations of the New Age being established. As the new temples rise and the green cities unfold and thrive, abundant place will be made for the romantic spirit and the desire of folks to connect. Excellent financial investments will be made, and organizations will be placed in talented and brilliant hands to make the trains run on time and our environment healed. Pluto will now have moved into outstanding prominence, and in the sign Cancer will focus all of Humanity on further restoring our Earth home for all species, and also on transforming our personal home and family life so that it nourishes the spirit instead of confining it as it has for millennia. We can expect our New Age ideas to transform ancient notions of patriotism into a higher purpose than national power and status. As the New Age becomes more of a concrete reality the people will be beautifying their local neighborhoods and towns instead of fighting for their country. These are the promises of Pluto in the New Age if we have sufficiently transformed ourselves. The 2160s provide us with the opportunity to actualize both the highest ideals of the 1960s and the romantic dreams and visions of the 2060s. This will be a profound moment when Humanity grounds itself again after our 2700-year adventure of conquering Nature, as we rediscover ourselves as connected to All in all our activities.

We will get more organized as Neptune passes into Aquarius in 2162, and reforms will flow like honey through our halls of power. Sometimes people may even knock over a few traces as they feel the walls to all possibilities falling. Anticipation and enthusiasm among the people will be contagious. Then Uranus follows Neptune into the sign Aquarius almost two years later, and the great cosmic event will be at hand. The golden light of the New Age will now be in full view. Remember, as Uranus comes closer toward its conjunction with Neptune, old conflicts that have simmered and occasionally broken out in previous decades are settled. We can expect conclaves of diplomats to assemble as Neptune crosses into Aquarius in 2162, most of them sincerely dedicated to building a new world of peace. Americans may take the lead in this, but Iran may be dragged kicking and screaming to the table. As Jupiter joins Uranus in January, and then Neptune in February 2163, breakthroughs for world harmony will happen. New opportunities for freedom and greater justice for all peoples and nations will quickly unfold. Remember this conjunction of **Uranus and Neptune in Aquarius in January 2165** comes exactly one 2140-year Age in the Precession Cycle since the time of Christ. As such, we can view the chart for this conjunction as in some sense THE Horoscope of the New Age. What does it say? Does it live up to the promise?

All conjunctions of Uranus and Neptune live up to their promise, even if some disappointments follow afterward. But it always indicates profound changes that are beneficial in the long run. Happening in the 7th degree of Aquarius, the 2165 conjunction aligns with the very degree where Mars turned stationary-direct in the progressed 1892 Chart of Humanity in 2022. You may remember that I entitled this the return of progress. So, we can predict that the reforms and revolutions that happen around 2165 will bring to full fruition what the leaders and activists envisioned all those years ago in the 2020s, and perhaps go far beyond their wildest dreams. Benefits of prosperity from this Aquarian Revolution will flow freely and easily to the people, who will share huge reservoirs of compassion with their fellows-- just as if they were themselves holding the urn from which Aquarius pours out the healing waters for Humanity. The Moon's position conjoining Jupiter in Pisces on the day of this conjunction promises this much. Those storied mystic crystal revelations will flow forth in abundance now in this time of romantic, bright inspiration and spiritual discovery, as the two most transcendent and creative planets in our universe combine forces and evoke the highest ideals of Humanity and the Spirit World. The visions we need to create the world of our dreams will vividly come to life and inform all our actions and plans.

But as I remarked at the start of this chapter, many of the key charts of the 22nd Century, such as the one for the climactic Neptune-Pluto opposition, and this one for the Aquarian Age conjunction too, show that if we haven't learned to pursue our aims in peace, we may still be in the habit of coming to blows. Mars and Saturn are in exact conjunction in Capricorn in this Horoscope of the New Age, and opposing Pluto, as if we are still likely to bring some baggage of old conflicts with us as we reach the other side of this golden marker in time. If powerful potentates are not restrained by the people, they could impose new burdens of bloodshed upon us in years to come. Regressive tyranny from the Middle East could still threaten us.

But this conjunction of Mars and Saturn could also indicate violence strictly restricted and controlled or judiciously channeled. It also suggests that enormous and gloriously-inspired artistic, constructive energy will flow toward building the incomparable green Emerald Cities and New Age temples that everywhere will rise and marvel the world in this period. Nothing so wonderful will have been done since the Taj Mahal, St. Peter's and St. Paul's were built during the previous era like this one of around 1650-1660. This time around, our lives will be lighted up in virtual realms too, and in rich, inward libraries of wisdom as well. But ideals were also betrayed by power seekers at that previous time in the 1650s and 60s, and will be again-- if we can't restrain ourselves

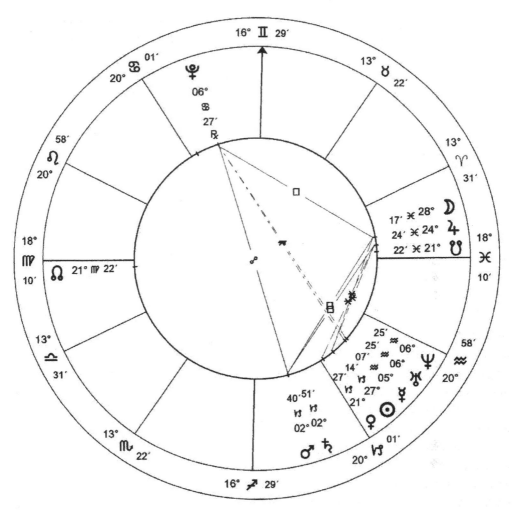

Uranus-Neptune Conjunction

January 17, 2165, cast for 2 AM UT, Washington DC. "Horoscope of the New Age"

and live according to the New Age principles that we have learned, and which great teachers are even now spreading out for Humanity at this very inspirational time.

Just as I predicted for the previous Uranus-Neptune conjunction in the early 1990s, this one in 2165 will usher in the Next World Order. By the 2080s much will have been done to improve our global security system, and a new world-wide financial and commercial network with a new world currency will at least have been considered, and perhaps even adopted, in the early 2040s. Along the way, local and national priorities will also have asserted themselves. In 2165 another great stride will be made in what is the principal project of our age begun in 1892, to develop world order and government with self-determination for all nations and peoples. In the sign Aquarius, this could well mean developing the first world parliament. More progress will be made toward a truly worldwide Aquarian financial system of commerce that is well regulated and dedicated to the social good of all.

Just what it means that **Pluto will be in exact quincunx, or at a 150-degree angle, with the Aquarian Age conjunction**, will be a matter of much discussion by astrologers before it happens. All the building, all the reforms, and all the reorganizations going on will run up against much that is incompatible with them. Powerful world organizations will find that they must respect the needs of the people and the planet for sustainable life. The conflicts between what we build anew and what we cherish from our traditions will promote a fruitful interaction between them, as we blend each side of the equation with the other. We will need to let go of any excess patriotism and nationalism so we can create the global foundations of a new world of justice and freedom for all. Demands of individuals for property rights and free enterprise will need to be placed within the context of an Aquarian humanitarian social system that pours out benefits equally for all.

The powerful Next World Order will constantly be challenged by the prerogatives of individuals and nations, but this will keep it perpetually honest, respectful of human rights, and safely controlled within the bounds of its proper authority. So although this quincunx to Pluto in Cancer may be difficult for the sometimes-stubborn and dogmatic Aquarian powers-that-be to deal with, that they *must* deal with it is a good thing. Ironically, the powerful Pluto in 7 degrees Cancer, perhaps the symbol of all the priorities that could conflict with this Next World Order, will align with the exact degree it last occupied when the League of Nations was formed in 1919 and 1920, implying that a world body that provides protection and security will be in vogue again, even as it challenges our attachments to our heritage and homelands. This connection emphasizes again that world unity, *with* proper respect for all people and local control, is the primary purpose and goal of our new global civilization that became a virtual reality for the first time back in those days.

We saw how world peace and order was restored in Vienna in 1815 while the conjunction of Uranus and Neptune approached, and yet was challenged immediately in 1821 during the exact conjunction by the new upsurge of liberal nationalism. We saw how right away ethnic conflicts became the bane of the New World Order established in 1991-1993 under Uranus-Neptune, and how religious and racist terrorism brought a feverish pain to the new global brain. Yugoslavia broke apart in 1992 and 1993, followed by a genocidal tribal massacre in Rwanda in 1994. Fanatic Islamic terrorism unleashed its fury on the world's capitol of New York City too, first in 1993 and then in 2001. In the 2010s many reactionaries ascended to power everywhere to stem the flow of refugees from revolutions and ethnic conflicts, which also pushed the British toward breaking with Europe. This time in 2165, Pluto's prominent position in Cancer, exactly quincunx the Aquarian conjunction, practically guarantees that the Next World Order will be challenged immediately by those who want to maintain their local control and national identity, and that this challenge will continue and be ongoing for decades. An ethnic or nationalist war could break out early in 2166, as Mars turns stationary direct in Cancer and aligns with Pluto and opposes Saturn, providing the new world parliament and its peace-keeping system with its first great test. Americans will likely be involved. This new conflict will wrap up in 2167 and 2168, as the new system takes hold and the people rise up and demand that peace and harmony be restored with all sides given their due.

As Saturn passes over Neptune and Uranus in Aquarius and brings the decade of the 2160s to its climactic end, Humanity will seek to make all the dreams of the preceding century real. Major events can be expected as Jupiter swings around to Leo and opposes all the planets in Aquarius in 2169. It will be quite some fireworks show! Inspired actions and projects will explode everywhere. As events continue to unfold after this glorious time, we'll discover whether we can hold the vision and keep the new age spirit alive in the years to come, or whether it just dithers away in useless arguments and cynical escapism in the 2170s and 80s, especially among a new disengaged generation. Probably some power struggles and rebellions can be expected in 2174, so how well the Next World Order keeps the peace and provides for change might get another test then. Readers can keep track of further possible rough spots for the Next World Order to handle for the rest of the century as indicated by Mars stationary in **Appendix F.**

The era's inventive genius will get more support when Jupiter, Saturn and Mercury join in another fabulous conjunction in Gemini in 2179. With Mars and Pluto conjoined in Cancer, we can expect the environmental movement to rev up, with improvements made to home and family life and swift communication and full education provided for all. With Moon conjunct Neptune in Pisces in the chart for the conjunction, we may see some advancement and generous support given for spiritual projects and for psychic kinds of communication as well as the technical kinds. Americans may take some generous, arrogant and probably successful actions abroad. The lingering baggage of conflict may come out again during a rebellious and cantankerous period around 2185-86. In January 2185, people who face harder times will rise up in an enthusiastic revolt, possibly motivated by religious zeal, but gloom and doom will make a comeback if it fails. Muddled management may make for a noisy and chaotic rattle of escapist rebellion through the land. At the same time though, public projects will be launched to stave off recession and provide for greater security for the people. We could call it the New Age New Deal.

I would expect the gloomy mood to lift rather soon, because as Century 22 ends civilization will move into its next phase. The social and economic provisions of this New Deal will bring back prosperity quickly. We will know how to do this by now, no matter where we are in any cycle. Neptune will begin its new cycle in Aries in 2189-2190, uplifting all the muddled moods and arousing the people into confident, feisty and reckless action again. Neptune will also be moving into what I call its rococo trine with Pluto, bringing a more optimistic and generous attitude among the people in the following years. As the trine continues up through the 2270s, much of the next century will be relaxed, complacent and enjoyable. The urge to conquer and do great things may not be as strong then, but the momentum from the 22nd Century's great projects will still resonate as the world blooms with peace and happiness and the new Aquarian Age wisdom is spread widely among the people. In 2199, Century 22 ends with a glorious bang, and with one more Aquarian conjunction of Jupiter and Saturn. Great blessings and climactic achievements will happen, as if the world is in a race to achieve all that it wants before the splendid century is over. There will be power struggles as it happens, but it looks like all will be resolved, and the New Age will continue to unfold its merry way forward.

Chapter 11

Itinerary for the New Age

Now that we have passed the Aquarian Conjunction of 2165 in our cosmic-eyed view of the future, what can we expect for the New Age that follows? What will the world be like after we have crossed over this border of time? If you think such a question is irrelevant, because it's so far in the future, just remember that if reincarnation is real, you may be back again and again in these times.

The famous song "Aquarius" speaks of harmony, sympathy and trust, of liberated minds bringing golden dreams to life, and of no further forces of derision. Whether the New Age will actually act out all these traits of Aquarius or not, we don't really know. But we know that a New Age has dawned. The spiritual and human potential movements that were launched in the 20th century have provided Humanity with all the means we need to unfold our highest qualities, if we turn our attention to them and use them. In the New Age we will benefit from greater understanding among all people. Global society will see the races increasingly blend into one and national borders become more fluid. We will have greater access than any people ever to all the resources of the spiritual realm, as well as to all the history and artistic treasures that were hidden and buried from us not so long ago-- which also remind us of how modern times have fallen short. We have all the physical, mental and spiritual tools we need to be fully realized human beings, and we have a new will to use them. We will have learned all the skills of management and global governance that we need to keep the peace and provide freedom and access for all people to the levers of power. We will have learned to live in peace and harmony with Mother Earth, and we'll have abundance in all things without excess and waste, and without destroying other living beings or the climate and environment that we all depend on. Having boldly traveled across the Valley of Transition, and then ascended and reached the climactic summit at the half-way point of Our Age in the Splendid 22nd Century, we have learned all that we need to survive and overcome our greatest obstacles.

The ignorance, anxiety, fear and greed within humans will not all disappear all at once in the New Age, however. Crime and tyranny will still threaten us, we'll still need some laws and police forces to protect us for some millennia to come. But we will have built the foundation from which further human development can be achieved. We may eventually gain some help from ETs, if it's true that they have been visiting us already, and that they are indeed the beings we expect them to be who have passed through the light barrier and become beings of light themselves. If they deem us ready to learn their ways, then we will join the Galactic Federation. But meanwhile, our own resources are already enough to build on. The rosy vision of paradise I presented in my previous book in the chapter entitled A Greener World will still be unfolding throughout the New Age, although perhaps not fully manifested so soon as the 22nd Century. I spoke there of the glowing but oft-forgotten flame of the Modern Spirit of Liberation that launched us on the path to the

New Age when the outer invisible planets began to be discovered at the end of the 18th Century. We can always tune into that spirit of Revolution anytime we choose as it continues to grow and spread across the Earth and arouse us to true freedom. Leaving aside trivial pursuits and arguments that numb and distract us, we can focus on our real desire to create love and beauty everywhere, as we tune in to the global spirit that resonates throughout the land and realize ever more clearly that the Divine Spirit is everywhere and within every being. Just as devoted followers of Christ were inspired by church bells that pealed across the farms and towns of Europe, or as Muslims heard the calls to worship that emanated from their minarets, or as Buddhists and Hindus heard the gongs and bowls that ring out from their temples, so in the New Age the World Spirit will be heard and felt by the people as it rings forth from all the ancient and New Age temples, through all the high-tech invisible links, and from all the reverberations that echo through our consciousness from our contact with psychic and spiritual realms and into the core of our connected Being.

Scanning the Map: Completing Our Age

As we review the highlights during the New "Aquarian" Age in the Precession Cycle as it unfolds over the next 2000 years, we know that they will follow the phases in the cycle of civilization as given in Chapter 2 and in **Appendix D**. In <u>Horoscope for the New Millennium</u> I also laid out the Cosmic Clock of Civilization in Chapter 5, featuring the Great Uranus Cycle. As each new 493-year cycle begins as defined by conjunctions of the two planets of civilization Neptune and Pluto, the Chart for that Age describes its main features. Uranus moves 1/8 of the way backwards at each conjunction. This creates an almost 4000-year cycle, starting with the triple conjunction of the three outer planets which marks an Axis Age of Enlightenment and a new beginning for Humanity. As Uranus traverses this long cycle it grants each 493-year Age a definite style and purpose, according to the general principles of astrology cycles. Saturn also travels backwards about ¼ of the way at each new age, giving that age a resonance with the one 2000 years before. The positions of the other planets in each chart of the age fill out all the other indications for each age. Throughout each 493-year cycle, Uranus makes conjunctions, oppositions and other aspects to the two great planetary carriers of Humanity, and each time it does this, eruptions of new ideas send the civilization of that Age into new directions. Some unique planetary patterns may happen along the way, including the Jupiter-Saturn conjunctions that launch us into a new element every 200 years or so, as we see right away as we begin our review of the rest of the Age of Aquarius.

In the 23rd and 24th Centuries, our current Age of Humanity will finalize and complete itself. In 2219 Jupiter and Saturn will align in the next great mutation into water signs, so that we'll be more preoccupied with unfolding our feelings and nourishing our souls than during the previous period that emphasized the intellectual air element, although the Uranus-Neptune cycle in air signs continues. Artists and designers will create more pleasant styles, and nations will form new diplomatic combinations and alliances, as the next cycle of revolution begins in 2221-22. With Uranus joining Pluto in Libra to start this new cycle, new media will emerge to promote pleasure and harmony among the people. The mystic vibrations of Neptune in Gemini will be joined to the planets of revolution Uranus and Pluto simultaneously through an expansive rococo trine in 2222. This will be a rare opportunity to bring more delicacy of feeling and fulfilling peace back into modern life.

In 2249-2253 the World System could experience tests to the new international order established around 2165 as Uranus opposes Neptune, and we could also experience new realms of musical and artistic creativity. Demands for more reform will come during a time of restless change and upheaval in c.2269 (especially in October), as new enlightened rulers emerge out of conflict to shift the global financial system. Then a full flowering of buoyant, delicate styles and vast interactions of ideas will sparkle across the globe in 2881-82, as the transcendental trinity of planets form a beautiful grand trine in air signs. Important prophets and creators will be born then too. Higher visions of Humanity and its powers of Divine Mind will unfold as never before and impart themselves into the halls of power as Saturn in Sagittarius joins the three outer planets in a kite formation or peace symbol. It should be an amazing time to be alive.

Another climax is still ahead, however, for just like in the 18th Century, new ideas of how to restructure our lives will have been floated about in salons and convocations for decades, and a new eruption of revolution, a generation of revolutionary change, will unfold from the visions of the grand trine as the 23rd Century ends in 2300. Seeds shall be planted at this time for the Age of Light yet to come, in which humans may travel to other dimensions and reach enlightenment as never before. In the signs Virgo and Pisces, with one in the series of these 5 Uranus-Pluto oppositions happening in the critical sixties revolutionary "stillness of spirit" 17th degrees, this revolution will further the 1960s human potential movement to release new powers of health and spiritual awareness. A new generation will break down the walls between themselves and experience fully the joys of communal relationship. As potent Pluto in Pisces is awakened to a fever pitch by Uranus opposing it in Virgo at this turn into the 24th Century, I foresee these new romantics breaking all boundaries to adventure and emotional experience, which had too often been kept under the covers during the 23rd century when the rational air signs so predominated. This revolution, therefore, will be primarily spiritual and cultural, but will be felt throughout society, and changes to the Establishment will be made in order to further the aims of the revolutionaries. And there's always the chance in this period of the civilization cycle that a leader will arise out of the movement who sets the course and plants the seeds within society for things to come. Instead of a new Napoleon, he or she could be someone like Constantine who institutionalizes principles of New Age religion within the state. Whether this would make it too repressive is the question that will be raised. This new reign may not last, though, as romantic impulses reach their climax when Neptune squares Pluto around 2310, plus more upheavals that challenge both old and new authorities in 2327. These events could seriously affect the world government system, which may not be able to satisfy all the demands that have been placed upon it. It may become too oppressive and rigid, neglecting human rights and resisting the new ideas it needs to truly dispense justice for all. Protests will happen that could reduce its power in 2327.

As the dissolving sextile appears in 2337 it will be time for the Age of Modern Maturing Humanity that began in 1892 to start falling apart. And yet as this sextile happens, Uranus will simultaneously join Neptune in its second conjunction in Aquarius since the first one lifted Humanity up into the New Age in 2165. This could mean that our dissolution proceeds more smoothly than usual. During this time many systems could crumble, but inventive new arrangements will be made to replace them and return more power to the people. Altogether this could be most fortunate and give the waning days of our Age a good review in the chronicles of history. Walls could fall at this time between peoples and even solar systems and universes, as huge migrations accelerate in the 2340s, and there may be many refugees from disasters and the failures in the world system. New changes in currency will be made, and it's possible that ET visits will intensify our connections to galactic civilizations, perhaps even psychic ones. But if this is too fanciful a prospect to entertain, then perhaps you might like the idea that migrations out to planets in the solar system could be expanding in this time, because during all of these Aquarian conjunctions among visible and invisible planets since 2020, much progress toward living in outer space will have been made. Meanwhile, as the "realist" conjunction of Uranus and Pluto in Taurus combines with a Jupiter-Saturn alignment in watery, protective Cancer in 2358, people will be preoccupied with property and survival. Rapid dissolving structures will rattle peoples' security as well as open new opportunities. With Neptune in Aries at this difficult time, competition and civil unrest could increase, and individualist activism may bring down many authorities. But wealth could swell among those lucky few who are sharp and greedy enough to make the most of their opportunities, and new kinds of industry (enhanced by our recent activities in outer space) will be exploding that change every aspect of our lives.

The Next Horoscope of Humanity: The Age of Light

When the next conjunction of Neptune and Pluto comes along around in about the years 2384 and 2385, it spells doom for many of the structures of society. Many nations and powers within our global civilization will fall. We can't go back, however, to a world of separate nations and countries; transition to a global civilization, effected in the cycle now ending, will be permanent. But the world system constructed in the 22nd Century, and which took shape at the time of the Aquarian conjunction in 2165, will undergo major changes and reorganizations, as powers and structures within it are swept away.

In this book, I'll cast the Chart of the Age of Humanity that begins with Neptune's conjunction to Pluto on May 21, 2385 for the solar eclipse on May 10 of that year. With Uranus in square to the conjunction, and Saturn aligned with it, I expect catastrophic change as this New Age of Humanity begins, somewhat similar to the time when Rome fell in the 5th Century CE. The eclipse chart suggests that the government of Iran is particularly due for a huge and permanently-fatal tumble. Uranus is directly opposite the Midheaven in Tehran, and in no other world capital is this opposition remotely as close! This should be good news, and it will likely mean liberation for the whole Middle East region soon after this conjunction. Meanwhile, the west coast of the United States may become the new nation of Pacifica. But if by now it has already done so, it may be due for a fatal tumble too since Uranus is on the Midheaven there in this chart. The entire United States of America is certainly liable to emerge from this new age of transition in a drastically new form from how we know it as of this writing. Overall, we can certainly predict that 2385 will be the "end of the world as we know it," but we'll feel just fine.

I expect things during this next 493-year cycle to be highly unstable and chaotic on many occasions, especially in its first century, and it will be a period of vast movements of peoples. With Mars squaring Saturn in the chart, I expect continual conflict of some sort will happen. But this will not be a new Dark Age, but the **Age of Light**. As it unfolds, the people will adapt to increased instability and movement. Humanity has already learned to live in a state of nearly constant revolution during much of the last cycle, so many of us will be well-prepared to live in a more airy and fluid world. Although life will be less structured and more spontaneous, new ideas will come to us easily, and we will launch ourselves into an age of constant enlightenment and discovery. Conflicts will more likely be battles of ideas rather than of weapons. We will learn to contact the Higher Mind directly, and everyone will develop immediate access to the wisdom of the spirit and all knowledge everywhere.

These are all implications from Uranus in a 9th house position in its great 4000-year cycle, and from the other aspects in this chart for this new age of 493 years. It strongly suggests that contact and exchange with extraterrestrials will come out into the open and grow, and that we'll gain greater access and relationship with beings from the afterlife and the other side. Many spiritual organizations and religions will be developed to educate us into this new reality over the next 493 years, and this will start right away, since the next religious dispensation in the 600 year cycle will happen just 40 years after this Age of Light begins, when Uranus and Neptune come into opposition between 2421 and 2422 in the signs of Virgo and Pisces. It's safe to say that in the Age of Light we will depend more on New Age religion and spirituality to guide our lives than on organizations and governments. The Age of Light will be a continual spiritual exploration, and the whole society and all its people will be on a difficult and ambitious hero's journey to enlightenment. Interestingly enough, about 5 years before the new dispensation, a great mutation of Jupiter and Saturn occurs, opening a new fire-element emphasis. Fire is the source of light, so the people will be enthusiastic and evangelistic in spreading the new religion and eager to keep the fires burning. Of course, fire can turn things into ashes too, which illustrates again how unstable and insecure this age might be.

As this new, new age religion gets under way, the E.T.s will have to decide when we have matured enough for contact and ready to learn how to teleport between star systems and dimensions. Such developments will depend of course on whether the E.T.s have really contacted us, whether they can really break through the speed of light ("break the light barrier"), and on whether as the Celestine Prophecy forecast during the inspirational Uranus-Neptune conjunction in the early 1990s, that we will actually be able someday to come and go between earthly and spiritual realms. It's at least safe to say that the new religion will probably teach that we can, and that many will believe they are being visited and can learn these skills. And it's possible that science might develop teleportation through quantum entanglement, or passing through worm holes, or whatever means will be invented, reverse-engineered or taught to us by the E.T.s. If science devotes itself to this task as fully as it did during the last 493-year cycle to Artificial Intelligence and the goal of turning us all into cyborgs, it will eventually make just as much rapid progress. And this new task will be much more valuable to Humanity, and much more in keeping with the fiery, adventurous spirit of the New Age of Light.

In any case, Uranus in the 9th House indicates we'll be ready to explore the solar system around us, but there's not a whole lot of reason to do so unless we are also learning to breach the light barrier and travel further out to the stars. Why should we be content just to mine a few asteroids and moons in our own solar system, when mining anything at all on Earth is going to be outdated anyway-- because we will have learned that mined resources run out, and because mining anything will have become too toxic for the sensibilities we will have developed since the Green Revolution? Why export that outdated industry to a few moons and asteroids? How much of our excess population can we really re-locate and export into space, if the only places we can go are a few smaller and colder places like Mars or the Moons of Saturn? I think the people will tire of such projects really quickly and will prefer these more ambitious and perhaps outlandish goals, whether they are only imaginary or truly possible.

The E.T.s will hesitate to help us, though, and we may not be able to help ourselves in these tasks either, unless we have eliminated both tyranny and war in our outer circumstances here on Earth, in *all* countries within our global civilization, and replaced them with peace, freedom, compassionate service and economic security for all people everywhere. Fortunately, in an age of constant change and abundant wisdom and knowledge, it will be harder at least for oppressive tyrants to reign and take away our liberties. The chart for the new cycle certainly suggests that disruption of old ideas and outdated structures will be as continuous during the Age of Light as they were back in the 1960s. We will just need inner peace and competent management to handle this more mobile, restless, insecure and chaotic society. We'll need more liberation within, and well as without. An amazing connection that will help us in this task is shown in the chart for the new cycle, because Uranus at the time of the May 2385 conjunction will be in exactly 16-plus tropical degrees of Virgo, the "sixties" and stillness of spirit degree.

I am not making this up, just because I liked the sixties! Uranus really *IS* in 17 Virgo in this chart, the exact degree in which it made its revolutionary conjunction to Pluto in 1966, the first invisible-planet conjunction ever to be experienced. This extraordinary coincidence *defines* the New Age of Light as a direct descendant of the sixties movements and the Green Revolution. Uranus in 17 Virgo will also be on the Midheaven in California and the West Coast of North America in this new Chart of Humanity, indicating that this

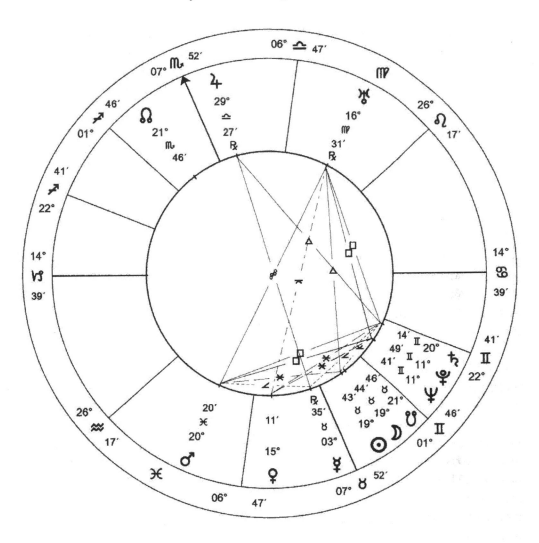

area could once again be the center of this spiritual revolution. This connection of the Age of Light to the 1966 conjunction suggests that the spiritual technology first explored in the 1960s, and further applied during the many awakening periods since then, will still be needed to achieve peace and freedom within. Since Virgo rules technology, and since Uranus is also placed in the 9th House of wisdom in the chart for the Age of Light, spiritual technology will be continually invented and developed during this quest. That technology will certainly include psychedelics, which were the means by which a new spiritual awareness burst through our commercial and tech-obsessed society in the 1960s. Remember, however, that as long as we are so immature psychologically and spiritually that we still *need* to use psychedelic chemicals, potions and plants to find inner peace and freedom and discover the spiritual universe, many people won't be able to safely use them without the proper set and setting.

Here are a few highlights from the cosmic map of time during the Age of Light. After economic disruption and reform in 2440, Uranus makes an interesting milestone on

June 6, 2444, the 500th anniversary of D-Day in World War Two, when it enters Gemini on that day. It indicates that key events will happen then in the relationship between North Americans and the world. Then a marvelous triple sextile of the three transcendental planets within a trine of Uranus and Neptune develops in the early 2450s that reminds me how the world emerged from depression and war in the mid-20th century. The new religion will be quickly unfolding then, and it will offer hope for the peace and freedom so desperately needed in this and restless age. The 2480 period will be another time of revolutionary breakthroughs, and a new shining city on the hill beckoning from the Uranus-Neptune conjunction in spiritual Pisces will be reached early in the next century in 2508, bringing a new world order and wonderful spiritual wisdom that restructures the world out of the ruins of the previous chaotic 120 years. This will put civilization on a new footing, but new conflicts will emerge from it too, including religious ones. What really propels the New Age of Light into orbit, however, will be the T-square in mutable signs starting with Uranus in 17 Virgo squaring Neptune in 2552, and then opposing Pluto in 2554 to indicate a generation of revolutionary change. If the Age of Light is able to contain all this chaos, it will be a miracle. But there's no limit to possible discovery at this time too. And as Neptune squares Pluto at that time, all of our potential for daring and possibly dangerous romantic adventure will be released then, and throughout the rest of the 2550s.

As the climactic high point of the Age of Light is reached in the early 2630s, with Neptune in spiritual and dreamy Sagittarius opposing Pluto in clever Gemini, more great schools and temples for the New Age Religion will be raised. At the same time, Jupiter and Saturn form their first in a new series of conjunctions in earth signs in 2636. This should bring the boundless and restless adventure of the first half of the Age of Light back down to earth more often in the second half. People will put more priority again on material security and mastering technology. The wisdom quests of the age will aim toward more pragmatic goals. But Uranus will again be in Virgo to square the planets of civilization during in the 2630s in yet another terrifying transcendental T-square, and this indicates that chaos will continue to disturb the following few decades at least. Wars may even erupt in the early 2650s, if you can "imagine" that! I'm sure the people will prefer to imagine peace instead, and more revolutionary change will follow in 2661 that topples some of these reckless war-like regimes. But when on Feb 15, 2676, Saturn and Pluto make exactly the same square from exactly the same degrees that they made on September 1, 1939, with Mars stationary making a hard aspect to them, just as it did then, it's difficult to escape the conclusion that another war may be upon us then, and it's hard to believe that it won't involve some kind of star wars too. But things will be settled quickly, and the age of peace and light will be restored in 2680 when Uranus and Neptune join together again just as they both begin a new cycle in Aries. The world order will be reshaped anew and infused with spiritual light so that war won't ever happen again; or at least not for a long, long time. Instead, we'll see lots of blessings of light distributed to all the world's peoples in the next century in a disciplined and constructive way, bolstered with greater material foundations. We may be ably assisted in this task by those from other dimensions and worlds, especially in the 2760s and 2790s. Finally though, reckless activism will return in a big way as the

29th Century begins, since in 2806 the three planets of civilization will orbit into still another rare and treacherous T-Square of the kind that seems to mark this unstable Age, and once again all the old ideas and values will be challenged. The next mutation of Jupiter and Saturn in air signs will follow in 2815, shifting preoccupations back to airy intellectual arguments and ideas, and thus removing the stabilizing earth-sign influence that had brought some order to this restless age. After this, the usual dissolution returns in a big way, and chaos will become uncontrollable. Yet at near end of the cycle in 2850 new seeds for the age to come will be implanted deep in the hearts of all humanity, even amidst all the strife and rebellion, by a new Saturn, Uranus and Neptune conjunction, and these seeds will bloom profusely in the years beyond. It will seem like a new Emerald City is being planned even while all the old cities are collapsing around it. Finally, as the next Neptune and Pluto comes in 2878, the lights will dim, and this restless and chaotic age will fall to depression and revolution in 2915.

The Two Final Cycles of Civilization Within the Aquarian Age

A more stable age of civilization will follow, as the wisdom imparted from the previous one inspires us to build a culture and society that will be the golden climax of the entire Aquarian Age, since Uranus reaching the 11th House position in relation to Neptune and Pluto in conjunction in 2878 is like being in Aquarius, the 11th sign of the zodiac. We can call it the **Age of Consummation**. I described it well in my first book in Chapter 5. Suffice to add here that it could be a rather narrowly-focused and complacent age, but also a generally comfortable and easy-going one, and fully devoted to the new spiritual values bequeathed to it by the Age of Light. Humanity will take many sighs of relief after the restless and romantic times of the previous cycle. This Age of Consummation and Peace will be well and securely established by about 120 years after the conjunction. Saturn in Pisces in the chart for this age stands out, indicating that like the corresponding Medieval period 2000 years before religion will prevail over the state and impose some uniformity of doctrine, but it will have to defend its authority later on as secular power rises again. Whereas in Medieval times those knights in shining armor followed a code of chivalry as they sought the lady's hand, this age will see salons, convocations and associations develop a code of friendship and fraternity among all persons, each one seen as a full manifestation of God and the Earth Spirit. Although genuine intimacy may be in shorter supply at times, individual rights and creative powers will be fully celebrated. The wisdom of the group will be supplemented by the glory of the individual as the sub-age of Leo unfolds-- and this is echoed by Uranus in Leo in the Age of Consummation Chart.

When the next religious dispensation arrives in 3024, with Uranus and Neptune joining in 7 degrees Taurus, the values of peace, stability and communion with the Earth Spirit will take hold in every corner of every land. The global spirit surrounding and enveloping the planet in love and devotion will become deeply rooted in the very hearts of all people and in every institution. The temples that rise to great heights in the 32nd Century will be well engineered and crafted and will make the Spirit accessible to all. The dramatic myths and glorious, resonant images that come forth in this age will contain and summarize all the heroic and romantic stories gathered through all ages of Humanity and weave them into a grand synthesis. Forms and archetypes will seem even more real than the objects of our senses. By 3314, however, a new Revolution will set human sights on a great breakthrough to come in the next age, and prepare the way for it, but in the meantime the Revolution's current failure will shake things up and bring on another time of transition in which the myths and codes of friendship and peace will begin to lose their resonant luster. As the Spirit grows weaker, the needs and desires of the body will get stronger. We will be dissolving this lovely, glittering but complacent and confining world to make way for the **next spectacular Axis Age**, when the three planets of the transcendental trinity will come together again.

Strangely enough, this next triple conjunction of Uranus, Neptune and Pluto in 3371 will be just as close as the last one in 578 BC, and so just as powerful. This 3944-year cycle has now become quite regular, even though the previous Axis Age conjunction was the first one since the dawning of the neolithic Agricultural Age somewhere around 7000 BC. That means that the Age of Enlightenment in the 6th and 5th Centuries before the Common Era will remain the greatest new beginning in human history. The next one starting in 3371 will just build on the previous one. Coinciding with Jupiter and Saturn closely aligned in Capricorn, this new Awakening will arrive into a more well-organized and well-managed world, and claims of power and authority will be made. Venus in Taurus in trine to Jupiter and Saturn promises that this will be a wealthy era full of sensuous delights and exquisite arts, as well as brimming over with great building projects, social reorganizations and abundant explosions of new ideas and revelations expressed in a profusion of literary arts. Perhaps the most interesting feature in the landscape of this cycle is that the next religious dispensation will be received by Humanity in 3623-27, near the climactic half-way point of the cycle in 3616-20, instead of at the beginning.

The great triple Axis Age conjunction of 3371 therefore will not be the next religious dispensation, like the 570s BC conjunction was, and we will not see the birth of great teachers and avatars like Buddha, Confucius and Socrates at that time, even though many philosophers will still appear. Instead, as the positions of Jupiter and Saturn in the chart for 3371 indicates, the new religious figures and prophets of this next Axis Age will arrive in a well-formed world at the peak of its performance, and they may have to challenge the existing powers of the age a lot more in order to get going. But this might also mean they don't have to shout from the outside in order to be heard. They might rise within the established order and be listened to and accepted by it during the Axis Age itself. Maybe when he comes back this time, Socrates won't have to drink the hemlock. This also means that the optimistic, confident attitude of the first half of this Axis Age, as in the Greek Golden Age, will not end after a spectacular imperial conquest followed by a shattered and dispirited Hellenistic-like period, but will be inspired by the new religious dispensation to ever greater heights of achievement and discovery in its second half, and provide a great foundation for the **Next Age of Unifying Order** that follows when the Neptune-Pluto alignment of 3864 comes. This religious dispensation in c.3625 will fulfill the 3600-year cycle since the time of Christ that I mentioned in Chapter 2. There won't be another extraordinary cosmic crucifix this time, but coming 200 years *before* the "New Rome" is built, the new religious impulse won't have to rise in opposition to it, and then in the end take it over and be distorted by its imperial trappings. It will have already come. Maybe this new dispensation, having been revealed at the peak of an Axis Age of Enlightenment, will be more compatible with the world into which it is born.

If the 2140-year Aquarian Age can be said to continue into this new Axis Age and beyond, then whatever new revelations come to us in the Aquarian Age's last days in about the year 4305 (2140 years after 2165) will be applied and added to all that Humanity has learned. If we learn to build on what has been revealed to us before, we won't have to reinvent the great spiritual wheels in the sky that the prophet Ezekiel discovered in 590 BC; they will already be turning within us here on Earth. God's chariot and *merkabah of ascension*, discovered by the prophet at the very beginning of the first Axis Age in history can now become a working vehicle in which we can travel between dimensions. Perfecting this discovery within each one of us will be one of the projects of the next 3940 years until the next Axis Age. We will need to do this eventually, because about one billion years from now our Planet Earth will no longer be habitable, and we will need to find a new foundation for our lives in God, the Omega Point that beckons us.

Rediscovering Our Own Age

Our own age, which I called the Age of Revolution in my previous book, is the most essential part of this quest, the linchpin of our journey. As we circle around in this chapter toward the return to a new Axis Age, it's valuable to turn around and look again at Chapter 5 in Horoscope for the New Millennium: the Cosmic Clock of Civilization and the Great Uranus Cycle. There I showed that while each succeeding conjunction of Neptune and Pluto every 493 years happened in almost the same place, from mid-Taurus to early Gemini, at each one Uranus moved backward about 1/8 of the way through the signs. In our Age it reached an 8th House position, which comes under the rulership of Scorpio. This means that in the hero's journey, we are now at the critical moment of facing death, which could happen unless we summon the will to rise up and meet the challenge successfully, and thereby become the true hero. We have faced death already on our time, through nuclear weapons and environmental disaster, and the threat won't go away anytime soon.

But the most amazing fact about our Age, is that on April 26, 1892, our birthday, as Neptune and Pluto joined together at 8 degrees Gemini, Uranus was located in the actual SIGN Scorpio too-- and in an *exactly corresponding degree*. The motion forward through the signs by Uranus in its 84-year orbit reached 4 degrees Scorpio, and met head-on its motion backward through the Houses, also at 4 degrees Scorpio, in the Great Uranus Cycle on the Cosmic Clock. What's more, the power of this symbol is magnified tremendously when we consider that Pluto is considered the ruling planet of Scorpio. As we have discovered since 1978, Pluto is a binary planet that is completely entangled with its Moon Charon, each one moving around the other, each one in the same place in respect to the other, so that it represents complete integration between two movements, and between the inward with the outward. Ours is therefore the Age when we are to learn the great lesson for which all the past has prepared us, and on which all the future depends; that the individual and the world, the local and the global, the assertive and the receptive, the male and the female, subject and object, breathing in and breathing out-- in fact, all polarities-- are interdependent. On this realization we will eventually build our Merkabah chariot and become gods.

We also saw that in the 22nd Century, our doorway to doom or paradise, the "New Age" will begin in earnest in the 2159 to 2165 period, first with the conjunction between the two great chronocraters Jupiter and Saturn in 8 degrees Scorpio in 2159, where it will be exactly in quincunx to the original conjunction that began our age in 1892, and then with another quincunx, exact within 1 or 2 minutes of arc, of Pluto at 7 degrees Cancer *exactly* quincunx to Uranus and Neptune in conjunction at 7 degrees Aquarius, which is also the "back to progress" degree where the progressed Mars in the 1892 chart is located as I write. It means that from now on as we move forward, we must simultaneously adjust toward where we've been. And the Aquarian conjunction of 2165 being in trine, within one degree, with the original conjunction of 1892 in Gemini, and Pluto in Cancer in 2165 being in trine, also within one degree, to the Scorpio conjunction of 2159, and within 2 degrees to the original Uranus position in 1892, will help us to make the adjustments.

As our quest continues toward the next Axis Age, we must go back and recover the ground and the roots we lost. We have needed to do this all along, and our myths about a lost Golden Age express it. Since Rousseau it has become the ideal and concern of all romantic souls.[86] We need it because in our quest to conquer Nature since 578 BC we separated ourselves from the world, and we placed God in a separate and higher realm from us. In Greece in the old Axis Age, Humanity liberated itself from the old gods and myths of the Archaic Ages and took it upon itself to think and reason in order to understand and manipulate the world, freed from the authority of superstitious belief. We began the long process of asserting our rights and becoming full individuals. This was an essential step, but after taking it we were no longer embedded in the organic world, which became disenchanted and stripped of its magic and wonder. And we will remain so alienated as long as we don't learn to step forward and backwards at once, as Pluto and Scorpio teach us.

We need to recover this. We have also undergone a sexual revolution, often attributed to the Scorpio sign influence, and this energy is very erotic and ecstatic. It is the kundalini energy that esoteric philosophy in east and west has tapped, and their teachers have taught as that we can bring this powerful energy up through the spine and the chakras and connect it with the divine at the crown above our heads to achieve spiritual liberation. But as Pluto reminds us, all movement goes both ways at once. Therefore, we also need to learn to tap into the divine spirit above, to experience the light and love of the pure divine consciousness, potent mind power and perfect wisdom, and bring it down into our bodies from above our crown chakras and outward onto Planet Earth. Only in this way can the new age of peace, harmony and understanding which we imagine and which we sing about

---

[86] Kenneth Clark, Civilization, Harper and Row, 1969, pp.272-275.

can be manifested. The Earth energy and the Spirit energy, moving together as one, will keep both alive.

Since the Axis Age, the Eastern world has delved deeply into the divine spirit, often freed from both the old archaic myths and superstitions, and genuinely open to the divine we experience directly. They connected with God within and understood our spiritual being, while the West tried instead to connect with God through yet another superstitious, mythical authority that the imperial churches imposed upon us. This meant that we separated ourselves too often from the divine. And the West repressed its own esoteric traditions as well, which could have given us that connection that we needed within our own culture. So, the West needs to turn toward the East and toward our own lost esoteric traditions in order to develop this wisdom and experience for ourselves, and to deepen it further. From these we can recover our lost souls and re-enchant the world, and we can re-integrate ourselves within it.

At the same time, our quest to control and understand Nature as objects gave us powerful technology and scientific knowledge, and in becoming free individuals we have developed a deep respect and love for the value of each person upon which free societies have been built. We don't want to lose this valuable heritage either. We don't need to embrace new superstitions; we need to ask questions and know truth for ourselves, as the great teachers of both East and West, both Buddha and Socrates taught us to do. And in the East today, too often their own heritage is being tossed aside so that they can become prosperous and free like The West. However, if all the peoples of the world aspire to be as wealthy and prosperous as the West has become since the industrial revolution, then our Earth home will no longer support us. Only by learning to live in harmony with the Earth can true and lasting prosperity be achieved. The West must set an example by rejoining its life to the Earth Mother, and the East needs to remember its heritage so it can follow that example and help lead the way.

And so, in both East and West today, the need for recovery and integration is uppermost. I have used the term "New Age" almost on impulse to label the journey we are on to a better today and tomorrow. It just means that a new way of life is at hand and available to us if we choose. I also referred to the "Modern Spirit" in my first book, which grew out of the Age of Revolution and the discovery of Uranus that gave it birth at the end of the 18th century. But these terms are temporary, because time passes quickly, and what is "new" and "modern" or even "post-modern" today will not be so tomorrow. I have found what I think are proper labels for the next two ages on our itinerary, the Age of Light, and the Age of Consummation. So, what would be a better name for our *own* 493 cycle, which at this writing has over 360 years still to run? It's not really an Age of Revolution anymore, since most of us are caught up in corporations, bureaucracies and even small non-profits to whose leaders we are subservient just as though they were medieval priests and kings and mother superiors or even ancient emperors. We defer to these rulers, and so we are spinning our wheels and locked in holding patterns for most of our lives, and our society hardly seems revolutionary any longer. Those whistle-blowers who speak out against it are cast out. Modern writers from 50 years ago, including many I have quoted in this book, spoke of our age as the first one ever to overthrow every authority and question every received tradition. That seems to be settling down now as our age matures. Under Scorpio, organizations may continue to get too big and powerful, even though reformed, for the next 400 years, until the overwhelming chaos and freewheeling spirit of the Age of Light knocks them down. And what exactly the "Age of Aquarius" means, we don't really know. It may be true, or it may be just another myth or superstition, even if a useful one.

But our need to transform still remains acute. The Revolution is our only real heritage, unless we can recover our past inheritance as well. We sing its patriotic songs at ball games, and we claim our dedication to our national creeds and our devotion to freedom and progress. We proclaim our latest flaming romantic rebellion or counter-culture too. Perhaps the Age of Transformation is a good label; at least it's what we need to do, and it fits the sign Scorpio which rules our current age almost as much as Aquarius does. *The Age of Integration*; that might be it, if we can live up to it. The Integral philosophers of Spiral Dynamics tell us that it's on the way. We don't seem to be carrying on constant revolution very well anymore, but we can still find that sacred alchemical marriage between all of our polarities that our esoteric tradition has taught us. We can transcend the past, and also embrace and include it. We can deepen our roots within the Earth and all its peoples, in our souls, and in our bodies, and simultaneously reach up above to the stars and the spirits. We can continue to build slowly and gradually, and sometimes explosively, and amid many reverses, and even from within the walls of our pent-up and subservient world, a just and harmonious society in which our spirits can grow. We can bring it all together into a greater whole. And so, onward and upward!

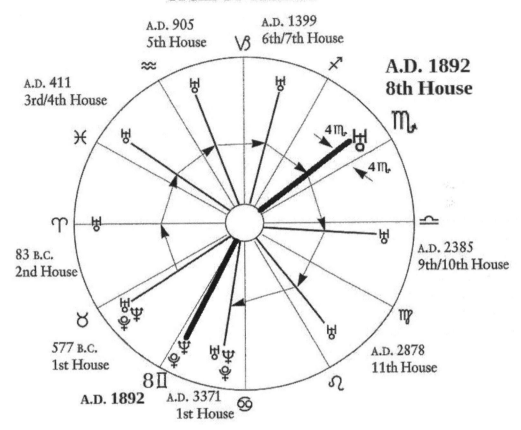

THE GREAT 4,000-YEAR
CYCLE OF URANUS

Chapter 12

Predicting Presidential Elections

Can presidential elections be predicted? Are there astrological methods that work, and which any reader can use to become a great presidential election prophet? I think so, but this chapter is an ongoing work in progress, and further updates will be found on my website philosopherswheel.com assuming it still exists when you read this.

The President of the United States has much to do with what happens in America, and in the world. Our system of government is set up to make it so. That makes it an important topic for a prophet to tackle, but presidential elections are a field where the unexpected can happen. Crystal balls can get cracked when it comes to predicting who will win. On the other hand, if the whole USA system changes, as it could in the upcoming years of potential revolution, then this chapter could become irrelevant. But so far, some people have been enthusiastic about what I have discovered.

For a while, my research into this question was rather unsystematic. I knew horoscopes for some of the presidents, and I studied the observations that Grant Lewi and others had made about them.[87] Lewi's cycles of Saturn in relation to horoscopes seemed to work, based on my cursory observations. Certain aspects between some planets seemed to appear more often in the charts of presidents than others, and Lewi had mentioned some of those. And I thought that liberals or Democrats would more likely get elected in times that were progressive, which were indicated when Uranus was more prominent, and when the outer planets were in liberal signs like Aquarius, while conservatives or Republicans might win when Saturn and conservative signs like Capricorn were more prominent.

That led me to predict that Al Gore would win the election in the year 2000, and I said so in my first book, published in 1997. That didn't quite work out; George W. Bush became president instead. On the other hand, when I tell people I predicted Al Gore would win, but was wrong, most people say, "But Eric, Al Gore DID win the election. You were right!" Election fraud and the Supreme Court just didn't allow him to take office, they say. Nevertheless, my assumption that the liberal candidate would become the president because 2 outer planets were in the "liberal" sign Aquarius at the time, didn't pan out.

Back to the drawing board, I thought.

---

[87] Lewi, <u>Astrology for the Millions</u>, Llewellyn Publications, 1940.

The Methods

So, in November 2003 I got more thorough in my research. I looked at hundreds of candidates and charts to see if any patterns could be found in them.[88] I tabulated the aspects (certain angles between planets) in the charts of all the winning and losing candidates from the time of Andrew Jackson to the time of Bush v Gore. I also looked at the various other methods I had thought about, and tabulated statistics for those too. From the patterns I saw, I was able to predict that Howard Dean would likely not be nominated in 2004, and that John Kerry was the best bet for the Democrats. I wrote an unpublished article with these findings. One month later Dean's candidacy imploded, and Kerry went on to win the nomination soon afterward. But although both Bush and Kerry had strong charts, or so I thought, the horary indicator I used, based on the New Moon before the election, predicted that Bush would be re-elected in November 2004. And so it was.

Here is a copy of the last paragraph of the article I wrote in 2003:

If we take a peak at the New Moon prior to election day, the planetary rulers give the advantage to the incumbent. This is bad news for those like myself who believe our nation has been put on a disasterous track. There is a chance to beat this fate, since Bush faces his Saturn Return on election day, but the Democrats need to pick the strongest possible candidate to do it. None of them, however, seem obviously destined to win the election. Kerry has the best chance of any in the field, and Gephardt would make the best president if he were chosen. Democrats would do well to heed the astrological indications and choose one of them, and not get starstruck by Howard Dean just because he's the most timely and outspoken about the war. His candidacy is not timely according to Saturn. Looking at the whole picture, Kerry and Gephardt have just as much chance to straighten out the mess as he does, and would do a better job overall.

When it was getting time for the 2012 election, I made a new list. Using those scores, I was able to predict that Obama would defeat Mitt Romney, and in fact I predicted the exact final electoral vote tally, beating all the pundits in that respect. On the Generations and Fourth Turning forum on the web, I successfully predicted each event in the election, including the ups and downs of all the candidates.

---

[88] I used solar fire, with data from wikipedia, to determine birth data and aspects for those candidates whose birth times are not known (Rodden rating X), or astrodienst at astro.com, to find the charts and their aspects of candidates whose birth times are given there. See **Appendix H** for more information. See **Appendix I** for historical references for this chapter.

I linked all these predictions, including the electoral vote tally forecast, to my website, http://philosopherswheel.com/predictions.html . They are now all stored at the Generational Dynamics Fourth Turning Forum Archive[89]

I further revised the scoring method 2016. I tallied up which aspects were in the charts of winning and losing candidates from the 1790s to 2012. I also observed which aspects were *not* in the charts of winning candidates, and which were *not* in the charts of losing candidates. If a candidate both won and lost election(s), their aspects were counted accordingly. I tightened up the requirements and came up with a list of favorable and unfavorable aspects for getting elected. Also, some of these aspects were even more favorable or unfavorable than others. Especially favorable, I decided, were the aspects most common in presidents who never lost an election. A candidate's horoscope score became the ratio between favorable and unfavorable aspects. The candidate with the highest favorable score is the most likely to win the general election. A candidate with a negative score (more unfavorable than favorable aspects) is very likely to lose it.

For example, Franklin D. Roosevelt's horoscope score was 21-4: 21 points for favorable aspects and 4 points for unfavorable. In 1936 FDR defeated Alf Landon, who had a score of 10-16, by a landslide. He went on to beat Wendell Willkie (8-9) in 1940, and Thomas Dewey (8-6) in 1944. In this example, Landon had what I call a "negative horoscope score" (more unfavorable than favorable aspects). From 1908 onward, no candidate with a negative score has been elected president. In fact, since 1932 every president elected but two has had a double-digit score of favorable aspects, compared to a single-digit score of unfavorable ones.

I was also aware that horary astrology is often used to predict the winner of contests such as sporting events, or to answer questions we put to the universe. Most horary charts look at the rising sign at the time of the event to make predictions about it. Since New Moon charts are used to predict the events of the upcoming month, I used the chart for the time of the New Moon before the election, cast for Washington DC, and applied the horary method to it. I theorized that the rising sign represents the candidate from the party out of power, or the challenger. The opposite descending sign represents the candidate from the party in power, or the champ. The winner is decided by which ruling planet is higher in the sky, the rising sign (or ascendant) ruler, or the setting sign (or descendant) ruler, compared to the horizon.

All signs are ruled by one of the planets. Mars rules Aries, Venus rules Taurus, and so on. But I used Mars as ruler of Scorpio, not Pluto. I used Uranus as ruler of Aquarius, and Neptune as ruler of Pisces. So, for example, if Aries is rising and Libra is setting at the time of the New Moon, then if Mars (ruler of Aries) is higher in the sky than Venus (ruler of Libra), the challenger wins. If Venus is higher, the champ wins.

Two methods based on Grant Lewi's work, from his book Astrology for the Millions, are useful. The first one is very powerful: the Saturn Return. If a candidate is thinking about running for office when (s)he is between the ages of 55 and 59, (s)he had

---

[89] http://generationaldynamics.com/tftarchive/

better think again! Saturn is returning to its horoscope position now, or it will be returning to it during the term in office (s)he is seeking. According to Grant Lewi, people who seek a high-status position during this time of life are pushing their luck, and they should dial down their ambition.

I wouldn't put it that way now. It is no longer the case that people past the age of 55 are too old to be ambitious. But it still represents a time to hold back and look at what you want to do with the rest of your life, and maybe shift course. Grant Lewi writes that "the few who have been in the White House through this transit or just prior to it have earnestly wished they weren't; and happy have been they who got out from under, even in defeat!"[90] Lewi wrote these words in the 1940s, and they could have been said by Lyndon Johnson after announcing he would not seek re-election-- right during his Saturn Return in March 1968! (as a matter of fact, he said those words almost exactly)

The second method also involves Saturn, the planet of ambition and destiny, and concerns which house the ringed planet is passing through in the candidate's chart at the time of the election. I cover this less reliable method on my website.

The List

Let's take a look at the list of planetary aspects I have developed that predicts which candidates are most-likely to win. If you are not interested in these technical details, feel free to skip to the next section Who Scored What.

First, let's define **aspects** again. These are the angles formed between the planets. They are like phases of the Moon, based on the lunar cycle between the Sun and Moon. A new moon is a conjunction between them, and a full moon is an opposition. The same applies to any two planets. Aspects are formed as they make their mutual cycles in relation to each other. The first and last quarter phases, when half the Moon is visible, are squares (90-degree angles), and a trine happens when they are 120 degrees apart, or 1/3 of the circle. There's a sextile when they are 60 degrees apart, or 1/6. Each pair of planets go through these same phases, forming these aspects. These are called the major aspects, and they are the most important ones. Other minor aspects are also scored as mentioned below.

The candidates who have done the best have the qualities that people in the USA like to vote for, or those who can wage good campaigns. These are usually indicated by the aspects in their birth charts. The optimism, confidence and generous spirit of Jupiter, the charismatic, eloquent, liberating energy of Uranus, the magnetism and radiance of the Sun all appeal to Americans; while the sulky anger and arrogance of Mars might not. Some of the aspects to Mars indicate recklessness and instability, which don't appeal. But just the right aspects to Mars or Saturn can show courage, energy and discipline which Americans admire. And no profit can be had in this approach by omitting Pluto!

From all my results, one thing is clear. Only skilled candidates ever win presidential elections in the United States of America. And it doesn't even take astrology

---

[90] Lewi, <u>Astrology for the Millions</u>, Llewellyn Publications, 1940, page 43; see also p.220-221

for most people to see which candidates these are. We can all observe them. We often like to think that people vote for candidates who propose the policies they agree with, and we also think that the candidate with the best policies is going to win. Especially those on the left and some on the right tend to think this. But it's not true. The candidates that win are those who have the strongest personalities; the most charismatic, the most likable, the most articulate and the most confident among the current candidates. Americans vote for the person, more than for policies. They are choosing a leader, and they vote for the candidate whom they think has the qualities of a leader. They don't generally vote for policy wonks unless they also have the other qualities. They sometimes make some pretty poor choices, in my opinion. In fact, the best candidates don't necessarily turn out to be the best presidents, although many times they do. The best candidates are first of all the most persuasive and likable; someone whom people want in their living room every night. If these personal qualities serve them well in office by helping them to get things done, then it's an added bonus if they are smart and actually propose the best policies that serve the current needs of the people.

This list of aspects is very largely based on which ones actually appeared in the charts of winning and losing candidates, and which ones did not. Some of these research findings might be surprising to a few astrologers. For example, some "inharmonious" squares and oppositions are better for competing and winning a presidential election than the "harmonious" or "easy going" sextiles and trines. But since past is usually prologue, but not always, astrological tradition and past knowledge by other experts may also affect some of these scores. Revisions were made for 2016 and may be made after future elections.

Anyone is invited to use this method to predict which candidates are likely to be elected president in the future, just by looking up a candidate's horoscope. This is a good site for many charts, and adding up the favorable and unfavorable points for any candidate you choose to look at. Sounds easy, doesn't it? Well, let's see!

Favorable aspects for getting elected president of the USA: (latest revision: Dec. 2016)

Sun conjunct or semi-square Venus, 1 point (attractiveness and artistry)
Sun trine or sextile Mars, 1 point (energy, audacity)
Sun opposite, square or conjunct Jupiter, 1 point (optimism, good fortune,
    confidence)
Sun trine or sextile Uranus, 1 point (charismatic leadership)
Sun opposite, square or conjunct Neptune, 1 point (vision, compassion in action,
    connection to the people)
Moon trine or sextile Mercury, 2 points (smart and comes across well through public
    media)
Moon conjunct Mars, 1 point (Lewi noticed this aspect; mobilizes people into action,

dynamic)

Moon opposite or square Jupiter, 2 points (connects with and uplifts the people)

Moon trine, sextile or conjunct Jupiter, 1 point (generous, and appeals to the feelings of the people)

Moon trine or sextile Uranus, 1 point (charismatic leadership, with feeling)

Moon opposite or square Pluto, 2 points (directs the power of the people, transformative, and may be hypnotic)

Mercury sextile Venus, 1 point (the candidate with the silver tongue)

Mercury trine or sextile Mars, 1 point (sharp mind and fast tongue)

Mercury trine, sextile or conjunct Jupiter, 1 point (communication skill)

Mercury in any aspect to Uranus, 1 point (charismatic eloquence)

Mercury opposite or square Neptune, 1 point (speaks to peoples' feelings, expert schemer)

Mercury opposite, square or conjunct Pluto, 2 points (convincing, thoughtful, perhaps revolutionary ideas)

Venus trine or sextile Jupiter, 1 point (good fortune and cheer; financial success)

Venus trine, sextile or conjunct Saturn, 1 point (steadiness, integrity, sacrifice; like George Washington)

Venus opposite or square Neptune, 1 point (the aspect of "divine discontent;" visionary empathy in action, but scandal is possible)

Venus trine or sextile Pluto, 2 points (ability to connect with people and power)

Mars trine or sextile Saturn, 2 points (disciplined energy and courage)

Jupiter trine or sextile Uranus, 2 points (the popular hero)

Jupiter trine, opposite or square Neptune, 2 points (expansive or compassionate; eloquent ideals)

Saturn trine or sextile Uranus, 1 point (strategic skills, practical ideals)

Saturn trine, sextile or conjunct Neptune, 1 point (visionary realism)

Unfavorable aspects for getting elected president of the USA:

Sun conjunct Mercury, 1 point (nervous instability)

Sun conjunct Mars, 2 points (restless energy, overworks, may be too combative)

Sun trine, sextile or conjunct Pluto, 2 points (may push too hard, or let energy run amok)

Moon opposite or square Mercury, 2 points (careless or radical speech)

Moon opposite or square Venus, 1 point (may have glamour, but lacks discipline)

Moon opposite or square Mars, 1 point (may be too angry, impulsive or moody)

Moon conjunct Saturn, 1 point (too cautious or negative)

Moon opposite or square Uranus, 1 point (unstable popularity, unconventional)

Moon opposite, square or conjunct Neptune, 2 points (malaise: muddled or lacks control of emotions)

Mercury conjunct Venus, 1 point (seems friendly enough, but too evasive)

Mercury trine or sextile Saturn, 1 point (thinking too rigid, or gets stuck in ruts)

Mercury trine or sextile Pluto, 1 point (may get carried away with radical ideas or rough speech)

Venus trine or sextile Mars, 1 point (may be distracted by passions and appetites)

Venus opposite or square Jupiter, 2 points (big ego; too showy, indulgent or unstable)

Venus opposite or square Saturn, 1 point (too cold, distant or conservative)

Venus trine, sextile or conjunct Uranus, 1 point (may be attractive, but unsteady)

Mars opposite or square Jupiter, 3 points (reckless prodigality; unfocused)

Mars opposite or square Saturn, 2 points (unstable, or cruel)

Mars conjunct Uranus, 1 point (powerful, reckless, willful)

Mars trine or sextile Neptune, 2 points (uncontrolled feelings, complacent, or too much of a crusader)

Mars trine, sextile or conjunct Pluto, 1 point (too passionate or unsteady)

Jupiter trine or sextile Saturn, 2 points (supposed to be good planner, but evidently way too cautious)

Jupiter opposite or square Pluto, 2 points (much like Mars-Jupiter; too careless)

Saturn opposite or square Neptune, 2 points (paranoia, pessimism)

Saturn trine, sextile, opposite or square Pluto, 2 points (ruthless domineering repels the people)

Minimum allowable orbs for aspects: Conjunctions, oppositions, trines and squares must be within 10 degrees to count for the horoscope score. Sextiles must be within 6 degrees.

For a strong aspect among any of these above: add 1 point each. This is important to remember. Stronger aspects are closer to being exact, and thus are more significant. Strong conjunctions, oppositions, trines or squares are those within exactly 6 degrees or less. Strong sextiles are those within exactly 3 degrees. To determine this requirement, you must look at the number of degrees and minutes indicated for the positions of the planets in the charts of the candidates, or else refer to aspect tables where these are listed.

Minor aspects:

Semi-squares are 45-degree angles, and sesqui-squares are 135 degrees. For these two aspects, score one point only for each aspect among any of the same 2 planets mentioned above in a square. The planets must be exactly 2 degrees apart or less. This applies also to the Sun-Venus semi-square already mentioned above. A quincunx is an aspect of 150 degrees. It's worth 1 point. Score the same as any opposition among the same planets in the above lists, but it must be within exactly one degree; no more. Semi-sextiles are 30 degrees and are also worth 1 point. Score the same as any sextile in the above lists, but only if it is within 1 degree. For example, among favorable aspects, Sun quincunx Neptune scores 1 point. Venus semi-sextile Jupiter scores 1 point. Among unfavorable aspects, for example, Mars quincunx Jupiter scores 1 point, and Mars semi-sextile Neptune scores 1 point.

If a candidate or president's birth time is not known, 12 Noon is used. But in that case, we can't be certain which lunar aspects (s)he has, because the Moon moves too fast. So, in those cases I don't count minor aspects to the Moon. For other lunar aspects that normally score 2 points, I only give one point if it's not a strong aspect (a strong aspect is 6 degrees apart or less; 3 for sextiles). If this becomes too much trouble, though, I would just score the major lunar aspects as indicated above. If I am certain that the aspect occurred all day, and it's worth 2 points, then I count 2 points.

Add up all the scores for the favorable aspects to obtain the first number in the candidate's horoscope score, the favorable number. Then add up all the scores for the unfavorable aspects to get the second number in the candidate's horoscope score, the unfavorable number.

The easiest way to score a candidate is to use an aspect chart, in which you can readily see each aspect and how far apart it is. Websites such as astro.com and many astrology programs have this feature. Be sure you have memorized the symbols for the planets and the aspects.

In President Obama's horoscope below, you can see his positive and negative-scoring aspects.[91] For example, Mars is at 22 degrees, 35 minutes Virgo and Saturn is at 25 degrees, 20 minutes Capricorn. That is a trine within 6 degrees between those two planets; worth 3 positive points from my list (representing disciplined energy). He has a close Moon-Jupiter trine (connects with people), worth 2 points. He also has a close Sun-Neptune square (vision, compassion), worth 2 points. Obama's Moon in Gemini is square to Uranus in Leo, within 10 degrees, but not 6. This gives him 1 negative point (representing unstable popularity). He also has a minor aspect from the list, a quincunx between Venus and Jupiter (showy), worth 1 negative point. Note that he just misses having an unfavorable conjunction of the Sun and Mercury.

[91] Source for Barack Obama's horoscope is his birth certificate. Rodden Rating is AA. Posted at
    https://www.astro.com/astro-databank/Obama,_Barack

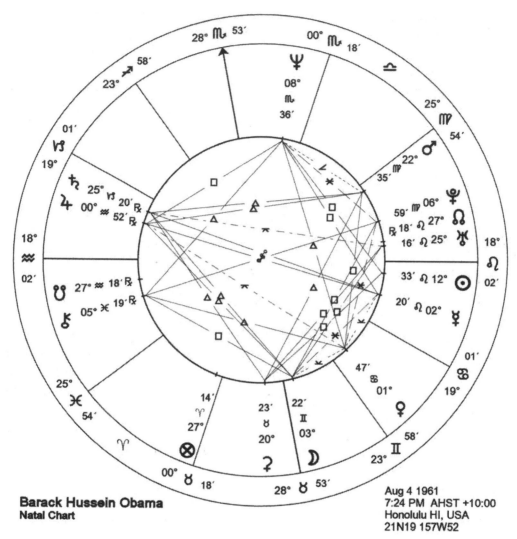

Barack Hussein Obama
Natal Chart

Aug 4 1961
7:24 PM AHST +10:00
Honolulu HI, USA
21N19 157W52

Who Scored What?

If you look at the scores for candidates who have run for president, you can see there's a consistent pattern. The candidates who won almost always had a higher score than the candidates who lost. A better margin of favorable over unfavorable scores compared to your opponent is a great advantage in a presidential election. The candidate with the higher percentage margin (positive score divided by negative score) usually wins. When the margins are close to each other, a close election is likely.

But sometimes the horoscope score may conflict with the other methods, as we will see, and a good prophet needs to take account of those and balance all the factors to make a prediction.

George Washington, the father of the country, set the pattern for a winning score with 18-5. James K. Polk had one of the best scores at 22-2. The first unknown "dark horse" candidate, he faced enormous odds against him to win and succeed as president. U.S. Grant followed in Washington's footsteps as a victorious general into the White

House with a formidable 17-3 score. History repeated itself when another victorious general, Dwight Eisenhower, won with a good 18-8 score.

On the other hand, most candidates who have too little recognition, or who are way out of the mainstream of opinion in their party or the country, are likely still at a disadvantage. A high score by itself is not enough to get you elected president. You still have to earn your way by getting yourself recognized and noticed. Third party and independent candidates are also at a disadvantage. A higher score may also indicate a greater chance of being nominated; but not necessarily. Some candidates with very bad scores have been nominated, only to lose the general election. Candidates who overcame great odds to win often had the highest scores.

A great score does not indicate a good president either; just a candidate who is good at getting elected. A bad score also does not indicate that someone can't get elected to other kinds of offices. Many candidates with low scores for the presidential election are elected governor or senator, for example. But someone with a negative score is unlikely to be elected president of the USA. No-one has done so since 1904.

In my database of aspects and candidates, I generally only included candidates I thought were significant; not those few (like for example Al Sharpton) who did very poorly. All candidates since 1968 in my database actually ran in primary elections and caucuses. Those who ran twice or more are counted only once for losing a nomination. I assume that these candidates did well enough to try again. For the same reason, I also did not count lost nominations by those who became nominees or presidents later. The aspects of those who never served are counted once for that, and for those who were never nominated are counted again for that. In my special new "win-loss" tally, one of my methods for calculating aspects scores, I observed these rules, but I only counted FDR's horoscope aspects for 3 wins. Eventually I will post all my research on my website.

In the list below, some scores are marked J, U, *, **, SN.

J = Jupiter rising, on the eastern horizon or in the first house, greatly helps a candidate's chances. This is called the Ascendant and indicates how your personality comes across. 8 major party candidates elected president had Jupiter rising (including Polk, Taylor, Lincoln, Grant, LBJ and Bill Clinton), and only 2 were never elected: Walter Mondale (12-12) and Hillary Clinton (9-11). Mondale also faced a Saturn Return. Bill Taft and Teddy Roosevelt both won and lost once (but they lost only when they ran both against each other-- *and* Woodrow Wilson). 3 others were from 3rd parties (unlikely to win) and 2 of those candidates had terrible losing scores otherwise (also unlikely to win). Americans like to vote for a buoyant, optimistic, generous personality, which Jupiter represents. Jupiter rising may be worth at least 6 points; maybe 10 (no more than 3 for an independent/third party candidate). But I don't include this in the official raw score, since I don't know the birth times of many of the candidates, especially the earlier ones. Lyndon Johnson's overwhelming personality was "larger than life;" his 5 rising planets (Jupiter, Mars, Sun, Moon, Mercury) represent perfectly the famous "Johnson treatment" which he used to get what he wanted from people.

These 5 rising planets probably helped him beat Barry Goldwater in 1964, who had a somewhat higher score. Tentatively you could give LBJ at least 10 extra points for these 5 rising planets; more than enough to beat Goldwater's score. Bill Clinton, who had 4 planets rising (Jupiter, Mars, Neptune and Venus) and is called a "gifted politician," is another famous example. These two guys had the most planets rising of any major candidates in history, along with the iconic Abraham Lincoln (4 planets rising). Jupiter rising also no doubt helped Teddy Roosevelt beat his lesser-known but higher-scoring opponent in 1904. But you'd have to give Walter Mondale about 30 extra points just for his Jupiter rising to make up for his much-poorer score than Ronald Reagan's, and Hillary Clinton would have needed at least 15 more points from Jupiter rising to beat Donald Trump's score.

In the charts of the two candidates with Jupiter rising who did the best, both winning big (although only once) in spite of having lower scores than their opponents, Jupiter was apparently in close conjunction to the rising degree. These were Lyndon Johnson and Theodore Roosevelt. By contrast, Walter Mondale's Jupiter is well below the horizon. Other candidates with Jupiter rising are in between these indications. Hillary's birth time is also in question, so her Jupiter rising is uncertain. How closely Jupiter is aligned with the Ascendant thus seems a factor in how much of an advantage it is. Note that astrologers consider conjunctions to the Ascendant to be important aspects in their own right.

U = The visionary charisma of Uranus rising may have helped presidents Monroe, W H Harrison and Taft get elected over their opponents. Uranus rising helped FDR get elected to 4 terms, but it didn't help the great orator William Jennings Bryan get elected; he lost 3 times. Legend has it that the "champions of democracy" Thomas Jefferson and Andrew Jackson had Uranus rising too, but this seems to be mere speculation.

* **The Saturn Return** is another major factor: from the time of Andrew Jackson onward, candidates who run with Saturn returning to its position in their horoscope from the election year until the next term begins 4 years later, are likely to lose. Many others with a Saturn Return happening or coming up soon choose not to run. Candidates who had a Saturn return are indicated by an asterisk in the first list below.

Sometimes, if Saturn returns to their natal position in the election year, or in the next election year (4th year of the term they seek), candidates can win, but the term is a disaster. If Saturn returns only during the 3 years after the election, they lose it. More details and statistics on the Saturn Return pattern later.

**As a rule, if both candidates are due for a return, the one whose return is earliest will lose the election. Woodrow Wilson was the one and only exception.

SN = Saturn at the Nadir. William Jennings Bryan lost 3 general elections. This may be explained by Saturn at the Nadir (SN) in his own horoscope. Ambitious Saturn is opposite to its natural position there. I know; I have this position, and I've not had an easy time with executive appointments. It turns out that only one elected president had Saturn at the Nadir or in the 4th house (the Nadir of Fortune) in his birth chart: William

Howard Taft. He had a good 12-8 score, enough to easily beat Bryan (5-4), who also had Saturn at his Nadir.

But Taft hated the office and was not re-elected. So far, I've counted 7 times when a nominee with Saturn at the Nadir/4th house lost the general election (including Thomas Dewey who lost twice); plus 5 other candidates who weren't nominated. Saturn was at the Nadir or in the 4th house in the charts of 9 candidates who were never elected president, out of 81 major party candidates whose birth times are known (11%); and in the chart of only one such candidate who was elected (Taft, but he lost re-election) (1.6%). The chances of anyone being born with Saturn in this position are 1 out of 12 (8.3%).

First, I'll list the scores of the winners and losers of each presidential election-- winner first.[92] It's true that, for elections up through 2016, these scores were mostly based on the same aspects that were in the horoscopes of all the candidates. But the results show how consistently the system has worked over time. From 1908 onward, no candidate with a negative score has won the general election. The candidate(s) with the lower score lost 24 out of 26 times since then. In 1964 Lyndon Johnson had a lower raw score than Barry Goldwater (not counting LBJ's Jupiter rising), but Goldwater faced his Saturn Return before LBJ did. In the close election of 1960, the loser (Nixon) had a slightly higher score than the winner (JFK).

Elections before 1932:

1789 and 1792: George Washington 18-5, unopposed
1796: John Adams 6-7 (Mars rising), Thomas Jefferson 5-0
1800: Thomas Jefferson 5-0, John Adams 6-7, Aaron Burr 5-9
1804: Thomas Jefferson 5-0, Charles Pinckney 9-15
1808: James Madison 12-7, Charles Pinckney 9-15
1812: James Madison 12-7, DeWitt Clinton 9-13
1816: James Monroe 7-5 U, Rufus King 7-12
1820: James Monroe 7-5 U, John Quincy Adams 8-3
1824: J Q Adams 8-3*, Andrew Jackson 9-3**, Henry Clay 6-13 (a 4th candidate,
     William Crawford (9-1) had a stroke and could not compete)
1828: Andrew Jackson 9-3, J Q Adams 8-3
1832: Andrew Jackson 9-3, Henry Clay 6-13*
1836: Martin Van Buren 9-4, William Henry Harrison 11-10 U
1840: W H Harrison 11-10 U, Martin Van Buren 9-4*
1844: James K Polk 22-2 J, Henry Clay 6-13
1848: Zachary Taylor 11-4 J, Lewis Cass 6-15, Martin Van Buren 9-4
1852: Franklin Pierce 15-14, Winfield Scott ("Old Fuss and Feathers") 8-23 (Mars rising)

[92] Election info from Sarah Janssen, senior ed., The World Almanac and Book of Facts, Infobase, 2018, p.504. Birth dates of presidents on p.487.

1856: James Buchanan 13-6, John C. Fremont 7-13 SN, Millard Fillmore 11-8*

1860: Abraham Lincoln 16-3 J, Stephen A Douglas 12-21, John Breckinridge 0-23 J, John Bell 3-15

1864: Abraham Lincoln 16-3 J*, George McClellan 10-16

1868: Ulysses S. Grant 17-3 J, Horatio Seymour 6-12*

1872: Ulysses S. Grant 17-3 J, Horace Greeley 4-11

1876: Rutherford B. Hayes 9-3, Samuel J. Tilden 3-14

1880: James A Garfield 8-9, Winfield Hancock 9-8*

1884: Grover Cleveland 10-9, James G. Blaine 7-9*

1888: Benjamin Harrison 14-8*, Grover Cleveland 10-9

1892: Grover Cleveland 10-9*, Benjamin Harrison 14-8**, James B Weaver 15-6

1896: William McKinley 13-3 (Mars rising), William Jennings Bryan 5-4 U, SN

1900: William McKinley 13-3*, William Jennings Bryan 5-4 U, SN

1904: Theodore Roosevelt (TR) 12-15 J, Alton B Parker 15-10

1908: William H. Taft 12-8 J/U, SN, William Jennings Bryan 5-4 U, SN

1912: Woodrow Wilson 10-6**, Theodore Roosevelt 12-15 J, William H. Taft 12-8 J/U, SN*

1916: Woodrow Wilson 10-6**, Charles Evans Hughes 7-11*

1920: Warren G Harding 13-10*, James Cox 8-8

1924: Calvin Coolidge 10-9, John W. Davis 8-16, Robert LaFollette 6-14

1928: Herbert Hoover 11-11, Al Smith 4-16*

Elections from 1932 to 2016:

1932: Franklin D Roosevelt (FDR) 21-4 U, Herbert Hoover 11-11*

1936: Franklin D Roosevelt 21-4 U*, Alf Landon 10-16

1940: Franklin D Roosevelt 21-4 U*, Wendell Willkie 8-9

1944: Franklin D Roosevelt 21-4 U, Thomas Dewey 8-6 SN

1948: Harry Truman 14-0, Thomas Dewey 8-6 SN

1952: Dwight Eisenhower 18-8, Adlai Stevenson 5-21

1956: Dwight Eisenhower 18-8, Adlai Stevenson 5-21*

1960: John F Kennedy (JFK) 13-6, Richard Nixon 18-7

1964: Lyndon B Johnson (LBJ) 8-6 J*, Barry Goldwater 20-11** (he had Mars in Scorpio rising, with inharmonious aspects: the perfect symbol of his stubborn "extremism")

1968: Richard Nixon 18-7*, Hubert Humphrey 9-5**, George Wallace 2-7 J (+ Mars rising)

1972: Richard Nixon 18-7*, George McGovern 9-10

1976: Jimmy Carter 12-4, Gerald Ford 12-8

1980: Ronald Reagan 22-6, Jimmy Carter 12-4*, John Anderson 14-8 J*

1984: Ronald Reagan 22-6, Walter Mondale 12-12 J/U*

1988: George H W Bush 14-6, Michael Dukakis 2-10*

1992: Bill Clinton 21-3 J, George H W Bush 14-6, Ross Perot 7-10 (his Jupiter rising is evident, but it was 10 degrees above his ascendant, so I didn't count it officially)

1996: Bill Clinton 21-3 J, Bob Dole 12-19, Ross Perot 7-10

2000: George W Bush 17-2*, Al Gore 10-9 (Mars rising)

2004: George W Bush 17-2*, John Kerry 8-12 (his score was much weaker in the revised system)

2008: Barack Obama 19-2, John McCain 15-13

2012: Barack Obama 19-2, Mitt Romney 4-10 U, SN

2016: Donald Trump 9-4 (Mars rising), Hillary Rodham Clinton 9-11 J

Best scores of any nominee: Harry Truman, 1948 (14-0), James K Polk, 1844 (22-2 J). Worst scores: John Breckinridge, 1860 (0-23 J), John Bell, 1860 (3-15), Michael Dukakis, 1988 (2-10). Lowest scores by winning candidates: Theodore Roosevelt ("TR"), 1904 (12-15 J), John Adams, 1796 (6-7), and James A Garfield, 1880 (8-9). Highest scores by losing candidates: Jimmy Carter (12-4), who defeated Gerald Ford (12-8) in 1976, was defeated by Ronald Reagan in 1980 (22-6). Thomas Jefferson, who had a perfect 5-0 score, lost in 1796 to John Adams-- although Jefferson also had the lowest total points of any candidate ever, and there was virtually no campaign that year. He came back to beat Adams in 1800 and won again in 1804.

Highest positive number in their scores among all candidates: James K Polk, Ronald Reagan, Franklin Roosevelt, Bill Clinton. Highest negative number: John Breckinridge, Winfield Scott, Chris Christie (not nominated).

In all 58 elections, only 3 winners had a negative horoscope score (John Adams, TR, Garfield; 5%). 54 had a positive score (93%), with one tie (Hoover). By contrast, 38 losers had a negative score (55% of 69). 28 losers had a positive score (41.4%), with 3 tie scores, but 15 of those with positive scores were also president of the USA. Candidates who ran more than once are tallied for each time they ran. I include in this list above all general election candidates who got at least 5% of the vote.

Here's how the pattern stacks up. Since 1932, out of 22 winners of presidential elections, only 2 had lower scores on this system than the loser: JFK (1960) and LBJ (1964) (9.5%). In all 58 presidential elections in US history through 2016, only 10 winners had lower scores than all their losing opponents (17.2%). 48 winners had higher scores (82.7%), and that's 20 since 1932 (90.5%).

Apparently, winning scores have gotten higher in elections for the modern presidency as we know it today. Only certain candidates have the skill to master a campaign in this difficult age of mass media and big money politics. Since 1932, all winners have had at least a 2-1 proportion in their winning score, except LBJ who had Jupiter and 4 other planets rising.

Another interesting fact related to this is that, from 1884 up to 2016, only one candidate with a positive number below 10 in their score had been elected (LBJ). The second is Donald Trump in 2016, who has a 9-4 score, which beat Hillary Clinton's 9-11 (+J). Trump and Hillary Clinton were considered the two most unpopular major candidates in modern history.

There were a few candidates with higher scores who lost to their opponents because of a Saturn Return. For example, Barry Goldwater, 20-11, lost to Lyndon Johnson, 8-6+J, in 1964. They both had a Saturn Return due during the upcoming term, but Goldwater's came first, and that made the difference. Of 13 candidates whose Saturn was returning to its place in their horoscope during *only* the first 3 years after the election, 11 of them lost (including Goldwater). 1 of them won-- only to be immediately assassinated. That was McKinley in 1900, who also had the highest score among these 13 candidates (13-3; this was also higher than opponent W.J. Bryan's score of 5-4). In 1968 Richard Nixon also beat Humphrey, whose Saturn Return came first.

Nixon (18-7) lost to a candidate with a lower score (JFK, 13-6) in 1960. The close scores between JFK and Nixon reflected one of the closest elections. But the closest ever by popular vote was when Garfield (8-9) beat Hancock (9-8) in 1880. In that case, Hancock also had a Saturn Return coming soon. Both JFK and Garfield were assassinated during these terms to which they were barely elected, by the way.

For all 58 elections in history through 2016, of the 10 losers on this list who had higher scores than the winners, only 5 of them did not have a Saturn Return coming to block them. That's only 5 losing candidates who had higher scores than their opponents, without any Saturn Return, out of 69 losing candidates, or 7%. These were Thomas Jefferson in 1796, John Quincy Adams in 1820, Alton B. Parker in 1904, and Richard Nixon in 1960 (this also includes 3rd-party candidate James Weaver in 1892). Jefferson and Nixon went on to become twice-elected president later, and Adams once. Parker lost to TR, who had Jupiter rising. You can see that two of these candidates who lost despite having higher scores were those from the early history of America, before elections campaigns and voters as we know them even existed.

Among the 5 losers who lost under a Saturn Return, despite having a higher score, 4 of them had their Saturn Return due only in the 3 years after the election. Only Benjamin Harrison lost re-election to his lower-scoring opponent Cleveland in the epochal, maverick year 1892 with his Saturn Return happening that year, and not in the next 3 years. A Saturn Return in the year of the election or the next election 4 years later evidently does not necessarily keep candidates from winning, although it means a very rough term ahead that destroys their presidency.

TR was an amazing fellow. He may have been the only candidate to transform himself in youth, beat the odds, and beat the swords in his chart into plowshares for himself and the country.

Conclusion: most of the time, the losing candidate had a lower score than the winner, and/or a Saturn Return coming in the next 3 years after the election.

Next, here's the list of recent and prospective candidates and their scores. Many scores are subject to minor change if birth time becomes known. Scores for newer potential candidates after this book is published are listed on my website[93] and are subject to correction for small errors in my count.

---

[93] http://philosopherswheel.com/presidentialelections.html

Republican potential or actual candidates 2012-2020 or later:

Donald Trump, 9-4 (Mars rising)

William Weld, 8-13 J

Joe Walsh, 11-13

Larry Hogan, 7-16

Mike Pence, 8-7

Mark Sanford, 5-7

Tom Cotton, 15-9

Nikki Haley, 8-15

Ben Sasse, 8-13

Rick Scott, 13-14

John Kasich, 3-12

Ted Cruz, 4-11 U

Marco Rubio, 11-10

Carly Fiorina, 16-7

Jeb Bush, 10-10

Chris Christie, 14-23*

Scott Walker, 10-9*

Rob Portman, 14-8

Ben Carson, 6-9

Jeff Flake, 12-12*

Newt Gingrich, 9-9 SN

Rick Santorum, 8-15

Rick Perry, 11-8

Michelle Bachman, 11-13

Herman Cain, 11-14

Buddy Roemer, 6-11

Rand Paul, 8-9*

Ron Paul, 14-9

Mitch Daniels, 18-17

Mike Huckabee, 9-18

Paul Ryan, 10-11

Bobby Jindal, 15-13

John Thune, 8-9*

Peter King, 9-7

Sam Brownback, 8-9

Kelly Ayotte, 13-8

Lindsay Graham, 1-5

Jim Gilmore, 10-16

George Pataki, 15-3

Sarah Palin, 5-5

George P. Bush, 4-7

Bob Corker, 11-21

Steve Bannon, 10-5

Jared Kushner, 10-4

Ivanka Trump, 16-2

(Donald Jr. 6-16, Eric 5-10)

Highest scores with no Saturn return due: Donald Trump 9-4, Ivanka Trump 16-2, Jared Kushner 10-4, Carly Fiorina 16-7, George Pataki 15-3. Carly Fiorina was barely known and had no experience in any public office when she ran against the celebrity Donald Trump in 2016, but she performed well-enough in the debate among lower-polling candidates to move up to the top tier for the next debate. Then Ted Cruz picked her as his potential running mate.

Democratic potential or actual candidates 2012-2020 and later:

Hillary Clinton, 9-11 J

Bernie Sanders, 14-7

Joe Biden, 14-7

Elizabeth Warren, 8-7

Mike Bloomberg, 7-5

Kamala Harris, 4-16*

Beto O'Rourke, 11-26

Pete Buttigieg, 7-9

Cory Booker, 6-7**

Amy Klobuchar, 7-7

Kirsten Gillibrand, 7-13*

("Mrs. Firebrand" would score 9-11 if born before 6 AM)

Joe & Julian Castro, 8-13

Tulsi Gabbard, 11-6

Steve Bullock, 10-7**

Marianne Williamson, 13-14

Deval Patrick, 9-6

Andrew Yang, 8-15

John Delaney, 7-5*

John Hickenlooper, 6-12

Bill DeBlasio, 12-17*

Jay Inslee, 3-7

Michael Bennet, 9-9*

Seth Moulton, 9-10

Tom Steyer, 11-7

Tim Ryan, 3-12

Joe Sestak, 3-10

Eric Swalwell, 4-6

Terry McAuliffe, 11-2

Stacey Adams, 13-7 (many

aspects uncertain, lower score if born in AM)
Mitch Landrieu, 16-2
Sherrod Brown, 19-8
Gavin Newsom, 7-1 U**
Mike Gravel, 5-10
Wayne Messam, 15-8
Martin O'Malley, 11-19*
Jim Webb, 11-7
Janet Napolitano, 11-5
Tammy Baldwin, 13-6*
Tim Kaine, 11-11
Michelle Obama, 6-6
Andrew Cuomo, 11-6
Brian Schweitzer, 9-5
Mark Warner, 7-11
Joe Kennedy III, 7-8
Eric Garcetti, 7-7
Howard Dean, 6-8 U
Jerry Brown, 5-10

Jason Carter, 10-4
Antonio Villaraigosa, 15-5
Joe Manchin, 6-10
Zephyr Teachout, 4-12
Lincoln Chafee, 15-9
Russ Feingold, 12-14
Tom Vilsack, 15-6
Al Franken, 9-9
Jack Markell, 14-9
Chuck Schumer, 15-8
Debbie Stabenow, 8-3
Roy Cooper, 10-6
Chris Murphy, 8-3 (if born before 10 AM) 8-4 (if born around Noon) 8-5 (if born after 2 PM) 7-5 (if born after 4 PM)
Jeff Merkley, 3-9
Eric Holder, 9-8

George Clooney, 11-19*
Michael Moore, 16-6 SN
Oprah Winfrey, 10-3
Stephen Colbert, 20-11*
Seth Meyers, 20-3
Bill Maher, 9-17
Chelsea Clinton, 9-5 U
Nancy Pelosi, 11-18
Doug Jones, 10-4
Nina Turner 12-7**
Alexandra Ocasio-Cortez, 13-19
Michael Avenatti, 13-4
Adam Schiff, 12-10
Robert F Kennedy Jr., 11-5
Conor Lamb, 13-17
Brian Schatz, 13-10
Richard Ojeda, 10-13
Richard Blumenthal, 11-6
Mark Kelly, 15-7*

More candidate scores will be added on my website.

Best scores, with no Saturn Return: Mitch Landrieu 16-2, Terry McAuliffe 11-2, Bernie Sanders 14-7, Joe Biden, 14-7, Gavin Newsom 7-1, Antonio Villaraigosa, 15-5, Tom Vilsack, 15-6, Jason Carter 10-4, Doug Jones 10-4. Sherrod Brown has a high positive number, and a good score: 19-8. Long shots Robert F Kennedy Jr. and Michael Avenatti have 11-5 and 13-4 respectively. Gavin Newsom (7-1) will have a Saturn Return for the election of 2024. If elected California governor in 2018, he would be well-advised to serve for 2 full terms before running for president.

McAuliffe was the recent governor of VA, former Democratic Party chair, and leader of the governors conference, as his friend Bill Clinton was before him when he ran. Note that Terry McAuliffe's score of 11-2 may be even higher if he was born in the morning. Another great choice appears to be the recently-retired Mayor Landrieu of New Orleans (16-2). Both McAuliffe and Landrieu have the energy, charisma and likability needed to win the presidency. Landrieu has a similar Jupiter-Uranus trine linked to the Sun and Moon as seen in both Bill Clinton's and Donald Trump's horoscope, but without Trump's negative factors. At this point, however, both Landrieu and McAuliffe have declined to run. This makes Donald Trump's re-election more likely, as none of the announced candidates have a higher score than his. I have predicted that only Bernie Sanders and Joe Biden have any chance to beat him. Although Elizabeth Warren is popular and may win the nomination, I have predicted that the Democrats will lose the

White House if she does. She is an example of a policy wonk who does not have the other personal qualities needed to get elected. But it would be a close election, and Donald Trump could still ruin his own chances.

In this new era when celebrities get elected president without any experience, maybe another one can save us! Late-night TV political comic Seth Meyers has indicated no interest in running, but if he did, he'd have a 20-3 score going for him (exact score subject to change, if birth time becomes known). Maybe "it's time for a closer look" at Seth Meyers! Late Night TV host Stephen Colbert (20-11), if he ran in 2020, would have a Saturn Return in his 4th year. Another media personality with a good score is documentary producer Michael Moore, 16-6, although he has Saturn at his Nadir (SN); and Oprah Winfrey has 10-3.

*Saturn Return due between 2020 and 2024   **Saturn Return due between 2025 and 2028.

Some other Independent/3rd party candidates:

Gary Johnson (Libertarian), 12-9 (ran in 2012, 2016)
Jill Stein (Green), 16-2 (ran in 2012, 2016; needs more qualifications, and major party backing; but an excellent candidate)
Evan McMullin, 6-2 (2016)
Ralph Nader (Green, Independent), 6-9 (ran in 2000, and 3 other times)
Sanders, see Democrats

Potential:

Mike Bloomberg (now Democrat), 7-5   Lawrence Kotlikoff, 13-2
Mark Zuckerberg (party unknown), 12-9   Dwayne "The Rock" Johnson, 8-9 U
Jesse Ventura, 14-13 U+Mars rising   Howard Schultz, 9-18
Mark Cuban, 8-10   Justin Amash, 9-11

Some past candidates not nominated:

Robert F Kennedy, 14-14
Eugene McCarthy, 11-5 U
Nelson Rockefeller, 14-13
Ted Kennedy, 8-15
Edmund S Muskie, 9-9
Gary Hart, 9-17 U
Rudy Giuliani, 6-15
John Edwards, 12-11 U
Dennis Kucinich, 7-8
Wesley Clark, 9-15
Chris Christie, 14-23

Of all candidates never nominated by a major party in my database, 30 had a negative score, 13 positive (usually narrowly), and 6 tie scores. Only two had a higher score than the winner of the elections in which they competed: Paul Simon, who was born with Saturn at the Nadir, barely beat George Bush I's score. Carly Fiorina barely tops Donald Trump's score.

The New Moon Before Election

Another major factor I use is the New Moon prior to the election. It has proved to be a very effective method. On the other hand, it seems to predict only the popular vote. As we have experienced twice in the 21st century so far, in cases where the popular vote conflicts with the electoral college, the New Moon before the election has been wrong.

I cast the chart for the exact time of the New Moon before the election for Washington DC.[94] If the rising sign's ruler is higher in the sky, the challenging party wins. If the setting sign ruler is higher, the party in power wins. Uranus at the Nadir (at the Sun's position at Midnight) also helps the challenger. Note that in 2000 the rulers were almost equally high. Gore's ruler (setting sign ruler, representing the party in power) was slightly higher.

I looked at new moon charts before the election going back to 1848, the first presidential election that was held nationwide on the same day. I am not using such charts for earlier elections, which lasted at least 5 weeks, and happened on different days in different states. The first two charts did not predict the election correctly (1848 and 1852). The New Moon was also incorrect in four other cases in the 19th century, including two that conflicted with the electoral college. In the 20th century however, the method usually worked. From 1900 onward through 2016, the new moon before the election has indicated the popular vote winner 26 times out of 29, a record of 90% correct. It was wrong only in 1952, 1968 and 1988. In all three cases, the winning candidate had a higher horoscope score than the loser, so the scores proved to be the deciding factor.

But in 2000 and 2016, although the new moon method indicated the popular vote winner, as it had in 1876 and 1888, the opposing candidate won the electoral college and became president. In all four of these cases, the electoral college winner was a Republican. Democrats have never won the electoral college without winning the popular vote. In the case of 2016, I thought Jupiter rising in Hillary's chart might give her an advantage, which along with her popular vote victory as the New Moon predicted, might help her overcome her much lower horoscope score than Trump's. But she proved to be a weak candidate in many ways, and her time of birth is uncertain anyway. The horoscope indicator prevailed and she lost the election.

---

[94] New Moon charts were cast using the solar fire program.

In 1904 the New Moon indicated that the lower-scoring candidate would win (Theodore Roosevelt). Also, in 1960, when John F. Kennedy was running against Vice President Richard Nixon, who had a slightly better horoscope score, the new moon also indicated that the challenger party would win, and it did. In 1964, the incumbent Lyndon Johnson won as the new moon predicted, although the challenger Goldwater had a higher score (but remember Johnson's powerful personality indicated by Jupiter and 4 other planets rising, and Goldwater faced a Saturn Return first).

If Uranus is at the Nadir or in the 4th house at the time of the new moon before election, that is a sign that the incumbent party could be toppled. The Nadir is the point below the horizon where the Sun is at Midnight. It signifies an electoral "revolution" by the people against their president. This happened in 1952, when it overpowered the rest of the chart which had predicted that the party in power would win. Eisenhower, a Republican, defeated Adlai Stevenson and succeeded Democrat Harry Truman as president. In this case also, Eisenhower's positive horoscope score easily overpowered Stevenson's very negative score. The intellectual Mr. Stevenson just didn't appeal as much to the people as the friendly and smiling old general. Another factor is that Ike did not pick a party to run in until it was time to run. A similar situation happened in 1848, when the new moon method also predicted an incumbent victory. Zachary Taylor, hero of the recent war with Mexico, picked the opposing party The Whigs even though he had served under Democrat James K. Polk. So, the challenging party won in both cases, although the party in power likely would have won if the war heroes had chosen to run in it.

Uranus at the Nadir also happened in 1932, when FDR kicked out the unpopular Herbert Hoover during the Great Depression, and in 1976 when Democrat Jimmy Carter turned out incumbent Gerald Ford, who had pardoned Nixon after he resigned in disgrace due to scandal. In these two cases the ruling planets of the Ascendant and Descendant also predicted a challenger victory, as normally indicated. Uranus was also at the Nadir in 1928. The rest of the chart indicated that the party in power would win, as it did. But Hoover had been in office for only 7 months when the Stock Market Crash came down on his stubborn head and ruined his chances for re-election.

So, Uranus at the Nadir worked 3 out of 4 times in the 20th century. The only other case was in 1868, when Republican Ulysses S. Grant succeeded Andrew Johnson, who had been a southern Democrat, but had been elected vice-president with Abraham Lincoln in 1864 on the "national unity" ticket. The Republican "radicals" of the time thus got their man in, toppling the party in power, even though they failed to convict and remove Johnson by one vote in the Senate earlier that year.

A new wrinkle appeared in the election of 2016, however. Uranus was at the Nadir again, if you count the houses only from the Ascendant. This is called the Equal House method by astrologers, and some say it's more accurate. In this case, it was. Uranus squared the Ascendant, and Donald Trump won a "revolutionary" victory and kicked the party in power, the Democrats, out of office. This was only the first time the New Moon showed Uranus squaring the Ascendant, but not in the Fourth House according to the usual chart methods. But here's another wrinkle: this will happen again, for the second time ever, in 2020. So, despite Trump's horoscope score, which is higher than all the announced candidates in 2020, he is still vulnerable to defeat as of this writing because Uranus will square the Ascendant (but not from the 4th House) in the New Moon before the election chart. But this being an unprecedented situation, it is no basis for a firm prediction.

Even though I thought Hillary might win in 2016, the fact remains that the two methods I rely on the most, the horoscope score and the new moon before the election, were both correct. Donald Trump always had a higher score than Hillary Clinton, and the New Moon before election correctly predicted the popular vote. Trump could be impeached and removed from office, because he often plays fast and loose with the law. If this happens, and Pence is the Republican candidate in 2020, his 8-7 score is easier for Democrats to beat.

Here's the outlook for the New Moon before the Election in the future. Remember, a candidate with a substantially higher score than an opponent, and who is less vulnerable to a Saturn Return, can still win in spite of the new moon indicator. The fact that the party in power is predicted to win the popular vote in 2020, and then the challenger is slated to win in 2024, could mean that Trump is re-elected and the Democrats win back the White House in 2024. It could also mean that if the Democrats win the presidency in 2020, they won't be able to hold it unless a candidate runs who has a great horoscope score, like Landrieu or McAuliffe. Meanwhile Trump could be thrown out of office before 2024. The midterm elections of 2022, which happen as the Pluto Return hits the USA horoscope, could reduce him or his successor to a figurehead. 6th-year midterm elections are usually a disaster for the party holding the White House anyway, and in this case Trump himself has been something of a disaster for the country in many peoples' minds. The sign Aquarius rules the legislature too, and we know how prominent that sign will become in the 2020s. Of course, all of this will be old news to those of you reading these words after 2024. Note that some indications may change if election day is moved, or extended through most people voting by mail.

Indications for 2016 and beyond for the new moon before election:
2016: party in power wins (popular vote win) (Uranus square the Ascendant; possible "revolution" indicator)
2020: party in power wins (Uranus square the Ascendant; possible "revolution" indicator)
2024: challenger wins
2028: party in power
2032: challenger
2036: party in power
2040: party in power
2044: "revolution" possible, favoring challenger (party in power ruler is higher, but Uranus is in 4th house and square the Ascendant)
2048: party in power

2052: challenger
2056: challenger
2060: party in power
2064: party in power
2068: party in power
2072: party in power favored in close election
2076: challenger
2080: party in power
2084: party in power
2088: party in power (Uranus square the Ascendant; possible "revolution" indicator)
2092: party in power
2096: party in power
2100: challenger, close election; 7 planets in 4th house

Jupiter and Saturn

Jupiter and Saturn may also upset the apple cart of expectations. In our time, zero election years like 2020 and 2040, when Jupiter and Saturn make a conjunction, frequently mean a change in the party in power, or a new direction of policy for the country. In fact, since real democracy was established in America in Andrew Jackson's times, in every zero-year election since 1840, the party in power changed, or the man elected died in office; or both. Let's look at what happened in the zero years when Jupiter and Saturn were making their conjunction:[95]

1800: Thomas Jefferson, Democratic-Republican, defeated incumbent John Adams, Federalist, in "the Revolution of 1800." Change in the party in power.

1820: James Monroe, incumbent Democratic-Republican, re-elected over John Quincy Adams.

1840: William Henry Harrison, Whig, defeated incumbent Martin Van Buren, Democrat. Harrison died in 1841. Change in the party in power, and death in office.

1860: Abraham Lincoln, Republican, defeated Stephen A Douglas, Democrat (party in power), and 2 others. Lincoln assassinated in 1865. Change in the party in power, and death in office.

1880: James A Garfield, Republican (party in power) defeated Winfield Scott Hancock, Democrat. Garfield assassinated in 1881. Death in office.

1900: William McKinley, incumbent Republican, defeated William Jennings Bryan. McKinley assassinated in 1901. Death in office.

1920: Warren G. Harding, Republican, defeated James Cox, Democrat (party in power). Harding died in 1923. Change in the party in power and death in office.

1940: Franklin D. Roosevelt, incumbent Democrat, re-elected over Wendell Willkie. FDR died in 1945. Death in office.

---

[95]   Sarah Janssen, senior editor, The World Almanac and Book of Facts, Infobase, 2018, pp. 487, 504.

1960: John F. Kennedy, Democrat, defeated Richard Nixon, Republican (party in power). Kennedy assassinated in 1963. Change in the party in power and death in office.

1980: Ronald Reagan, Republican, defeated Jimmy Carter, Democrat (party in power). Ronald Reagan survived assassination attempt "by inches" in 1981. Change in the party in power.

2000: George W Bush, Republican, defeated Al Gore, Democrat (party in power). Change in the party in power.

But since Reagan survived an assassination attempt soon after his election in 1980, and George W Bush survived in office after being elected in 2000, the zero year no longer automatically means that the president elected that year will die in office. And a change in party rulership only happened 7 out of 11 times from 1800 to 2000. So, a change in the party in power is not guaranteed by this conjunction. It's interesting though that when one party was predominant (1820: the Democratic-Republicans, 1880 and 1900: the Republicans, 1940: the Democrats), the change in the party in power did not happen in the zero year. Therefore, if the current party in power is not predominant, it will probably lose a zero-year election. Because the Republicans were not predominant in the divided USA in 2020, it seemed possible that President Trump might lose his re-election bid despite the new moon indicator and his higher horoscope score than the other candidates.

The 2020s are likely to be a progressive decade. It starts with Jupiter and Saturn joining together in Aquarius. With Pluto also in Aquarius starting in 2024, and Neptune in Aries starting in 2025-26, and with all three outer generational planets returning to or opposing their USA horoscope positions, indicating a possible revolution or civil war, as of this writing it's hard to see a typical Republican getting elected in these conditions.

It's no secret, however, that the voters are not happy with either of the two major parties. A strong independent candidate could beat both of them in the years ahead. Even Ross Perot, who had the money and charisma to win, but not a favorable horoscope, was able to rack up a good percentage of the vote as far back as 1992.[96] A progressive takeover of the Republican Party seems less likely, but already Donald Trump was at least unconventional. To predict future elections, an astrological prognosticator will need to balance all the various factors. Also, bear in mind that by the 22nd Century the conjunction will have moved back into a "9" year instead of a zero one.

The Saturn Return

The third major factor is the Saturn Return. This pattern was first reported in 1940 by Grant Lewi in his book <u>Astrology for the Millions</u>. It generally boils down to this warning for aspiring candidates: if Saturn returns to its position in your horoscope during the next three years after you run for president, you will lose the election. You may win if it happens in your 4th year as president or when you run for re-election (if

---

[96] Sarah Janssen, <u>op.cit.</u> p.504.

you have a positive horoscope score), but in that case sooner or later you'll wish you hadn't won! The Saturn Return happens to everyone when they are about 55 to 59 years old.

The Saturn Return didn't seem to bother the founding fathers, however. Of the first 6 presidents of the United States, five were elected just before their Saturn Return. The other, John Adams, lost his re-election bid even though his Saturn Return had already passed. These presidents were all chosen by the electoral college (except the 6th, chosen by the House of Representatives). The presidency was considered a job for a detached, comfortable, retired gentleman, according to Alexander Hamilton; not for an ambitious, Saturnian power-seeker like Aaron Burr. Once modern democracy was introduced in Andrew Jackson's time, however, American presidents were subject to all its rigors, temptations and tribulations, and therefore apparently to the Saturn Return too. In the election of 1824, the first during which the popular vote was a major factor, no candidate won the electoral college. John Quincy Adams beat Jackson in the House of Representatives, despite losing the popular vote. Both faced their Saturn return two years later, but Jackson's was due sooner. Since then, in fact, if both leading candidates face the Return, the one who faces it first is the one who generally loses.

Here is the list of all nominees who faced a Saturn Return, with the year in parentheses:[97]

- Andrew Jackson (1825), the first "democratic" candidate, lost in 1824 to John Quincy Adams (1826), but won in 1828 and 1832.

- Henry Clay (1835-36) lost to Andrew Jackson in 1832. He also lost in 1824 and 1844.

- Martin Van Buren (1841) lost to William Henry Harrison ("Tippecanoe") in 1840.

- John Tyler (1848-49), who succeeded Harrison, chose not to run in 1844 after a rocky term.

- Millard Fillmore (1858-59) lost to James Buchanan in 1856. John C. Fremont, the first Republican Party nominee, also lost. Fillmore had succeeded Zachary Taylor as president in 1850 and served 2 years.

- Abraham Lincoln (1868) was re-elected in 1864 but assassinated in 1865 at the end of the Civil War.

- Andrew Johnson (1868), who succeeded Lincoln, resisted post-civil war radical reconstruction and was impeached in 1868, but survived in office by 1 vote. He did not run for re-election that year.

- Horatio Seymour (1869) lost to Ulysses S. Grant in 1868.

- Rutherford B. Hayes (1881) was elected in 1876 but didn't run again in 1880.

- Winfield Scott Hancock (1882) lost to James A Garfield in 1880.

---

[97] Sarah Janssen, Ibid.

- Chester A. Arthur (1888) succeeded Garfield in 1881 but was not nominated for re-election in 1884.

- James G. Blaine (1888) lost to Grover Cleveland in 1884.

- Benjamin Harrison (1892) beat Grover Cleveland in the electoral college in 1888, but he was not re-elected in 1892 amid much public unrest.

- Grover Cleveland (1896) won in 1892 but was shoved aside for William Jennings Bryan in 1896. Upon his election in 1892, Cleveland was immediately saddled with the worst financial panic of the century in 1893, and a farmer-labor populist revolt, which he tried to repress.

- William McKinley (1902) was re-elected against Bryan in 1900 but was assassinated in 1901. He was also facing a revolt in the Philippines after his army had conquered it in 1898.

- William Howard Taft (1916) was elected in 1908 but defeated for re-election in 1912, after his sponsor Theodore Roosevelt rejected him and ran against him.

- Woodrow Wilson (1915-16) was elected in 1912 and re-elected during his Saturn Return in 1916. He immediately faced World War I, and then collapsed under the strain with a stroke in 1919 while campaigning for the League of Nations.

- Charles Evans Hughes (1920) was defeated by Woodrow Wilson in 1916.

- Warren G. Harding (1924) was elected in 1920, but he died in 1923 under the strains of scandal.

- Calvin Coolidge (1931) succeeded and won re-election in 1924. He wisely chose "not to run in 1928."

- Al Smith (1932) was defeated by Herbert Hoover in 1928.

- Herbert Hoover (1933) lost his re-election bid to FDR in 1932.

- Franklin D. Roosevelt (1940) won in 1932 and was re-elected in 1936. He won re-election in 1940 and 1944, only to die under the strains of World War II (1939-1945) in 1945.

- Adlai Stevenson (1959) lost his second run for president to Dwight Eisenhower in 1956.

- Barry Goldwater (1967) lost to Lyndon B. Johnson in 1964. His Saturn Return happened before LBJ's.

- Lyndon B. Johnson (1967-68) succeeded John F. Kennedy in 1963 and was elected in 1964, only to drop out of the presidential race in 1968 under the strains of the War in Vietnam and protests against it.

- Hubert Humphrey (1970) lost to Richard Nixon in 1968.

- Richard Nixon (1971-72), elected in 1968, invaded Cambodia and continued the War in Vietnam, despite continued protest. But upon publication of the Pentagon Papers in 1971, revealing the war's lies, he set up "the plumbers" to spy on Daniel Ellsberg, who had published them. Many of these plumbers then carried out a burglary at his opponent's headquarters at the Watergate Hotel in 1972, and Nixon covered up this crime. Although he was re-elected in 1972, scandal erupted immediately, and he was forced to resign in 1974.

- Gerald R. Ford (1972) was chosen by Nixon in 1973 to potentially succeed him, and once in office Ford pardoned him. He lost to Jimmy Carter in 1976.

- Jimmy Carter (1982) was elected in 1976, but he lost his bid for re-election to Ronald Reagan in 1980. (John Anderson, losing independent candidate, also faced his Saturn Return in late 1980 and 1981)

- Walter Mondale (1986) lost to Ronald Reagan in 1984.

- Michael Dukakis (1992) lost to George H W Bush in 1988.

- George W Bush (2004), son of George H W Bush, became president in 2000 through the electoral college after the Supreme Court stopped a recount in Florida against Al Gore, who had won the popular vote nationally. Bush's Saturn Return was due on election day 2004, at the end of the 4th year of his first term. During it, he was saddled with two wars, one against Afghanistan after the September 11, 2001 attack on the World Trade Center by Al Qaeda, and another of his own making in 2003 against Iraq. Neither war was completed by the end of his 2nd term. He also mishandled the Hurricane Katrina disaster in 2005 and had to deal with the financial crash and Great Recession in 2008.[98]

As you can see, anyone between 55 and 59 years old should think twice about running for president, and they should probably remember that if they run between the ages of 51 and 55, they might also not be re-elected and/or they may face disaster in office. In general, people of those ages should not press their luck regarding their ambitions for power in the next 4 years, especially around the time of their exact Saturn Return.

Summarizing the pattern, then, we see that from 1824 onward, 30.5% of the losing major party candidates, and/or former or sitting presidents who lost, 18 out of 59, faced a Saturn Return. You can see the full pattern in the list in part 1, with candidates who faced a Saturn Return indicated by * or **. Given that the potential age at which candidates can run is about 35 to 75, and the age at which they face a Saturn return is 55 to 59 (a 5-year period), that's about a 1 in 8 chance (12.5%). Saturn Returns therefore cost a candidate the election 2.5 times the chance rate.

---

[98] See **Appendix I** for references for the historical events mentioned related to presidents and their Saturn Return. See References for Chapter 12

10 candidates won the election despite their imminent Saturn Return. 8 of these were candidates who faced a Saturn Return during the 4th year of their term. Some of these unlucky winners were re-elected too. These 4th-year survivors all faced disaster while in office. This pattern does not include the founding fathers, Washington through John Quincy Adams.

11 out of 13 candidates who ran for president in the general election while facing a Saturn Return which was due only in the first three years after the election, lost it. (84.6%). One of those who made it into office under this condition, William McKinley in 1900, was assassinated in the first year. These 11 candidates were: Andrew Jackson, Martin Van Buren, Millard Fillmore, Horatio Seymour, Winfield Scott Hancock, Herbert Hoover, Adlai Stevenson, Barry Goldwater, Hubert Humphrey, Jimmy Carter, Walter Mondale. This pattern excludes the first 6 presidents. Richard Nixon experienced his Saturn Return in 1971 in his 3rd year, *after* Hubert Humphrey's in what would have been his second year. Saturn also returned to within 2 degrees of Nixon's position in 1972.

7 other candidates were not even re-nominated by their party or chose not to run again when their Saturn Return was happening or due within 4 years, as if they knew what was coming. These presidents were: John Tyler (with his Saturn Return due before what would have been his next term began), Andrew Johnson, Chester Arthur, Grover Cleveland, Calvin Coolidge, and Lyndon Johnson; plus, Rutherford B Hayes also honored his original pledge not to run for re-election to a term in which his Saturn Return was due. Only 6 other presidents since 1824 chose not to run or were not chosen to run again, with no imminent Saturn Return (Polk, Fillmore, Pierce, Buchanan, TR, Truman). 54% of those presidents who didn't run again or were dumped faced a Saturn Return, compared to the 12.5% chance rate. This does not include the presidents who upheld the two-term tradition and chose not to run after 2 full terms (4 of the founding fathers, Jackson, Grant, and the incapacitated Wilson).

4 others who faced a Saturn Return during the term to which they were elected, died while still in office due to the strains and conflicts they faced. These presidents included: Abraham Lincoln, William McKinley, Warren G Harding and Franklin D. Roosevelt. These men all died, of course, after being elected in a zero year. That's 29 candidates so far who lost, didn't or couldn't run again, or died while facing their Saturn Return.

6 other presidents faced a long and grueling war during the term to which they were elected; a war during which their presidencies were destroyed. These were: Abraham Lincoln, Woodrow Wilson, FDR, Lyndon Johnson, Richard Nixon and George W. Bush. Wilson suffered a stroke, FDR died, Lyndon Johnson did not run again, and Richard Nixon resigned; only George W Bush survived more-or-less intact, but with his and his family's reputation shattered. Abraham Lincoln did not suffer his Saturn Return until his second term, when a man who could not accept that the Civil War was over shot and killed him just one week after the war ended, and only a month after the second term began.

Kamala Harris is the only 2020 candidate who faces a Saturn Return, and so I predict she will not win. She has a very low horoscope score too. Others such as Gavin Newsom and Steve Bullock would encounter their Saturn Return if they ran in 2024.

Nixon resigns in 1974, after facing his Saturn Return in 1971 and in the election year of 1972 (Watergate)[99]

Some presidents faced no Saturn Return during wars that were less taxing on them, including John Adams (war with France), James K. Polk (Mexican War), Harry Truman (Korean War) and George H W Bush (Gulf War). They did not face Saturn Returns during their time in office. James Madison faced a Saturn Return just before a war (War of 1812), although this was before the democratic era began in 1824, and his presidency wasn't destroyed by this war, even though the war was poorly fought. William McKinley's war in 1898 was called "splendid," but it resulted in a long colonial war in The Philippines starting in 1899. He faced a Saturn Return due during this war two years after his re-election in 1900, and he was assassinated in 1901.

Benjamin Harrison was elected in 1888 despite an upcoming Saturn Return due 4 years later, but then lost his bid for re-election in 1892. Like John Quincy Adams, he did not win the popular vote when he was elected. Harrison faced a recession and a lot of labor rebellion during his term. It only got worse for his successor Grover Cleveland, who was also elected with his Saturn Return due in the 4th year of his term. The birth of the modern "populist" or "pro-labor" Democratic Party that we know today followed from these years of turmoil and transformation under the epochal Neptune-Pluto conjunction of 1892.

All bets are off under this unique, once-in-500-years cataclysmic cosmic event. The fortunes of civilization and all who tend to it are up in the air. Consider some of the events under past conjunctions between Neptune and Pluto: Sulla overthrowing the Roman Republic. The Fall of the Roman Empire. The Fall of the Tang Dynasty. Henry Bolingbroke overthrew Richard II. The Fall of Bismarck. Fortunes are not great for those

---

99   Photo: https://www.cavaliergalleries.com/artist/Harry_Benson/works/624

in power during Neptune-Pluto conjunctions! No wonder Benjamin Harrison could not win in 1892, despite some advantages in the indicators.

From this list of Saturn Return victims you can see how heavy it weighs on presidents and candidates who encounter it. Almost all major party nominees and presidents who experienced it since 1824, 33 of them in all, were defeated, didn't run again, died in office or suffered a debilitating disaster. Only ONE candidate faced a Saturn Return while running for or in office who managed to avoid landing on this list: the very first one, and one of the first 6 presidents, John Quincy Adams in 1824, who won his election in the House despite losing the popular vote, beat a candidate who suffered a Saturn Return before he did, and then lost to him anyway four years later!

Saturn represents the state, and ambitions for power. Power corrupts, and it's addictive too. It's hard to let go of it. Presidents are no different; they often suffer for their ambitions, as do we all.

Connections to the USA Horoscope

Another method astrologers sometimes use is conjunctions with the US horoscope by planets in candidates' charts. Using the birthday for the USA of July 4, 1776 at about 5 PM, I compared the planets' positions in the horoscopes of 44 presidents, and 97 other candidates who never served as president, with the US chart. I found that presidents had such a connection 1.7 times more often than did defeated candidates, when restricting the orb (amount of exactitude) of their conjunctions to US planets to only one degree. When I extended the orb to 2 degrees, I found only a 1.06 times difference. In this method, I used a time of 12 PM to cast charts for candidates whose birth times were not known.

Perhaps this method might explain some unusual and unique attractions Americans have had to some presidents, and some of the talents they have offered the nation. For example, maybe the fact that George W Bush and Calvin Coolidge both have their Sun in Cancer (sign of home, motherhood and apple pie) exactly aligned with America's Sun, accounts for why the people like their home-spun, simple and complacent personalities. Teddy Roosevelt's connection between his rising Jupiter and the USA's Mars certainly illustrates how TR expanded our aggressive and courageous spirit and our penchant for waving a "big stick" around in other nations' faces. Another aggressive leader was George Bush's father H.W., whose Sun was aligned with and stimulated the nation's Mars to "overcome the Vietnam syndrome" and get us into wars again; successfully in his case. Maybe Richard Nixon's conjunction of mysterious Neptune with America's "tricky magician" Mercury explains our fascination with all his nefarious and secretive activities. Thomas Jefferson certainly awakened the country's ability to transform itself by reminding us that a little rebellion is a good thing now and then. His natal Uranus was conjunct America's Pluto. And James Madison certainly kept the common people's spirit of freedom alive through the connection between his Uranus and the nation's Moon in Aquarius. Barack Obama tried to clean up the international mess left by George W. Bush, and to advance health care too, perhaps because his warrior planet Mars was right on top of the nation's Neptune in health-conscious Virgo in the 9th house of foreign affairs.

Donald Trump's Saturn connects within 1 degree to America's Mercury in the 8th house (financial dealings) in Cancer (a sign of nationalism and racial heritage), which might go a long way to explain the appeal of his promise to "build a wall" on America's southern border (Saturn = limits and barriers) and "make America great again" through tough deal-making. Venus is also close to this US Mercury, with his Sun close to the US Mars in Gemini. Elizabeth Warren's Mars connects to the nation's Uranus. Joe Biden misses this connection to Uranus from his Saturn by 2 minutes of arc. No other current candidates have a strong US chart connection. It may have given Trump an advantage, but this indicator may not be as powerful as the others, since the ratio of winners to losers is only 1.70. (This percentage rose by .05 with Trump's victory).[100]

The Spirit of the Times: Uranus, Neptune and Pluto

Another connection I found was very interesting, however. From the time of Teddy Roosevelt, who launched the USA's career as a world power able to make progressive reforms, until the reign of Ronald Reagan, who helped end the Cold War that had kept us so involved in the world, but also turned our nation away from the progress that TR and his cousin FDR had launched, the outer three planets connected our presidents to the zeitgeist, or spirit of the times. ALL 14 out of the 14 presidents between and including TR and Reagan experienced a visit of Uranus, Neptune and/or Pluto over one or more of their most personal indicators, the Sun, Moon or Ascendant, within orb of a conjunction and in the same sign, sometime during their time in office or on the campaign trail. This is more than twice the chance rate. This connection put them in touch with the spirit of the times and the thrust of world progress, and they were called upon to serve this higher calling. Plus, JFK had a special posthumous connection, as Uranus and Pluto joined together exactly on his Moon in Virgo 2 years after his death, showing how his revolutionary work lived on in the efforts of his successors (LBJ also had Moon and Sun in Virgo, giving him another huge boost in the mid-sixties; Nixon had Virgo rising).

After Reagan, and probably because of the direction he took the country, the next 3 presidents didn't have this connection; not either President Bush, nor Bill Clinton. This indicates what we all know; that these 3 recent presidents failed to lead us toward the high potential that lies within the spirit of these times.

Note however that Reagan may not have had this connection either. It is based on a birth time of about 4 AM with a Sagittarius Ascendant, which would have connected him to Uranus and Neptune transits during his 2 terms. However, this birth time is uncertain. Note also that Herbert Hoover just barely had Neptune transiting over his Sun in Leo when he ran for president; but then lost it once he entered the White House and

---

[100] See Appendix I for historical references to presidents and connections to the USA
    horoscope. See References for Chapter 12

the Depression hit. Something similar happened to Richard Nixon. Uranus and Pluto were still in Virgo, his rising sign (same degree as JFK's Moon), for his first year or two, but once he went down the Watergate path starting in 1971, he was off track. Barack Obama was also connected to Neptune through his Ascendant, (which we now know, thanks to Trump's pressure on him to release his birth certificate). Jupiter and Chiron (the centaur asteroid called "the wounded healer") joined Neptune as it moved very close to Obama's Ascendant in Aquarius in December 2009-- just before the health care reform often named after him was passed. Because I used that conjunction to successfully predict that Obamacare would pass, among other successful predictions I had made, I decided to write this book.

It should be no surprise however that with Trump's election in 2016, we in the USA are again now seriously off-track from the world spirit of progress. It seems very fitting that Trump has a strong connection to the nation, but not to the world. He puts "America First," especially in trade and immigration issues, and specifically opposes the global revolutionary spirit.

I hope that any future presidents we elect will keep us "on the road again" to world peace and progress. Among known potential candidates with positive scores, many of them have connections to the revolutionary planet Uranus in the years ahead, which may in fact be revolutionary times. Republican Mike Pence (8-7) would have a connection to Uranus in Gemini late in his term if he were elected or re-elected in 2024. Among Democrats, Mitch Landrieu (16-2) would probably have a similar connection to Uranus through his Gemini Moon if he won that year. Terry McAuliffe (at least 11-2) also connects to Uranus through his Gemini Moon if he wins in 2024. Joe Biden (14-7) has Moon in early Taurus, so he would have a lunar connection to Uranus early in his term if elected in 2020. Since an independent or third-party candidate might win in 2024, that opens up a slight chance for Green Party candidate Jill Stein (16-2), whose Uranus connects with her Sun that year. I don't expect a Green Party candidate to have a real shot until the 2040s, but you never know; especially if Stein does something before 2024 to elevate her status in the world. Tulsi Gabbard (11-6) would not have a connection of Neptune to her Sun in Aries until the early 2030s.

Chapter 13

Your Life in the New Age

Now that you know some of how the New Age will unfold for humanity and the Earth, it's time to bring the focus to the individual. This chapter will cover just some of what may lie ahead for you in the years from 2020 to 2100, showing how the major planetary cycles interact with your Sun sign and your rising sign. Be sure not to interpret these indications too narrowly, as they must be somewhat general. Of course, the forecast for the entire period may not apply to you personally if you are not on Earth then, but if not, it will be relevant for others born under the same sign as you. The usual birth dates for each sun sign are given below, along with the forecast. A complete reading by an astrologer for your birthday, time and location would give you more detailed information than what's in this book. But I do include an approximate *table of houses* in **Appendix B**, so that you can find and apply your rising sign to the forecasts below if you think it fits you better. Some ideas from Chapter 20 of my first book may help as well, though it only covers the years up to 2050. Remember that astrologers don't have sufficient information to make forecasts of unalterable fate. Even if we did, we could not say how each person would respond. We are always free to do the best we can with what destiny gives us.

Most people want to know which years will be the best ones for us. To follow the ups and downs of your life, with its **lucky years**, and the years of fruitful hard work and useful lessons, you can turn ahead to the section on the rhythms of Jupiter and Saturn, further in this chapter. Here we begin with the overall forecast for each sign, starting with what the great conjunction of those two planets in December 2020 portends for you. This conjunction of Jupiter and Saturn in the first degree of Aquarius (also joined by Pluto) opens a 200-year era of repeating alignments of these two planets in air signs every 20 years, making it what we call the great mutation. The 2020 conjunction could set the stage for much that is to come for all of us. So focus your 2020 vision now on how you can unfold your potentials in the New Age of Aquarius, as it continues to dawn through the 21st Century. I skip through the years pretty fast in this review, but after all, time really flies for us all.

ARIES (March 21-- April 20) The New Age begins for you with Jupiter and Saturn inviting you to make contributions to the larger world. Your natural spirit of activism will find much to do, and you may be reaching for a higher status in the years ahead. Later 2020 may find you especially active and aggressive. Then the powerful conjunction of Jupiter and Neptune in 2022 provides the chance to get away and refresh your spiritual life.

Neptune in your sign from 2025-26 to 2039 will find you more starry-eyed than usual. Dreams may be more important to you than realities, and you may get confused and discouraged if they don't come true. Those born under the early degrees of the sign may be involved in some momentous world events or crucial decisions in 2025-26 that will affect the rest of your life. Aries natives will find their minds stimulated and their networking proclivities extended as Uranus moves through Gemini in harmony with the other planets in the late 2020s and early 2030s. 2029 will be a very active year, with some disputes, but 2035 could be a very inspirational year for you. Changes in home and family life will be your focus in the later 2030s, with many generous and rewarding ideas concerning your property and your heritage unfolding in 2037. With the next Jupiter-Saturn conjunction in 2040 opposing your Sun in your 7ᵗʰ house, your plans and fortunes will depend on your relations with others in the following years. Shore up your marriage and choose your partners wisely in the 2040s, since by the 2050s they will often be under strain from your desire for independence. You will apply the Green Revolution to your health and spiritual life in the late 2040s, which may help your personal relationships, and you will meet many new visionaries who expand your mind in the 2050s. But Spring 2046 and all year in 2056 could be times for quarrels.

After the next Jupiter-Saturn conjunction in 2060 in Gemini, with Neptune there as well, you will continue to focus on expanding your education and networking skills in the years ahead. 2061 will be an active year. Neptune enters Cancer in 2066, urging you for the next 14 years or so to seek the ideal home, and to get in touch with your subconscious and inner self. Your imagination may stimulate you to create and to travel. You are very restless and aggressive in later 2067. Then in 2068 Pluto comes into your sign for most of the rest of the century. You can apply all you have learned and discovered to unfold your personal powers of leadership and offer it to others, especially in Feb. 2074 which could be a time of a glorious struggle and victory. As Uranus squares Pluto in the early and mid-2070s you may be involved in some revolutionary and innovative schemes that lead to power struggles in Feb. 2076 and in 2077 and more quarrels in June 2078. But breakthroughs occur in the 2080s, as these relationships get easier for you after the next Jupiter-Saturn conjunction in Aquarius. By then Aries natives will be able to cultivate their personal power and style and express it in their active dedication to the great ideals and causes they support. After a break to restore your health in the early 2090s, it's full speed again for Aries, as Uranus visits your sign and stimulates the best of your creative and pioneering leadership abilities. In late 2099, you are eager to get into as many fights as you can.

TAURUS (April 21 – May 20) You can begin the New Age in 2020 by expanding your connections to the wider world and growing in wisdom and status within it. You may be taking many courses of higher learning or shifting your religion. If you are born early in the sign, these years could find you reaching for new power and authority. Uranus in Taurus means that all born under this sign will experience their creative genius unfolding in the early 2020s. At first some of your new ideas could conflict with those in authority that you hope will help your rise in status, but as the 2020s proceed, you'll be getting more and more support and making connections that help you financially. At the end of the decade, however, extra burdens and power struggles could occur, so prepare for the battle. In the mid-2030s you may transform your home life and career at the same time, with attendant difficulties, as you seek to align your soul purpose with your place in the world. Spiritual help will come to your aid in this quest, and you may pursue this theme of your life again in the early 2050s.

In 2038 Neptune enters your sign, so for the next 14 years your spiritual quest will be a larger part of your life, and your soul quest will deepen. As a Taurus, communion with Nature and Earth spirits will be important in this adventure. You will be more foggy-headed, dreamy, imaginative and unrealistic than usual. Since it is squared by Uranus for the first 7 of these years, changes in home and family could arouse you to find your spiritual home amidst the chaos of life. At the same time, the next Jupiter-Saturn conjunction in 2040 will find you focusing on work and health and being more of service. In 2043 you may find others opposing your generous, idealistic and innovative activities for a while. In 2045 this only stimulates those born late in the sign to be more to be resourceful and innovative. The Green Revolution of the mid/late 2040s urges you be a creative leader in the higher causes of the time, including environmental ones. In 2047 your ebullient generosity and compassion will know no bounds, as Jupiter joins Neptune in a powerful and historic conjunction in your sign, connecting you to important events. Pursue your creative paths again in 2052 and they will be successful.

As a Taurus you can get stuck in your ways, and you may be in something of a rut in the mid-2050s. You may be subject to fits of rage or explosions of energy in late 2052, as Mars visits your sign. Uranus may pull you out of any ruts you're in when sudden changes and breakthroughs happen as Uranus opposes your sign in the early and middle 2060s. This could get quite disturbing in 2063, but many new connections and new ideas will help you financially in these years. As mystical new age ideas come to you in the 2070s, they could lead to disruptions, revelations, and new directions in your religious life around 2073. Under the powerful planetary configurations of 2079-2080, the theme of blending your soul purpose and your career emerges again, as you once again pursue wealth and power in the world and at the same time seek to express your spirit. In 2084 as Mars visits your sign you could get quite rebellious and aggressive about all this. But your soul purpose rises to predominance over other interests during the Jupiter-Neptune conjunctions in Leo in 2085-86, and your perspective evens your temper. But perhaps because of this turn in your life, you may neglect your finances, and they may get very chaotic in 2090. As the century comes toward a close in 2096-97, you gain a new sense of power as Pluto enters your sign and Saturn-Neptune trines it. You'll enter a winning track then if you can release yourself from old habit patterns and discover new sources of energy within, and wealth without.

GEMINI (May 21-- June 20) Financial dealings and investments will be important to you as the New Age opens in 2020, as you seek a firm foundation for the exciting years to come. You will fight for recognition and to have your say in 2023, as Mars visits your sign. A period of liberation will be bubbling up for you in 2023-24 in your dreams and your subconscious, or through institutional investments. Your creativity explodes in 2025, with Uranus entering your sign for 7 years of good luck. It's time to be a leader in the exciting new developments that change America and the world in the next few years, and to help others through our troubles. Your tremendous writing and speaking skills are at their best, and connections with associates and with world networks are buzzing and bursting with life, so don't let the 2020s pass without making them a highlight of your life.

In 2030-2031, you'll assess and make decisions about what you've accomplished, and focus on the new opportunities that others may present to you. Changes in your family and finances may occur in the 2030s, with some resulting conflicts likely in Summer 2033 and Fall 2037. The Jupiter-Saturn conjunction of 2040 happens in your 5th house, so romance, relationships, children, or entertainment and sports may come into prominence in your life, along with more opportunities to share your writing and journalistic talents. As the Green Revolution comes along in the later 2040s, you'll be making changes in your career and your home life, which may be disrupting and surprising, especially in the Summer of 2048. You may be experimenting with lifestyles, teaching methods, or ways to live more sustainably on the land and in harmony with Nature.

Neptune enters your sign in 2052 for 14 years, with Uranus in trine to it for 7. Expect your imagination to be stimulated and your vision to be either fogged up or starry-eyed. Brilliant works could stream from your pen. In 2053-54 you will be working hard to advance your career and status. This could be a struggle, leading to possible anger or overwork as Mars visits your sign in late 2054 and early 2055. But you may accomplish much that can help transform the world around you. The next Jupiter-Saturn conjunction in 2060 happens in early Gemini, bringing you both luck and life lessons that could change your life. Around July 1 could be an especially expansive and energetic time, and your eloquence will be boundlessly inspiring. This may propel you into a position of leadership. Pluto in Pisces in your 10th house from 2043 all the way through 2068 will be a continual energetic stimulus to bring career dreams to fruition. But at other times you may waste your talents and reputation through escapism, indulgence, resentment and deception, depending on your soul own development. In the early to mid-2060s the situation could get intense, especially for those born later in Gemini, as Neptune in your sign squares Pluto. The question is, after 2066 as Neptune enters Cancer, will your quest for achievement or escape under Pluto in Pisces affect your home and finances? And will new stimulation from Uranus in Sagittarius opposing your sign in 2065 and in the late sixties further disrupt your life, or unfold more of your brilliant ingenuity that enables you to master it? As Mars visits your sign in late 2069 and early 2070, you will find out how intelligently you can deal with your problems and outwit your opponents.

In the 2070s and early 2080s, planets in Aquarius, Aries and Leo bring lots of opportunity to unfold your talents as things become smoother and your world expands. Wonderful adventures and friendships await you in this period, if you can keep potential quarrels to a minimum. Your eloquence swells to a peak again in 2085-86. The following year Uranus enters Pisces in your 10th house, and this could see you challenging authority or rising to status as a brilliant spokesperson. During the tense T-square of June 2090 you'll be involved in sharp controversy. It will be a difficult year, but you may learn a great deal about the chaotic conditions of life. Around 2096 confusing roadblocks come up. As the century ends it may be time to slow down, reconnect, restore your spirits, and develop creative talents.

Cancer (June 21 – July 21) Making new connections with visionary friends and partners will one of your pursuits as the 2020s begin. This may mean changes in your current relationships though. Connections you make may help with innovative financial investments and partnerships in the following years. In 2022 you will find much spiritual and artistic inspiration that expands your view of the world. In 2025 Neptune enters Aries, and in the next 20 years or so (those early in the sign will see this earlier, later years later) your visions will be directed outward. Career goals will be idealistic, or just aimless and impractical. Rises and falls in status in about 2026 may be in store for those born early in the sign. In 2031-32 it may be time to take a breather to restore your spirits and health.

While Uranus is in your sign from 2033 to 2040 it's time to break through your shyness and share your sensitive genius. 2035 will be a fortunate time for your idealistic ventures. Your financial position may rise and fall a bit in this period due to unstable world conditions later in the year and in 2036. Your 7-year up and down roller coaster ride with Uranus is much more fun in 2037 and 2038 when Jupiter comes along. But in late 2039 and early 2040 you may be subject to temperamental fits and family issues. In the early 2040s you settle things down, as the next Jupiter-Saturn line-up indicates more focus on establishing a more harmonious and stable home life. Later in the decade you will travel, learn and write about what's going on in your community and your world, and at decades end and into the next you will make some amazing personal connections and discoveries.

By the mid-2050s you'll be changing home and family life and reorganizing your relationship to the land and your partners too. Discovering your new soul-purpose could result, which may conflict with what your bosses and authorities want you to do. If you're born early in the sign, be especially watchful of your temper in dealing with these conflicts, and take new initiatives, as Mars visits your sign in late 2054. Those born later in the sign Cancer may do a rebellion against authority of sorts in early 2057, as Mars makes its visit to you guys then and turns stationary in your sign. In the 2060s many Cancers will experience a stimulating love life and friendships, and perhaps motivated by this, your philosophical and spiritual searches will also intensify under Pluto in Pisces. This could lead to a quest into dark spaces by mid-decade, and it could even be like a hero's journey-- and it could be a long one as Neptune enters your sign in 2066 for a 14-year stay. Many discoveries await you, and you may come out of all these years transformed and renewed if you were prepared and ready for the adventure, and if you can remain as sober, clear-minded and optimistic as you can be. As Pluto enters Aries in 2068, you may be ready to confront the world again, but don't be disillusioned by defeat, as Neptune in your sign from 2066 to 2080 will inspire you to have very big and even over-inflated dreams and expectations. You'll be especially feisty and dreamy in early 2072, 2073-74 and 2077. By working with others, your previous dreams of accomplishment can come true in 2079 and the early 2080s. You may make a new initiative in November 2086, but watch and stay safe that month. Religious disputes motivate your search for emotional security in mid-2090, and new inspirations come in 2093 to further your quest. Your transformative career goals could gain support from imaginative financial dealings in the 2090s. New ambitious ideas and conflicts at work could affect your status as the decade comes to a close.

Leo (July 22 – August 22) As the 2020s begin you will focus on your work, which may be stimulating and idealistic in nature. Many new directions will open up. Early Leo natives will be encouraged to travel widely and meet new people in the mid-2020s and aroused to become more energetic and assertive in December 2024. The people may need your inspirational Leo confidence, so be sure to put it on display. At decade's end Leos may be sparring with some worthy opponents and bosses, and you will likely do so again in 2035-36. But your visionary ambitions will be powerful then, so unleash them to help you win.

The Jupiter-Saturn conjunction in Libra, Neptune in your 10th house *and* Uranus in your sign in the 2040s impels you to develop your knowledge and communication skills, unfold your performing genius and bring your inspiration into your work and career. You may go to extremes and test your boundaries, so don't let your success go to your head or tilt at too many windmills, especially in early 2042 as Mars visits your sign for its stationary turns, or in 2043-44 you may be taken down a notch, and your property, home and family could be affected. The upheavals, awakenings and changes of the late 2040s will inspire you to seek personal and financial independence, and you may emerge as an entirely new person with transformed relationships, although there may be breakups in the process. The July 2047 conjunction and eclipse highlights this rebirth, as you get another opportunity in 2047-48 to share your charming presence and your resources with others, and thereby boost your own status and wealth, especially by the Fall of 2049. Your skill in dealing with partners and bosses will be tested in 2050-52, but this challenge will expand your networking skills and thus your realm of influence in the following years. There will be many opportunities to expand the good times in the 2050s, and Leos are always the life of the party. And you will also discover how much more you need to learn about the world and other people, including those in your circle of friends. You may be aroused to activism as Mars turns stationary and moves retrograde in Leo in early 2057. Be sure and control temperamental and ego-defensive outbursts or risky adventures.

2059 may see some disturbing changes at home, and a new spiritual interest surging within you. Summer Solstice 2060 may see you leading the charge in a great cause. Leos born early in the sign are in a position to experience breakthroughs in sports and romance or in an entertainment career in 2066. You'll be more and more eager to explore the world from the time Pluto enters Aries in 2068, and maybe bring your act on tour. Those born early in Leo should be careful of conflict and control temper in December 2071. Some real success and fame could come in your expressive pursuits in early 2074. Don't miss that opportunity in mid-February.

An especially visionary period for you could begin as Neptune enters your sign in 2079. As the 2080s proceed things will get more complicated, if indeed very exciting, with many break-ups and new relationships, many opportunities to work or quarrel with others over your imaginative schemes, and maybe the danger of disillusionment if others don't support you. So be sure to take your ego down a little and ask for divine or expert guidance in these years. You may well be rewarded with fame and fortune again in 2085-86 if you come through this confusing and stimulating time well. And the following years should be smooth and inspirational overall, although early Leos will have to control their rebellious temper in August and September of 2097.

Virgo (August 23 – September 22) The 2020 conjunction finds you expanding your personal power beyond what you have known. You may seek positions of authority, or you may have writing, crafts or music to share. It's time to apply your talents and your skills and see what you can do. You will also carefully speculate financially and make investments that also help others. Partners may help you expand in 2022, and travels and education widen your perspective in 2024, which helps you make financially beneficial connections. The next year early Virgos may become visionary pioneers in investment schemes or help others in this work with new ideas. Keep your usual practical perspective and don't be deceived by false promises and impossible dreams. The connections Virgos have made will open new original and absorbing career paths for you guys in the later 2020s. Your work will help put society on a more reliable and practical path during this time of disturbing change. You are a rock of stability amid chaos. Work out conflicts between old ideologies and new discoveries. Powered by a spark of new energy as Mars turns direct in your sign in 2029, you will climb toward higher status in the early 2030s. Meanwhile, restore your spirits by expanding and nourishing your family life, and find a place for it amid the challenging demands of your work. Your success will enable you to help higher causes and find new friends in 2038-39.

In the 2040s, your work with others helps your financial independence. You dream of traveling to exotic natural places as Neptune travels your 9th house. You may become an ecological tour guide. Your love of wild places involves you in controversies with institutions that become important fights during the green revolution a few years later. Early Virgos may face a power struggle or break-up late in 2044 which pushes you to develop new green ideas in managing your home and land that others can learn from. With Uranus in your sign, expect to emerge as an experienced leader in the movement in the later 2040s, to be an advocate for change and transformation, and to provide many inventive ideas on how to make the world sustainable and help the people regain power. You can be an important resource in your community. Make the most of this time and shine. Spread your example to the world in 2047.

Virgos will advance their wealth and career through innovation and imagination in the 2050s. Even so, legal challenges happen in 2053-54, so keep your career affairs above board and know what associates are doing. Be careful and practical in your business dealings in the late 2050s and early 2060s to keep out of trouble. In the 2050s and 60s, education and new ideas widen your interests. In the Summer of 2060, your career as a great charismatic speaker or teacher expands, which you can offer to the world or to any spiritual movement that's going on. Many disputes over new ideas, and legal battles with authority over issues important to the world, could consume your time in the 2060s, as you pursue impossible dreams in your idealistic career. Later in the decade, changes in your home and family life crop up too, as well as mind-expanding travels.

The great configurations of 2079-2081 put you more in the background, as most Virgos like it. Be creative and imaginative in your work or for an organization. Impress your teacher with your innovative and analytical mind and find rewards through science and technology. Become a leader in an institution that serves people with compassion. Shocking and stimulating changes in relationships will knock you out of your rut in the late 2080s and 2090s. By the mid-2090s Virgos will expand beyond their well-analyzed world, as Neptune visits your sign and opens your imagination. But Neptune brings possible drift, delusion and addiction for those Virgos less prepared for the unknown. Widen your worldview beyond analysis and fear and it will be a wonderful excursion of discovery.

Libra (September 23-- October 22) The new Aquarian Age in late 2020 finds Libras working at home and managing family issues. Ground yourself within your soul purpose. Dealing with opponents or assertive partners may present problems. Afterward, first early Libras, and then later ones, will share creative gifts and find romance, as well as make creative investments. As you become a great performer, you'll contribute to the progressive and tumultuous second half of the 2020s, especially in the amazing Summer of 2026 (especially early Libras), and during the active time in early 2029 (Mars and Jupiter stationary-retrograde in Libra). But quarrels with those who misunderstand you may lead to neurotic suspicions in 2025, so center yourself and don't depend too much on others' approval. You may be changing the world through legal exploits, magnificent speeches or diplomatic efforts that sometimes take you to foreign places or concern very fundamental ideas. As Libras perform these feats, they need to be realistic about assertive partners and opponents (Neptune in Aries opposite your Sun 2025 through 2039). Financial power struggles may be an issue in 2028. Bring new ideas to your work or strike out in new career paths as Uranus transits Cancer from 2033 to 2040. Be ready for unexpected changes. In early 2035 associates expand your life or lead you into amazing and unrealistic adventures.

In 2040 the next conjunction of the two great chronocraters happens in your sign. New opportunities test and challenge your self-identity as you shift your whole life and work. You may be involved in the controversial and visionary world financial reorganization schemes of the early 2040s, and they may affect your own fortunes. Apply your idealistic sense of balance to the projects of the time. The changes and upheavals of the late 2040s will inspire you to advance new ideas for a sustainable and healthy environment, and to work in and reform the organizations and institutions that serve the higher good. You may be seeking your own spiritual and physical rebirth as well now, and for many years to come. In the early and mid-2050s, Uranus is in your sign. New ideas and visions flow through you, and friendship and romance multiply. You may find a chance to unfold your genius and share it with the world. This life-changing Uranus aspect usually only comes once in a lifetime, and it's rare to have Neptune supporting it in a trine at the same time, so make the most of it.

You will be challenged by others to learn more in 2056, and to make your new ideals real. But the next chronocrater conjunction in 2060 opens up more opportunity for Libras to widen your experience and travel the world. In Summer you join world-changing adventures and causes. More adventures come your way as Mars visits your sign in early 2061, so be sure and keep safe and be prepared. Meanwhile your quest for greater health and self-renewal gets more intense through the sixties, as your worldview is dissolved and illusions fall. Learn philosophy and delve into mystical religion. You may emerge in the later 2060s as a teacher and writer. From 2068 on, with Pluto in Aries, you will boldly challenge opponents to the truths you have discovered and try to transform them. In the process you will be transformed as well. In the late 2060s and early 2070s you will express your imaginative insights in new careers. The fiery grand trine of Feb.15, 2074 may impel you to redesign your community or the world. Later that year and in 2077 you may need to focus on conflicts in your home and family. How-ever these family relations and partnerships are reconstructed, the great alignments of 2079-2081 will provide more fabulous opportunities for Libras to share their creative gifts and experience wonderful, life-changing romance and friendship. Go forth and share your enthusiasm for change in late 2085 and through 2086. Battles for status may happen in the early 2090s, and be careful about reckless plans, power struggles or needless quarrels as Mars visits your sign in May, 2093. You may return to self-searching until century's end, when more Martian adventures and misfortunes in November 2099 reshape your whole life and open new directions for you in the new century (another Jupiter-Saturn conjunction in your sign in Sept.2100, opposed by Uranus).

Scorpio (October 23 – November 21) As the new era opens, you are getting an education, learning new skills and discovering your boundless creative imagination. Some of you Scorpios, being natural investigators, could make new discoveries in your own neighborhood. Your new quest for knowledge and inner roots could take many years and transform your life. You will soon apply what you learn in the 2020s to improve your home and family life and make interesting new connections to people who advance important movements in the world. You will need more knowledge of family subjects, because Uranus will shaking up some of your relationships and family affairs in the early 2020s. You will deal with some conflict with partners and family members in early 2029, and this extends to authorities you deal with in 2035-36. You will have much work to do in the 2030s to find a rewarding place in the world where you can be of service, and yet still be true to your ongoing spiritual quest to transform yourself and your relationships from within. You discover wide connections to distant realms that call you home.

In the 2040s you will have much to do to help others reshape their finances. Your own ambitions will bring struggle and conflict in 2042-43. Meanwhile your artistic inspirations will unfold as you commune with Nature and express its beauties. You will seek dreamy, ideal relationships that take you to mysterious and wonderful places. But others may not live up to your ideals around 2043, and you may project your fears onto them and seek to control them. Fortunately, the liberating and awakening energies of the later 2040s stimulate your friendships and associations, and this not only eases your fears and softens your demands on people, but it offers opportunities to share your developing artistic talents. You may be involved in the great causes and movements of this time to restore the Earth and transform human suffering into blessed abundance and divine consciousness. In the 2050s this may extend to occult interests and to enlightening, secret research projects. As 2059 leads into the early 2060s, with Uranus in your sign, your genius unfolds from these quests and your mystical or scientific investigations lead you to major discoveries. Your romantic and sex life may be aroused as well. These romantic adventures could get pretty intense, confusing and mysterious during the 2060s, as Neptune squares Pluto. Your power and confidence in 2063 may be extraordinary (Mars in your sign with Uranus), so relax and unwind as much as you can so you don't explode. Learn that you don't always have to have your way, and that others have valuable opinions too. In the later 2060s your discoveries could make you some money. Travel and higher learning and wisdom could restore your soul.

The 2070s are a steadier time, as you focus on making visionary ideas practical and useful to people and families. But the big aspects of 2079-81 are more of a challenge for you than for other signs. You have big career dreams and ambitions now, but they may be subject to frequent changes and blocks for a while. The 2080 conjunction focuses you closer to home. Family responsibilities may limit your ability to fulfill your dreams. But powerful impulses will well up from your subconsciousness and inner life that must be expressed in the world. Conflict with others at home and at work is likely late in 2084. Working out these complications in the 2080s will encourage you to really apply yourself to your health, fitness, work and career, and your new skills may pay off with new opportunities early in 2086. In the late 2080s hard work will pay off and you'll find many creative outlets, and your lucky year 2089 will be especially fortunate. Take care to keep your finances in order and ready for the following year though, as the chaotic events of June 2090 may put them at risk. As the century ends, if your money stays intact, you can devote yourself to more generous causes and pursuits for the benefit of your community and humanity. You may find that your service is much needed, as this could be a time of suffering for many. Find time to maintain your own health too.

Sagittarius (November 22 – December 20) As the New Age begins in Dec.2020, you are putting your finances on a stronger footing, and new resourceful ideas will abound. Communication networks open up for you in the following years, and you can transform your life through education. Partners may lure you into exploring new ideas, or you may grow beyond your partners, as Uranus opposes your Sun from Gemini starting in 2025. Neptune in Aries will open up your romantic and creative life from the mid-2020s onward. You can become an inspirational agent for the changes rolling through society at this time, and your wise perspective and prophetic wisdom is needed. In 2030-32 you need to reconcile your own expansive and adventurous impulses with what others want from you or think you need. Investment opportunities in innovative real estate projects may be a route to riches in 2038.

The next Jupiter-Saturn conjunction in 2040 indicates you'll make many friends and partners as you share your wealth and wisdom. Financial situations may benefit from your brilliant advice and counsel. Early Sagittarians, however, may also face some power struggles on the home front in 2044, as you seek to establish your own security. Then as the revolution unfolds in the later 2040s, your career and status may go through major upheaval. You'll land on your feet as you generally do, but you'll need to make changes that fully satisfy your spirit and which align with your ideal of a fully-sustainable and just economy. Establishing new relationships with the land, and labor practices fair to all, will concern you, and you may even start a new career for many years as a farmer or fisherman. Financial stability may be restored to you as the 2040s end, and a career breakthrough may happen in 2051-52. From then onward you'll meet many stimulating, extraordinary and visionary people, and cycles of dreamy ideal partnerships followed by disillusionment will happen as Neptune in Gemini opposes your Sun sign for 14 years, perhaps especially in 2056 and 2061. The conjunction of Jupiter and Saturn in 2060 will help put these affairs on a stable footing, as your working life absorbs you. Your dreamy relationships will get some cold water of reality. But in the Summer of 2060, you may be swept up into some kind of crusade, perhaps engaging in verbal combat or legal battles. This adventure will pass, but power struggles may result with your partners or family if they disagree with your new activities and interests. The choices you make on these matters in the early and mid-2060s will be fundamental and life changing. You are being challenged to look deep to release outdated ideals and habit patterns. Our society will be going through a wet and windy challenge, and you will be involved. As long as you are not carried away by depression or indulgence, you'll come through fine.

Better times are ahead for you guys. You'll be feeling increasingly liberated by the mid-60s, as inspiration flows to you abundantly. Uranus in your sign from 2065 to 2072 will be a time of discovery, freedom and independence, and the ball really gets rolling in 2066. You will be a truth-teller and ambassador for your pioneering new ideas. Deep and adventurous affairs may happen. In the early 2070s new financial opportunities will open up in innovative fields. Be sure your dealings are all open and above board. The great grand trine on Feb 15, 2074 encourages you travel widely to establish a new secure basis for expressing your wisdom to all. This era could be unstable for the world, however, due to Uranus square Pluto, so protect your finances and don't speculate abroad in this period. Avoid financial quarrels, especially in 2077. Be conservative with your funds and invest close to home. The great alignments of 2079-2081 open up fascinating times for you, especially if you're an early-degree Sagittarian. You'll have so much to learn and share, and you can look forward to dreamy travels. You may even become a tour guide, or even an ambassador into the virtual world or outer space. The rapid advances of the time will sweep you up, and you'll take others with you. Your rhetorical and literary genius will unfold. As the 2080s unfold, all Sagittarians will share in this bounty of beauty.

Dizzying chaos could explode all around you in June 2090, and you are called upon to bring your perspective and generosity to bear. Home and family life could change. The world will enter a more difficult time in the 2090s, and your career will be devoted to compassionate service to all in need. You could step out and be a creative leader in this task in the Fall of 2099 and in 2100.

Capricorn (December 21 – January 19) Practical and reliable, most Capricorns are usually focused on achievement in the world and attaining or defending authority. Now it's time to get a stronger sense of *yourself*. Can you find a deeper ground for your life than recognition by society? Take care of yourself in 2021; boost your fitness and fine-tune your presentation. Discover what is unique about you, and how can you express it. Can you develop your own initiative beyond what authority requires? Can your ambitions be aligned with higher social values and ideals? Unfold your creative insight and strike out on new paths. In the next few years, your new confidence will pay off with a better job and more stable income.

The revolutions going on as the decade proceeds might open up even more new income opportunities for you. As Neptune enters Aries in 2025-26, you may also be on a long 14-year quest to find or further develop your ideal home and family. You gain a deeper sense of place, and you may apply your organizational talents to defend our Earth home or your traditional heritage. Dedication to your work and taking care of your health will be top concerns in 2030-32. In the mid and late 2030s though, unstable conditions may prevail in your home and marriage. Stay steady and calm with those you love in May and June of 2033, and if necessary decide whether it's best to stay together or not. If you have a deep connection with your partner, things will be fine. Financial dealings could be a tug of war in 2036-37. Political conditions might cause a downturn in your investments then, but this will pass. Be practical and unwavering in your quest for security and analyze potential financial partners well.

The 2040 conjunction indicates a rise in status for you due to your ability to negotiate and work with others. Organizational and diplomatic talents serve you well. Your love of beauty and harmony in Nature and art expands, and you can develop a career as an artist or art dealer and investor. Watch for how world financial reorganization schemes of 2042-43 may affect you, and whether you can help people adjust or reorganize. This may also be a career path to follow for those born during the latter part of Capricorn. Contribute to the green revolution of the late 2040s by learning, networking and sharing information through travel and teachings. Become an ecological tour guide. In the 2050s you can apply many of your best creative and visionary insights in your work and career, and you can develop your own original solutions. Your position or status could shift in 2056, but your work continues to preoccupy you in the 2060s as you dedicate it to serve others and fulfill your dreams. Don't lose faith and keep hope alive in what you are doing. Make lasting partnerships and friendships that serve higher causes. Meanwhile, continue a long-term quest to transform yourself and acquire power through deeper knowledge, as Pluto passes through Pisces.

In the late 2060s you are again seeking the ideal home and family and a place by the sea or in faraway lands to retreat to. From 2068 on, Pluto is in Aries, which indicates you can transform your land or city and lead the way in projects to restore the Earth as an eco-pioneer. Upsets in family life may be a recurring theme from then on, and you may depart from your parents' wishes and strike out on independent paths in search of your soul. The 2070s are an important time for you with Uranus in your sign, as you further develop your original ideas on how to organize your community and society and revolutionize home and family life. You may break with some traditions. During the alignments of circa 2080 you'll have new ideas on how to make money and to help others make their ideas more practical. Property management may be a financially rewarding job. The year 2086 may be a milestone in how you organize your home and uphold your heritage. After Neptune enters Virgo in 2093, you can help people through science education and travel. Making money through expressing yourself will be a favorite pursuit for Capricorns into the new century. Meanwhile, as the 21st century ends you will have much work to do to reconcile personal and family needs with your career ambitions, and to conjoin your search for spirit with your search for power.

Aquarius (January 20 – February 19) "Harmony and understanding; sympathy and trust abounding" the song says. That's the Age of Aquarius we have been promised. Some Aquarians I have known personally are not such sterling examples of the ideal, whatever their claims. But in this respect Aquarians in general are probably no worse, no better and no different than people born under other signs. I tell you though, with all that's going on cosmically, with this Jupiter-Saturn conjunction on Dec.21, 2020, and then transformative, no nonsense Pluto exploding forth in your sign for the next 20 years, and much later on even further conjunctions in 2080, 2140, and the great one in 2167, all marking this era as truly the dawn of the New Age, it may be time now for Aquarians to face up to themselves. For most of you, this conjunction will come in your 12th house, in which people dredge up the truth about themselves of which they are unconscious. That is the project now for Aquarians; a spiritual and psychological quest. Release some of your karma, forgive your secret enemies, let go of your pretensions, and become more of an example of what the new age will be. People may even expect it of you. But for those born early in the sign, this conjunction means you have done some of this work already, and so it's time to come out of your shell and shine. Be all that you can be, organize your life and your personality and assert your independence. You may now be called upon to step forward and play a significant leading role in the affairs of this crucial and exciting decade. And those of you born later in the sign can do this too after you've cleared up some of the debris in your inner closet, and you will do even better after you have gone through some changes close to home. And no doubt there will be restrictions and burdens to deal with on that front a few years later in 2028-29.

Meanwhile the great planetary figure at mid-decade certainly will bring a bundle of abundance into your life and deliver to your door a wealth of ideas with which you can go forth and change the world. You really do need to be ready for these years, because you will literally be called upon to help bring about the New Age itself. Speaking, writing, performing, teaching, promoting; you'll be very busy and almost dizzy doing all this and even more. You may even attract some unusual fun and romance, if that's something you wish. With all the changes going on, our society will certainly need Aquarians to show us the right paths forward. There's so much to do, and you have the ingenuity and altruism to lift us out of our mis-directed confusion, if only you can be true to who you are beneath the programming which society has laid down on top of all of us. You may take an even more organized approach in 2030-32, and you'll need it, because the powers that be of the Old Age are not going away quietly. You'll have to defeat some serious dragons and people who restrict you as Saturn opposes Pluto-- still in your sign in 2035-36.

If you can navigate the stressful times of breaks, ambitions and power struggles in the early 2040s, you'll likely be ahead of the game during the green revolution due later in the decade. You'll be more sensitive than others then to your own home environment and the land, and your love of Nature will expand beyond anything you have known. You will certainly be an advocate for balance and cooperation with Nature, and your financial and ecological advice will be much needed and listened to. And you'll do your best to see to it that the financial re-organizations of the early 2040s are made sustainable for the planet, and not just for government, banks and businesses. That may even be a rewarding career path for you. And no doubt these financial changes in the world will shake up your own property and partnership arrangements in this period. In the late 2040s you will reorganize your own financial affairs, and help people adjust to changing times as well. You may find at the end of the decade that your dedicated activities have created the authenticity you sought 30 years before, as you take stock and go within to restore your spirits.

Naturally there's more to say about your sign than about the others, since you are at the eye of the storm, so to speak, of the New Age that's coming on. The 2050s will be an exuberant time of awakening for many people, and especially for you. In the Summer and Fall of 2050 you'll burst out assertively, but don't push too hard (Mars visits your sign). It looks like some of you may initiate some trends then that bring the New Age closer. Lots of travel, romance and adventure awaits that will enrich your life beyond measure, and you'll be bursting at the seams to share it all. In 2060 you literally step onto the stage, as sports or the entertainment world is opened up to you through all the latest technological communication channels. Besides possibly your own performance career, you'll be an agent, ambassador and network organizer for new games or new pop stars or classical artists, whatever is your pleasure. Your career will reach new heights, and also experience many shake-ups and start-ups, as you will settle for nothing less than radical innovation in every work you pursue. The malaise of the 2060s will unsettle your finances, but they will emerge transformed as you transform the world. Promoting the healthy benefits of Nature and the cause of preserving the outdoors may be your favorite vocation or avocation in the later 2060s. In early 2074 an influx of exuberant network connections and friendships will enrich and deepen your life.

The highlight of the century for Aquarians still lies ahead, as the 2079-82 period approaches. Expect a flood of innovative ideas and powerful, confident energy as Uranus visits your sign along with Jupiter and Saturn. Multiple discoveries await you in science or the arts. Watery Neptune in Leo invites you to pour your gifts out for the benefit of your fellows, like the Aquarius symbol shows. Be careful with those waters though; don't let your dreams of romance or fruitful partnership turn to illusions. Your ingenious creative and scientific abilities are at your height around 2080, so use them to discern the truth in all your affairs. Fabulous liaisons follow you in 2086, but also reminders to keep your tongue polite. As you zealously promote your agenda in the 2070s and 80s, Pluto in Aries advises you not to grind your axe too stubbornly, as Aquarians are sometimes prone to do. As the century winds toward its close around 2090 and beyond you may be getting off your high horse and winding down your crusades, seeking to keep your finances and working partnerships on an even keel as chaos swarms all around you. At the turn of the century though, it looks like you'll be getting right back up into the saddle to ride off into the battle.

Pisces (February 20 – March 20) Neptune in your sign shows that you have been more intuitive and inspired than ever before, but you may also have been adrift and confused. The 2020 conjunction should impel you to rise out of chaos and share your new revelations with friends and associates and in groups you think will bring forth the new age of harmony and understanding. Those born late in the sign, and possibly other Pisceans as well, may still be seeking solace and retreat in order to delve deeper into religious and spiritual contemplation. You'll find your spiritual life infinitely expanding in 2022 as Jupiter joins Neptune in your sign. While early Pisceans will continue to pray for peace and try to calm the waters of the gathering storm of the times, and to protect your finances from the confusion, those of you born late in the sign may be jumping into the fray with zealous enthusiasm as Neptune enters Aries in 2025-26. But with Uranus in Gemini at that time, joined by Saturn around 2030-31, many frazzled Pisces people will still need to retreat, hold back and settle upheavals happening around the house, and continue their contemplative ways until they find the inner stability they seek. In the early 2030s you can help the world situation through study, learning, networking and teaching at home. Then you can express your sensitivity through the arts and find innovative ways to help or educate young people as Uranus travels though Cancer for 7 years starting in 2033. You may get involved in health or spiritual disputes in Fall 2035 through 2036.

The Jupiter-Saturn alignment in 2040 focuses on your 8th house of shared resources, so partnerships and investments should pay off for you. Your financial research could unveil useful insights in the early 2040s. Pluto in Pisces for 20 years starting in 2044 will impel you to discover new strength within yourself and lead you to explore vast realms of experience. The green revolution should be a big deal for you, and you'll be doing some research, analysis, teaching and speaking about the needed changes. Originate and promote new ideas about how to restructure society so that it's fulfilling, sustainable and equitable for all. Your speeches will be eloquent and inspired beyond measure now, so don't be shy. Be sure and stay close to your soapbox in 2047; the world awaits your shimmering voice. Your compassion and dedication to service will be powerful. Wilder and less-disciplined Pisces people may wander off into chaotic adventures or headstrong rebellions in this era. Break-ups with partners could occur.

Nature, environmentalism and ideas about land reform and sharing resources will continue to interest you through the 2050s and 2060s. Find investment partners in the

2050s who can help you build security, because in the early 2060s you'll be so hypersensitive and intoxicated you won't care much about making money. As a Pisces you are at heart a hippie beatnik bohemian, and you may be so disappointed with city life now that you just want to swim away with the dolphins. Or you may just want to stay home to read and study or hang out in neighborhood bars. Later in the decade you can apply your inspiration to the arts as a painter or musician, and develop an innovative career helping others to travel and discover the exotic delights of the wider world before they all disappear. By the 2070s you'll join with others and learn skill at fundraising to support the organizations you believe in. Some of you will raise your voice and become dangerous, reckless radicals around 2073-74, while others of you will find that your financial organizing powers are improving your status. But your performing arts skills will be expanding too then, and they'll continue to develop in the later 2070s. Discover secrets to rejuvenate your life and health in the 2080s and dedicate yourself to a service or charity institution. Build sturdy financial foundations and prepare for a sudden change or crisis in your life and career that may happen around June 2090. Uranus in your sign from 2087 to 2094 will liberate your imagination and stimulate your psychic and intuitive abilities. You may be subject to sudden flashes of insight or to disturbing dreams. You feel the mounting chaos of the times, and as Neptune enters Virgo in 2093 you will double down on compassion in service. Your ideal relationships may be disappointing though, and charitable organizations that you dedicate your life to in this period may not always be honest and trustworthy, so be sure to know all about them so you can join only the best ones with the best people. The high integrity and compassionate empathy you have developed and demonstrated over the years has now made you a model citizen of the New Age that we can all learn from. And you can be the perfect teacher for us.

Your Lucky Years

Jupiter and Saturn provide the basic rhythms of life. We call them the ups and downs of our roller coaster ride of life. Sometimes, especially when these planets are in your sun sign or rising sign, you can feel them in your body, which itself is connected to the Earth and to the greater organism that is our solar system. In cosmic terms, the planets are not that far away from us. In every atom, the distance between a quantum energy packet called an "electron" is as far from its nucleus as a planet is from the Sun, and yet it adheres together. But remember, astrology does not determine your life. Rhythms and cycles are not dispensers of certain fate; they are something to dance to. There are too many variables in life to make absolutely certain predictions for individuals, and astrology is not an exact enough science to decree exactly and in full detail what will happen to you, or when. You have the freedom to decide.

Jupiter's rhythm is buoyant and invigorating. When he visits you, you feel more expansive. When Jupiter is in your sign, or making a lucky trine to your sign, it can be a **lucky year**. Take advantage of opportunities, enjoy life, spread your wings, and make new connections. First though, look at the birth dates of your sign listed here. If you were born early in the sign, the benefits might come early in the year, and may even start at the end of the previous year. If you were born later in the sign, they may come later, or even extend a bit into the beginning of the next year. Check also the appendix for your *rising sign*, and check the lucky years listed here for that sign too. That's two chances for good luck!

If two years are listed here with a dash between them, like 2022-2023, then the luck most-likely comes in the latter part of the first year listed, and/or the earlier part of the second year, depending on your birthday. The same applies if your rising sign is in a low-numbered degree below 15 or a high numbered degree above 15. The earlier the birthday, and the lower the degree, the earlier Jupiter visits you. But Jupiter moves around pretty fast, so if you want a more accurate reading about *exactly when* Jupiter is scheduled to bring you the most luck, please consult an astrologer. Be open, and don't take your fortunate year for granted. Don't be complacent or reckless. We all make our own luck. And, good luck!

Fair warning though, if **Saturn** decrees that a **year of lessons** is coming right during or right after your lucky one, he might throw some cold water on your plans for good fortune. You will need to handle the problems and learn the lessons of Saturn to get the full benefits of your lucky year. So be sure and check that listing below too.

I've included some years before 2020 for both Jupiter and Saturn, so that those who lived through those years can see how the schedule has worked for them. The same would apply to those reading this list after the year 2020. Remember too: younger people are probably more susceptible to these transits of Jupiter and Saturn than those who have been around the block a lot of times. Some people over 60 are more set in their ways and might not notice much difference from year to year.

ARIES (March 21-- April 20) 2002-2003 2007 2011 2014-2015 2019 2022-2023 2026-2027 2030-2031 2034-2035 2038-2039 2042 2046-2047 2050 2054 2058 2061-2062 2066 2070 2073-2074 2078 2082 2085-2086 2090 2094 2097-2098

TAURUS (April 21 – May 20) 2003-2004 2008 2011-2012 2015-2016 2020 2023-2024 2027-2028 2032 2035-2036 2039-2040 2043 2047-2048 2051 2055 2059-2060 2063 2067 2071 2074-2075 2079 2083 2086-2087 2091 2094-2095 2098-2099

GEMINI (May 21-- June 20) 2000-2001 2005 2009 2012-2013 2016-2017 2021 2024-2025 2028-2029 2033 2036-2037 2040-2041 2044-2045 2048-2049 2052 2056 2060-2061 2064 2068 2071-2072 2076 2080 2083-2084 2087-2088 2092 2095-2096 2099-2100

CANCER (June 21 – July 21) 2001-2002 2006 2010 2013-2014 2018 2022 2025-2026 2029-2030 2034 2037-2038 2041-2042 2045-2046 2049 2053 2057 2061 2065 2069 2072-2073 2077 2081 2084-2085 2089 2093 2096-2097

LEO (July 22 – August 22) 2002-2003 2007 2011 2014-2015 2019 2022-2023 2026-2027 2030-2031 2034-2035 2038-2039 2042 2046-2047 2050 2054 2058 2061-2062 2066 2070 2073-2074 2078 2082 2085-2086 2090 2094 2097-2098

VIRGO (August 23 – September 22) 2003-2004 2008 2011-2012 2015-2016 2020 2023-2024 2027-2028 2032 2035-2036 2039-2040 2043 2047-2048 2051 2055 2059-2060 2063 2067 2071 2074-2075 2079 2083 2086-2087 2091 2094-2095 2098-2099

LIBRA (September 23-- October 22) 2000-2001 2005 2009 2012-2013 2016-2017 2021 2024-2025 2028-2029 2033 2036-2037 2040-2041 2044-2045 2048-2049 2052 2056 2060-2061 2064 2068 2071-2072 2076 2080 2083-2084 2087-2088 2092 2095-2096 2099-2100

SCORPIO (October 23 – November 21) 2001-2002 2006 2010 2013-2014 2018 2022 2025-2026 2029-2030 2034 2037-2038 2041-2042 2045-2046 2049 2053 2057 2061 2065 2069 2072-2073 2077 2081 2084-2085 2089 2093 2096-2097

SAGITTARIUS (November 22 – December 20) 2002-2003 2007 2011 2014-2015 2019 2022-2023 2026-2027 2030-2031 2034-2035 2038-2039 2042 2046-2047 2050 2054 2058 2061-2062 2066 2070 2073-2074 2078 2082 2085-2086 2090 2094 2097-2098

CAPRICORN (December 21 – January 19) 2003-2004 2008 2011-2012 2015-2016 2020 2023-2024 2027-2028 2032 2035-2036 2039-2040 2043 2047-2048 2051 2055 2059-2060 2063 2067 2071 2074-2075 2079 2083 2086-2087 2091 2094-2095 2098-2099

AQUARIUS (January 20 – February 19) 2000-2001 2005 2009 2012-2013 2016-2017 2021 2024-2025 2028-2029 2033 2036-2037 2040-2041 2044-2045 2048-2049 2052 2056 2060-2061 2064 2068 2071-2072 2076 2080 2083-2084 2087-2088 2092 2095-2096 2099-2100

PISCES (February 20 – March 20) 2001-2002 2006 2010 2013-2014 2018 2022 2025-2026 2029-2030 2034 2037-2038 2041-2042 2045-2046 2049 2053 2057 2061 2065 2069 2072-2073 2077 2081 2084-2085 2089 2093 2096-2097

Saturn is called the rhythm of the world. Without the archetype of Saturn, our bodies would have no backbone. We could not have orderly expectations or make any plans and structures. Saturn is our teacher and task master. When he visits, circumstances or other people may appear that challenge you. If you can meet those challenges, you may grow as a person. You can also get depressed and let troubles get the best of you. We all face some difficulties and problems in life. Without them, we could never master any subject or acquire any skill. Saturn is the rhythm of discipline and practice. Good luck is great, but we make more progress when we apply ourselves and solve problems. It is said that successful people don't depend on luck, and that obstacles and failures made their good fortune possible. So, Saturn may be even more valuable to your success than Jupiter.

In the New Age, we are not throwing over old determinist, materialist and physicalist paradigms only to embrace new ones. Astrology does not cause the events of your life. It helps you to connect with your larger being. Although Saturn is known as the planet of limits and burdens, it does not determine your fate. There are too many variables and uncertainties in life for astrology to claim to know your destiny in detail. Saturn is the indicator of your cycles of personal growth into maturity. It is your planet of mastery. So watch for these years of lessons, and take advantage of them.

Also take note of your **Saturn Return** when you are 29 and 59 years old, and the years immediately prior. At these times you are moving into a new phase of life, but you may need to be forced out of old situations that keep you down, and this can be a difficult time. Around 44 years of age is a good time to be achieving a higher status in the world, with all the privileges and challenges pertaining thereto.

When Saturn is in your sign or making a hard square or opposition aspect to your sign, it's a **year of lessons**. You'll need to pay careful attention to what you say and do. People and circumstances may come your way that offer opportunities to learn to handle adversity. You'll probably make some mistakes anyway, unless you are a really lucky and skilled individual. You may have some hard work to do in these years, but if you do it well, it will pay off handsomely for you. Remember that success comes through persistence and resilience. If you fail, or if others oppose you or treat you unfairly, remember who you are: an expression of Divine Being. Learn a lesson or two from your own and others' mistakes-- and keep on going! The way out is the way through. And be courageous; relish the challenge, and you'll get stronger. Tests build character, and that's what Saturn is all about. And divine help is always available to you, so pray and call on it often. And if you know that one of these years is coming, you can prepare. Saturn also reminds you that situations don't last forever; in a year or two this phase will be over. And some of these years are better than others.

Two or three years are listed for each hard aspect of Saturn to your sign, as in 2003-2005. If you were born early in your sign, the challenges and lessons may come in the earlier years listed; if you were born later in your sign, then later. For more exact indications, consult a professional astrologer, and take heed of his or her advice. (S)he can give you more accurate information on just when Saturn's transit is the most significant for you. Or consult an ephemeris if you can. Check this list also for your rising sign. If your rising degree is a low number below 15, then the early years listed here for your rising sign will be the tougher ones. If it's a higher number over 15, then the later years listed will be the tougher ones. If you were born early in the sign, things may get challenging even in the year before the first one listed here; if you were born later, then perhaps things may stay challenging for a bit later. And if one of these years listed here is also a lucky year, Jupiter may provide some relief and good luck. Check the listing above for Jupiter's lucky years too.

ARIES (March 21-- April 20) 2003-2005 2010-2012 2018-2020 2026-2028 2032-2034 2039-2041 2047-2049 2055-2057 2062-2064 2068-2070 2077-2078 2084-2086 2091-2093 2098-2100

TAURUS (April 21 – May 20) 2000-2001 2005-2007 2012-2014 2021-2022 2028-2030 2035-2037 2042-2043 2050-2052 2057-2059 2064-2066 2071-2073 2079-2081 2087-2089 2093-2095

GEMINI (May 21-- June 20) 2001-2003 2007-2009 2015-2017 2023-2025 2030-2032 2037-2039 2044-2046 2052-2054 2060-2062 2066-2068 2074-2076 2082-2084 2089-2091 2096-2097

CANCER (June 21 – July 21) 2003-2005 2010-2012 2018-2020 2026-2028 2032-2034 2039-2041 2047-2049 2055-2057 2062-2064 2068-2070 2077-2078 2084-2086 2091-2093 2098-2100

LEO (July 22 – August 22) 2000-2001 2005-2007 2012-2014 2021-2022 2028-2030 2035-2037 2042-2043 2050-2052 2057-2059 2064-2066 2071-2073 2079-2081 2087-2089 2093-2095

VIRGO (August 23 – September 22) 2001-2003 2007-2009 2015-2017 2023-2025 2030-2032 2037-2039 2044-2046 2052-2054 2060-2062 2066-2068 2074-2076 2082-2084 2089-2091 2096-2097

LIBRA (September 23-- October 22) 2003-2005 2010-2012 2018-2020 2026-2028 2032-2034 2039-2041 2047-2049 2055-2057 2062-2064 2068-2070 2077-2078 2084-2086 2091-2093 2098-2100

SCORPIO (October 23 – November 21) 2000-2001 2005-2007 2012-2014 2021-2022 2028-2030 2035-2037 2042-2043 2050-2052 2057-2059 2064-2066 2071-2073 2079-2081 2087-2089 2093-2095

SAGITTARIUS (November 22 – December 20) 2001-2003 2007-2009 2015-2017 2023-2025 2030-2032 2037-2039 2044-2046 2052-2054 2060-2062 2066-2068 2074-2076 2082-2084 2089-2091 2096-2097

CAPRICORN (December 21 – January 19) 2003-2005 2010-2012 2018-2020 2026-2028 2032-2034 2039-2041 2047-2049 2055-2057 2062-2064 2068-2070 2077-2078 2084-2086 2091-2093 2098-2100

AQUARIUS (January 20 – February 19) 2000-2001 2005-2007 2012-2014 2021-2022 2028-2030 2035-2037 2042-2043 2050-2052 2057-2059 2064-2066 2071-2073 2079-2081 2087-2089 2093-2095

PISCES (February 20 – March 20) 2001-2003 2007-2009 2015-2017 2023-2025 2030-2032 2037-2039 2044-2046 2052-2054 2060-2062 2066-2068 2074-2076 2082-2084 2089-2091 2096-2097

Chapter 14

Prescriptions for a New Age

I know there might be some people out there who might wonder about this chapter. What business does this crazy quack Eric Meece have telling us what we need to do in the New Age? But those people probably aren't reading this book anyway. I have done my best to separate my progressive biases from what I think the planets and signs actually say about what's going to happen in the future, without at the same time hiding all of my views. However, a "prophet" in the old and proper sense not only says what might happen, but also provides visions of what *can* happen if we do what we need to do, and gives warnings about what might happen if we don't.

So, after all these pages talking about what's in our future, I also need to say how we can come out of all our troubles in reasonably good shape. I am a student and observer of history and the current scene, and also some sort of philosopher and visionary, so I feel qualified, even though I have no title before my name, and no MD or even a PhD (but only an MA) after it, to make some prescriptions. I know they aren't the only ones that can be given, but the title of my book does imply a vision for the future, and what I have predicted in these pages does seem to indicate that we may not be on the way to doomsday, but that instead a New Age could be dawning. So, although this book covers primarily what *might* happen, I need to conclude this book with some recommendations about what *needs* to happen. This chapter is largely written from my current perspective from circa the year 2020, but it may apply for the entire New Age in some respects.

First of all, in fact, we need to catch the vision and realize that doomsday is not our destiny. We are bigger and better than that. Our destiny is our divinity. All souls have within themselves direct access to the Divine Mind. Our very being is a hologram of the cosmos and of Divine, the very Infinite Spirit itself. Long ago the Brahman priests who wrote the Upanishads at the beginning of the Axis Age of Enlightenment in the 570s BC taught that our very soul, the most intimate part of ourselves, is the Brahman and the Godhead Itself. In The West if someone claims to be God he is often written off as a crazy egotist; or even accused of blasphemy, as Jesus himself was. But in India you are congratulated upon finding out. It's a different idea about the divine than we in The West are used to. We can experience ourselves as individual expressions and incarnations of God, just as Jesus did, and just as he taught. We can discover that we have access to power to create a better life for ourselves and to contribute to the common good. Each person has a unique contribution to make. Without your own special light, the New Age will not be as bright, and only you can make it shine.

Cultivating our imagination gives us access to infinite realms of potential to bring into being. We can at any time tune in to our most lovely subtle impressions and intimations, let them waft their way through our mind and help us recall our most intimate and uplifting moments and our highest aspirations. Our lives are incredibly rich. The metaphysical principle is that whatever you can feel and imagine, you can bring into being. There are obstacles within ourselves and in the world, but we grow by accepting and relishing the challenge. Without some kind of mystery, or some sort of goal to reach, life is too boring. All good stories have a villain to master or an uncertainty to resolve. We humans will always be reaching out for the next adventure, the next frontier. Some-how we can never just rest on our laurels and do nothing. Ultimately, we can say yes to life with all its troubles.

That means we all need to ditch the cynicism that is so prevalent as I write this. The popular music and entertainment styles of our time often strike me as expressing anger and hopelessness, when we need to be uplifted and sensitized. Our arts can be more than a commercial appeal to teenie-boppers. We need to rise up and remember that people have overcome far more difficult obstacles than we face today, and that humans have scored amazing victories. Our achievements in the past still astound us. We have achieved so much in our time that we can be proud of and admire ourselves for today as well. We make products and machines that can fill any need, and we have learned so much about the world. We have made much social progress. Many of us live in relative peace, freedom and prosperity that people could not have imagined centuries ago. We don't have any excuse to run ourselves down.

Don't reject what was made available to us in the awakening years of the 1960s and 70s. We lose their benefits when we only focus on the problems that those years brought us. We don't need to settle for less than the best now, or in the future. We can open our media to the real talent that is not allowed to be expressed by commercial interests. We can aspire to greatness; what we create does not always need to be based on our pessimism. The best art, music and literature transforms our problems into statements of timeless truth and illustrations of the heroic journeys of life.

These days trends come and go. They erupt powerfully and seem to make a difference, and then are just thrown over for the next trend or are immediately reversed. We sons and daughters of the modern spirit reject what our parents did, instead of following in their footsteps. That can be great and liberating, but it seems to be a prime malady of our age since the Revolution. The result is that we are always reinventing the wheel, or spinning our wheels, especially in politics and culture. It seems like I have predicted here that the same reforms and revolutions have to happen again and again before they ever become established. But if we are ever to really make progress as a people, we need to learn and grow, building on what came before as well as striking out in new directions. We can't just be rebels or reactionaries all the time. We need to value permanence as well as transience, the timeless as well as the timely.

We need to value arts more highly than we value money. Technology is only a means to the end of expressing ourselves creatively. This shift requires learning to handle our fear of not surviving. If you can make some of your money in ways that don't conflict with your values, then maybe you can save and invest so that someday you have enough. Then you can do the creative things that support your values. The great challenge of spiritual work is to become aware of the voices in our minds, our social programming, and the anxious impulses that we have allowed to dominate us. Then we can be free of the fear that impels us to dominate others. Indulging and escaping from life can't make troubles go away. Sometimes the way out is the way through. Spiritual practice is becoming a necessary part of our lives every day. It is Job One for all of us to use the tools given to us since the sixties and since the Axis Age to grow spiritually. Quiet the incessant mental chatter through meditative practice and become aware of what's going on inside you and around you. Knowing that you are pure consciousness, and not just your experiences, is healing. We can discover our chakra centers, and be centered in our center of centers, following the heart's guidance instead of just the head's alone. To be authentic and fulfilled, we need to do more than what is asked or expected of us, and we need to live according to our genuine inner promptings. "Follow the Leader" is not an adequate prescription for the New Age. Heed your inner light as if it's the only lamp. Exercise, eat right and stay forever young and easily aroused. It's never too late. 70 is the new 40. The New Age depends on all of us unfolding our best.

One prevalent obstacle to catching the vision of the possible is dogmatic science. A worldview that proclaims that everything is running down to inevitable heat death does not inspire confidence. If we want to feel that our lives are worthwhile, then we need to see ourselves as greater than small biological mechanisms trapped for a few years on an insignificant planet in an infinite universe until our own death ends everything. Empirical science will not give us all the answers someday. Such methods only give us observations after the fact and cannot explain the creative. Science is wonderful; it helps us verify facts and provides a grand view of our unfolding world. It allows us to manipulate objects for our benefit. But the ultimate answers to life already lie within us, not out there in the objective world. Science has too long ignored the scientists and the observers themselves and their inward lives. Once we understand that science can never explain life or consciousness and can't account for our freedom or the wonder of our love and imagination, we can begin to realize just what a miracle life really is, and how amazing we are. When we do that, we won't be destructive or treat others merely as objects to be used. We will be grateful and appreciate everything. We will respect our fellow miraculous beings as inherently valuable, from the smallest fly and every beautiful flower to all kinds of human beings, and we'll see the divine in each one. We can open up to the spiritual realms and recognize the angels and the faeries too. We can see miracles everywhere and make them happen. We can treat others as we wish to be treated. To do this, need a new world view. And, need I say, we need to accept astrology as more than superstition and make it a part of our lives. It is an inexhaustible fountain of wisdom to be poured out for the benefit of all.

We need to recall President Obama's slogan: *yes we can*. Si se puede! To do this we need to expect big things not only from ourselves as individuals, but from society. For too long politics has been captured by ideologies that are long-outdated, but which serve the interest of a powerful rich 1% minority. We don't need to be subservient to these ideologies or let them convince us that politics and public service are useless. We must be willing to question our received assumptions!

Number One on the list of ideologies to be overthrown is trickle-down economics. It has many other names: neo-liberalism, free market fundamentalism, libertarian economics, social darwinism, rugged individualism. It's the best way to fool the people into allowing a few fat cats to hoard all the wealth. Providing tax breaks and cutting regulations to the so-called job creators does not boost the economy. The last time they promised us a trickle, only the richest people got any of it. Reagan's prescription missed the mark. Government is not the problem; it's part of the solution. Until we each are ruled by the better angels of our nature, laws and governments are still needed. Libertarianism and anarchism are attractive doctrines. Who likes to be controlled, forced and ordered around by the government? But government does more than control us; it organizes society and makes the world run. It can't do this without taxes, and when taxes are cut too far, it swells the national debt. The USA has accumulated so much debt now that it's hard to see how it can remain solvent. Fiscal responsibility must be a prime prescription for the New Age, on both a personal and public level. We can generously support the values and the causes we like, and we can spend our money prudently too. Nations need to budget for what's really needed, and government needs to operate efficiently. Our taxes need to be fair, and we need to be willing to pay them.

The problem in our country is that the rich have too much, not that the poor get too much welfare. Entrepreneurs and inventors make things happen and must not be hampered too much. Maybe we can't depend on taxing the rich for everything we want. But we need to be willing to pay for what works. Social programs provide cash and benefits to people who actually spend it, and this stimulates the economy and creates jobs. When these programs are cut, people suffer, the economy weakens, and everyone becomes vulnerable. The social safety net protects each individual from capricious business practices and from economic crashes over which we have no control. Claiming that the wealthy use their breaks to create jobs only allows them to pay themselves 300 times more than the workers who make their wealth possible. They often use their extra funds to speculate, buyout, install robots, and hire cheap labor abroad.

We can no longer afford this free market shibboleth. Because of it, today's younger generation may be the first in USA history not to do as well as their parents. Wages are too low, and prices are too high. We need to free our political parties from this ideology so that our government can help the people. We can't allow gerrymandering, voter suppression and unrestrained corporate money to stifle the peoples' will, and still expect to create the New Age. We need reform-minded progressive leaders instead. After 40 years (so far, at this writing) of stalemate and regression by neo-liberal ideology, we need to end forever the blockade which the reactionaries erected against every reform and program, from affordable health care to better democracy and infrastructure. Yes, we need to come together and find common ground, and to understand the feelings of everyone in our country and in our world. Yes, we need to respect all opinions and all people as much as we can. But we don't need to be dominated by a stupid ideology that just plain doesn't work.

One of the best examples of the power of rich corporate lobbies to destroy the peoples' will in the name of freedom and liberty is failure to pass gun control in the USA. 90% of the people support it because of the epidemic of ongoing mass shootings, and yet nothing gets done even when 20 innocent children are killed. You can't consistently be against war, and then support the right of domestic terrorists to keep and bear arms, or of anyone to buy military weapons. Someday the USA will repeal the ill-conceived Second Amendment and join the rest of the world in creating a non-violent and gun-free society.

As much as the free-market ideology never really worked in the first place, it will be even useless in a world where computers and machines are taking over. The work ethic has been a bastion of neo-liberal ideology. It is claimed that our tax money is given to people who are lazy and have no character. But what happens to work when it is no longer available, and no longer needed? Why should all the benefits of increased productivity go just to the owners? Machines were advertised to us as labor saving devices for everyone, not just a few. Unless income support is provided to the people through taxing these benefits, we will have no money to spend, companies will go bankrupt, the owners themselves will go broke, and the whole economy will collapse. At a minimum, wages must be raised and hours reduced to make more jobs available, and for those who are not needed or who do work that doesn't usually pay well, like charity or creative arts, some support must be given. If we guarantee equal opportunity to all ethnic and gender groups, wealth disparity will be reduced.

Being told that welfare goes to "those people" to "create dependency" was once a "dog-whistle" that appealed to closet racism. But by 2017 it was being stoked intentionally by the President of the United States. The Pope said it better; we need to build bridges, not walls. Scapegoating ethnic groups has to end if we are ever to enter the New Age. The globalization of civilization cannot be stopped! It's very true that it needs to be managed and directed so that it benefits the people and the environment, and not just the rich corporations, and we need preserve local control and community economies. Some trade regulations are needed so that workers can start out on a level playing field with other countries, so that companies don't just depend on cheap labor abroad. But our primary loyalty now must be to the whole Earth and all its peoples, not to one exceptional nation or one ethnic group.

"Imagine there's no countries, and no religion too," sang John Lennon in 1971. A lot of us had similar visions come into our minds simultaneously and spontaneously in the sixties. It didn't really mean we have to get rid of religion, but it doesn't have to erect walls. All religion is based on the mystical realizations of its original prophets, not on texts and dogmas passed down from on high. Religion in the New Age is an inside job, and the responsibility and project of each one of us. The truth lies within, not in the mouths and words of authorities. There is no one exceptional and right religion that everyone should believe, and to which everyone must be converted. There is only one spiritual truth that lies at the heart of all religions and spiritual teachings. We have inherited from religious and other authorities, who threatened to punish us if we didn't behave, the habit of putting people in boxes and labeling them as right or wrong. But we can liberate ourselves and each other by observing people as they actually are, expressions of the divine, and then treating people and speaking with each other from the heart, and respectfully.

Beware of conspiracy theory. Most of it is false. The claims about agenda 21 or the new world order that is spreading communism, or the deep state and secret government that is behind such disasters as assassinations, terrorist attacks and mass shootings, mostly just fall flat through lack of evidence when you research them. The lesson for the New Age is that even we astrologers and new agers need to make sense and look at the evidence. Holding beliefs that have no basis is bad for our reputation. There is a good balance between what can be known by science and what cannot. It's up to the New Age to discover and describe that balance. Conspiracy theories distract and deflect us from real problems, and real solutions.

Preserving our Mother Earth and protecting the lives of all beings on the planet is the top New Age priority as of this writing. This is another example of how we need to value science, as well as the miracle of life that it can't explain. Global measurements show that the Earth is still warming as of this writing, and that humans emitting too much carbon and methane is the cause. Cynicism will not work here either; we can't give up and say it's too late. But we can't ignore reality either. Sea levels, storms, floods, fires, droughts, heat waves and more are rising and becoming ever-more catastrophic. Acid is killing the life in our precious oceans, which are filling up with plastic, and many other species are dying because of habitat loss. We have no right to kill other beings. We need to change our own lifestyles and spending habits, and we need to elect effective government leaders who will control pollution and encourage investments in solar energy, wind power, electric cars and batteries. Regulations are needed to restrain and phase out dirty fuels. Much needs to be done to research and further perfect alternative energy so it doesn't pollute or hurt life in turn, but it is much better than the current system, and we need to switch to it right away. Other sources of energy may be needed too that don't contribute to the greenhouse effect. Farming methods need reform as well. We also need to be more efficient and stop basing our economy on growth, including the unending expansion of our population. The New Age must be one where climate change is not constantly wreaking havoc on the lives of people all over the world. It must be a world where our environment supports and inspires us and keeps us safe and healthy; a world of great architecture and design, of inviting human and natural spaces, and of abundant resources preserved and available to all. There is no limit to our potential, but we can't achieve it by being reckless and wasteful. We can be our best by being smart, strong and compassionate. Perhaps by the time you read this, we will be well on our way toward this sustainable and nurturing society. If we aren't, then perhaps it might indeed be too late.

Nature restores our spirit, and we need to restore Nature. The New Age is not going to be dominated by runaway technology; it will celebrate the organic. The living world nourishes our body and soul. The prescription for the New Age is to admit Nature back into our lives. A gentle breeze flows into our mind like nectar and connects us to the world. Visiting wild places takes us back to when Earth was new, and we are renewed too. Our bottom line is not financial, it is spiritual. What have we given is more valuable than what we have taken. The measure of our being is what we create, not how much we have. Music and the arts are as important as food in keeping us alive. When all else fails, good music rescues us and reminds us of what we can be.

Although a New Age is dawning that is opening up our abilities to fully imagine and bring into being our highest potential, we also need to confront our shadow. We can't take things for granted or ignore our problems. We are still emerging from those times, not so long ago, when the societies we lived in were oppressive, unjust and violent, and we still live in the midst of some of these disabilities and relics. If my predictions indicate that we are not about to suffer doomsday, they also indicate that we have a long way to go before we become spiritual masters fully at peace with ourselves. We need to take some courage and some conscience along with us on our long journey into utopia. We each need to create an ethical foundation of right action for our lives and consider the needs of others as well as ourselves. At each period in the years ahead that I have described, many tasks and causes will call to us, and we need to be ready and willing to fulfill them as the time comes.

As we get into the flow of life through spiritual knowledge, the right actions will emerge, and we will be guided by higher forces. We will learn to accomplish that age-old alchemical task of the great work: to marry the assertive with the receptive as our guru planet Pluto inspires us to do. We will surf the polarities of life and find that magical balance which is astrologically indicated by the age we live in, as I described at the end of the last chapter; to flow in a simultaneous balance of expressing outwardly and being impressed inwardly all at once. The revelation for our age is to know ever more vividly that we are each interconnected holograms of the whole cosmos; each of us dependent on our world just as our world depends on each of us.

In the 1960s this new alchemical and visionary spirit moved among younger people, and many older ones too. It started with civil rights movements and peace demonstrations, surfing and dance crazes, and folk and rock music events. Then it spontaneously grew into communities of acid tests, hippie cultures, be-ins, the Summer of Love, and music festivals like Woodstock (the Aquarian Exhibition); and then to thousands of other music and art festivals and to expos and fairs in all the decades ever since, and to rainbow gatherings, raves, diversity liberation movements, and the vast Earth Day demonstration and the ecology movement; and then into the New Age movement, the Harmonic Convergence, Live Aid, and Hands Across America; and to Occupy Wall Street and the Arab Spring at Tahrir Square and people power movements all across the world, and to the Women's Marches against Trump and to the March for Our Lives for gun control, and more. It is a building tradition that still lives within us and moves us. Tune in to it! The Spirit that is moving us toward a New Age is not only people being aware of themselves, or even taking action by themselves, but also people feeding off of each other, combining their energy, seeking togetherness, breaking through the walls to our common life, and responding to what is greater than ourselves. It is Spirit speaking through us together as One; a Spirit that seeks something bigger and better than our normal restricted lives; a Spirit *rising up* and moving beyond the injustice and oppression perpetrated against us. It is our inherent urge for communion that can move mountains and build civilizations and cultures based on higher spiritual principles of peace, love and inner wisdom. It is the vast energy of the cosmos and the solar system and the Planet Earth moving through us.

We need to recognize, celebrate, organize, and catalyze this group energy of Spirit. It takes people deciding to make it happen, people resonating with the spirit of what has gone before, and people catching the vibe that is swirling through us now and blowing in the wind, helping us to see beyond what we lack in ourselves and what we condemn in others. It is the inner moving with the outer; it is the outer planets holding the spirit of the times and dispensing the tide of cosmic energy down into our world and our individual being, and it's our own individual and group spirit moving, resonating and evolving the planets' meanings in turn. The New Age needs to unfold from this transforming energy that has existed since the sixties, and often in earlier forms too, at various times around the world-- in religious, spiritual and revolutionary movements, creative cultural trends, and magnificent civilizations everywhere and throughout history. It's the force of Humanity evolving and coming to birth, and it's paradise manifesting. And it needs to be directed into all of our government and business affairs, filling them and moving them, and as it were, overgrowing them with the new age spirit, and making it real through the nuts and bolts of our practical everyday lives.

I am looking forward to humans continuing the evolutionary development that has gotten us this far. We have come a long way, as I mentioned at the start. I remind my readers of this fact again at the end. We don't have to settle for a world on a downward spiral. We can ditch all the ideologies that deny our enormous potential and affirm instead the sacred nature of life and the infinite divine power that is our very being and birthright. We can affirm all our life-giving principles. Those of us who aspire to bring forth the light within and create a brighter world are much needed today. With our help, Humanity can keep moving forward from the momentum of the great Age of Revolution that launched the Modern Spirit, into the Ages of Light and Consummation, and over ever-farther horizons out to the stars and the galaxies and all the visible and invisible dimensions of life. I hereby predict that we can, and that we will!

My best wishes to all, and keep the spirit alive everyone

Appendix A: Predictions and Events, 1997-2020

The following table is a comprehensive list of the predictions I made in my January 1997-published book <u>Horoscope for the New Millennium</u> at the end of Chapter 15, "The Modern Spirit's Journey: Part 2," pages 250-255, covering the first years after my book was published, 1997-2000, and in Chapter 17, "Looking Over the Edge, Into the Third Millennium, 2000-2020". I list them in the order they appear in the book, together with actual events at or near the time predicted, and the astrological basis for the prediction (mostly as mentioned in the book). This is not a scientific statistical study; readers can judge for themselves whether the predictions are specific enough to make a difference, and how closely the actual events matched the forecasts. Astrologers may also get some clues about what the various planetary positions might mean for future events, and which ones worked out as predicted in the past.

Information listed in this table under "Actual Events" is taken from well-known chronicles of major events, such as <u>The World Almanac</u>, from the website News and Events Year by Year by Infoplease https://www.infoplease.com/yearbyyear , from notes taken on the nightly network TV news, and from occasional on-line searches for more details about the events. Since these events were found from these easily-available major sources, they are important events, and just dredged up to fit the predictions. These were not the only events that happened during these years; many other events happened which I didn't predict. As you can see however, many of the most memorable events of these times are included here.

Date	Prediction in my Jan.1997 book	Actual events	Astrology
Early 1997	Another Middle or Far East war (page 250, Horoscope for the New Millennium)	March-May: Israel-Hamas clashes	Mars Libra SR Feb.6 opp Saturn Feb.16
Early 1997	Domestic violence simmering;	April 27: Texas separatist revolt	" + Mars SD April 27.
Early 1997	Another terrorist attack in US	Jan 15: abortion clinic bombed; Feb 24 lesbian club bombed	" plus conj charts for Jupiter-Uranus/Neptune
Early 1997	Another Clinton scandal	Feb.15 China accused of giving funds to him; inviting contributors to White House	"
Early 1997	Clinton may take anti-terrorist actions	No	Mars Libra SR, Feb.6 opp Saturn
Early 1997	Clinton should be careful of violent attacks	No	Mars 5 Libra SR, Feb.6 opp Saturn
April 27 1997 and soon afterward	Time of great riot, revolution, "rev up the Marseillaise." Russian states may try to be independent, initiatives to help US cities	April 27 Texas revolt. May 18: Kinshasha falls to rebels in Zaire; becomes Congo. May 15: labor unrest in Paris; strike in Belgium. May 25 Sierra Leone coup June 2 socialists win in France	April 27: Mars SD 17 Virgo, soon after total solar ecl in 18 Pisces
Early & Spring 1997	Health breakthroughs; AIDS cure; health care debates, plagues, labor reforms (page 251)	May 1 AIDS vaccine announced. Feb 23 Dolly the Sheep cloning controversy. Mar 2 Monkey cloned. June 20 tobacco suits settled.	6th and 12th house emphasized in important charts of the period.
April 27 1997 ff	Saddam Hussein's foolish action could be excuse for US attack	No, not yet	Mars SD 17 Virgo
Feb or Apr 1997	Chinese may attempt to unify with Taiwan	No	" + SR 5 Libra, opp Sat. in Feb.
Late Aug/early Sept 1997	Transportation accident could dominate news. Communications controversy, terrorist attack could happen	Princess Diana dies in car crash Aug 31. Funeral Sept.6. Sept.8: Haiti ferry crash kills 100s. Sept.28: Borneo fires since Sept 23 cause major crash.	Mars opp Saturn late July; late Aug. Mars sq Uranus & Mercury-- SR 16 Virgo, ecl. Sept 1.
Early Oct or late Dec.	Promising times for	Oct 7 campaign finance	Oct.8 Jupiter SD, Mars

1997	diplomacy. Progress & financial innovation in US	reform attempted but blocked by Republicans.	conj Pluto Sag.Late Dec. Venus SR conj Mars-Ura. Aqu.
October, 1997	Space travel exploits	July 4: Pathfinder lands on Mars (not Oct.)	Mars conj Pluto in Sagittarius
October, 1997	Enlightened religious movement may sponsor conference	Oct 1997: Promisekeepers rally in D.C.	"
October, 1997	Global cooperation on major problems	Dec.11: Kyoto Treaty	"
Feb-Mar 1998	Major peace breakthrough	Feb 16-22: Kofi Annan negotiates bombing cease-fire between US & Iraq. April: N. Ireland agreement	Feb 5: Venus SD 19 Cap, Feb 26: ecl. conj Jupiter in 9th.
1998	Spiritual revivals	No?	Pluto in Sag sq Jup in Pisces
1998	More scandals; secret military misdeeds	Monica Lewinsky scandal	"
1998-99	Health care transformed, breakthroughs by century's end	April 1998: new drugs: Timoxifin, Viagra, Evista. Jan 1998: medicare expanded. May 1998: Cancer cure in rats. June 11 1998: TB cure.	" + lunar ecl in Virgo March 13, 1998, & see Spring eq. ch. 1998
1999, "as century ends"	Workplace issues; anxiety about free trade and immigration	WTO protests, the "Battle in Seattle" Nov.30, 1999	Mars conj Neptune, sq Saturn
1998	International agreements in ocean or space travel (page 252)	Kyoto Treaty on global warming Dec.11, 1997	Venus SR Dec. 1997
Spring 1998	Presidential diplomacy very active; aggressive moves controversial.	US response to Al Qaeda attacks (bombing Sudan & Afghanistan) Aug 20 called "wagging the dog"	Ecl. Aug 22 1998, Mars-Saturn SR-Neptune T-sq Aug.1998
August, 1998	Violence due to religious cults, repression of protests (page 253)	Al Qaeda attack on US embassies in Kenya & Tanzania, Aug 7. Rwanda-Uganda war Aug.16. President's controversial moves I predicted for the Spring happened after these attacks in August.	Ecl Aug 22 1998, Mars-Saturn SR-Neptune T-sq Aug.1998
1998	Panic over econ & ecol. Uncertainties; unusually	Sept-Oct 1997, panic over Asia fires. 1998 "warmest	Saturn in Taurus sq Neptune in Aq,

	severe weather	year of the millennium"--Jones, British Researcher. Hurricane Mitch, El Nino, China & Bangladesh floods; worldwatch says 1998 was record disaster year.	Pluto opp conj of 1892.
1999	New Millennium fears of "end of the world"	Y2K	Saturn sq Neptune
August, 1998	Disillusion with progress may cause radical change, some of corporate/oil power structure dissolves	?	Pluto opp US Uranus, Neptune conj US Pluto
1990s/2000s	Economy rebounds in 1990s; but unsettled due to radical upheavals in the first few years after 1998. Severe catastrophe not due until at least 2008.	Spot on; boom in 90s, dot.com bubble burst in 2000 and 9-11 in 2001; housing bubble and speculation brings severe crash and recession in 2008.	Neptune and Pluto transits
Around Aug 1999	Major multi-national Balkan conflict.	See below	See below
February, 1999	Nations get more aggressive; major religious, revolutionary upheavals due in April & July in Middle East or Balkans; perhaps SE Asia or Central Africa. See also April 1999 below. Also p.247: "look for Bosnia to come apart again in 1998-99"	Kosovo March 24-June 3 1999	Uranus & Neptune in places like 1914. Mars SR March 18; SD Libra June 4 (predicted on website)
Late 1998	Major diplomatic efforts to deal with upheavals in E. Europe and SE Asia. (Middle East?)	Oct 8 Albania rebels cease fire in Kosovo. Albright ultimatum to Serbs. Mid-Oct. Md. Mideast summit with Clinton. Oct 23 Wye agreement for Israel withdrawal from West Bank. Dec.14 Palestine removes anti-Israel language. Clinton in Gaza. Nov 16 Saddam backs down on inspections. Dec. 16 Iraq bombed.	Eq chart active 7th,9th,3rd house incl. Jupiter opp Venus.
November, 1998	Major religious/moral controversy breaks out	Lewinsky scandal leads to impeachment. Falun Gong protests in China April 1999	Nov. 1998: Mars sq Jupiter SD Pisces, sq Mercury SR

April, 1999	Major religious/revolutionary upheavals in Balkans & Middle East, perhaps Southeast Asia or Central Africa.	Kosovo War between Muslim Albanians and Orthodox Serbs. Niger revolt April 9. Falun Gong, see above.	Mars SR March 18. April 6 Saturn sq Neptune.
July, 1999	Major religious/revolutionary upheavals in Balkans & Middle East, perhaps Southeast Asia or Central Africa.	June 13 N & S Korea clash. July 24: Serbs rise up against Milosevic. Falun Gong persecution July 20, East Timor independence clashes Aug. and Sept.	Lunar ecl July 28 Mars-Jup.-Nep T-sq. mid-July, & w/ecl.. July 18: Saturn sq Uranus
August 11, 1999	Upheavals in Balkans, Russia (breakup of fed?), Mexico revolution, revolutionary civil war. Religious war, probably in Iran. Purges, massacres; Balkan earthquakes predicted in my 1976 article in AFA and on my website. Art experiments.	July: Iran protests. Aug.6-16: Dagestan & Chechnya revolts; Sept 9 Apartment bomb in Moscow. Russians attack Chechnya Oct 22 & Jan.2000. Huge Serb rally Aug 19. Aug 9 Putin is new Russian PM, Yeltsin cronies criticized. Earthquakes: Turkey Aug 17 kills over 17,000. Sept 7 Greece, Sept 20 Taiwan. Sept. 30 Mexico, + Japan nuc accident. July 2, 2000: PRI loses power in Mexico after 7 decades. Aug., Al Qaeda plans 9-11 attack.	"Eclipse of the century" opposes Uranus and squares Mars & Saturn, Aug.11. "Terror from the Sky" predicted-- Nostradamus.
August 11, 1999	Transportation accident, student uprising, terror bombing or labor unrest in US. Corporate or economic restructuring, health innovations. (page 254)	Roller coaster accidents, late August 1999. Nov. 1999: Battle in Seattle June 29, 1999: Clinton proposes Medicare drug plan, anti-poverty initiative. Nov.5: Microsoft ruled a monopoly.	Aug 11 1999 ecl. in Leo (youth, amusement) in 12th, Uranus in 6th (labor, health). Saturn sq Uranus in fixed money signs.
After Aug.11	Upheavals may cause financial panic	Financial Panic, Sept.23	Aug 11 1999 eclipse
February 5, 2000	Outbreak in or US clash with Iran	no	Feb 5 2000 eclipse conj Uranus in 17 Aquarius
February 5, 2000	Another presidential scandal	?	"
February, 2000	More troubles erupt in same places as in August	Kosovo clash Feb 18. Russians capture Grosny Feb.6	"

Year 2000	A hopeful moment for new opportunities realized	Gore announces we have reached "the mountain top," the greatest economy ever seen. Stocks at record, but dot com bust begins in March.	The "valley of transition" is passed, as we reached the "mountain top" which I and Dr. King predicted.
2000-2020 era	Health, safety & transportation re-regulated (page 263)	Affordable Care Act, 2010	May 28, 2000 Jupiter-Saturn conj chart #4 at Midheaven in US, forecasting new 20-year era.
2000	Democrat or progressive elected president	Republican GW Bush becomes president instead, but Gore was actually "elected," as everyone says.	Uranus in Aquarius squares 2000 conj. in Tau
2000-2010	Financial system reformed	Dodd-Frank, 2010	Conj. in Taurus sq Uranus in Aq
2000-2010	Electronic superhighways & planet-friendly tech receives govt support	Mostly at decade's end under Obama, 2009-2010.	" Jupiter-Saturn opposition in 2010 was climax of 2000 cycle.
2000-2010	Restructured mass media to help democracy	Not yet	"
2000-2002	Best time for political changes	No, because Gore didn't become president	Uranus in Aq
2000-2003	New agencies and economic controls could be oppressive	"	"
2000-2010	Hidden powerful influences cause scandals (page 264)	Torture and spying on Americans secretly OK'd, 2002. Abu Ghraib prison torture scandal, 2003.	Jupiter-Saturn conj, new moon in 12th house in USA, June 2, 2000
2000, 2001, 2003, 2005	Danger to president, or to candidates before election (page 265)	No personal danger, just disastrous attacks (9-11) and resulting wars (Afghanistan, Iraq).	Mars at 20 Gemini (conj US Mars) in the Jupiter-Saturn conj. new moon chart, plus eclipses
2000s	Creative ferment high (page 266)	No, except in tech media	Planets in Aq
Fall 2000	US gearing up for war	USS Cole attacked by Al Qaeda, Oct.12	Jupiter in Gemini on Desc. in Fall eq ch with Mars sq Saturn
Date	**Prediction in my Jan.1997 book**	**Actual events**	**Astrology**
2001	Conflicts that exploded in 1999 will probably come to	March 13 ethnic Albanians in Kosovo attack	Saturn opp Pluto

	a head. Continuing ethnic strife in Europe seems likely.	Macedonia; March 26 & June 6, Albanians attacked.	
Summer 2001	Uncle Sam feeling righteous again in a big way. Religious & trade issues involved. Attacks on Latin neighbors. Nuclear accident can't be ruled out. "Star wars" tech used.	Sept.11 Al Qaeda attack on America; US declares War on Terror; Afghan War starts Oct.7. Drones used later.	Saturn opp Pluto on US Asc/Desc, conj Mars stationary July-Aug. 2001
Nov.2 & Dec 22, 2001	Turning points in the confrontations begun in Summer 2001. US suffers losses in naval engagement.	Oct 25: Patriot Act passed. Nov.9 Northern Alliance defeats Taliban in northern cities; takes Kabul Nov.13. Dec.16: Tora Bora caves fall but bin Laden escapes; Dec.22 shoebomber Richard Reed stopped. Late 2001: Pakistan vs India confrontations heat up.	Nov.2 Saturn exact opp Pluto; Dec.14 ecl. Dec.22 Mars sq Saturn
May-June 2002	Another decisive moment in the war	June 6: President Bush proposes Homeland Security Dept.	Eclipse aligned with Saturn and Pluto
After Oct 2002	Outlook for peace improves; if we are lucky we will escape further conflict	We weren't lucky. (Gore didn't become president, after all; Bush did)	Venus SR; Saturn opp Pluto beyond orb
December, 2002	Agreements, especially in Mid-East or Balkans	Dec.8: Iraq turns over its list of weapons.	Jupiter in Leo SR trine Pluto/ecl.
Late Feb 2003	If we aren't lucky, another flare-up	War in Iraq begins March 19	Saturn opp Pluto in orb again, conj Mars
2001-2002	Breakthroughs in space travel. Progress toward manned expedition to Mars may happen. (page 267)	Not until Jan 3 & 23, 2004, when rovers land on Mars.	Pluto in Sagittarius, Jupiter prominent, etc.
2001-02	Conflicts over space dealt with.	no	"

Late 2002 through Spring 2003	Significant, innovative health & welfare programs could be approved. Good time to streamline bureaucracy to help safeguard the security of the people.	Medicare prescription drug program, prop. May 2003, passed in June/July, conference Nov.21-25, signed Dec.8, 2003; largest overhaul of Medicare in its history so far.	Jupiter opp Neptune Feb & June 2003; June: Saturn trine Uranus. August Jupiter in Virgo opp Uranus in Pisces. In Fall eq 2003, Mars SD conj Uranus in 6th house. Nov 23 ecl, Mars opp Jupiter
Late 2002-Spring 2003	Electronic media will be used to give everyone access to work and education	Beginnings of social media: Friendster begun in 2002. My Space, Linked-In, itunes begun in 2003. Facebook begun in 2004.	Saturn in Gemini trine Uranus in Aquarius in April 2003.
April 2003 – March 2004	New constitutions in defeated nations after wars begun in 2001, const. changes may come to nations established in WWI. Iran & Vietnam may see advances to democracy.	After Iraq "defeated" in mid-April, new parliamentary government is begun. EU adds 10 nations.	Saturn trine Uranus, air/water cusp.
2003	Another mid-east clash	Iraq War	Saturn opp Pluto in orb again, conj Mars
2003	Disaffection with change; reformers will have to scale back their expectations.	N/A	Uranus enters Pisces March 10
Late 2002, early 2003	Swelling enthusiasm among the people for reforms; dangerous demonstrations in Feb 2003	Largest-ever anti-war protests (or any protests?) Jan 18, Feb 15, 2003. Probably delayed Iraq invasion to March.	Jupiter opp Neptune Feb 16, Mars opp Saturn Feb 20
Sept 2003	Another great social or foreign aid program will be proposed	Oct.23: Donors conference & USA donate 33 billion for Iraq reconstruction.	Aug 27 New Moon in 9th conj Jup in Virgo opp Uranus in Pisces. In Fall eq 2003, Mars SD conj Uranus in 6th house
Fall 2003	Season of discontent; war/mid-east troubles could trigger recession or shortages	Discontent with the war; recovery from 2001 recession is slow. We didn't have shortages, but we did have blackouts! (Aug 2003)	Saturn in Cancer like 1974
Fall 2003	Plague, famine, protests (I renounced this prediction at New Age publishing conference in Denver, Summer 1997). Efforts to improve public health.	See Medicare prescription drug program, above	Mars stationary conj Uranus at 0 Pisces, opp Jupiter in Virgo

Around Nov. 23, 2003	Political & social passions; purges shake US govt.	Rose Revolution in Georgia, Nov.23. Shevernaze resigns. Nov.20: 200,000 protest Bush visit to Britain. Miami trade talk demonstrations.	Mars 17 Pisces opp Jupiter 16 Virgo
Around Nov. 23 2003	Travel mishaps and naval battles may occur	Oct 15: Staten Is. Ferry crash kills 70. Nov.13: Accident on Queen Mary II under construction kills 13.	Mars 17 Pisces opp Jupiter 16 Virgo
Late 2003, early 2004	President lost at sea and unable to handle troubles	I predicted that the War in Iraq would turn out to be a quagmire. It did.	Uranus in Pisces, Saturn in Cancer
Early 2004	Unrest in LA; demands for economic recovery (page 268)	March 14: socialists win in Spain	Mars in Aries
April 19, 2004	Renewed struggles over religious issues like abortion	Gay marriage issue, responding to SF marriages Feb 12 & March 11. March 25: law makes killing a fetus in pregnant woman murder. May 17: gay marriage legalized in MA.	Eclipse April 19 feat. Pluto in Sag SR, opp Mars over US Mars rising. Uranus in Pisces MH opp Jupiter in Virgo
Sept/Oct 2004	Minorities demand rights, social measures could be taken	No known correlation	Mars conj Jupiter in Virgo
Spring or Fall 2004	Military altercations could occur in Mid-East or Asia	Ongoing war in Iraq	Spring, Mars in Aries; Fall, Mars in Virgo
Winter 2004-2005	More severe economic shortages, new financial policies and social programs gradually bring relief	No	Saturn singleton in Cancer
November 1, 2004	Progressive president re-elected in close vote	No, reactionary president re-elected in close vote. I said incumbent Bush had the advantage in an unpublished article.	Oct.28: total lunar eclipse. Previous new moon Oct 14 indicated incumbent winning.
2005-2008	Economic restructuring and financial reform in this presidential term	Banks forced to take bailouts in exchange for making some changes, Fall 2008	Oath of Office chart shows Mars-Pluto in 8th, etc.
Spring 2005	Better ways to live on the land get attention; debate over "progress"	No known correlation	Saturn in Cancer SD in 4th of eq chart

Spring 2005	Breakthrough in economic diplomacy, involving Europe. President secures resources, opens trade.	No known correlation	Spring eq chart: Pluto in Sag SR, Jup in Libra
After July 2005	Gov't supports creative projects, education improved	No	Saturn in Leo
After July 2005	Death of major entertainers; youth act out cynicism	No known correlation	Saturn in Leo
Oct 2006 to May 2007	Government focused on creative investment and long-term growth	no	Saturn in Leo singleton
Oct 2006 to May 2007	Economy should be bouncing along again by then	July 19, 2007: Dow Jones peaks at 14,000	"
Early Oct 2005	Economic restructuring	No	Mars SR in Taurus; eclipse
Early Oct 2005	US quarrel over land and fuel with Mid-East or Balkan countries	Sept.2005: IAEA says Iran fails to verify that its nuclear program is peaceful	Mars SR in Taurus
2004-05	Religious fundamentalists may wage war on the USA	On-going wars against Taliban in Afghanistan and Al Qaeda in Iraq	Pluto in Sag opposing US Mars
2004-05	Turks perturbed by economic and ethnic turmoil; East Indian ethnic problems	Ongoing Kurd revolt	Mars in Taurus SR
circa 2005	President energized by messianic zeal	Bush seeking to "spread freedom"	Pluto in Sagittarius
2005-06	Sensational crime stories of entertainment figures	Michael Jackson on trial for molestation March 2005; acquitted June 13. Robert Blake (Baretta) found innocent of murder, March 16, 2005. Baseball stars testify in steroid scandal, Mar 17.	Saturn in late Cancer SD spring equinox, and in Leo
Mar.29, 2006, late June 2006	Eclipse could make Al Gore a marked man (page 269)	Actually, it energized him to make movie (I.T. rel. May 24) that won awards. Divorce came later in 2010.	Total solar ecl. March 29, 2006 near Gore's solar degree; Saturn return in Leo.

March 29, 2006	Purge or scandal in courts or State Dept., proposals to transform our legal system; concerns for human rights in America. (page 270)	CIA secret prisons confirmed, Sept.6, 2006. Bush reveals Jan 17 2007 that NSA monitors Americans' conversations with suspected terrorists. Immigration: see below	Eclipse portended these things in coming months, since Pluto was on MH in Sag at the time
Late 2006, early 2007	Xenophobia grows over world trade or immigration; president may rally paranoia against Iran, other enemies	Immigration reform failed; new border fence funded, Oct.26, 2006.	Saturn opposing Neptune
Sept 2007	President may respond to violent incidents in Iran against Americans with a strike	No, not until Aug.1, 2009 (3 student hikers arrested)	Saturn in Virgo; ecl. in Virgo sq Mars at 21 Gemini & opp Uranus
2007, especially in March	Nations liberated in 1989 may see changes, powered by mass movements for human rights. This may include China.	April 1: Romanian leader suspended. Polish govt. falls Oct.26. July: Chinese food safety scandal; official executed July 10.	Solar ecl March 19, 2007; Saturn opposite Neptune.
March 19, 2007	President may face unmasking in major scandal; may involve Iran or economy. Assassination attempt could reveal links to JFK.	Scooter Libby guilty in Valerie Plame spy-outing scandal, March 6. Atty. Gen. Alberto Gonzales resigns Aug.27 after scandal in March & April over firings of US attorneys. He was also involved earlier in human rights violations in war on terror.	Solar ecl March 19, 2007; Saturn opposite Neptune & Mars in 17Aq
2007	Ecology and oil issues brought to the fore again by environmental accidents	Global warming arouses concern and action. Green trends mushroom. Dec. 2007: fuel standards raised.	Uranus in 17 Pisces
2007	US aggressive military moves resisted by peace movement	Surge in Iraq is protested but goes forward	Uranus in 17 Pisces
Nov/Dec. 2007 and following Spring	Realignment of policies toward fundamentalist nations; national defense concerns and fear of	April 1, 2008: Justice Dept. revealed the 2003 policy to torture Al Qaeda detainees. Surge of war in Iraq. Also	Saturn enters Virgo Sept.2, 2007. Mars stationary & singleton in Cancer, Oct-Jan.. Jupiter

	foreigners. Climax of legal and court reforms mentioned above for March 29, 2006. (page 271)	see Gonzales resignation Aug. 27, 2007.	conj Pluto in Sag. Dec.2007. See Spring eq. chart.
August 1, 2008	Shady US dealings abroad	Czechs July 8, and Poles Aug.20, agree to US missile defenses	Solar ecl with Mars in 18 Virgo opp Uranus
August 1, 2008	Resurgent counter-culture, unrest among the poor. (page 272)	No known correlations	"
November, 2008	Tight & bitter election race; demagogue foments fear of foreigners. Religion and drugs may be issues. Republican will win.	No, Bush upset the pendulum swing. Power shifted the other way. Some say Obama was a cult figure, but the opposite kind to the prediction. Trump didn't come along until 2016.	Saturn in Virgo opposes Uranus on election day.
Jan.26, 2009	Mushrooming anxieties played upon by new president. Tech and engineering applied to social and financial problems. (page 273)	Anxieties at height over great recession. New president passes stimulus program that boosts new technology and stops economic slide.	Annular eclipse puts powerful Saturn in Virgo singleton on Midheaven, opp. Uranus.
November 26, 2008	Start of important, painful period. Status quo vs. revolution.	Great Recession in USA, depression in Europe follows. Governments fall by 2010.	Pluto enters Capricorn, Saturn opposite Uranus
Nov.26, 2008 and 2009	New religious reformation begins. Church targeted for radical change; moral debates. Famous prophecy of the end of the Papacy could come true.	2009: scandal of church officials protecting priests who molest children hits Pope Benedict. In 2013 he becomes the first Pope to resign in 500 years; succeeded by friend of the poor, the popular Pope Francis.	Stellium in Sagittarius in the chart for Pluto entering Capricorn
From 2009 on	Science and religion must make ecological peril their first priority above all else.	Global warming concerns among scientists and activists rise due to severe weather. Governments take action (US fuel standards, China encourages solar/electric cars, Europe goes solar), but global	Stellium in Sagittarius in the chart for Pluto entering Capricorn

		agreement is not reached.	
November 6, 2008	Pluto entering Capricorn will set off powerful changes, like the Reformation & peasant revolt of 1517 and Age of Democratic Revolt in 1762, complete with a new Luther (or Rousseau, as I mentioned in my talks, but not by name on this page of my book)	In Fall 2008, 94-year old French WWII hero Stephane Hessel gives a lecture, which becomes a short book called "Time for Outrage" in 2010 that sells 3 million copies immediately and helps inspire 2011 Arab Spring and Occupy movements.	Pluto enters Capricorn, Saturn opposite Uranus
After 2008	Enlightened despots or visionary leaders appear who will seek to reform society in the following years.	Did Obama qualify? Merkel? I'm not sure who.	Pluto enters Capricorn, Saturn opposite Uranus
2009 and next several years	Passionate debates over immigration; refugees caused by famine and revolution in many places that get worse. Fear doesn't help.(p.273)	July 6: US sues AZ over new law; supreme court modifies it. New proposal 2013. Refugees from Syria civil war starting in 2011 demand attention; fear of inflaming the war deters help to rebels and victims. African refugees killed in Mediterreanean, Oct.2013.	Pluto enters Capricorn, Saturn opposite Uranus; Neptune entering Pisces 2011-2012
May 2009 through Jan 2010	Fear somewhat superseded by philanthropy and idealism. Compassion toward healing humanity and solving global problems of the Crisis. High hopes for political reform may be disappointed.	Health care reform (ACA/Obamacare): Obama holds summit March 5; bill passes committees in July; passes Senate in Dec and congress in Jan. 2010 on close partisan votes. Many are disappointed with the reforms. Financial reforms like Dodd-Frank deal with causes of recession; introduced July & Dec. 2009; passed July 2010 after being watered down in May by the Senate. Jan.19: Scott Brown elected to Ted Kennedy's Senate seat to oppose the reforms.	Jupiter begins powerful long close conj with Neptune and Chiron in late Aq. in May 2009 through Jan. 2010. Dec. 2009 Mars SD opposes exact conj. Dec/Jan: Saturn sq Pluto.

Early April or late May 2009	There may be some major sea disasters	No known correlation	Jupiter conj Neptune; Mars opp Saturn early April; Mercury SD sq Mars, Jup, Nep. late May.
2009	Spiritual and humanitarian movements in Europe, leading to increased conflict between those who want to help the starving millions and those who fear them.	As European debt crisis grows in 2009-2010, conflict between govt austerity policies and many popular uprisings against it.	Jupiter conj Neptune; Saturn opp Uranus and approaching T-sq with Pluto.
Around July 6 and/or August 19, 2009	Peoples' unhappiness may cause conflict & civil unrest	July 5-7: Uighar-Han clash in Xinjiang China. June 28: Honduras coup. Disruptive US town-hall meetings over health care reform in August. June 12-29 & late July, Iran mass protests against election fraud	July 6: Mars sq Jup/Neptune. Aug 19: Mars-Mercury-Uranus T sq.
October, 2009	More unmaskings of presidential misdeed or terrorist actions; more trouble with Iran. (page 274)	Afghan election fraud. US hands-off approach to Iran uprising is controversial.	Jupiter SD at 17 Aquarius, Oct.13
December 1, 2009	Revolution may rise to fever pitch in Fall 2009 and become international by 2010. Religious reformation may become a crusade. US, Iran, Central Asia, France, Israel, India, California might be involved.	Late Nov. violence in Philippine elections. Dec. 1 Obama announces surge in Afghanistan will begin in Jan.2010. European debt crisis explodes late 2009 and early 2010. Nov.4 and Dec.7 more Iran election protests.	Dec.20: Mars SD 20Leo (near 1999 ecl degree) opposes Jupiter-Neptune in "Marseillaise" figure in Dec.; Saturn sq Pluto
Date	**Prediction in my Jan.1997 book**	**Actual events**	**Astrology**
Jan,15, 2010	Another "deadline day" similar to 1991 might occur. Peace may have a better chance. Economic clashes.	Haiti earthquake Jan.12. Jan 19 Citizens United Decision. European debt crisis explodes late 2009 and early 2010.	Solar eclipse. Saturn sq Pluto, etc.
Spring 2010	Peasants and the poor rise up worldwide in June; governments besieged with demands for change.	April 7: Kyrgyzstan president flees capitol riots. May 3-19: Thai riots. May 11 UK P.M. Brown resigns. April-May Greece, see	Jupiter joins Uranus entering Aries. Mars in Virgo opp Neptune, June 2010. Saturn, Uranus and Pluto T sq.

		below.	
July, 2010	Major, worldwide financial collapse. 2010 looks like a year of sudden, cataclysmic changes and drastic, forced new beginnings	Greece requests bailout and takes austerity measures in April and May 2010. People resist. Irish economy crashes in August. Portugal bond rating cut in Summer 2010; bailout requested and new elections called in Nov.	Solar ecl July 11. 2010: Saturn-Uranus-Pluto T sq in cardinal signs, & Jupiter opp Saturn; "like Gt. Depression"
July 2010 & next months (remember that powerful eclipses with big aspects can be significant for months up to a few years)	Corporations go bankrupt. Economic troubles will bring down many governments with dizzying speed as revolutions sweep the globe. (page 274-75)	Nov. 2010, the ruling Irish Party since 1930s calls elections, and is defeated in Feb.2011. Power shifts in Portugal (March 2011), Greece (Nov. 2011), Italy (Nov.2011), Spain (Nov.2011), Slovenia (Sept.2011), Slovakia (Oct.2011), Belgium (Dec.2011), France (May 2012). Revolution in Tunisia Jan 2011 ignites Arab Spring; Feb 2011: Egypt govt falls, uprisings in Bahrain, Yemen, Libya, Iran "days of rage;" March 2011: Syria.	Solar ecl in July. 2010: Saturn-Uranus-Pluto in Capricorn T sq in cardinal signs, 2010-2011. Jupiter-Uranus conj/solar eclipse Jan.4, 2011.
2010	Common people may be in retreat; xenophobia and fear of radicals. (page 275)	Tea Party arises in Spring 2010, wins US House in Nov. Austerity and racial strife in Europe.	Saturn sq. Pluto, new moon in progressed horoscope of humanity.
July 11, 2010	Economic changes forecast for the USA similar to the Great Depression of the 1930s	Great Recession ongoing. Dodd-Frank financial reforms passed July 15.	July 11: total solar eclipse, Saturn-Uranus-Pluto T sq in financial houses.
2010, esp. Summer after eclipse	Ecological disasters. Global warming and climate change will begin to seriously affect agriculture in many places and magnify 2010 Crisis/revolutions. Shortages and famines. (page 276)	April 20: BP oil spill in Gulf of Mexico; worst environmental disaster in US history. July 30: huge & rare Pakistan flood. Early Aug. unprecedented fires and drought in Russia. Food prices cause global shortages.	July 11 ecl. T sq of 2010-2011 plus Neptune entering Pisces 2011-2012.

2011-2012	All these catastrophes will produce unprecedented steam of refugees	Syria civil war 2011-13 produces millions of refugees. Pakistan floods and other disasters leave thousands homeless.	Neptune entering Pisces
2010s	Countercultures will expand as people seek alternatives to despair and conformity. New rebels will be inspired by high tech, and be altruistic and spiritual, but more committed to realizing their dreams.	Spiritual aspect growing in late 2010s; youth have been inspired, and their revolts such as the Arab Spring, facilitated, by twitter and facebook. Occupy movement (Sept-Oct. 2011) was like a new counter-culture, but directed toward economic and political goals. New social-media inspired pop music is more upbeat and escapist (e.g. Bieber Fever 2010 and 2012 pop stars). High tech wikileaks website and anonymous groups reveal gov't secrets.	Neptune in Pisces, Uranus sq Pluto
August, 2010	Major war may break out, mostly likely in Central Asia.	No known correlation	Saturn sq Pluto
Early 2011	Further breakdown of financial institutions. Collapsed governments may be reimposed. More refugees, disillusion. Conservative politicians benefit.	European debt crisis at peak; govts were still falling as per July 2010 eclipse/Tsq. Some reimposed later (Bahrain, Syria dictators resist), bringing refugee crisis. Tea Party at peak of power in US House.	Neptune entering Pisces, like 1848. Saturn singleton.
Fall of 2010	Huge fireworks of change (page 277)	Arab Spring, early 2011. Nov.2010, new elections called in Ireland and Portugal.	Jupiter conj Uranus
Late 2010 and 2011	Great opportunity for reform movements to mobilize action and swift progress	Arab Spring, early 2011. Occupy movement, Sept.-Oct.2011. Eurozone leaders meet Oct.2011 to solve debt crisis. Many governments fall in Europe in Nov.2011 (see above)	Jupiter conj Uranus, and Uranus sq Pluto; Mars opp. Neptune late Oct.-Nov.
Nov.2010 to Aug 2011	Damper on economic recovery. Right-wing conservatives will try to	Recovery stalls. US credit rating downgraded in August due to Republican	Saturn singleton in Libra; Neptune in Pisces.

	bring another celebration of greed, as indicated by 30-year Saturn cycle. But these are more compassionate times, so they might fail.	default threat by Tea Party House. Europe and UK austerity.	
November, 2010	Great chance to resolve international disputes	No! North Korea attacks South. No known correlation. But lame-duck US congress passes bills before new Tea Party House takes office. ("Pray" by Bieber)	Venus and Jupiter stationary in own signs on same day.
Around April 23 or Aug 25, 2011	Americans calling for making the world safe for democracy, leading to US intervention by 2012	US and NATO help Libya rebels with bombing and no fly zone beginning March 19, 2011. Qaddafi killed Oct.20. Osama bin Laden killed May 1. No new intervention in 2012 except drone attacks.	Jupiter in 7th house in US Spring eq. chart. April 23: Mars opp Saturn (& sq Pluto). Aug 25 Mars sq Saturn. 2012: Jupiter in Gemini
2010s	"depression diplomacy" Global depression requires diplomatic solutions. UN, global free market and help for poor nations are issues.	European nations negotiate growth vs. austerity; develop central bank. US trade talks with Europe begin in 2013.	Saturn in Libra 2010-2012; also to re-enter Libra in progressed chart of humanity in 2017.
Sept-Oct 2011	Some swift and decisive revolutionary or military actions	Syria: 1st armed insurrection June 4. Free Syrian Army formed July 29. Rastan uprising in Syria Sept.27. Armed clashes "spread "in Sept-Oct acc to wikipedia. Occupy Wall Street begins Sept.17, peaks in October.	Mars makes grand cross to T-sq planets. Nov., Mars enters Virgo.
May, 2012	US military action, fulfills its role as peace-keeper, may keep Mid-East nation from using nuclear weapons.	US restraining Israel from nuclear attack on Iran. But no military action yet.	Solar ecl. with Mars in Virgo at MH, Jupiter in late Taurus on Desc.
June, 2012	US probably supporting or opposing a revolution (page 278)	No, US stays out in June 2012	June 2: Uranus' first exact sq to Pluto.
Spring 2013	Expect revolutionary wave crashing through Europe, Mid-East and parts of the Far East	Arab Spring already came in 2011 and troubles on-going. Wave of bombings and explosions in mid April (Boston, Iraq, etc). Turkey rebellion, Brazil mass protests, and largest-yet	Uranus sq Pluto, many planets in Aries at Spring eq Mercury sq. Uranus in June/July

		protests in Egypt in June topple President Morsi July 3.	
December 21, 2012	Birth of one human Great Mind; new spirituality will heal humanity and bridge to higher consciousness	Limited evidence of this so far. World focus on baby killed in Mediterranean Sea migrations	Neptune enters Pisces in Feb.2012; "end of Mayan Calendar" in Dec.
November, 2012	Disillusion would help Republicans win White House	No, but I predicted the election correctly in all its details on The Fourth Turning Forum, 2012 election thread.	Neptune in Pisces
Nov.2012 ff	More mistakes in foreign policy; many US soldiers could die	No known correlation	Neptune in Pisces
July 2013	Constitutional changes, and massive new world-wide connections ease chaos	Late June/early July: Negotiations begin in Afghanistan. New Iran president seeks nuclear deal. Obama gives aid to Syria rebels. Syria conference. Obama offers nuc deal with Russia; summit later canceled due to Snowden affair. Largest demonstrations yet target Morsi and Muslim Brotherhood; army intervention forces new government July 3. Violent protests follow. July 27-29: Pope Francis visits Brazil. July 29: new Israel-Palestine peace talks begin.	Jupiter, Saturn and Neptune grand trine, starting in June, exact on July 17 and effective in August. Mars sq Uranus-Pluto in early August.
2013-2014	Economy recovers, new world-wide connections	Economy recovering as predicted; US-Europe and TPP trade deals in works	Jupiter prominent singleton
November, 2013	More troubles for US troops abroad, more protests at home	no	Total eclipse with Mars in Virgo at Midheaven in USA
Early 2014, May 2014	Crescendo of discontent. Problems for and in the USA as world's top cop. Uprisings and constitutional changes, maybe in Korea.	Ukraine Revolution, invasion of Iraq and Syria by Islamic State group in April-May. Later this caused fear of Muslim	Jupiter at 10 Cancer, grand cross with Uranus, Pluto, stationary Mars in May

	Immigration challenges for USA result.	immigration in the USA.	
Late 2014, early 2015	Possible space flight breakthrough. Loosening social inhibitions	no	Jupiter prominent and trine to Saturn in Sagittarius
Mid-2010s	Mind expanding drugs back in vogue	Marijuana legalization (Washington state Dec.2012, Colorado Jan.2014) with consequent increase in use and new cannabis tourism in some states.	Mercury-Neptune conjunctions in important charts
Spring 2015	More trouble in the Middle East	Iraq and Iranian militias attack Islamic State Mar.2. Yemen war escalates, Mar.19	Mars conj Uranus sq Pluto, and Jupiter singleton in Leo, in equinox chart
August, early Sept.2015	Short-lived peace agreements (in Middle East)	Cuba and USA re-open embassies July 1, flag raising ceremony in Cuba Aug 14. Iran nuclear deal July 14. Paris climate agreement Dec.	Venus stationary
2015 (especially Sept)	Religious reformation causes tremendous turmoil in Middle East as reformers clash with fundamentalists; Israel a target of attacks.	Palmyra ancient temple destroyed by IS Aug. 24. Taliban captures Kunduz, first city in Afghanistan they take in over a decade, Sept.21. Counter-attack follows. Worst Israel-Palestine violence in years over temple mount, early-mid Oct.	Sept 28 lunar eclipse: Mars in Virgo conj Jupiter sq Saturn in Sagittarius square Neptune in Pisces
2016	The above conflicts could disrupt world diplomacy	US air strike hits hospital in Kunduz Oct.3, UN condemns	Saturn sq Neptune
October, 2015	Uprisings among the poor against church and health authorities. Moral crusades.	no	Mars in Virgo opposite Neptune and conj Jupiter
Oct 2015, mid-April 2016	Religious terror attacks or trade wars	TPP trade agreement Oct.5, later withdrawn by President Trump	Mars in Sagittarius stationary, conj. Saturn sq. Neptune and Jupiter
April, 2016	Separatist battle in Spain	Catalonia Parliament votes to secede, Nov. 2015. Big demonstration on Sept.11, 2016. Measures to secede	Saturn in Sagittarius, conj Mars SR in April, conj Saturn again in Sept. and Saturn sq

		in late 2015 and 2016 blocked by Spain, binding referendum blocked Oct.2017	Neptune exact Sept.11, 2016
2016, through Fall	Cult or church financial scandals and clashes in USA and Latin America; could affect US economy	Panama papers reveal secret assets, April 3, 2016. Maduro declares state of emergency in Venezuela in May, huge protests follow. Scandal in Brazil, Pres. Rouseff removed from office Aug.	Saturn in Sagittarius, sq Neptune and Jupiter; Neptune's positions in Fall Equinox and eclipse charts. Jupiter opp Neptune in April and May.
2016 era	$millions in damage from global weather crisis	Canada wildfire, May. Hurricane Matthew Oct. Even worse in 2017; same aspect still in effect. Fires and hurricanes.	Saturn sq Neptune
Spring 2016	USA takes health and ecology measures in concert with other nations	no	Mars in Sagittarius stationary, conj. Saturn sq. Neptune and Jupiter
circa 2017	New USA president to face religious strife in the world	Trump takes office and bans travel to US from 6 Muslim countries.	Saturn sq Neptune, Jupiter opp.Neptune in Jan. Jupiter sq Pluto in Summer
Late 2010s	USA offers itself as ineffective instrument in world peace-keeping and diplomacy. Small muddled sea battles and scandals	Trump fails to stop N. Korea nuclear program, tries to force new Iran deal; crisis with Iran in Gulf results in June 2019.	Saturn sq Neptune
2017	Religious battles in court	US Supreme Court hears oral arguments over baker's refusal to provide a cake for same sex wedding in Dec., preceded by months of private conferences through 2017, acc. to USA Today; inconclusive ruling June 2018.	Jupiter in Libra sq Uranus-Pluto sq.
February 26, 2017	Unrest by poor or religious rebels; US should stay out	no	Eclipse with Mars conj Uranus opp Jupiter
2017	Start of constitutional reforms, ecological reforms, human rights for refugees	Constitutional reforms in Kazakhstan reduce presidential powers; Turkey increases them. Also in Thailand and Sri Lanka. I expected more and better; perhaps this will mature as Saturn moves further into	Jupiter in Libra sextile Saturn in Sag. Saturn enters Libra in 1892 prog., chart of humanity

		Libra in progressed chart of 1892.	
August, 2017	International bridge building, space breakthroughs, or US bombing strike	India and China resolve border dispute Aug.28. Not as much bridge-building as I expected, because of who was President of the USA. No US bombing or space breakthrough.	August 2017 great American eclipse, with Mars in 9th trine Saturn SD in Sag. rising, sextile Jupiter
Sept.2017	Israel or USA bombing strike or rescue attempt, strike or tax revolt by poor people	no	Mars in Virgo opposite Neptune
Spring, Summer 2018, also March 2019	USA leaders and activists promote new Earth-friendly vision	Green New Deal proposed Jan-March 2019	Uranus enters Taurus, Neptune at 16 Pisces, Mars station in Aquarius on June 26, 2018
2018-19	Better economy, helped by new green industries, fewer revolts	Economy doing well.	Uranus enters Taurus
Summer 2018	Global responsibility sacrificed to materialism, as people feel pulse of progress	Trump administration ignores climate change, pulls out of Paris Agreement June 1/Aug.4, 2017	Uranus in Taurus, Mars stationary in Aquarius
January 21, 2019	Popular upheavals against the government and religious disputes, but not war with USA	Another women's march against Trump that day. Yellow Vests protest in France, Jan. Hindu protests shut down India, Jan. "Re-elected" Maduro cuts Venezuela ties with USA.	Lunar eclipse sq Uranus, Venus-Jupiter sq Neptune
early 2019 era	Many governments may crack down on upheaval with oppression	Reactionaries and tyrants coming into power: Erdogen, Deterte. Xi Jinping, Sisi, Assad, Bolsonaro, Morrison, Trump, Salman, Netanyahu, Putin; it's a long list.	Saturn conj Pluto in Capricorn
January, 2019	Financial scandals cost investors money in heady green-boom climate	no	Lunar eclipse sq Uranus, Venus-Jupiter sq Neptune

March 2019 era	Natural psychedelics in vogue	Marijuana legalization proceeding	Uranus entering Taurus
2019	We face karmic results of our battle with nature and racist delusions	Trump arouses hate crimes and stokes racism, climate change causing massive floods	Uranus at 1 Taurus, Neptune in 17 Pisces, key degrees
Mid-June 2019	Escalating ethnic conflicts over natural resources	US crisis with Iran in Persian Gulf and Straight of Hormuz over oil ships and drones attacked, mid-June through July 2019.	Mars opp Saturn and Pluto
2019	USA neighbors helping to trigger conflict in America later.	Controversy in USA heats up over refugees from Central America fleeing regimes, crime and climate change, flooding the border.	July 2, 2019 eclipse with Mercury-Mars in 9th, Saturn-Pluto in 3rd
circa March 2020	Economy may be out of whack again. Again, troubles with other American nations affect US economy		Mars, Jupiter, Saturn and Pluto conj in Capricorn at Spring Equinox
January, 2020	Some kind of resource conflict, postponed by diplomacy		Lunar eclipse conj Saturn-Pluto in 9th
Sept.2020	Major conflict brewing, with roots on June or Jan 2019, that will challenge New World Order established in 1991.		Mars in Aries SR square Saturn-Pluto
After Nov. 14, 2020	Another Day of Infamy begins war in Iraq, India or Central Asia. US plays supportive role, but crisis begins that threatens it.		Mars station in Aries, square Jupiter-Pluto

Appendix B: Abridged Table of Houses

If you know your birth time, use this table to help you understand the meaning of the great planetary cycles in your life. These tables are cast for Washington, D.C., but are generally workable for everyone born in northern temperate longitudes. If you wish greater accuracy, have your chart cast by an astrologer or chart service.

Use the table with the date closest to your birthday, then look for the closest time listed to your own birth time. The tables will show which sign and degree is on each angle (Ascendant, Midheaven, Descendant, and Nadir) for the time listed. If you wish to, you may interpolate using your own estimates. Since these tables assume standard time, you should subtract four minutes from your birth time for each degree west your birthplace is from your standard time meridian (east: add) to get your true local time. If you were born during war or daylight savings time, don't forget to subtract an hour!

January 1

Time	Ascendant	Midheaven	Descendant	Nadir
12:42 A.M.	17 Libra	19 Cancer	17 Aries	19 Capricorn
3:08	16 Scorpio	25 Leo	16 Taurus	25 Aquarius
4:28	2 Sagittar.	16 Virgo	2 Gemini	16 Pisces
4:58	8 Sagittar.	24 Virgo	8 Gemini	24 Pisces
5:36	16 Sagittar.	5 Libra	16 Gemini	5 Aries
7:55	19 Capric.	12 Scorpio	19 Cancer	12 Taurus
9:25	16 Aquarius	4 Sagittar.	16 Leo	4 Gemini
9:42	22 Aquarius	8 Sagittar.	22 Leo	8 Gemini
10:43	16 Pisces	22 Sagittar.	16 Virgo	22 Gemini
11:55	16 Aries	9 Capricorn	16 Libra	9 Cancer
12:38 P.M.	3 Taurus	19 Capric.	3 Scorpio	19 Cancer
1:15	16 Taurus	26 Capric.	16 Scorpio	26 Cancer
2:26	8 Gemini	15 Aquarius	8 Sagittar.	15 Leo
2:57	16 Gemini	23 Aquarius	16 Sagittar.	23 Leo
4:26	7 Cancer	16 Pisces	7 Capricorn	16 Virgo
5:25	19 Cancer	2 Aries	19 Capric.	2 Libra
7:37	16 Leo	8 Taurus	16 Aquarius	8 Scorpio
9:40	11 Virgo	8 Gemini	11 Pisces	8 Sagittarius
10:06	16 Virgo	14 Gemini	16 Pisces	14 Sagittarius

January 15

Time	Ascendant	Midheaven	Descendant	Nadir
2:12 A.M.	16 Scorpio	25 Leo	16 Taurus	25 Aquarius
3:33	2 Sagittar.	16 Virgo	2 Gemini	16 Pisces
4:03	8 Sagittar.	24 Virgo	8 Gemini	24 Pisces
4:41	16 Sagittar.	5 Libra	16 Gemini	5 Aries
7:00	19 Capric.	12 Scorpio	19 Cancer	12 Taurus
8:30	16 Aquarius	4 Sagittar.	16 Leo	4 Gemini
8:47	22 Aquarius	8 Sagittar.	22 Leo	8 Gemini
9:48	16 Pisces	22 Sagittar.	16 Virgo	22 Gemini
11:01	16 Aries	9 Capricorn	16 Libra	9 Cancer
11:44	3 Taurus	19 Capric.	3 Scorpio	19 Cancer
12:21 P.M.	16 Taurus	26 Capric.	16 Scorpio	26 Cancer
1:31	8 Gemini	15 Aquarius	8 Sagittar.	15 Leo
2:02	16 Gemini	23 Aquarius	16 Sagittar.	23 Leo
3:31	7 Calncer	16 Pisces	7 Capricorn	16 Virgo
4:30	19 Cancer	2 Aries	19 Capric.	2 Libra
6:42	16 Leo	8 Taurus	16 Aquarius	8 Scorpio
8:45	11 Virgo	8 Gemini	11 Pisces	8 Sagittar.
9:11	16 Virgo	14 Gemini	16 Pisces	14 Sagittar.
11:44	17 Libra	19 Cancer	17 Aries	19 Capric.

February 1

Time	Ascendant	Midheaven	Descendant	Nadir
1:05 A.M.	16 Scorpio	25 Leo	16 Taurus	25 Aquarius
2:26	2 Sagittar.	16 Virgo	2 Gemini	16 Pisces
2:56	8 Sagittar.	24 Virgo	8 Gemini	24 Pisces

February 15

Time	Ascendant	Midheaven	Descendant	Nadir
12:10 A.M.	16 Scorpio	25 Leo	16 Taurus	25 Aquarius
1:31	2 Sagittar.	16 Virgo	2 Gemini	16 Pisces
2:01	8 Sagittar.	24 Virgo	8 Gemini	24 Pisces

February 1

Time	Ascendant	Midheaven	Descendant	Nadir
3:34 A.M.	16 Sagittar.	5 Libra	16 Gemini	5 Aries
5:54	19 Capric.	12 Scorpio	19 Cancer	12 Taurus
7:23	16 Aquarius	4 Sagittar.	16 Leo	4 Gemini
7:40	22 Aquarius	8 Sagittar.	22 Leo	8 Gemini
8:41	16 Pisces	22 Sagittar.	16 Virgo	22 Gemini
9:54	16 Aries	9 Capricorn	16 Libra	9 Cancer
10:37	3 Taurus	19 Capric.	3 Scorpio	19 Cancer
11:15	16 Taurus	26 Capric.	16 Scorpio	26 Cancer
12:24 P.M.	8 Gemini	15 Aquarius	8 Sagittar.	15 Leo
12:55	16 Gemini	23 Aquarius	16 Sagittar.	23 Leo
2:24	7 Cancer	16 Pisces	7 Capricorn	16 Virgo
3:21	19 Cancer	2 Aries	19 Capric.	2 Libra
5:36	16 Leo	8 Taurus	16 Aquarius	8 Scorpio
7:38	11 Virgo	8 Gemini	11 Pisces	8 Sagittarius
8:04	16 Virgo	14 Gemini	16 Pisces	14 Sagittarius
10:37	17 Libra	19 Cancer	17 Aries	19 Capric.

February 15

Time	Ascendant	Midheaven	Descendant	Nadir
2:39 A.M.	16 Sagittar.	5 Libra	16 Gemini	5 Aries
4:59	19 Capric.	12 Scorpio	19 Cancer	12 Taurus
6:28	16 Aquarius	4 Sagittar.	16 Leo	4 Gemini
6:45	22 Aquarius	8 Sagittar.	22 Leo	8 Gemini
7:46	16 Pisces	22 Sagittar.	16 Virgo	22 Gemini
8:59	16 Aries	9 Capricorn	16 Libra	9 Cancer
9:42	3 Taurus	19 Capric.	3 Scorpio	19 Cancer
10:20	16 Taurus	26 Capric.	16 Scorpio	26 Cancer
11:30	8 Gemini	15 Aquarius	8 Sagittar.	15 Leo
12:00 P.M.	16 Gemini	23 Aquarius	16 Sagittar.	23 Leo
1:29	7 Cancer	16 Pisces	7 Capricorn	16 Virgo
2:26	19 Cancer	2 Aries	19 Capric.	2 Libra
4:41	16 Leo	8 Taurus	16 Aquarius	8 Scorpio
6:43	11 Virgo	8 Gemini	11 Pisces	8 Sagittarius
7:09	16 Virgo	14 Gemini	16 Pisces	14 Sagittar.
9:42	17 Libra	19 Cancer	17 Aries	19 Capric.

March 1

Time	Ascendant	Midheaven	Descendant	Nadir
12:36 A.M.	2 Sagittar.	16 Virgo	2 Gemini	16 Pisces
1:06	8 Sagittar.	24 Virgo	8 Gemini	24 Pisces
1:44	16 Sagittar.	5 Libra	16 Gemini	5 Aries
4:04	19 Capric.	12 Scorpio	19 Cancer	12 Taurus
5:34	16 Aquarius	4 Sagittar.	16 Leo	4 Gemini
5:51	22 Aquarius	8 Sagittar.	22 Leo	8 Gemini
6:51	16 Pisces	22 Sagittar.	16 Virgo	22 Gemini
8:04	16 Aries	9 Capricorn	16 Libra	9 Cancer
8:47	3 Taurus	19 Capric.	3 Scorpio	19 Cancer
9:25	16 Taurus	26 Capric.	16 Scorpio	26 Cancer
10:35	8 Gemini	15 Aquarius	8 Sagittar.	15 Leo
11:06	16 Gemini	23 Aquarius	16 Sagittar.	23 Leo
12:34 P.M.	7 Cancer	16 Pisces	7 Capricorn	16 Virgo
1:31	19 Cancer	2 Aries	19 Capric.	2 Libra
3:46	16 Leo	8 Taurus	16 Aquarius	8 Scorpio
5:49	11 Virgo	8 Gemini	11 Pisces	8 Sagittarius
6:14	16 Virgo	14 Gemini	16 Pisces	14 Sagittarius
8:47	17 Libra	19 Cancer	17 Aries	19 Capricorn
11:12	16 Scorpio	25 Leo	16 Taurus	25 Aquarius

March 15

Time	Ascendant	Midheaven	Descendant	Nadir
12:10 A.M.	8 Sagittar.	24 Virgo	8 Gemini	24 Pisces
12:48	16 Sagittar.	5 Libra	16 Gemini	5 Aries
3:08	19 Capric.	12 Scorpio	19 Cancer	12 Taurus
4:38	16 Aquarius	4 Sagittar.	16 Leo	4 Gemini
4:55	22 Aquarius	8 Sagittar.	22 Leo	8 Gemini
5:56	16 Pisces	22 Sagittar.	16 Virgo	22 Gemini
7:08	16 Aries	9 Capricorn	16 Libra	9 Cancer
7:51	3 Taurus	19 Capric.	3 Scorpio	19 Cancer
8:29	16 Taurus	26 Capric.	16 Scorpio	26 Cancer
9:39	8 Gemini	15 Aquarius	8 Sagittar.	15 Leo
10:10	16 Gemini	23 Aquarius	16 Sagittar.	23 Leo
11:39	7 Cancer	16 Pisces	7 Capricorn	16 Virgo
12:35 P.M.	19 Cancer	2 Aries	19 Capric.	2 Libra
2:50	16 Leo	8 Taurus	16 Aquarius	8 Scorpio
4:53	11 Virgo	8 Gemini	11 Pisces	8 Sagittar.
5:19	16 Virgo	14 Gemini	16 Pisces	14 Sagittar.
7:51	17 Libra	19 Cancer	17 Aries	19 Capric.
10:16	16 Scorpio	25 Leo	16 Taurus	25 Aquarius
11:37	2 Sagittar.	16 Virgo	2 Gemini	16 Pisces

April 1

Time	Ascendant	Midheaven	Descendant	Nadir
2:01 A.M.	19 Capric.	12 Scorpio	19 Cancer	12 Taurus
3:31	16 Aquarius	4 Sagittar.	16 Leo	4 Gemini
3:48	22 Aquarius	8 Sagittar.	22 Leo	8 Gemini

April 15

Time	Ascendant	Midheaven	Descendant	Nadir
1:06 A.M.	19 Capric.	12 Scorpio	19 Cancer	12 Taurus
2:36	16 Aquarius	4 Sagittar.	16 Leo	4 Gemini
2:53	22 Aquarius	8 Sagittar.	22 Leo	8 Gemini

April 1

Time	Ascendant	Midheaven	Descendant	Nadir
4:49 A.M.	16 Pisces	22 Sagittar.	16 Virgo	22 Gemini
6:01	16 Aries	9 Capricorn	16 Libra	9 Cancer
6:44	3 Taurus	19 Capric.	3 Scorpio	19 Cancer
7:22	16 Taurus	26 Capric.	16 Scorpio	26 Cancer
8:32	8 Gemini	15 Aquarius	8 Sagittar.	15 Leo
9:03	16 Gemini	23 Aquarius	16 Sagittar.	23 Leo
10:32	7 Cancer	16 Pisces	7 Capricorn	16 Virgo
11:29	19 Cancer	2 Aries	19 Capric.	2 Libra
1:44 P.M.	16 Leo	8 Taurus	16 Aquarius	8 Scorpio
3:47	11 Virgo	8 Gemini	11 Pisces	8 Sagittarius
4:13	16 Virgo	14 Gemini	16 Pisces	14 Sagittarius
6:44	17 Libra	19 Cancer	17 Aries	19 Capricorn
9:09	16 Scorpio	25 Leo	16 Taurus	25 Aquarius
10:30	2 Sagittar.	16 Virgo	2 Gemini	16 Pisces
11:00	8 Sagittar.	24 Virgo	8 Gemini	24 Pisces
11:38	16 Sagittar.	5 Libra	16 Gemini	5 Aries

April 15

Time	Ascendant	Midheaven	Descendant	Nadir
3:54 A.M.	16 Pisces	22 Sagittar.	16 Virgo	22 Gemini
5:07	16 Aries	9 Capricorn	16 Libra	9 Cancer
5:50	3 Taurus	19 Capric.	3 Scorpio	19 Cancer
6:27	16 Taurus	26 Capric.	16 Scorpio	26 Cancer
7:37	8 Gemini	15 Aquarius	8 Sagittar.	15 Leo
8:08	16 Gemini	23 Aquarius	16 Sagittar.	23 Leo
9:37	7 Cancer	16 Pisces	7 Capricorn	16 Virgo
10:34	19 Cancer	2 Aries	19 Capric.	2 Libra
12:48 P.M.	16 Leo	8 Taurus	16 Aquarius	8 Scorpio
2:51	11 Virgo	8 Gemini	11 Pisces	8 Sagittar.
3:17	16 Virgo	14 Gemini	16 Pisces	14 Sagittar.
5:50	17 Libra	19 Cancer	17 Aries	19 Capric.
8:14	16 Scorpio	25 Leo	16 Taurus	25 Aquarius
9:35	2 Sagittar.	16 Virgo	2 Gemini	16 Pisces
10:05	8 Sagittar.	24 Virgo	8 Gemini	24 Pisces
10:43	16 Sagittar.	5 Libra	16 Gemini	5 Aries

May 1

Time	Ascendant	Midheaven	Descendant	Nadir
12:03 A.M.	19 Capric.	12 Scorpio	19 Cancer	12 Taurus
1:33	16 Aquarius	4 Sagittar.	16 Leo	4 Gemini
1:50	22 Aquarius	8 Sagittar.	22 Leo	8 Gemini
2:51	16 Pisces	22 Sagittar.	16 Virgo	22 Gemini
4:04	16 Aries	9 Capricorn	16 Libra	9 Cancer
4:47	3 Taurus	19 Capric.	3 Scorpio	19 Cancer
5:25	16 Taurus	26 Capric.	16 Scorpio	26 Cancer
6:34	8 Gemini	15 Aquarius	8 Sagittar.	15 Leo
7:05	16 Gemini	23 Aquarius	16 Sagittar.	23 Leo
8:34	7 Cancer	16 Pisces	7 Capricorn	16 Virgo
9:31	19 Cancer	2 Aries	19 Capric.	2 Libra
11:46	16 Leo	8 Taurus	16 Aquarius	8 Scorpio
1:48 P.M.	11 Virgo	8 Gemini	11 Pisces	8 Sagittarius
2:14	16 Virgo	14 Gemini	16 Pisces	14 Sagittarius
4:47	17 Libra	19 Cancer	17 Aries	19 Capricorn
7:11	16 Scorpio	25 Leo	16 Taurus	25 Aquarius
8:32	2 Sagittar.	16 Virgo	2 Gemini	16 Pisces
9:02	8 Sagittar.	24 Virgo	8 Gemini	24 Pisces
9:40	16 Sagittar.	5 Libra	16 Gemini	5 Aries

May 15

Time	Ascendant	Midheaven	Descendant	Nadir
12:38 A.M.	16 Aquarius	4 Sagittar.	16 Leo	4 Gemini
12:55	22 Aquarius	8 Sagittar.	22 Leo	8 Gemini
1:56	16 Pisces	22 Sagittar.	16 Virgo	22 Gemini
3:09	16 Aries	9 Capricorn	16 Libra	9 Cancer
3:52	3 Taurus	19 Capric.	3 Scorpio	19 Cancer
4:30	16 Taurus	26 Capric.	16 Scorpio	26 Cancer
5:40	8 Gemini	15 Aquarius	8 Sagittar.	15 Leo
6:10	16 Gemini	23 Aquarius	16 Sagittar.	23 Leo
7:39	7 Cancer	16 Pisces	7 Capricorn	16 Virgo
8:36	19 Cancer	2 Aries	19 Capric.	2 Libra
10:51	16 Leo	8 Taurus	16 Aquarius	8 Scorpio
12:53 P.M.	11 Virgo	8 Gemini	11 Pisces	8 Sagittar.
1:19	16 Virgo	14 Gemini	16 Pisces	14 Sagittar.
3:52	17 Libra	19 Cancer	17 Aries	19 Capric.
6:16	16 Scorpio	25 Leo	16 Taurus	25 Aquarius
7:37	2 Sagittar.	16 Virgo	2 Gemini	16 Pisces
8:07	8 Sagittar.	24 Virgo	8 Gemini	24 Pisces
8:45	16 Sagittar.	5 Libra	16 Gemini	5 Aries
11:05	19 Capric.	12 Scorpio	19 Cancer	12 Taurus

June 1

Time	Ascendant	Midheaven	Descendant	Nadir
12:49 A.M.	16 Pisces	22 Sagittar.	16 Virgo	22 Gemini
2:02	16 Aries	9 Capricorn	16 Libra	9 Cancer
2:45 A.M.	3 Taurus	19 Capric.	3 Scorpio	19 Cancer

June 15

Time	Ascendant	Midheaven	Descendant	Nadir
1:08 A.M.	16 Aries	9 Capricorn	16 Libra	9 Cancer
1:51	3 Taurus	19 Capric.	3 Scorpio	19 Cancer
2:33 A.M.	16 Taurus	26 Capric.	16 Scorpio	26 Cancer

June 1

Time	Ascendant	Midheaven	Descendant	Nadir
3:23 A.M.	16 Taurus	26 Capric.	16 Scorpio	26 Cancer
4:34	8 Gemini	15 Aquarius	8 Sagittar.	15 Leo
5:05	16 Gemini	23 Aquarius	16 Sagittar.	23 Leo
6:34	7 Cancer	16 Pisces	7 Capricorn	16 Virgo
7:31	19 Cancer	2 Aries	19 Capric.	2 Libra
9:46	16 Leo	8 Taurus	16 Aquarius	8 Scorpio
11:49	11 Virgo	8 Gemini	11 Pisces	8 Sagittarius
12:14 P.M.	16 Virgo	14 Gemini	16 Pisces	14 Sagittarius
2:48	17 Libra	19 Cancer	17 Aries	19 Capricorn
5:13	16 Scorpio	25 Leo	16 Taurus	25 Aquarius
6:33	2 Sagittar.	16 Virgo	2 Gemini	16 Pisces
7:03	8 Sagittar.	24 Virgo	8 Gemini	24 Pisces
7:42	16 Sagittar.	5 Libra	16 Gemini	5 Aries
10:02	19 Capric.	12 Scorpio	19 Cancer	12 Taurus
11:32	16 Aquarius	4 Sagittar.	16 Leo	4 Gemini
11:48	22 Aquarius	8 Sagittar.	22 Leo	8 Gemini

June 15

Time	Ascendant	Midheaven	Descendant	Nadir
3:39 A.M.	8 Gemini	15 Aquarius	8 Sagittar.	15 Leo
4:10	16 Gemini	23 Aquarius	16 Sagittar.	23 Leo
5:39	7 Cancer	16 Pisces	7 Capricorn	16 Virgo
6:36	19 Cancer	2 Aries	19 Capric.	2 Libra
8:51	16 Leo	8 Taurus	16 Aquarius	8 Scorpio
10:54	11 Virgo	8 Gemini	11 Pisces	8 Sagittar.
11:19	16 Virgo	14 Gemini	16 Pisces	14 Sagittar.
1:53 P.M.	17 Libra	19 Cancer	17 Aries	19 Capric.
4:18	16 Scorpio	25 Leo	16 Taurus	25 Aquarius
5:39	2 Sagittar.	16 Virgo	2 Gemini	16 Pisces
6:09	8 Sagittar.	24 Virgo	8 Gemini	24 Pisces
6:47	16 Sagittar.	5 Libra	16 Gemini	5 Aries
9:07	19 Capric.	12 Scorpio	19 Cancer	12 Taurus
10:37	16 Aquarius	4 Sagittar.	16 Leo	4 Gemini
10:53	22 Aquarius	8 Sagittar.	22 Leo	8 Gemini
11:56	16 Pisces	22 Sagittar.	16 Virgo	22 Gemini

July 1

Time	Ascendant	Midheaven	Descendant	Nadir
12:05 A.M.	16 Aries	9 Capricorn	16 Libra	9 Cancer
12:48	3 Taurus	19 Capric.	3 Scorpio	19 Cancer
1:26	16 Taurus	26 Capric.	16 Scorpio	26 Cancer
2:36	8 Gemini	15 Aquarius	8 Sagittar.	15 Leo
3:07	16 Gemini	23 Aquarius	16 Sagittar.	23 Leo
4:36	7 Cancer	16 Pisces	7 Capricorn	16 Virgo
5:33	19 Cancer	2 Aries	19 Capric.	2 Libra
7:48	16 Leo	8 Taurus	16 Aquarius	8 Scorpio
9:51	11 Virgo	8 Gemini	11 Pisces	8 Sagittar.
10:16	16 Virgo	14 Gemini	16 Pisces	14 Sagittar.
12:50 P.M.	17 Libra	19 Cancer	17 Aries	19 Capric.
3:15	16 Scorpio	25 Leo	16 Taurus	25 Aquarius
4:36	2 Sagittar.	16 Virgo	2 Gemini	16 Pisces
5:06	8 Sagittar.	24 Virgo	8 Gemini	24 Pisces
5:44	16 Sagittar.	5 Libra	16 Gemini	5 Aries
8:04	19 Capric.	12 Scorpio	19 Cancer	12 Taurus
9:34	16 Aquarius	4 Sagittar.	16 Leo	4 Gemini
9:51	22 Aquarius	8 Sagittar.	22 Leo	8 Gemini
10:53	16 Pisces	22 Sagittar.	16 Virgo	22 Gemini

July 15

Time	Ascendant	Midheaven	Descendant	Nadir
12:30 A.M.	16 Taurus	26 Capric.	16 Scorpio	26 Cancer
1:41	8 Gemini	15 Aquarius	8 Sagittar.	15 Leo
2:11	16 Gemini	23 Aquarius	16 Sagittar.	23 Leo
3:41	7 Cancer	16 Pisces	7 Capricorn	16 Virgo
4:37	19 Cancer	2 Aries	19 Capric.	2 Libra
6:52	16 Leo	8 Taurus	16 Aquarius	8 Scorpio
8:56	11 Virgo	8 Gemini	11 Pisces	8 Sagittar.
9:21	16 Virgo	14 Gemini	16 Pisces	14 Sagittar.
11:55	17 Libra	19 Cancer	17 Aries	19 Capric.
2:19 P.M.	16 Scorpio	25 Leo	16 Taurus	25 Aquarius
3:41	2 Sagittar.	16 Virgo	2 Gemini	16 Pisces
4:11	8 Sagittar.	24 Virgo	8 Gemini	24 Pisces
4:48	16 Sagittar.	5 Libra	16 Gemini	5 Aries
7:08	19 Capric.	12 Scorpio	19 Cancer	12 Taurus
8:38	16 Aquarius	4 Sagittar.	16 Leo	4 Gemini
8:54	22 Aquarius	8 Sagittar.	22 Leo	8 Gemini
9:57	16 Pisces	22 Sagittar.	16 Virgo	22 Gemini
11:08	16 Aries	9 Capricorn	16 Libra	9 Cancer
11:53	3 Taurus	19 Capric.	3 Scorpio	19 Cancer

August 1

Time	Ascendant	Midheaven	Descendant	Nadir
12:34 A.M.	8 Gemini	15 Aquarius	8 Sagittar.	15 Leo
1:04	16 Gemini	23 Aquarius	16 Sagittar.	23 Leo
2:33	7 Cancer	16 Pisces	7 Capricorn	16 Virgo

August 15

Time	Ascendant	Midheaven	Descendant	Nadir
12:09 A.M.	16 Gemini	23 Aquarius	16 Sagittar.	23 Leo
1:38	7 Cancer	16 Pisces	7 Capricorn	16 Virgo
2:35	19 Cancer	2 Aries	19 Capric.	2 Libra

August 1

Time	Ascendant	Midheaven	Descendant	Nadir
3:30 A.M.	19 Cancer	2 Aries	19 Capric.	2 Libra
5:45	16 Leo	8 Taurus	16 Aquarius	8 Scorpio
7:49	11 Virgo	8 Gemini	11 Pisces	8 Sagittar.
8:14	16 Virgo	14 Gemini	16 Pisces	14 Sagittar.
10:48	17 Libra	19 Cancer	17 Aries	19 Capric.
1:12 P.M.	16 Scorpio	25 Leo	16 Taurus	25 Aquarius
2:34	2 Sagittar.	16 Virgo	2 Gemini	16 Pisces
3:04	8 Sagittar.	24 Virgo	8 Gemini	24 Pisces
3:41	16 Sagittar.	5 Libra	16 Gemini	5 Aries
6:01	19 Capric.	12 Scorpio	19 Cancer	12 Taurus
7:31	16 Aquarius	4 Sagittar.	16 Leo	4 Gemini
7:48	22 Aquarius	8 Sagittar.	22 Leo	8 Gemini
8:50	16 Pisces	22 Sagittar.	16 Virgo	22 Gemini
10:02	16 Aries	9 Capricorn	16 Libra	9 Cancer
10:45	3 Taurus	19 Capric.	3 Scorpio	19 Cancer
11:23	16 Taurus	26 Capric.	16 Scorpio	26 Cancer

August 15

Time	Ascendant	Midheaven	Descendant	Nadir
4:50 A.M.	16 Leo	8 Taurus	16 Aquarius	8 Scorpio
6:53	11 Virgo	8 Gemini	11 Pisces	8 Sagittar.
7:18	16 Virgo	14 Gemini	16 Pisces	14 Sagittar.
9:52	17 Libra	19 Cancer	17 Aries	19 Capric.
12:17 P.M.	16 Scorpio	25 Leo	16 Taurus	25 Aquarius
1:38	2 Sagittar.	16 Virgo	2 Gemini	16 Pisces
2:08	8 Sagittar.	24 Virgo	8 Gemini	24 Pisces
2:46	16 Sagittar.	5 Libra	16 Gemini	5 Aries
5:06	19 Capric.	12 Scorpio	19 Cancer	12 Taurus
6:36	16 Aquarius	4 Sagittar.	16 Leo	4 Gemini
6:53	22 Aquarius	8 Sagittar.	22 Leo	8 Gemini
7:55	16 Pisces	22 Sagittar.	16 Virgo	22 Gemini
9:07	16 Aries	9 Capricorn	16 Libra	9 Cancer
9:50	3 Taurus	19 Capric.	3 Scorpio	19 Cancer
10:28	16 Taurus	26 Capric.	16 Scorpio	26 Cancer
11:38	8 Gemini	15 Aquarius	8 Sagittar.	15 Leo

September 1

Time	Ascendant	Midheaven	Descendant	Nadir
12:31 A.M.	7 Cancer	16 Pisces	7 Capricorn	16 Virgo
1:28	19 Cancer	2 Aries	19 Capric.	2 Libra
3:43	16 Leo	8 Taurus	16 Aquarius	8 Scorpio
5:46	11 Virgo	8 Gemini	11 Pisces	8 Sagittar.
6:11	16 Virgo	14 Gemini	16 Pisces	14 Sagittar.
8:45	17 Libra	19 Cancer	17 Aries	19 Capric.
11:10	16 Scorpio	25 Leo	16 Taurus	25 Aquarius
12:31 P.M.	2 Sagittar.	16 Virgo	2 Gemini	16 Pisces
1:01	8 Sagittar.	24 Virgo	8 Gemini	24 Pisces
1:39	16 Sagittar.	5 Libra	16 Gemini	5 Aries
3:59	19 Capric.	12 Scorpio	19 Cancer	12 Taurus
5:29	16 Aquarius	4 Sagittar.	16 Leo	4 Gemini
5:46	22 Aquarius	8 Sagittar.	22 Leo	8 Gemini
6:48	16 Pisces	22 Sagittar.	16 Virgo	22 Gemini
8:00	16 Aries	9 Capricorn	16 Libra	9 Cancer
8:43	3 Taurus	19 Capric.	3 Scorpio	19 Cancer
9:21	16 Taurus	26 Capric.	16 Scorpio	26 Cancer
10:31	8 Gemini	15 Aquarius	8 Sagittar.	15 Leo
11:02	16 Gemini	23 Aquarius	16 Sagittar.	23 Leo

September 15

Time	Ascendant	Midheaven	Descendant	Nadir
12:33 A.M.	19 Cancer	2 Aries	19 Capric.	2 Libra
2:48	16 Leo	8 Taurus	16 Aquarius	8 Scorpio
4:51	11 Virgo	8 Gemini	11 Pisces	8 Sagittar.
5:16	16 Virgo	14 Gemini	16 Pisces	14 Sagittar.
7:50	17 Libra	19 Cancer	17 Aries	19 Capric.
10:15	16 Scorpio	25 Leo	16 Taurus	25 Aquarius
11:36	2 Sagittar.	16 Virgo	2 Gemini	16 Pisces
12:06 P.M.	8 Sagittar.	24 Virgo	8 Gemini	24 Pisces
12:44	16 Sagittar.	5 Libra	16 Gemini	5 Aries
3:04	19 Capric.	12 Scorpio	19 Cancer	12 Taurus
4:34	16 Aquarius	4 Sagittar.	16 Leo	4 Gemini
4:51	22 Aquarius	8 Sagittar.	22 Leo	8 Gemini
5:53	16 Pisces	22 Sagittar.	16 Virgo	22 Gemini
7:05	16 Aries	9 Capricorn	16 Libra	9 Cancer
7:48	3 Taurus	19 Capric.	3 Scorpio	19 Cancer
8:25	16 Taurus	26 Capric.	16 Scorpio	26 Cancer
9:36	8 Gemini	15 Aquarius	8 Sagittar.	15 Leo
10:07	16 Gemini	23 Aquarius	16 Sagittar.	23 Leo
11:36	7 Cancer	16 Pisces	7 Capricorn	16 Virgo

October 1

Time	Ascendant	Midheaven	Descendant	Nadir
1:45 A.M.	16 Leo	8 Taurus	16 Aquarius	8 Scorpio
3:48	11 Virgo	8 Gemini	11 Pisces	8 Sagittar.
4:13	16 Virgo	14 Gemini	16 Pisces	14 Sagittar.

October 15

Time	Ascendant	Midheaven	Descendant	Nadir
12:50 A.M.	16 Leo	8 Taurus	16 Aquarius	8 Scorpio
2:53	11 Virgo	8 Gemini	11 Pisces	8 Sagittar.
3:18	16 Virgo	14 Gemini	16 Pisces	14 Sagittar.

October 1

Time	Ascendant	Midheaven	Descendant	Nadir
6:47 A.M.	17 Libra	19 Cancer	17 Aries	19 Capric.
9:12	16 Scorpio	25 Leo	16 Taurus	25 Aquarius
10:33	2 Sagittar.	16 Virgo	2 Gemini	16 Pisces
11:03	8 Sagittar.	24 Virgo	8 Gemini	24 Pisces
12:18 P.M.	16 Sagittar.	5 Libra	16 Gemini	5 Aries
2:01	19 Capric.	12 Scorpio	19 Cancer	12 Taurus
3:31	16 Aquarius	4 Sagittar.	16 Leo	4 Gemini
3:47	22 Aquarius	8 Sagittar.	22 Leo	8 Gemini
4:50	16 Pisces	22 Sagittar.	16 Virgo	22 Gemini
6:02	16 Aries	9 Capricorn	16 Libra	9 Cancer
6:45	3 Taurus	19 Capric.	3 Scorpio	19 Cancer
7:22	16 Taurus	26 Capric.	16 Scorpio	26 Cancer
8:33	8 Gemini	15 Aquarius	8 Sagittar.	15 Leo
9:04	16 Gemini	23 Aquarius	16 Sagittar.	23 Leo
10:33	7 Cancer	16 Pisces	7 Capricorn	16 Virgo
11:30	19 Cancer	2 Aries	19 Capric.	2 Libra

October 15

Time	Ascendant	Midheaven	Descendant	Nadir
5:52 A.M.	17 Libra	19 Cancer	17 Aries	19 Capric.
8:17	16 Scorpio	25 Leo	16 Taurus	25 Aquarius
9:38	2 Sagittar.	16 Virgo	2 Gemini	16 Pisces
10:08	8 Sagittar.	24 Virgo	8 Gemini	24 Pisces
10:46	16 Sagittar.	5 Libra	16 Gemini	5 Aries
1:06 P.M.	19 Capric.	12 Scorpio	19 Cancer	12 Taurus
2:36	16 Aquarius	4 Sagittar.	16 Leo	4 Gemini
2:53	22 Aquarius	8 Sagittar.	22 Leo	8 Gemini
3:55	16 Pisces	22 Sagittar.	16 Virgo	22 Gemini
5:07	16 Aries	9 Capricorn	16 Libra	9 Cancer
5:50	3 Taurus	19 Capric.	3 Scorpio	19 Cancer
6:27	16 Taurus	26 Capric.	16 Scorpio	26 Cancer
7:38	8 Gemini	15 Aquarius	8 Sagittar.	15 Leo
8:09	16 Gemini	23 Aquarius	16 Sagittar.	23 Leo
9:38	7 Cancer	16 Pisces	7 Capricorn	16 Virgo
10:35	19 Cancer	2 Aries	19 Capric.	2 Libra

November 1

Time	Ascendant	Midheaven	Descendant	Nadir
1:46 A.M.	11 Virgo	8 Gemini	11 Pisces	8 Sagittar.
2:11	16 Virgo	14 Gemini	16 Pisces	14 Sagittar.
4:45	17 Libra	19 Cancer	17 Aries	19 Capric.
7:10	16 Scorpio	25 Leo	16 Taurus	25 Aquarius
8:31	2 Sagittar.	16 Virgo	2 Gemini	16 Pisces
9:01	8 Sagittar.	24 Virgo	8 Gemini	24 Pisces
9:39	16 Sagittar.	5 Libra	16 Gemini	5 Aries
11:59	19 Capric.	12 Scorpio	19 Cancer	12 Taurus
1:29 P.M.	16 Aquarius	4 Sagittar.	16 Leo	4 Gemini
1:46	22 Aquarius	8 Sagittar.	22 Leo	8 Gemini
2:48	16 Pisces	22 Sagittar.	16 Virgo	22 Gemini
4:00	16 Aries	9 Capricorn	16 Libra	9 Cancer
4:43	3 Taurus	19 Capric.	3 Scorpio	19 Cancer
5:20	16 Taurus	26 Capric.	16 Scorpio	26 Cancer
6:31	8 Gemini	15 Aquarius	8 Sagittar.	15 Leo
7:02	16 Gemini	23 Aquarius	16 Sagittar.	23 Leo
8:31	7 Cancer	16 Pisces	7 Capricorn	16 Virgo
9:08	19 Cancer	2 Aries	19 Capric.	2 Libra
11:43	16 Leo	8 Taurus	16 Aquarius	8 Scorpio

November 15

Time	Ascendant	Midheaven	Descendant	Nadir
12:51 A.M.	11 Virgo	8 Gemini	11 Pisces	8 Sagittar.
1:16	16 Virgo	14 Gemini	16 Pisces	14 Sagittar.
3:50	17 Libra	19 Cancer	17 Aries	19 Capric.
6:14	16 Scorpio	25 Leo	16 Taurus	25 Aquarius
7:36	2 Sagittar.	16 Virgo	2 Gemini	16 Pisces
8:06	8 Sagittar.	24 Virgo	8 Gemini	24 Pisces
8:44	16 Sagittar.	5 Libra	16 Gemini	5 Aries
11:04	19 Capric.	12 Scorpio	19 Cancer	12 Taurus
12:33 P.M.	16 Aquarius	4 Sagittar.	16 Leo	4 Gemini
12:50	22 Aquarius	8 Sagittar.	22 Leo	8 Gemini
1:52	16 Pisces	22 Sagittar.	16 Virgo	22 Gemini
3:04	16 Aries	9 Capricorn	16 Libra	9 Cancer
3:48	3 Taurus	19 Capric.	3 Scorpio	19 Cancer
4:25	16 Taurus	26 Capric.	16 Scorpio	26 Cancer
5:36	8 Gemini	15 Aquarius	8 Sagittar.	15 Leo
6:06	16 Gemini	23 Aquarius	16 Sagittar.	23 Leo
7:36	7 Cancer	16 Pisces	7 Capricorn	16 Virgo
8:33	19 Cancer	2 Aries	19 Capric.	2 Libra
10:47	16 Leo	8 Taurus	16 Aquarius	8 Scorpio

December 1

Time	Ascendant	Midheaven	Descendant	Nadir
12:13 A.M.	16 Virgo	14 Gemini	16 Pisces	14 Sagittar.
2:46	17 Libra	19 Cancer	17 Aries	19 Capric.
5:11	16 Scorpio	25 Leo	16 Taurus	25 Aquarius

December 15

Time	Ascendant	MidHeaven	Descendant	Nadir
1:51 A.M.	17 Libra	19 Cancer	17 Aries	19 Capric.
4:16	16 Scorpio	25 Leo	16 Taurus	25 Aquarius
5:37	2 Sagittar.	16 Virgo	2 Gemini	16 Pisces

December 1

Time	Ascendant	Midheaven	Descendant	Nadir
6:33 A.M.	2 Sagittar.	16 Virgo	2 Gemini	16 Pisces
7:03	8 Sagittar.	24 Virgo	8 Gemini	24 Pisces
7:41	16 Sagittar.	5 Libra	16 Gemini	5 Aries
10:00	19 Capric.	12 Scorpio	19 Cancer	12 Taurus
11:30	16 Aquarius	4 Sagittar.	16 Leo	4 Gemini
11:47	22 Aquarius	8 Sagittar.	22 Leo	8 Gemini
12:49 P.M.	16 Pisces	22 Sagittar.	16 Virgo	22 Gemini
2:01	16 Aries	9 Capricorn	16 Libra	9 Cancer
2:45	3 Taurus	19 Capric.	3 Scorpio	19 Cancer
3:22	16 Taurus	26 Capric.	16 Scorpio	26 Cancer
4:33	8 Gemini	15 Aquarius	8 Sagittar.	15 Leo
5:03	16 Gemini	23 Aquarius	16 Sagittar.	23 Leo
6:32	7 Cancer	16 Pisces	7 Capricorn	16 Virgo
7:30	19 Cancer	2 Aries	19 Capric.	2 Libra
9:44	16 Leo	8 Taurus	16 Aquarius	8 Scorpio
11:48	11 Virgo	8 Gemini	11 Pisces	8 Sagittar.

December 15

Time	Ascendant	MidHeaven	Descendant	Nadir
6:07 A.M.	8 Sagittar.	24 Virgo	8 Gemini	24 Pisces
6:45	16 Sagittar.	5 Libra	16 Gemini	5 Aries
9:05	19 Capric.	12 Scorpio	19 Cancer	12 Taurus
10:35	16 Aquarius	4 Sagittar.	16 Leo	4 Gemini
10:52	22 Aquarius	8 Sagittar.	22 Leo	8 Gemini
11:54	16 Pisces	22 Sagittar.	16 Virgo	22 Gemini
1:06 P.M.	16 Aries	9 Capricorn	16 Libra	9 Cancer
1:49	3 Taurus	19 Capric.	3 Scorpio	19 Cancer
2:26	16 Taurus	26 Capric.	16 Scorpio	26 Cancer
3:37	8 Gemini	15 Aquarius	8 Sagittar.	15 Leo
4:08	16 Gemini	23 Aquarius	16 Sagittar.	23 Leo
5:37	7 Cancer	16 Pisces	7 Capricorn	16 Virgo
6:34	19 Cancer	2 Aries	19 Capric.	2 Libra
8:49	16 Leo	8 Taurus	16 Aquarius	8 Scorpio
10:52	11 Virgo	8 Gemini	11 Pisces	8 Sagittar.
11:17	16 Virgo	14 Gemini	16 Pisces	14 Sagittar.

Appendix C: The Houses of The Horoscope

The horoscope figure is divided into twelve "Houses," representing the twelve "departments of life." They are closely related to the twelve signs, and they have corresponding meanings. The houses represent the "theaters of activity" in which the planets interact.

The 1st House takes its meaning from the Ascendant, and represents the self, personality, initiative, personal power, health, appearance, the people, and their behavior and attitudes. It is linked to Aries.

The 2nd House represents all financial affairs, desires for stability, constructive talents, financial independence, and values. It is linked to Taurus.

The 3rd House represents travel, communications, trade, journalism, the media, the mind, writings, intellectuals, education, youth, ideas, speech, neighbors, and relatives. It is linked to Gemini.

The 4th House takes its meaning from the Nadir. It represents private institutions, home, family, ethnic pride, the personal and national soul, the land, and the weather. It is linked to Cancer.

The 5th House represents self-expression, youth, romance, pleasures, financial speculation, sports, games, children, education, ambitions for power, imperial expansion, the Senate, royalty, and nobility. It is linked to Leo.

The 6th House involves public health, welfare, work, civil and military service, bureaucrats, employees, labor unions, volunteers, servants, and the service industries. It is linked to Virgo.

The 7th House takes its meaning from the Descendant, and rules international relations, diplomacy, politics, war, disputes, legal affairs, marriage, divorce, contracts, enemies, and public scandals. It is linked to Libra.

The 8th House rules financial dealings, corporations, taxes, insurance, mortgages, inheritance, group management of funds, communes and communism, stock markets, and debts. It also stands for death, rebirth, rebuilding, renewal, and the occult. It is linked to Scorpio.

The 9th House rules foreign affairs, trade, distant travels, higher education, philosophy, the law, the courts, the Church, and prophecy. It is linked to Sagittarius.

The 10th House takes its meaning from the Midheaven. It stands for status, career, achievement, the government, the administration, the king, and public life. It is linked to Capricorn.

The 11th House represents group cooperation, idealistic associations, the legislature (lower house), government finance, social programs, theater, friends, hopes for the future, and profitable inventions. It is linked to Aquarius.

The 12th House rules personal and national karma, hidden forces, secret enemies, big institutions, prisons, asylums, monasteries, hospitals, occult interests, spirituality, exile, and the search for refuge and self-renewal. It is linked to Pisces.

Appendix D: Phases of The Cycle of Civilization

Neptune-Pluto **conjunctions**, discussed in Chapter 2 of this book, are just the beginning (and most important) milestones in the fortunes of civilization; the moments of endings and beginnings. Other aspects mark the important phases of rise and decay that follow and are accurately reflected in civilization by the arts. The years stated are approximate.

The **opening sextile** (sixty-degree aspect), when Neptune and Pluto are two signs apart, is a "crescent moon" phase, in which the creative energy of the new civilization is flowering and its first crises are overcome. In the arts this is called the "classical" phase, when original themes are stated in a confident but restrained and balanced style. The sextile often lasts many years because Pluto is moving faster in its eccentric orbit. They occurred in:

435 B.C. during the Age of Pericles in the Greek golden age.
20 B.C. (approximate aspect) and A.D. 60 during the golden age of Rome and the building of Teotihuacan. In 17 B.C. the "saeculum" was celebrated in the Augustan Age, as Virgil wrote his epic, the Aeneid.
A.D. 550 at the height of the Byzantine golden age under Justinian.
960-995 in the time of Otto the Great and the founding of the Sung Dynasty, and again in 1046 when the first great cathedrals were built.
1450-1500 during the creative flowering of the Renaissance and the voyages of Columbus, and again around 1537 at the time of Copernicus, Henry VIII, Suleiman the Magnificent.
1940-2040 during the crisis of our own emerging New Age.
2430-2530 will be the time of the next "creative flowering" under the sextile. Future opening sextiles will occur in about 2975 to 3020, 3410 to 3430 (and approximately from 3480 to 3510), and in 3910 to 3920.

The **opening or waxing square** (ninety-degree aspect, three signs apart) represents a serious early crisis in the new civilization. Its foundations are tested or rebuilt and firmed up, and "ghosts from the past" are confronted. Such first quarter waxing squares occurred in:

405 B.C. at the end of the Peloponnesian War and the trial of Socrates.
A.D. 91 during the "reign of terror" under Roman Emperor Domitian.
583 as new barbarian invasions ended the Byzantine golden age.
1077 during the height of church-state rivalry when Holy Roman Emperor Henry IV capitulated to the Pope.
1570 during the height of the Wars of Religion and witch burnings.
2063 is the time of the next square and the next crisis. After that, waxing squares will happen in about 2556, 3050 and 3540.

The **waxing trine** or 120-degree aspect (four signs apart) is like a gibbous moon. It represents a period of confident expansion when the energies of civilization are moving toward their climax. In the arts it brings the baroque phase: an elaborate, lively, more rhythmic interpretation of the original classic themes. Waxing trines occurred in:

380 B.C. in the time of Plato's dialogues, and of conqueror Philip of Macedon. Greek art became less restrained and more dynamic in style.

A.D. 115 when Trajan and Hadrian expanded the Roman Empire in its silver age, when the Pantheon was built.

607 in the time of Pope Gregory the Great, who brought Christianity to Britain. Khmer Empire was founded. Soon afterward, Mohammed founded Islam.

1100 during the First Crusade and the height of the Romanesque style. Kenneth Clark called this period "a similar outburst to the Baroque." You can see it in the lively, elaborate sculptures on southern French cathedrals.

1595 in the time of Shakespeare and the first Baroque artists and composers such as El Greco, Rubens, and Monteverdi.

2090 will bring the next lively baroque expansion. Further trines will occur in about 2580, 3075 and 3565.

The **opposition** marks the half-way point and climax of the cycle. It is the "full moon" (or in this case a "full Neptune"), a time of expansion when the civilization is becoming fully and consciously developed. Schisms may occur, and as its ideas and formulas begin to rigidify, the civilization may begin to lose touch with its original sources of inspiration. Decline may set in afterwards. During the opposition, crucial events occur which affect the rest of the cycle. Oppositions occurred in:

330 B.C. in the time of Alexander the Great's conquests, which spread Greek culture all over Eastern Europe and Western Asia. World trade expanded in the first global economy. After Alexander died, his empire crumbled and the less secure Hellenistic Age began.

A.D. 166 in the time of Marcus Aurelius, the "philosopher-king" of Rome. After his reign, Rome began its decline and civil wars started.

660 during the conquests and expansion of Islam, when it divided into the Sunni and Shi'ite sects. The Synod of Whitby opened the way to the Northumbrian renaissance in England, climax of Dark Ages culture.

1153 during the Crusades and the first Gothic cathedrals.

1645 as imperial Europe expanded its colonies. Baroque art reached its summit in Rembrandt, Bernini and Borromini, as well as in the reign of the "Sun King" Louis XIV. Our view of the physical cosmos was vastly expanded. The artist Jan Vermeer embodied this full moon phase as the "clear light of the fully conscious mind." The Manchu Dynasty was founded.

2140 is when the next climactic opposition is due. Further oppositions are due in 2630, 3125 and 3616.

The Neptune-Pluto opposition was also clearly significant in the archaic times before the Axis Age. The opposition of 823 B.C., for example, came at about the time of Homer and the start of early Greek culture. In China after 800 B.C., the strong Chou dynasty began its decline while the Upanishads (the final stage of the Vedas) were being written. Around the time of the opposition of 1320 B.C., the temple of Seti at Abados and other great temples were built during the height of New Kingdom civilization in Egypt in the reign of Ramses II. It was the last great period of ancient Egypt. The opposition of 1810 B.C. marked the fall of Egypt's Middle Kingdom to Hyksos invaders and is close to the time of Hammurabi's law codes. At the opposition of 2305 B.C., the pharaoh's power started to decline, as authority was dispersed throughout the Old Kingdom. Civil wars began there around 2260 B.C. 2305 B.C. is also very close to the time of the first expansive Mesopotamian Empire of Sargon I (c.2325 B.C.).

The **waning gibbous trine** (which often lasts many years because Pluto is moving faster in its eccentric orbit) establishes, distributes or disseminates ideas and benefits from the period of the opposition. It may mark a time of "frivolity and decadence" with a rococo art style, especially in its early years, but toward the end more decisive events and expressions occur, anticipating the square (see below). This aspect occurred in:

280-240 B.C. (approximate orb) and
190 B.C. when Rome was first inspired by Greek art and drama. Ashoka put Buddhist ideas into effect in his Mauryan Empire of India, and the Chin and Han emperors established Confucian morals in China.
A.D. 220-260 (approximate orb) and
306 in the "decadent" period of Rome and its final recovery under Constantine, when Rome converted to Christianity.
710-750 (approximate orb) when Europe repelled Moslem invaders, and
796 when Charlemagne became emperor and restored European civilization.
1200-1305 (exact in 1230 and 1290) when Gothic architecture and philosophy were developed along the lines laid down during the opposition. The lighter "rayonnant" style also developed. The cults of the virgin and courtly love were popular.
1695-1795 (exact in 1712, 1730 and 1783) when the Enlightenment philosophers popularized the ideas of the new science and applied them to help liberate society. The result was the American and French Revolutions. Art became delicate, light and decadent in the Rococo style, reflecting the frivolous attitudes in society.
2190-2280 will bring the next closing trine. Future waning trines will happen from 2680 to 2700 and 2730 to 2770, 3170 to 3190 plus an approximate trine from 3240 to 3260, and 3660 to 3680.

The **closing, last quarter square** generally follows quickly after the trine. It represents a final climax in the cycle, but also may mark the start of its final crisis or schism. Art is romantic, emotional and dramatic, as it nostalgically sums up the past, bemoans the present and/or anticipates the future. Waning squares occurred in:

155 B.C. as Rome struggled for dominance over other Mediterranean states. In 146 Rome conquered Greece. Sculpture at this time consisted of dramatic, monumental, exaggerated depictions of tragic heroes.

A.D. 340 just after Constantine's reign, as schisms in the new Christian faith began to appear. The more emotional Christian art began to dominate.

830 as Charlemagne's empire declined after his death. It split up soon afterward in 843.

1325 just before the Hundred Year's War. Giotto's paintings reflected the dramatic, emotional style of this phase.

1815 during the Congress of Vienna and the defeat of Napoleon, events which resulted in nationalistic movements. Romantic artists became estranged from the new industrial society and depicted monumental disasters at sea.

2311, 2830, 3323 and 3815 are the dates of future closing squares.

The **closing sextile** or "balsamic" phase accelerates the process of dissolution and destruction, as the cycle crashes toward its close. Invasions and/or rebellions begin. New economic methods and innovations develop. It marks the period of realism, when the arts accurately depict the sufferings of the people. For example:

130 B.C. as peasant revolt in the Gracchian Revolution opened the final crisis in the Roman Republic. The troubles were reflected in the realistic sculpture of the time, like the works of the Laocoon Group.

A.D. 363 in the time of Julian the Apostate, when Christian schisms accelerated. Barbarians began their full-fledged invasions of Rome soon afterward.

857 as Viking and Saracen invasions began. Feudalism took root in Europe.

1350 as the Black Plague spread through Europe, destroying the old Medieval Christian society. The Middle Class began to develop. Medieval art also reflected the realist trends.

1844 just before the Irish Potato Famine and the resulting revolutions, causing massive migrations from Europe. Industry expanded explosively. Realist artists and writers included Courbet, Daumier, Dickens, Marx, and others.

2338, 2830, 3323 3815 are the dates for future closing sextiles.

Appendix E: Progressions and Precessions in The Chart of Humanity

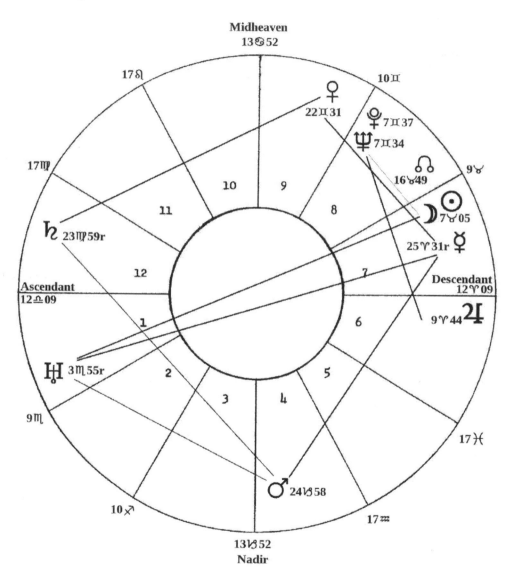

Pictured above is the Horoscope for Modern Humanity, the chart for the conjunction of Neptune and Pluto and solar eclipse on April 26, 1892, cast for Washington DC at 9:47 PM Universal Time (Greenwich Mean Time). Note the connections to the planetary positions in the US horoscope pictured on page 26, especially to the positions of the transcendental trinity.

Progressions are based on one day following April 26, 1892 equals one year after 1892. The chart is also **"precessed"** backwards showing how modern humanity developed "pre-natally" before the start of our age. The major historical events happening at the time of each progressed planetary event are listed, along with the actual corresponding transits in the sky at the time. The most important positions are noted in bold type, and corresponding transits are noted in italics. Notice that the current transiting positions of the outer planets are often similar or related to the progressed positions of the inner planets.

PRECESSED CHART

1760: Mars conjunct Uranus (beginning of industrial revolution/steam engine; Seven Years' War).

1784: Mercury stationary-direct at 28 Sagittarius.

1785: Saturn stationary-retrograde at 0 Libra (U.S. Constitution embodied ideals of justice).

1788: Mercury square Saturn.

1789: Sun sextile Mars; Sun in 24 Capricorn (French Revolution).

1789: Full Moon in Cancer (active awareness of common people is at its height during the Full Moon).

1791: Venus in Aquarius square Mars in Scorpio (emotions ran wild in reign of terror) *Similar to transit of Neptune entering Scorpio, 1792*

1795: Sun entered Aquarius; Venus entered Pisces (sign changes indicate shifts of energy. In this case, the reign of terror ended). *Corresponds to transit of Pluto in Pisces from 1799*

1798: Saturn re-entered Virgo (Napoleon betrayed the revolution; work began to make ideals of justice a reality).

1800: Mars entered Sagittarius (romantic age expanded) *Neptune entered Sagittarius in 1806.*

180l: Sun square Uranus (revolutionary aspect which was in orb ten years before and after 1801; it dominated the age of revolution).

1804: New Moon in Aquarius (Napoleon crowned emperor; common people in retreat at New Moon).

1810: Mars opposite Neptune-Pluto (quest of the sublime in the climax of the Napoleonic wars) *Pluto in Pisces, square Neptune.*

1811: Venus conjunct Jupiter in Pisces (another symbol of romanticism).

1813: Mercury entered Aquarius (students and soldiers [Mercury] were inspired by the "war of liberation" against Napoleon in 1813 to expand their activism.).

1815: Uranus stationary retrograde at 6 Scorpio (revolution ended with defeat of Napoleon and restoration by Vienna Concert).

1817: Mercury square Uranus (peak of student activism at Wartburg Festival, etc.). *Jupiter conjunct Uranus; Uranus square Pluto.*

1819: Full Moon in Leo (common people active, especially youth).

1819: Venus entered Aries (age of pioneers opened) *Pluto entered Aries 1822-23.*

1824: Sun entered Pisces; Neptune and Pluto stationary-direct (romantic age climaxed; dissolving industrial forces started moving us toward the modern age).

1830: Sun trine Uranus (revolutionary year) *Uranus in Aquarius opposite Saturn.*

1831: Sun square Neptune-Pluto.

1832: Mercury entered Pisces (worker unrest increased) *Uranus entered Pisces 1834.*

1834: New Moon in Pisces (post-1830 activism crushed; people retreated into disillusionment).

1844: Jupiter opposite Saturn (ongoing economic crisis in this era).

1844: Venus entered Taurus; *Mars square Saturn; Sun sesqui-square Uranus*

1846: Mars square Jupiter (westward ho/manifest destiny/roaring '40s enthusiasms). *Jupiter-Uranus in Aries, 1844.*

1847: Mercury entered Aries, conjunct Jupiter, square Mars (the many aspects in mid-late '40s stand for industrial expansion and crisis).

1848: Mars entered Capricorn at exact time of the beginning of the 1848 revolutions. (Revolutions' failure opened the age of realism).

1848: Full Moon in Virgo, conjunct Saturn (common people, especially workers, rose again, but had to confront reality).

1849: Venus opposite Uranus (Eureka! the gold rush, in many ways). *Uranus conj. Pluto entering Taurus, 1850.*

1851: Sun opposite Saturn (heavy hand of repression crushed the revolutions; realpolitik; industrialism) *Saturn conj. Uranus-Pluto in Taurus.*

1854: Sun entered Aries, conjunct Jupiter (Crimean War ended international cooperation; prosperity exploded as industrial revolution expanded in the 1850s) *Neptune in Pisces; Jupiter singleton.*

1863: New Moon in Aries (new beginning, as governments moved toward individualism).

1864: Sun in Aries square Mars (age of aggression; U.S. Civil War and Indian wars; Wars of German Unification; Darwinism popularized) *Neptune in Aries in 1860s.*

1865: Mercury entered Taurus (civil war ended; gilded age began) *Pluto in Taurus inaugurates age of materialism.*

1871: Venus entered Gemini (new diplomatic era [Venus] opened in the wake of the Franco-Prussian war).

1876: Mercury stationary retrograde, opposing Uranus (telephone invented, international crises were early signs of the Great War, which came when Mercury opposed Uranus again later on) *Uranus square Pluto/Saturn*

1877: Venus conjunct Neptune-Pluto (impressionism; first economic combinations and dissolutions during 1870s depression). *Neptune in Taurus.*

1877: Full Moon in Libra (common people active in Granger movements, etc.; diplomatic moves by Bismarck followed).

1885: Sun entered Taurus (age of materialism continues).

1885: Sun conjunct Mercury; Mercury re-entered Aries (inventions at a peak; international crises). *Pluto entered Gemini, mercurial sign, 1884.*

1890: Sun opposite Uranus (labor unrest dominated this period).

1890: Mars trine Saturn *Mars-Saturn-Pluto T-square*
1892: Mercury square Mars (Schlieffen plan for the Great War; Populist activism). *Year of the Neptune-Pluto conjunction.*

PROGRESSED CHART:
1892: The solar eclipse in Taurus.
1893: Venus square Saturn; Sun sesqui-square Saturn (panic and depression of 1893).
1900: Mercury stationary direct at 24 Aries (Marconi invented radio; Muckrakers attacked corporations). *Uranus opposite Pluto in Gemini.*
1900: Venus entered Cancer (Freud opened subconscious; conservation movement began; nationalism heated up). *Neptune entered Cancer 1901.*
1902: Mars entered Aquarius (active progress and progressivism) *Uranus opposite Pluto, 1901*
1907: Lunar eclipse in Scorpio (increasing upheaval and activism in this era; financial panic; this eclipse was a sign of impending doom).
1909: Mars square Uranus (series of pre-war crises began in 1908) *Saturn in Aries square Uranus*
1909: Sun trine Saturn.
1911: Mercury re-entered Taurus (Balkan Wars).
1914: Mercury opposite Uranus (World War I began.) *Jupiter conjunct Uranus in Aquarius.*
1916: Sun entered Gemini.
1918: Mercury square Mars, completing T-square in fixed signs (final battles of World War I).
1918: Mars sesqui-square Saturn (final battles of World War I).
1922: New Moon in Gemini (common people in retreat during reactionary '20s; new beginning after war).
1922: Mars trine Neptune (roaring '20s enthusiasm, powered by alcohol prohibition, disillusionment). *Uranus in Pisces trine Pluto.*
1923: Saturn stationary-direct at 23 Virgo (Fascist takeovers and conservative trends world-wide). *Jupiter-Saturn conjunction at 21 Virgo in 1921.*
1925: Sun conjunct Neptune-Pluto (peak of disillusionment, gangsterism, moral decay, surrealism in arts, self-expression, and deceptive prosperity). *Neptune in Sun's sign Leo.*
1927: Sun trine Mars (energy of roaring '20s peaks; sports heroes) *Jupiter & Uranus enter Aries.*
1929: Mercury trine Saturn (depression sign).
1932: Mercury entered Gemini (materialism ends in depression).
1932: Venus sextile Saturn (depression).
1934: Sun sesqui-square Uranus (Nazism and New Deal). *Uranus square Pluto.*
1935: Sun sextile Jupiter ("happy days are here again"?).
1937: Full Moon in Sagittarius (common people active).
1937: Mercury conjunct Neptune-Pluto (worker unrest) *Saturn in Pisces opposite Neptune*

1940: Sun square Saturn (dominated entire depression/war period; peak of Nazi repression) [FDR's aspect]. *Jupiter-Saturn square Pluto.*

1940: Mercury trine Mars (World *War II, a swifter moving war than World War I under Mercury-Mars square; led to aviation advances*). *Uranus entered Gemini, 1941, trine Neptune.*

1945: Venus stationary retrograde at 26 Cancer (World Wars ended; U.N. and Cold War began). *Jupiter conj. Neptune in Libra.*

1945: Mercury square Saturn (The UN charter, post-war austerity.)

1947: Sun conjunct Mercury (age of anxiety; first computer 1946).

1947: Sun and Mercury entered Cancer (Cold War; Defense Dept., baby boom). *Uranus entered Cancer, 1948.*

1949: Sun trine Uranus; Sun sesqui-square Mars (Red revolution in China; atomic arms race opened). *Uranus-Pluto parallel and semi-square.*

195l: New Moon in Cancer (common people retreat into domestic concerns in conservative 1950s; new beginning as post-war austerity ended).

1954: Venus sextile Saturn.

1958: Mercury square Jupiter (space race opened) *Saturn in Sagittarius.*

1958: Mercury conjunct Venus.

1959: Venus square Jupiter (this ongoing aspect of the post-war era represented exaggerated materialism and wasteful prosperity).

1962: Mercury entered Leo (youth became prominent in Kennedy years).

1963: Mercury square Uranus (youth and civil rights activism) (Kennedy's aspect).

1962-63: Mars stationary-retrograde at 17 Aquarius (Missile crisis; Kennedy assassinated; progress arrested). *Great 1962 eclipse-conjunction, 15-17 Aquarius; Saturn at 17 Aquarius Nov. 22, 1963; Neptune in Scorpio, Mars' ruling sign.*

1966: Uranus stationary-direct at 2 Scorpio (liberation movements of the 1960s exploded; transcendental awakening of new consciousness, non-conformist counterculture). *Uranus conjunct Pluto.*

1966: Sun conjunct Venus (Cold War/defense establishment went haywire in Vietnam; flower children appeared; women's movement began).

1966: Full Moon in Capricorn (Activism of the people in the 1960s against the all-powerful Capricornian "system" is largely defeated).

1972: Mercury opposite Mars (Nixon's aspect) (Watergate dirty tricks; war in Vietnam continued).

1972: Sun square Jupiter (inflation; diplomatic breakthroughs). *Jupiter conjunct Neptune in Sagittarius, 1971.*

1973: Sun semi-square Neptune (Watergate scandal; oil embargo).

1974: Sun sextile Saturn (depression brought on by events mentioned in the above two aspects).

1979: Sun entered Leo.

1980: New Moon in Leo (common people in retreat in the reactionary 1980s).

1981: Sun square Uranus (revolutions in Iran and Nicaragua; Reagan counter-revolution in U.S.).

1982: Mercury entered Virgo (high-tech yuppies; computer mania; AIDS emerges).

1989: Venus stationary-direct at 10 Cancer (Cold War ended; nationalism revived; earth activism resumed). *Jupiter singleton stationary at 10 Cancer, Gorbachev's position, in fall, 1989.*

1990: Sun sextile Neptune (idealism re-awakened worldwide).

1991: Sun opposite Mars (resurgent activism; Persian Gulf War; ethnic wars in 1992-93). *Saturn square Pluto in Scorpio 1992-93.*

1992: Mars sesqui-square Saturn (see above).

1992: Sun semi-square Saturn (economic panic in early 1990s).

1994: Mercury sextile Venus (liberalized trade and peace breakthroughs).

1996: Full Moon in Aquarius, conjunct Mars (peak of the 1990s resurgent activism) *Uranus enters Aquarius.*

1996: Mars trine Neptune (the creative energy of the 1990s).

1997: Mercury square Neptune (disinformation, scandal).

1999: Mercury stationary retrograde at 11 Virgo (literary, health and scientific breakthroughs).

1999: (Sun in same degree as prophetic Leo eclipse, August 11, 1999).

2001: Mercury square Neptune again.

2001-02: Jupiter stationary-retrograde in 25 Aries, conjunct Moon (holy war climaxes; optimism at dawn of a new millennium of peace) *Pluto in Sagittarius opposite Saturn in Gemini.*

2005: Sun trine Jupiter (prosperous period).

2010: Sun enters Virgo; New Moon in Virgo (people retreat again in period of disillusionment and economic breakdown, as medical and ecological disasters loom). *Neptune enters Pisces 2011, Saturn in Virgo.*

2013: Sun sextile Uranus (year of revolutions). *Uranus square Pluto, 2011-14.*

2014: Sun conjunct Mercury retrograde (anxiety, inventions created to meet the world crisis).

2017: Saturn re-enters Libra (Dreams of justice realized).

2017: Mercury re-enters Leo (re-discovery of youthful creativity).

2020 (year of this writing): Venus square Jupiter (prosperity may return; diplomatic tensions).

2022-23: Mars stationary-direct at 7 Aquarius (progress resumes at full speed in its renewed form; possible U.S. Civil War or break-up, drastic reform, etc.). *Pluto enters Aquarius, Neptune enters Aries.*

2022: Sun square Neptune (idealist activism).

2024: Mercury direct at 28 Leo (outspoken journalism, entertainment, travel and networking inventions) *Uranus enters Mercurial Gemini*

2025: Full Moon at 15 Pisces (people awake with compassion and a new spiritual impulse)

2026: Venus enters Leo (a new romantic expressiveness)

2028: Mercury re-enters Virgo (deeper concern with health, technology) *(powerful Jupiter singleton in Virgo that year)*.

2028: Venus sextile Saturn (economic tensions, stability returning). *Saturn enters Taurus.*

2029: Sun semi-square Uranus (possible revolutions or quick reforms).

2030: Venus square Uranus (cultural or financial inventions and disturbances).

2032: Mercury sextile Uranus (a period of reform and social adjustment). *Saturn-Uranus conjunction in Gemini/Cancer.*

2033: Neptune and Pluto turn retrograde.

2034: Sun sesqui-square Mars (more activist upheavals). *Uranus sesqui-square Pluto; Neptune in Aries.*

2035: Venus opposite Mars (pioneering and extremism; passions hot). *Jupiter-Neptune in Aries.*

2037: Mercury square Neptune *Uranus square Neptune.*

2038: Venus sextile Neptune (quieter period begins; dissolving of economic structures). *Neptune enters Taurus.*

2040: New Moon in 29 Virgo (common people in retreat).

2042: Sun enters Libra.

2044: Sun conjunct Saturn (conservatism or repression; depression; constitutional reform) *Saturn square Pluto.*

2047: Mars trine Neptune (active idealism surges). *Uranus opposite Pluto in Pisces.*

2048: Venus trine Jupiter (prosperity, diplomacy, or expansion in the arts). *Jupiter conjunct Neptune in Taurus.*

2050: Mercury conjunct Saturn (more constitutional reforms; recession). *Saturn in Aquarius, trine Uranus and Neptune.*

2053: Sun trine Neptune (idealism). *Saturn conjunct Pluto in Pisces.*

2054: Mercury trine Neptune. *Neptune enters Gemini, 2053.*

2055: Full Moon in 14 Aries; Sun trine Mars (energetic, progressive).

2056: Mercury trine Mars; Venus enters Virgo.

2057: Sun conjunct Mercury (inventive, inquisitive).

2059: Mercury opposite Jupiter (travel, communication advances).

2061: Sun opposite Jupiter (over-optimism).

2065: Mercury enters Scorpio.

2066: Venus square Neptune (basic conflict of values; apathy and malaise). *Neptune square Pluto.*

2068: Mars sextile Jupiter.

2069: Partial eclipse at 28 Libra; Mercury conjunct Uranus.

2071: Sun enters Scorpio (Pluto enters Aries, 2067).

2073: Mars sesqui-square Saturn.

2078: Sun conjunct Uranus (revolutionary year). *Uranus opposite Neptune.*

2082: Venus enters Libra.

2084: Lunar eclipse at 13 Taurus (possible economic or ecological catastrophe).

2084: Mercury square Mars (controversy, unrest).

2085: Mercury enters Sagittarius.

2089: Mars enters Pisces (end of "progress"; new religious enthusiasm). *Uranus enters Pisces, 2087-88.*

2090: Venus conjunct Saturn (depression threatens).

2091: Mercury sextile Saturn.

2092: Venus trine Neptune.

2096: Mercury trine Jupiter.

2097: Venus opposite Jupiter (more optimistic mood returning?).

2099: New Moon in Scorpio *Uranus in Aries, 2095-2102.*

2101: Sun enters Sagittarius (a new Baroque period).

2103: Mars trine Uranus *Uranus conjunct Pluto.*

2105: Saturn trine Neptune *Uranus trine Neptune.*

2106: Mars square Neptune.

2108: Venus enters Scorpio.

2111: Sun opposite Neptune-Pluto.

2113: Mercury retrograde at 29 Sagittarius.

2114: Full Moon In Gemini *Uranus in Gemini.*

2116: Sun trine Jupiter.

2120: Jupiter turns direct at 15 Aries (a period of crusades and expansion).

2121: Sun square Mars at 20 Pisces (religious conflicts). *Neptune enters Scorpio.*

Appendix F: Mars Stationary 2020-2200

The significance of Mars is intensified as it passes close to Earth every 2 years-plus. As it does, it appears to slow down and start going backwards (retrograde), because the Earth is passing it in orbit. In a couple of months it turns direct again. When stationary retrograde (SR), and especially when stationary direct (SD), its significance is magnified, and wars sometimes start or major violent events often happen in the several weeks afterward, especially if when stationary it made major aspects to Saturn, Pluto and sometimes other planets. Mars-Saturn and Saturn-Pluto hard aspects are also significant indicators of wars. If Mars turns stationary in a **critical degree** (as indicated in bold type), in a national (usually the USA) chart, or of a previous conjunction, it could stimulate related events. In personal charts, it may indicate a time to initiate bold, well-planned action, or may counsel caution against impulsive, aggressive behavior or protection against crime and accidents. The strongest planetary aspects to the Mars stations listed here are shown in **bold**. If, when Mars is stationary, it stands alone in half the sky, it is also a rare and powerful **singleton**, magnifying its cosmic power further. Degrees listed are rounded up. See also Appendix F in Horoscope for the New Millennium for Mars stations from 1775 to 2050, with corresponding events up through the 20th Century.

Sept 9, 2020: Mars SR **29 Aries sq Saturn**, Pluto
Nov 14, 2020: Mars SD 16 Aries sq Pluto/Jupiter
Oct 30, 2022: Mars SR 26 Gemini sq Jupiter and Neptune
Jan 12, 2023: Mars SD **9 Gemini** sesqui-sq Saturn, conj. 1892 conj./US Uranus
Dec 6, 2024: Mars SR 7 Leo opp Pluto
Feb 24, 2025: Mars SD 17 Cancer trine Saturn
Jan 10, 2027: Mars SR 11 Virgo
April 2, 2027: Mars SD 21 Leo **conj Jupiter** trine Saturn
Feb 14, 2029: Mars SR **14 Libra** trine Uranus and Pluto, opp Neptune conj US Saturn
May 5, 2029: Mars SD **25 Virgo** conj US Neptune
Mar 29, 2031: Mars SR 22 Scorpio
June 13, 2031: Mars SD **5 Scorpio**
May 26, 2033: Mars SR 13 Capricorn **opp Saturn** sq Neptune/Venus
Aug 2, 2033: Mars SD 30 Sagittarius opp Uranus
Aug 15, 2035: Mars SR 29 Pisces
Oct 15, 2035: Mars SD **18 Pisces** quincx Saturn, trine Uranus, opp. 1966 conj.
Oct 12, 2037: Mars SR **7 Gemini sq Saturn** conj 1892 conj.
Dec 23. 2037: Mars SD 21 Taurus **sq Pluto** tr Saturn sextile Uranus
Nov 23. 2039: Mars SR 22 Cancer
Feb 9, 2040: Mars SD 4 Cancer **sq Saturn**
Dec 28, 2041: Mars SR 28 Leo **opp Pluto** sq Jupiter

Mars 18, 2042: Mars SD 9 Leo **sq Saturn conj Uranus sq Neptune**

Jan 31, 2044: Mars SR 1 Libra sext Saturn quincx Pluto

Apr 21, 2044: Mars SD 12 Virgo

Mar 11, 2046: Mars SR 7 Scorpio **tr Pluto**/Mercury opp Neptune

May 28: 2046: Mars SD 19 Libra sext Saturn opp Jupiter

Apr 30, 2048: Mars SR **21 Sagittarius** opp US Mars

July 10, 2048: Mars SD 6 Sagittarius **sq Uranus and Pluto**

July 15, 2050: Mars SR 27 Aquarius **sq Neptune**

Sept 15, 2050: Mars SD **17 Aquarius** opp Jupiter

Sept.23, 2052: Mars SR 14Taurus

Nov.29, 2052: Mars SD **29 Aries**, sext. Saturn

Nov. 9 2054: Mars SR **6 Cancer**

Jan.23, 2055: Mars SD18 Gemini **square Pluto 14Pis, sq Saturn 23Pis**

Dec.15, 2056: Mars SR 15 Leo, **trine Saturn** (SD 16Aries)

Mar 5 2057: Mars SD 26 Cancer, **sq Uranus 24Lib, sq Saturn 21Ari**

Jan 18, 2059: Mars SR **18 Virgo, opp. Pluto 18Pisces**

April 9, 2059: Mars SD 29 Leo

Feb.23, 2061: Mars SR 22 Libra trine Jupiter SD, trine Neptune SD

May 14, 2061: Mars SD 4 Libra

April 9, 2063: Mars SR 2 Sagittarius **sq Jupiter**

June 23, 2063: Mars SD 15 Scorpio **trine Saturn, conj. Uranus**

June 13, 2065: Mars SR 28 Capricorn sext.Uranus, Pluto

Aug.16, 2065: Mars SD 16 Capricorn

Aug.31, 2067: Mars SR 16 Aries

Nov. 2, 2067: Mars SD 5 Aries, conj Pluto 30 Pisces

Oct.23, 2069: Mars SR 18 Gemini, **opp Uranus 17 Sag**, sq Jupiter

Jan.4, 2070: Mars SD 1 Gemini

Dec.2, 2071: Mars SR 1 Leo, sq Saturn

Feb.19, 2072: Mars SD **12 Cancer**, **trine Saturn SR 14Sco, conj Neptune 13Can**

Jan.5, 2074: Mars SR 6 Virgo, **sq Saturn** 4Sag

March 27, 2074: Mars SD 16 Leo

Feb.9, 2076: Mars SR 9 Libra, conj Jupiter 15Lib, **opp Pluto** 9Ari

April 30, 2076: Mars SD 20 Virgo

March 21, 2078: Mars SR 16 Scorpio

June 7, 2078: Mars SD 28 Libra, **sq Uranus 27Cap, sq Neptune 27Can, sq Saturn 22Cap**

May 15, 2080: Mars SR 3 Capricorn

July 23, 2080: Mars SD 19 Sagittarius sextile Jupiter

Aug.2, 2082: Mars SR 15 Pisces conj Saturn 8Pis

Oct.1, 2082: Mars SD 5 Pisces, **conj Saturn 4Pis**

Oct.5, 2084: Mars SR 28 Taurus

Dec.13, 2084: Mars SD 12 Taurus, sq Uranus 19Aqu

Nov.18, 2086: Mars SR 16 Cancer
Feb.2, 2087: Mars SD 28 Gemini trine Uranus
Dec.23, 2088: Mars SR 23 Leo **conj Neptune, square Saturn**
March 13, 2089: Mars SD 3 Leo
Jan.26, 2091: Mars SR 26 Virgo sq Saturn 19Gem
April 17, 2091: Mars SD 7 Virgo
March 4, 2093: Mars SR 1 Scorpio, sextile Neptune
May 22, 2093: Mars SD 12 Libra
April 22, 2095: Mars SR 13 Sagittarius **trine Saturn** (SD Apr 16, 15Leo)
July 4, 2095: Mars SD 27 Scorpio **(singleton)**, **sq Saturn** 20Leo
July 1, 2097: Mars SR 13 Aquarius sextile Uranus
Aug.31, 2097: Mars SD 4 Aquarius **(singleton) sq Pluto 3Tau**
Sept.14, 2099: Mars SR 3 Taurus **conj Pluto 5Tau**
Nov.18, 2099: Mars SD 20 Aries **conj Uranus 19Ari, opp Saturn 22Lib**, opp Jup 15Lib
Nov.3, 2101: Mars SR 29 Gemini sext. Ura 28Ari
Jan.16, 2102: Mars SD 11 Gemini, opp Jupiter 15Sag
Dec.11, 2103: Mars SR 9 Leo, **sq Pluto, trine Saturn**
Feb.28, 2104: Mars SD 20 Cancer
April 5, 2106: Mars SD 23 Leo
Feb.18, 2108: Mars SR 16 Libra, trine Jupiter
May 9, 2108: Mars SD 27 Virgo **conj Nep 2 Lib**, **trine Saturn SR 29 Cap,** trine Uranus 24Tau, trine VenusR 21Tau, sq Jupiter 23Gem
April 2, 2110: Mars SR 24 Scorpio **sq Saturn 20Aqu**, sq Ura, sq Jup 18Leo
June 17, 2110: Mars SD 7 Scorpio opp Pluto 15Tau
June 1, 2112: Mars SR 16 Capricorn, **sq Jupiter 18Lib (SD June 14), sextile Saturn 17Pis**
Aug.6, 2112: Mars SD 4 Capricorn
Aug.20, 2114: Mars SR 3 Aries, conj Saturn11Ari
Oct.20, 2114: Mars SD 22 Pisces, **sq Uranus 24Gem, sq Jupiter 25Sag, opp Venus SD 27Vir**
Oct.17, 2116: Mars SR 10 Gemini
Dec.27, 2116: Mars SD 23 Taurus, **conj Pluto 19Tau**
Nov.27, 2118: Mars SR 24 Cancer, sq Neptune 28Lib
Feb.13, 2119: Mars SD **6 Cancer conj Uranus 8Can**
Dec.31, 2120: Mars SR 0 Virgo sext. Saturn, sext. Neptune
March 22, 2121: Mars SD 11 Leo
Feb.4, 2123: Mars SR 3 Libra, conj Jupiter, sext. Saturn-Uranus
April 26, 2123: Mars SD 14 Virgo
March 14, 2125: Mars SR 10 Scorpio **conj Neptune 12Sco**
June 1, 2125: Mars SD 21 Libra, sextile Saturn 25Leo
July 16, 2127: Mars SD **9 Sagittarius**
July 20, 2129: Mars SR 1 Pisces, **opp Uranus 27Leo, sq Pluto 3Gem**

Sept.18, 2129: Mars SD 21 Aquarius **trine Saturn 22Lib**

Sept.28, 2131: Mars SR 17 Taurus, **opp Saturn 14 Sco**, opp Nep 23 Sco, trine Ura 10Vir

Dec.5, 2131: Mars SD 3 Taurus

Nov.12, 2133: Mars SR 9 Cancer

Jan.27, 2134: Mars SD **21Gemini, sq Uranus 22Vir, sq Saturn 18Sag**

Dec.19, 2135: Mars SR 17 Leo

March 8, 2136: Mars SD 28 Cancer, sextile Ura

Jan.21, 2138: Mars SR 21 Virgo trine Sat 28Cap, sq Jup 27Sag

April 12, 2138: Mars SD 1 Virgo

Feb.27, 2140: Mars SR 25 Libra, opp Venus, trine Jup, trin Sat, conj Ura

May 17, 2140: Mars SD 6 Libra

April 13, 2142: Mars SR 5 Sagittarius

June 27, 2142: Mars SD 18 Scorpio opp Jup, trine Saturn

Feb.12, 2155: Mars SR 11 Libra

May 4, 2155: Mars SD 22 Virgo, **sq Pluto 26Gem**, Uranus 29Sag

March 25, 2157: Mars SR 19 Scorpio

June 10, 2157: Mars SD 1 Scorpio trine Pluto

May 20, 2159: Mars SR 7 Capricorn opp Pluto 1Can

July 28, 2159: Mars SD 24 Sagittarius

Aug.7, 2161: Mars SR 20 Pisces

Oct.6, 2161: Mars SD 1 Libra

Oct.9, 2163: Mars SR 2 Gemini

Dec.18, 2163: Mars SD 16 Taurus sq Jupiter

Nov.21, 2165: Mars SR 19 Cancer

Feb.6, 2166: Mars SD 1 Cancer conj Pluto

Dec.27, 2167: Mars SR 26 Leo opp Uranus

March 16, 2168: Mars SD 6 Leo **opp Saturn**

Jan.29, 2170: Mars SR 29 Virgo

April 20, 2170: Mars SD 10 Virgo **conj Jupiter** opp Saturn opp Uranus

March 7, 2172: Mars SR 4 Scorpio trine Uranus-Neptune

May 25, 2172: Mars SD 16 Libra **sq Pluto 14Can**

April 25, 2174: Mars SR 16 Sagittarius **sq Uranus** trine Saturn

July 7, 2174: Mars SD 1 Sagittarius sq Neptune

July 6, 2176: Mars SR 19 Aquarius **sq Saturn**

Sept.5, 2176: Mars SD 9 Aquarius

Sept.18, 2178: Mars SR 7 Taurus

Nov.23, 2178: Mars SD **24 Aries sq Pluto 25Can**

Nov.5, 2180: Mars SR 3 Cancer

Jan.19, 2181: Mars SD 15 Gemini sq Neptune

Dec.13, 2182: Mars SR 13 Leo **conj Saturn 19Leo**

March 2, 2183: Mars SD 23 Cancer **sq Jupiter 22Lib conj Pluto 28Can** sq Uranus 17Ari

Jan.16, 2185: Mars SR **17 Virgo conj Saturn 16Vir** sq Jupiter 15Sag opp Neptune 20 Pis

April 7, 2185: Mars SD 27 Leo trine Uranus 27Ari

Feb.21, 2187: Mars SR 20 Libra conj Saturn 11Lib

May 12, 2187: Mars SD 1 Libra **conj Saturn 6Lib**

April 4, 2189: Mars SR 29 Scorpio

June 19, 2189: Mars SD 12 Scorpio **sq Uranus 16Tau sq Pluto 6Leo** opp Jupiter 7Tau

June 5, 2191: Mars SR 21 Capricorn

Aug.10, 2191: Mars SD 9 Capricorn opp Jupiter 14Can sq Neptune 7Ari

Aug.24, 2193: Mars SR 8 Aries conj Neptune 12 Ari

Oct.24, 2193: Mars SD 27 Pisces opp Jupiter

Oct.20, 2195: Mars SR 14 Gemini **conj Uranus 12Gem**

Dec.31, 2195: Mars SD 28 Taurus opp Jupiter 21Sco

Nov.29, 2197: Mars SR 28 Cancer **opp Saturn 4Aqu**

Feb 15, 2198: Mars SD 10 Cancer

Jan.3, 2200: Mars SR 4 Virgo opp Saturn 29Aqu conj Jupiter 5Pis conj Pluto 25Leo

March 25, 2200: Mars SD 14 Leo conj Pluto 23Leo

Appendix G: List of Planetary Aspects

Main planetary conjunctions and other most important aspects from 2020 until 2170, with some notable simultaneous eclipses:

Jan 12, 2020: Saturn conj Pluto 22Cap46 conj Mercury (ann.lunar ecl Jan.10, 19:10 20Cap)

Apr 5, 2020: Jupiter conj Pluto (3 times through Nov.12)

Dec 21, 2020: Jupiter conj Saturn 0Aquarius28 (total ecl Dec.14, 2020 16:14 23Sag08)

Apr 12, 2022: Jupiter conj Neptune 23Pisces58

Apr 21, 2024: Jupiter conj Uranus 21Taurus50 (partial ecl Apr.30, 20:29 10Tau28)

Aug 29, 2025: Uranus sextile Neptune 1Ari25

Nov 20, 2025: Uranus sextile Neptune

Feb 20, 2026: Saturn conj Neptune 0Aries45 (ann. Ecl. Feb.17, 2026 12:02 28Aqu50)

July 15, 2026: Uranus sextile Neptune 4Ari24 (several times through June 6, 2027)

July 18, 2026: Uranus trine Pluto (1st)

July 20, 2026: Jupiter opp Pluto 4Leo/Aqu26

July 25, 2026: Neptune sextile Pluto (many times through Feb 28, 2032)

Nov 29, 2026: Uranus trine Pluto 3Gem/Aqu30

Jan 13, 2028: Uranus trine Pluto

May 10, 2028: Uranus trine Pluto (final)

June 24, 2028: Saturn square Pluto 8Tau/Aqu23 (also Nov.15)

Sept 28, 2028: Jupiter opp Neptune 7Lib/Ari30

Mar 29, 2029: Saturn square Pluto 10Tau/Aqu03

Dec 22, 2029: Jupiter opp Saturn (through Oct 6, 2031)

Jan 20, 2031: Jupiter opp Uranus (3 times through Oct.30, 2031)

Sept 1, 2031: Uranus sesqui-square Pluto (several times through May 3, 2034)

Oct 6, 2031: Jupiter opp Saturn 23Sag/Gem01

Oct 30, 2031: Jupiter opp Uranus 26Sag/Gem56 (ann.lunar ecl Sept.30, 7:34 6Tau41)

June 28, 2032: Saturn conj Uranus 28Gemini01

Feb 4, 2033: Jupiter conj Pluto (14Aqu48)

Sept 16, 2033: Saturn square Neptune (3 times through June 25, 2034)

June 25, 2034: Saturn square Neptune 22Can/Ari07

Mar 24, 2035: Jupiter conj Neptune 21Ari20 (ann.ecl. Mar.9, 2035 23:11 19Pis12)

Oct 17, 2035: Saturn opp Pluto 17Leo/Aqu31 (also Jan 1, 2036)

July 28, 2036: Saturn opp Pluto 20Leo/Aqu29 (partial ecl July 23, 10:18, 1Leo09)

Sept 26, 2036: Uranus quincunx Pluto (several times through Mar 19, 2039)

Sept 8, 2037: Jupiter conj Uranus 23Cancer02 (new moon Sept.9, 18:27, 17Vir25)

Oct 12, 2037: Jupiter square Neptune (3 times through June 16, 2038)

Feb 19, 2038: Jupiter conj Uranus (also March 30 @ 20Cancer05)

Sept 25, 2038: Jupiter opp Pluto (3 times through June 11, 2039)

Oct 3, 2039: Uranus square Neptune 2Leo/Tau49 (several times through July 25, 2041)

Oct 31, 2040: Jupiter conj Saturn 17Libra56 (partial ecl Nov.4, 2040, 19:09, 12Sco58)

Oct 12, 2041: Jupiter opp Neptune 7Sco/Tau10 (ann. Ecl Oct.25, 2041 1:32 2Sco01)

Oct 29, 2042: Saturn opp Neptune 9Sco/Tau01 (several times through Aug 15, 2043)

Jan 8, 2043: Saturn square Uranus 16Sco/Leo31 (several times through Nov 21, 2043)

Nov 4, 2044: Saturn square Pluto 0Sag/Pis27

Feb 28, 2045: Jupiter opp Uranus 24Aqu/Leo11 (ann. ecl Feb.16, 23:52 28Aqu43)

Apr 12, 2045: Jupiter conj Pluto 3Pisces31

Sept 22, 2046: Uranus opp Pluto 3Vir/Pis45

July 22, 2047: Jupiter conj Neptune 21Taurus19 (partial ecl July 22, 22:36 0Leo05)
        (total lunar ecl July 7, 10:35 15Cap17)

Aug 16, 2047: Uranus opp Pluto 6Pis

Nov 16, 2047: Jupiter conj Pluto

Feb 24, 2048: Jupiter conj Neptune 19Taurus0

Apr 12, 2048: Uranus opp Pluto 7Pis27

June 30, 2048: Uranus opp Pluto   7Virgo/Pisces59 (ann.ecl   June 11, 2048   12:58 21Gem17)

Aug 14, 2049: Jupiter opp Saturn 22Cap (3 times through July 1, 2050

August 15, 2051: Jupiter opp. Pluto 11Pis

Nov.9, 2051: Jupiter conj. Uranus 28Virgo55

Nov.18, 2051: Uranus trine Neptune 29Tau (many times through Aug.7, 2054)

May 26, 2052: Jupiter conj. Uranus 26Virgo13

April 1, 2052: Saturn square Neptune 1Gem57 (through Jan 13, 2053)

June 16 and July 10, 2053: Saturn conj. Pluto 14Pisces30

Jan.28, 2054: Jupiter opp. Neptune 2Gem22 (3 times through Oct.21, 2054)

Feb.2, 2054: Saturn conj. Pluto 13Pisces13

May 2, 2056: Saturn opp Uranus 17Lib

Oct.7, 2056: Saturn opp. Uranus 20Lib

Jan.26, 2057: Uranus sesqui-sq Neptune (several times through Sept.23, 2060)

March 24, 2057: Saturn opp Uranus 23Lib

April 26, 2057: Jupiter sq Neptune 14Gem (3 times through Dec.25)

Jan.26, 2058: Jupiter conj Pluto 18Pis

April 6, 2059: Jupiter opp. Uranus 3 Scorpio

Nov.10, 2059: Uranus sesqui-sq Pluto 19Pis49 (several times through June 15, 2061)

April 8, 2060: Jupiter conj Saturn 1 Gemini, also conj. Venus (tot ecl Apr.30 10Tau50)

June 27, 2060: Jupiter conj. Neptune, 19Gemini,

June 30, 2060: Mars conj Neptune 20Gem,

July 1, 2060: Mars conj. Jupiter 20Gem

June 7, 2061: Saturn conj. Neptune 21 Gem

July 6, 2061: Saturn sq Pluto 25Pis

Sept.19, 2061: Neptune sq Pluto (several times through May 30, 2065)

Jan.9, 2064: Uranus quincunx Neptune 25Gem31 (several times through Oct.27, 2066)

Oct.31, 2064: Uranus trine Pluto 25Sco/Pis54 (through June 1, 2065)

Jan.20, 2066: Jupiter conj. Uranus 4Sag43 (through Aug 21, 2066)

Feb.12-- Aug.6, 2066: Jupiter conj Uranus singleton in Sagittarius

Aug.31, 2066: Saturn sq Uranus (3 times through July 3, 2067)

Jan.28, 2067: Jupiter opp Neptune 2Can (through Oct.17, 2067)

Jan.3, 2068: Saturn opp Pluto 30Pis (through April 10, 2069)

Jan.11, 2069: Saturn sq Neptune (through June 15, 2070)

March 13, 2070: Jupiter conj Pluto 2Ari38

April 5, 2070: Jupiter sq Neptune 8Can

May 1, 2070: Jupiter opp Saturn 15Lib (3 times through March 13, 2071)

July 24, 2072: Jupiter opp Uranus 3Cap (3 times through April 26, 2073)

Feb.16, 2073: Uranus sq Pluto 6Ari (several times through Oct.24, 2074)

June 17, 2073: Jupiter conj. Neptune 16Can35

Nov.21, 2075: Jupiter opp Pluto 8Ari (3 times through Aug 7, 2076)

Oct.24, 2076: Jupiter sq Neptune 26Can35

March 12, 2077: Saturn square Pluto 10Ari3 (3 times through Dec.4, 2077)

March 7, 2078: Uranus opposite Neptune 26Can15 (through Dec 13, 2081)

Oct.5, 2078 to April 6, 2079: Neptune singleton in Cancer/Leo

Feb.17, 2079: Saturn opp Neptune 29Can (through Dec 24)

Feb.26, 2079: Saturn conj Uranus 29Cap49 (also Aug 31 and Oct 22)

Jan.29, 2080: Jupiter opp Neptune 1Leo39

Jan.31, 2080: Jupiter conj Uranus 2Aqu16

March 15, 2080: Jupiter conj Saturn 11Aqu52, Ura 4Aqu31

Sept.4, 2081: Uranus opp Neptune 6Leo/Aqu32 (total ecl Sept.3, 2081 9:08 11Vir35)

April 21, 2082: Jupiter conj Pluto 16Ari10

March 21, 2083: Uranus sextile Pluto 16Ari25 (through Sept.8, 2084)

March 23, 2083: Jupiter sq Neptune 7Leo15

Oct.12, 2085 -- May 15, 2086: Jupiter conj. Neptune singleton in Leo

Nov.1 2085: Jupiter conj Neptune 16Leo26 (through June 10, 2086

April 9, 2086: Saturn conj Pluto 19Ari54

Aug.17, 2086: Jupiter opp Uranus 28Aqu

Nov.13, 2087: Neptune trine Pluto 20Leo/Ari40 (1st)

May 17, 2088: Saturn sq Neptune 18Leo15

Feb.3, 2089: Uranus semi-sq Pluto 21Ari37 (through Nov.9, 2089)

Aug.21, 2089: Saturn sq Uranus (3 times through June 13, 2090)

Nov.1, 2089: Jupiter sq Neptune 25Leo10

Dec.21, 2089: Jupiter opp Saturn 6Gem (through Nov 20, 2090)

May 30, 2090: Jupiter sq Uranus 15Pis44

June 5, 2090: Jupiter opp Saturn 14Sag/Gem45

July 29, 2091: Neptune trine Pluto SR, 26Leo/Ari29

June 14, 2092: Jupiter 27 Aquarius SR, almost opp. Neptune 28Leo

Nov.14, 2092: Saturn sq Pluto 27Ari

Jan.23, 2093: Jupiter opposite Neptune 1Vir17

May 17, 2093: Jupiter conj Uranus 27Pis (3 times through Dec.6)

July 28, 2093: Saturn sq Pluto 28Ari27 SD

May 30, 2094: Jupiter conj Pluto 28Ari51

March 8-- Sept.26, 2095: Mars singleton in Sagittarius/Scorpio

April 26, 2095: Uranus quincunx Neptune 3Vir40 (many times through Nov.4, 2098)

July 1, 2095: Jupiter sq Neptune (through Feb.25, 2096)

Dec.16, 2095 Saturn conj Neptune 9Vir (through May 13, 2097)

Dec.31, 2095-- June 1, 2096: Saturn conj Neptune singleton in Leo/Virgo

May 13, 2097: Saturn conj Neptune 8Vir

July 6, 2097 to Sept.27, 2097: Mars singleton in Aquarius

Oct.16, 2098: Jupiter conj Neptune 14Vir9 (through May 10, 2099)

Dec.30, 2098: Saturn opp Uranus 13Ari46 (through Sept.13, 2100)

Dec.7, 2099: Jupiter opp Uranus 17Ari53 (also Sept.15 Ura @ 25Ari)

March 22, 2100: Jupiter opp Uranus (at equinox, Moon sq both)

Aug.12, 2100-- Feb.11, 2101: Uranus and Pluto singleton, 10-11 deg. apart

Sept.13, 2100: Saturn opp Uranus 25Ari (total ecl Sept.4, 8:49, 11Vir57)

Sept.19, 2100: Jupiter conj Saturn 25Lib33, Saturn in 24Aries45

Nov.10, 2100: Neptune sesqui-sq Pluto

Nov.27, 2100: Saturn opp Pluto 4Tau (3 times through Sept.16, 2101)

May 2, 2101: Saturn opp Pluto 5Tau

July 6, 2101: Saturn opp Ura 30Ari

July 19, 2102-- Jan.22, 2103: Uranus conj Pluto singleton in Taurus/Aries

Nov.17, 2102 to April 9, 2103: Neptune singleton in Virgo

June 17-19, 2103 Mars conj Uranus and Pluto

Aug.13, 2103: Uranus conj Pluto, SR (Aug.8) 8Tau12

April 24, 2104: Uranus conj Pluto 7Tau36 (sq Mars, conj Venus May 2)

July 2, 2104-- Jan.13, 2105: Uranus conj Pluto singleton in Taurus

Dec.11, 2104 to May 28, 2105: Neptune singleton in Virgo

April 4, 2105: Saturn sq Neptune 27Vir (3 times through Sept.4, 2106)

April 23, 2105: Jupiter opp Neptune 26Vir

Feb.19, 2107: Jupiter conj Pluto 9Tau14

April 7, 2107: Jupiter conj Uranus 18Tau15, trine Saturn 17Cap43

Dec.8, 2107 to July 2, 2108: Mars conj Neptune singleton in Libra/Mars also in Virgo

Oct.6, 2108: Jupiter opp Saturn 23 Cap (three times through March 16, 2110)

May 21, 2109: Saturn sq Pluto 12Tau51

Jan.21, 2110: Saturn sq Pluto

March 16, 2110: Jupiter opp Saturn 18Aqu9

June 15, 2110: Jupiter opp Saturn 22Aqu31

June 27, 2111: Uranus trine Neptune (through April 8, 2114)

Oct.18, 2111: Jupiter conj Neptune 11Lib37, trine Uranus 11Gem

Feb.27, 2112: Saturn sq Uranus (3 times through Jan 4, 2113)

Jan.6, 2114: Jupiter opp Uranus, trine Nep (Jan.13)

April 8, 2114: Uranus trine Neptune, 17Lib

July 24, 2114: Saturn opp Neptune 16Lib (through Feb.27, 2116)

Aug.16, 2114: Jupiter opp Uranus 24Gem

Oct.28, 2115: Saturn opp Neptune 21Lib, Mars 24Lib, sq Jup 25Cap

Aug.13, 2117: Saturn conj Pluto 22Tau (through April 6, 2118)

April 1, 2119: Jupiter conj Pluto 21Tau02

July 16, 2119: Jupiter conj Saturn 14Gem52

Aug.17, 2120: Jupiter conj Uranus 18Can49

Feb.10, 2123: Saturn conj Uranus

April 28, 2123: Saturn conj Uranus 26Can09

July 21, 2123: Saturn sq Neptune in Scorpio

April 10, 2124: Saturn SD 10Leo sq Neptune 9Sco; Ura SD 1Leo

Sept.18, 2124: Uranus sq Neptune in Scorpio (through May 12, 2127)

Oct.20, 2124: Jupiter conj Neptune 9Leo

Oct.21, 2124: Uranus sq Neptune, sq Jupiter

Oct.21, 2124: Saturn sq Pluto 28Tau (through July 20, 2125)

June 18, 2129: Jupiter opp Saturn (through Jan.10, 2131)

Nov.1, 2129: Uranus sq Pluto 2Vir/Gem13 (through May 11, 2131)

May 6, 2131: Jupiter conj Pluto 2Gem48

May 11, 2131: Uranus sq Pluto 3Gem, sq Jupiter 4Gem, opp Mars 5Pis

Feb.8, 2132: Saturn conj Neptune 27Sco (through Oct 11)

Feb.16, 2132: Mars opp Saturn & Neptune

Dec.26, 2132: Saturn opp Pluto (through Oct 16, 2133)

Dec.22, 2133: Jupiter opp Pluto 6Gem

March 6, 2134: Saturn sq Uranus (through Nov 24, 2135)

Oct.15, 2134: Jupiter conj Uranus

Nov.24, 2135: Saturn sq Uranus 0Cap/Lib42

Jan.10, 2137: Uranus trine Pluto 8Gem, sext. Nept 7Sag02

Jan.30, 2137: Neptune opp Pluto 7Gem34 (through Sept.28, 2141, 14Gem15)

March 22, 2137: Jupiter conj Neptune 8Sag, opp Pluto 8Gem

Sept.7, 2137: Uranus sextile Neptune (through July 22, 2138)

Oct.18, 2137: Jupiter conj Neptune 6Sag14

April 6, 2138: Uranus trine Pluto

June 20, 2139: Uranus SD 12Lib46, trine Pluto 12Gem16, sext.Nep 11Sag, Jup 12Aq, sext.Mars 12Gem

Aug 20, 2139: Saturn in Aquarius, trine Uranus 13Lib26

Sept.5, 2139: Saturn trine Pluto 12Gem20

Jan.14, 2140: Jupiter conj Saturn 17Aqu03

Jan.15, 2141: Jupiter sq Neptune 16Sag

June 22, 2141: Saturn sq Pluto 14Gem, sq Nep 15Sag

Aug.14, 2141: Jupiter opp Uranus 23Lib
Sept.28, 2141: Neptune opp Pluto 14Gem15
Feb.18, 2142: Saturn sq Pluto 12Gem18
April 13, 2142: Saturn in Pisces sq Neptune in Sagittarius (through Jan.19, 2143)
Nov.3, 2142: Saturn sq Neptune 18Sag (Saturn SD Nov.20) sq Pluto 15Gem

And leading up to that beacon, that shining city on a hill:

Nov.26, 2155: Uranus opp Pluto 27Gem43
July 26, 2157: Saturn sq Pluto 29Gem40
Dec.21, 2159: Jupiter conj Saturn 7Sco58
Jan.17, 2165: Uranus conj Neptune 6Aqu26, quincunx Pluto 6Can27
Nov.26, 2165: Saturn opp Pluto 9Can
Feb.6, 2169:Saturn conj Neptune15Aqu40
July 24, 2169: Jupiter opp Saturn 23Aqu
Feb.16, 2170: Saturn conj Uranus 27Aqu09

Appendix H: Chart Sources

See http://philosopherswheel.com/chartsources.html (as long as it's up) for information on the sources of the horoscopes of the presidents and candidates mentioned in Chapter 12. When available I used horoscopes posted at http://astro.com/astrodatabank Posted at the website are the sources, Rodden rating, Ascendant and Midheaven for all charts with given birth times.

Otherwise, if birth time was not available, the birth date is listed. This Appendix is also the reference for the website http://philosopherswheel.com/presidentialelections.html and any other articles I published on this subject.

Appendix I: Historical References

This book updates <u>Horoscope for the New Millennium,</u> and focuses more on predictions and prophecies, so the new book contains mainly historical data already presented there. Providing a footnote or endnote for every single fact mentioned in this book would be cumbersome for the reader. I have not added a new bibliography, since it would be almost the same as the one in the old book, but I have compiled a list of books referenced in this appendix at the end. This appendix briefly describes events I mentioned in three of the historically-oriented chapters, and their documentation. Many more sources were used to find this data over the years than are listed here. I have included online sources too, which are more current than the books I refer to here. Most of my recent reading and study has been online, where finding information has become easier. If you are reading this book in book format, you may need to type the listed URLs in on your own device separately to visit these sites. If these websites no longer exist, you can try a search for another related site. You can probably find information on-line about the books I mention here too, but they might be expensive or hard to find now.

Given space and time limitations, I have decided to provide references for just the historical review chapters 2 and 3, and the presidential election chapter 12. These days it is easy to pick up a device and search for a reputable website that can verify historical and astronomical facts, so if you have a question about historical events mentioned in the other chapters, I invite the reader to check online. But I have also included footnotes for quotes and for references to published works (not to websites) for historical events not covered in the historical review in Chapters 2 and 3.

Note that I often prefer to use **AD** for dates after the birth of Christ, just because it's visually easier to the tell the difference between AD and BC or BCE, than between **CE** and the others, which makes both terms easier to read. I think many readers are still used to seeing AD, and many of my sources use it. By using AD, I am not *necessarily* claiming that Christ is "our Lord." I also use BC a lot more than BCE, because BCE, although politically correct, is cumbersome and redundant. You can read "BC" as "Before the Common-era."

References to Chapter 2: Discovering the Great Cycles.

Cautionary note: some astrological correlations with earlier dates in history may be approximate, due to the paucity of historical accounts for these times. Unknown related events and conditions probably occurred leading up to or just after the times listed for the astrological event. If my previous book should ever become famous, it would be a good example of this. As I related in Chapter 2, its inspiration came from the Uranus-Pluto conjunction of June 1966, but its main ideas were conceived in 1971 during Jupiter's conjunction with Neptune. It was finished in 1993 during the exact Uranus and Neptune conjunction, and then published in shorter form in 1997 just when Jupiter joined it. So which conjunction gets the credit?

As I suggested in Chapter 2, the conjunctions and other aspects between planets are not isolated events. They are not mechanical causes of events that follow on Earth. They indicate the rhythm of unfolding cycles, and they are the main phases of an entire cycle when their meaning comes into high focus, like huge, swelling crests of historical waves, and they are forever interacting with the other cycles going on within the whole being that is our solar system and its wonderful living being we call Planet Earth.

The Discovery of the Outer Planets, and synchronistic events

Uranus discovered March 13, 1781. http://coolcosmos.ipac.caltech.edu/ask/134-Who-discovered-Uranus- https://en.wikipedia.org/wiki/Uranus

Cornwallis surrender at Yorktown, Oct 19, 1781, Thomas A Bailey, The American Pageant, D.C. Heath and Company, 1956, p.121. Bailey reports that after Yorktown the British were getting weary of war. The synchronicity of USA independence and Uranus' discovery is amazing, as related in these two cited sources. First the surrender at Yorktown in 1781, then a preliminary agreement in 1782, and finally an official treaty in 1783. First Herschel, who discovered Uranus in 1781, thought it was a comet and wanted to name it after King George. Lexell and Bode determined that it was a planet in 1782, and Bode proposed Uranus as the name. In 1783 Herschel accepted its status as a new planet.

The sensational *Oath of the Horatii* was painted in 1785 by J. L. David. Kenneth Clark called it the "supreme picture of revolutionary action." Kenneth Clark, Civilization, Harper and Row, 1969, p. 262-263.

Immanuel Kant's Critique of Pure Reason, 1781, Will and Ariel Durant, The Story of Civilization, Rousseau and Revolution, Simon and Schuster, 1967, pp.535-540. This massive series is good for history up to 1815, though hard to plow through. More on Kant at https://en.wikipedia.org/wiki/Immanuel_Kant

Galvani discovered electric current, 1786; Volta's battery, 1799; Chemistry invented, 1789, E,J Hobsbawm, The Age of Revolution 1789-1848, The New American Library, 1962, p.331-32. Beginning of Industrial Revolution dated as 1780 to 1800 in Britain: Ibid., p.45-46.

William Herschel discovered infrared light in 1800, 19 years after he had discovered Uranus: https://en.wikipedia.org/wiki/Infrared

Inspired by Herschel's discovery, Johann Ritter discovered ultra-violet light in 1801, and he also continued the development of batteries. http://coolcosmos.ipac.caltech.edu/cosmic_classroom/classroom_activities/ritter_bio.html

Montgolfier Brothers first balloon flights 1783-1786:
https://www.thevintagenews.com/2016/11/29/montgolfier-brothers-the-inventors-of-the-hot-air-balloon/

First radio-active element Uranium discovered in 1789 and named after Uranus:
https://en.wikipedia.org/wiki/Uranium#History

"Mesmer's theory attracted a wide following between about 1780 and 1850"--https://en.wikipedia.org/wiki/Franz_Mesmer

The American Revolution inspired the French to make theirs, which spelled out the rights of man in 1789: https://www.history.com/news/how-did-the-american-revolution-influence-the-french-revolution

USA Bill of Rights: Martin Shapiro, ed. The Constitution of the United States, Appleton Century Crofts, Meredith Publishing Company, 1966, p.19. "The first 10 amendments were adopted in 1791"--

William Langer, ed., J.H.Hexter, Western Civilization: The Struggle for Empire to Europe in the Modern World, Harper & Row, 1968, p.249.

J.L.Talmon, Romanticism and Revolt Europe 1815-1848, Harcourt, Brace and World, 1970, cites the important figures of romanticism, including Turner p.147-155, Delacroix p.158, Blake and Wordsworth p.150 and p.165. See also Clark, op.cit., on Wordsworth. pp.276 and 296; Turner, p.284 and 308; Beethoven, p.305; and Byron p.307. And see https://youtu.be/BDRDsXgVOAA   https://youtu.be/pq56Kzc3jI4

Discovery of Neptune in 1846. Zim, Baker, Stars, Simon and Schuster, 1956, p.122. Also see: https://en.wikipedia.org/wiki/Discovery_of_Neptune

We started sailing the oceans: The first regular steamship crossings started in the 1840s: https://americanhistory.si.edu/onthewater/exhibition/2_3.html

The main form of migration was overseas; it was largest population movement in recorded history, beginning in 1846-1847 with the Irish Potato Famine: William Langer ed., Richard Pipes, Western Civilization: The Struggle for Empire to Europe in the Modern World, Harper and Row, 1968. p.445-446.

The 1850s was the golden age of the merchant marine. Frantic demands for rapid passage to the gold fields of California and Australia: Bailey, op.cit. p.315: p.376.

Nationalism in the 1848 revolutions: called "the springtime of the peoples." They unleashed the first full-scale nationalist wars in Europe. The political experience of 1848 and the advance of industrialism were needed for nationalism to spread: George Fasel, Europe in Upheaval, The Revolutions of 1848, Rand McNally, 1970, p.35-36.

Conditions were so alike in the countries of Europe that a revolution in one would set off the rest: Gordon A. Craig, Europe, 1815-1914, The Dryden Press, 1972, p.124.

The Communist Manifesto was written on the very eve of the revolutions of 1848; "it created the modern socialist movement": Ibid., p.272-73.

Marx, Engels, Dickens; Humanitarianism as the most significant civilizing achievement of the nineteenth century, Clark, Civilization, p.327-329.

Florence Nightengale, founder of modern nursing: Bailey, <u>The American Pageant</u>, p.561: Clara Barton; https://en.wikipedia.org/wiki/Florence_Nightingale

Birth c.1825 of the founders of Bahai Faith and Christian Science, Charles A, Jayne Jr, "Cycles" in <u>Encyclopedia of Astrology</u>, Nicholas Devore, editor.

History of New Thought: https://en.wikipedia.org/wiki/History_of_New_Thought

Theosophy established in 1875: https://en.wikipedia.org/wiki/Theosophy_(Blavatskian)

Beethoven as the sound of Europe going beyond eighteenth-century classicism, Clark, <u>op.cit.</u>, p.293.

Impressionism, <u>Ibid.</u> pp.341-343.

Beethoven's final works as a transition from classicism to romanticism. Craig, <u>op.cit.</u>, p.62.

The Romantic Spirit: Joseph Machlis, <u>The Enjoyment of Music</u>, W.W. Norton & Co., 1963, pp.71-77.

Pluto discovered in 1930 and Charon in 1978. Sarah Janssen, senior editor, <u>The World Almanac and Book of Facts</u>, Infobase, 2018., p.346.

Pluto known only by an astrologer to be a dual or binary planet: Brunhubner, Fritz, <u>Pluto</u>, American Federation of Astrologers, 1934, 1966, pages 13 and 16.

The Great Depression. Bailey, <u>op.cit.</u>, pp.818-824. The New Deal p.831ff.

Second Global War. Stewart Easton, <u>A Brief History of the Western World</u>, Barnes & Noble, 1966, pp.374-377: Devolution of the Western Empires. <u>Ibid.</u>,pp.384-391.

The Secrets of Quantum Mechanics: https://youtu.be/TftGVf5345g John and Mary Gribben, <u>Schrodinger's Kittens and the Search for Reality</u>, Little Brown and Company, 1995, pp.10-14.

Modern Thought: William Langer, ed. Richard Pipes, <u>The Expansion of Empire to Europe in the Modern World</u>, American Heritage Publishing, Harper and Row, 1968, pp.639-657.

Wilhelm Reich: https://en.wikipedia.org/wiki/Wilhelm_Reich "his idea of muscular armour—the expression of the personality in the way the body moves—shaped innovations such as body psychotherapy, Gestalt therapy, bioenergetic analysis and primal therapy; influenced generations of intellectuals; he coined the phrase "the sexual revolution" and according to one historian acted as its midwife." Reich published <u>Character Analysis</u>, 1933.

Gestalt Psychology: https://en.wikipedia.org/wiki/Gestalt_psychology "The visual Gestalt principles of grouping were introduced in Wertheimer (1923). Through the 1930s and '40s Wertheimer, Kohler and Koffka formulated many of the laws of grouping through the study of visual perception."

Human Potential Movement: https://en.wikipedia.org/wiki/Human_Potential_Movement

New Age Movement: https://www.britannica.com/topic/New-Age-movement

Green Movement: Charlene Spretnak, <u>The Spiritual Dimension of Green Politics</u>, Bear and Company, 1986.

Planetary Dynamics

    Spiral Dynamics: http://spiraldynamicsintegral.nl/en/overview-value-systems/
Don Beck, Spiral Dynamics, John Wiley and Sons Ltd., 2005.
Steve McIntosh, Integral Consciousness and the Future of Evolution, Paragon House, 2007.
    Planetary Dynamics: http://philosopherswheel.com/planetarydynamics.html

The Cycle of Civilization: Neptune-Pluto Cycle
References for *Neptune conjunct Pluto* correlations that are mentioned in Horoscope for
the New Age, Chapter 2.
Reference for dates of all the conjunctions and aspects:
https://www.astro.com/swisseph/swepha_e.htm

c.3057 BC

    Mesopotamia timeline: https://www.ancient.eu/timeline/Mesopotamia/
    Egypt timeline:
https://www.worldatlas.com/webimage/countrys/africa/egypt/egtimeln.htm Upper and
Lower Egypt unified by Pharaoh Narmer, 3100 BC Early Dynastic Period began;
hieroglyphics were developed as a formal writing system.

c.2560 BC

    The Great Pyramids of Egypt were built in Dahshur and Giza, 2575 BC; the 4th
dynasty was founded that year by Sneferu:
https://www.worldatlas.com/webimage/countrys/africa/egypt/egtimeln.htm
    Mature Harappan (Indus Valley Civilisation) flourished c.2600 – 1900 BCE.
https://en.wikipedia.org/wiki/Indus_Valley_Civilisation, Most other dates of early and late
Indus Valley Civilization listed in this article don't resonate very well with the Cycle of
Civilization. Early Harappan civilization was established c.3300 BCE according to this
source. Sometimes events in India may better correlate to the Neptune-Pluto opposition
dates half-way (about 247 years) between these dates mentioned here.

c.2064 BC

    The age of the Middle Kingdom began, 2055 BC: See Egypt timeline link above.
    The Minoan civilization flourished in the Middle Bronze Age on the island of Crete
located in the eastern Mediterranean from c. 2000 BCE until c. 1500 BCE:
https://www.ancient.eu/Minoan_Civilization

According to this website, palaces were centers for the nation's activities and power. They date from 2000 BCE, were rebuilt c.1700 BCE and survived until between 1500 BCE and 1450 BCE.

First evidence of building structures at Mycenae, c.2100 BCE: https://www.ancient.eu/timeline/Mycenaean_Civilization

The rise of the Olmec civilization, the source for many features of later Maya culture, 2000: https://www.historymuseum.ca/cmc/exhibitions/civil/maya/mmc09eng.html

The Dark Age of Mesopotamia, c.2083 BCE - c. 2050 BCE; Amorite period (Babylon) in Mesopotamia, c.2000 BCE – 1600 BCE: https://www.ancient.eu/timeline/Mesopotamia/

Hsia Dynasty in China.,1994 BC – 1523 BC;. L. Carrington Goodrich, A Short History of the Chinese People, Harper and Row, 1943/1969, p.5. This book reveals parallels in Chinese history with The West, and reports dates that often correspond to the Cycle of Civilization. See table of contents for timeline: p.v.

Chinese history timeline: http://afe.easia.columbia.edu/timelines/china_timeline.htm

c.1568 BC

The New Kingdom began under the ruling of Ahmose I, 1550 BC: See Egypt timeline link above.

First evidence of elite buildings at Mycenae, c. 1600 BCE, Mycenae at its peak of influence, c. 1500 BCE – 1200 BCE: https://www.ancient.eu/timeline/Mycenaean_Civilization/

Aryan invasions of India, first hymns of Rig Veda composed, c.1500-1200, Wm. Theodore De Bary, ed., Sources of Indian Tradition Volume I, Columbia University Press, 1958, p. xx

Shang Dynasty, 1523 BC – 1028 BC: Goodrich, op.cit., p.7.

c.1073 BC

Dorian invasion of Greece, 1103 BC, Will Durant, The Story of Civilization, The Life of Greece, Simon and Schuster, 1939, pp. 62-63.

Saul was born c.1076 BC; became first King of Israel circa 1046 BC by uniting the tribes and turning back enemies: https://www.biography.com/religious-figure/saul

Chou Dynasty, 1046-256 BC, Goodrich, op.cit., pp.18-30.

c.578 BC Axis Age

Siddhartha Gautama, The Buddha: c.563-483 BC. Death of Mahavira, c.468, Wm. Theodore De Bary, ed., Sources of Indian Tradition Volume I, Columbia University Press, 1958, p. xx:

The Upanishads were foundational to Hindu religious thought. The most important of them that deal with the basic Hindu philosophy were written between about 600 and 300 b.c., says this source: https://www.encyclopedia.com/philosophy-and-religion/eastern-religions/hinduism/upanishads#3490900494 The Upanishads were begun in 1000-900 BC, according to some other sources; probably the earlier portions not as foundational were written then.

The Chou Dynasty Chinese classical age, in middle Chou, 770 -475 BC and late Chou, 475-221 BC, produced milestones in literature, thought and discovery: Goodrich, <u>A Short History of the Chinese People</u>, Harper & Row, 1943/1969, p.23-24.

It is said Confucius was born on September 28, 551 BC: https://en.wikipedia.org/wiki/Confucius

Lao Tzu has usually been said to be a 6th-century BC contemporary of Confucius, but some modern historians say he lived during in the 4th century BC: https://en.wikipedia.org/wiki/Laozi

The prophet Ezekiel's visions occurred during his exile in Babylon from 593–571 BC: https://en.wikipedia.org/wiki/Book_of_Ezekiel

Deutero-Isaiah, an anonymous priest who wrote chapters 40–55 of Isaiah, including the "first clear statement of monotheism" and some of the most famous prophetic verses of the Bible; see: https://en.wikipedia.org/wiki/Book_of_Isaiah Also see Will Durant, <u>The Story of Civilization: Our Oriental Heritage</u>, Simon & Schuster, 1935/1954, p.325.

In the early sixth century BC, Thales and his successors Anaximander and Anaximenes pioneered the idea that an "underlying rational unity and order" existed: Richard Tarnas, <u>The Passion of the Western Mind</u>, Ballantine Books, 1991, p.19: *The Birth of Philosophy.*

Thales of Miletus, c.624/623– c.548/545BC was one of the Seven Sages of Greece; many, most notably Aristotle, regarded him as the first philosopher in the Greek tradition… He is the first known individual to whom a mathematical discovery has been attributed: https://en.wikipedia.org/wiki/Thales_of_Miletus

Pythagoras of Samos (c.570 – c.495 BC) was an ancient Ionian Greek philosopher; see https://en.wikipedia.org/wiki/Pythagoras. He taught the transmigration of souls, and planetary motion according to mathematics (the music of the spheres). Pythagoras influenced Plato, ancient Greek art, and European scientists like Copernicus, Kepler, and Newton. European esoteric philosophy used Pythagorean symbols.

c.83 BC

Sulla becomes dictator and master of Rome, 82 BC, Donald R. Dudley, <u>The Civilization of Rome</u>, Mentor Book, New American Library, 1960, p.82.

Composition of <u>Bhagavad Gita</u> c.100 BC to 100 AD, Wm. Theodore De Bary, ed., <u>Sources of Indian Tradition Volume I</u>, Columbia University Press, 1958, p. xxi.

The First Empires, Ch'in, 221BC, Han 206 BC – 9 AD, Eastern Han 25-220 AD, Goodrich, <u>op.cit.</u>, pp.31-43.

Tsin Empire led hazardous existence, 265-420 AD. <u>Ibid.,</u> p.81.

c.411-412 AD

Alaric the Visigoth conquered Rome in 410: Will Durant, <u>The Story of Civilization, The Age of Faith</u>, Simon and Schuster, 1950., p.36.

Visigoths rule Spain 420; reconquered it in 456-466, Odoacer replaces Roman emperor in Italy 476, Ostrogoths under Theodoric the Great succeed Odoacer 493 , Merovingians in France 511: Ibid., pp.92-97.

Theodosius II rules East, 408-450 AD; Anastasius makes Constantinople impregnable and wealthy, 491-518. Ibid., p. 103. See also https://en.wikipedia.org/wiki/Theodosius_II

Huns invade west, Fall of Rome, new barbarian kingdoms, including Vandals in Africa 435 AD, end of 4th to end of 5th century, Stewart Easton, A Brief History of the Western World, Barnes and Noble, 1966, p.97-99.

In 395 the empire was divided and the final stages of dissolution of the western empire began. Western emperor moved to Ravenna. Europe was overwhelmed with the greatest folk migrations thus far in history, including the Huns. "The capture of Rome by Alaric in 410 sent a shudder through the world."-- Donald R. Dudley, The Civilization of Rome, New American Library, 1960. p. 219. Augustine in *The City of God* (413) thereupon pronounced that on Earth we have no abiding city; Ibid.

Ghana: traditional beginning in the 4th century CE: https://www.britannica.com/place/Ghana-historical-West-African-empire

Mayans: Many websites claim 250 AD as the start of the Mayan golden age. But its two greatest cities, Tikal (see below) and Copan, started their golden age in circa 400-500 AD: https://en.wikipedia.org/wiki/Cop%C3%A1n

500 Tikal becomes first great Mayan city: https://www.historymuseum.ca/cmc/exhibitions/civil/maya/mmc09eng.html

Teotihuacan near today's Mexico City has a different and earlier timeline; it was established in 100 BCE and built its major monuments until 250 CE; the city was sacked and burned around 550 CE: https://en.wikipedia.org/wiki/Teotihuacan

c.905

Last Carolingian king of Germany died 911, his successor appointed Henry the Fowler in 919 to consolidate the realm. Alfred the Great (871-899) lost territory to the Vikings; his son recaptured it soon after 900, and grandson Edgar ruled all England 959-975. Hugh Capet founded French monarchy 987 (but its territory was often small – E.A.M.)-- Stewart C. Easton, A Brief History of the Western World, Barnes and Noble, 1966, p.122-123.

The 10th century created art as splendid as that of any other age, in astonishing quality, Kenneth Clark, Civilization, Harper and Row, 1969, p.35.

The Abbey of Cluny was founded in the tenth century, and from 1049 to 1109 was the greatest church in Europe and a great power – mostly benevolent, Ibid., p. 24.

In about 910 twelve monks established the Abbey of Cluny from which the great monastic reforms came, Will Durant, The Story of Civilization, The Age of Faith, Simon and Schuster, 1950, p.537.

The Sui and T'ang Dynasties, 590-906, L. Carrington Goodrich, A Short History of the Chinese People, Harper & Row, 1943/1969, p.125. The T'ang had brought Buddhism and

Taoism to maturity, and was poetic and cosmopolitan, but it collapsed in 906, followed by an era of cruel banditry, Ibid., p.143. Sung (Song) Dynasty established in 960 and lasting to 1279, brought renewal, Ibid., p.146.

The Classic Period of Maya history ends, as southern lowland cities collapse, 900 AD. The Toltecs ruled Mayan central Mexico circa 900s to 1100s A.D: https://www.historymuseum.ca/cmc/exhibitions/civil/maya/mmc09eng.html

As a federation of united tribes, Hungary was established in 895, some 50 years after the division of the Carolingian Empire at the Treaty of Verdun in 843, and just before the unification of the Anglo-Saxon kingdoms: https://en.wikipedia.org/wiki/Hungary

c.1399/1400

The Florentines felt like gods in 1400, and showed how civilization's rise depends on a burst of confidence, Clark, op.cit., p.89. Ghiberti won the contest in 1401 to design the door to the Florence Cathedral Baptistry, inaugurating the Renaissance: https://courses.lumenlearning.com/suny-arthistory2/chapter/bruelleschi-ghiberti-the-sacrifice-of-isaac/

The West was turning away from its previous interests; Stewart Easton, A Brief History of the Western World,, Barnes & Noble, 1966, p.193. Great Schism, 1377-1414, Ibid., p.195-96.

Turk invasion of Byzantium in the early 15th century, Ibid., pp. 177-179.

Henry the Navigator begins Portuguese explorations and conquests, 1415. Columbus 1492, Balboa 1513, Magellan 1520, Cortez 1519, Pizarro 1530-- William Langer, ed. J.H. Hexter, The Expansion of Empire to Europe in the Modern World, American Heritage Publishing, Harper and Row, 1968, p.26-33.

Navigation by explorers fueled the development of the scientific revolution: https://www.enotes.com/homework-help/how-did-age-european-exploration-help-pave-way-530463

Aztec Empire, In 1428 Itzcoatl created the Aztec Triple Alliance that ruled until the Spanish came in 1519: https://www.historyonthenet.com/overview-of-the-aztec-empire

The Inca Empire flourished in South America, c. 1425 CE – 1532 CE: https://www.ancient.eu/timeline/Inca_Civilization/

Ming Dynasty, 1368-1644, Goodrich, A Short History of the Chinese People, p.189. First reign repaired defenses and irrigation, and brutally suppressed dissent; devastation followed in 1398-1403, Ibid., p.190. After 1403, Chu Ti (the Yung-lo era) "brought glory to Chinese annals." Naval expeditions, Ibid., pp.192-195.

(cycle continues from Nept.Pluto opposition) Ching, or Manchu 1644-1912, Ibid., p. 214. Early Manchu writing asked fundamental philosophical questions, just like those happening in the West at the same time, Ibid., p.227. Ku Yen Wu (1613-1682) was typical of the age by emphasizing "the necessity of observation (and) evidence..."-- Ibid., p.228. Revolutionary movement begins, 1900; establishes the Republic in 1912, Ibid., p.224-25.

Fall of Khmer empire to Siamese invasion, 1431:
https://en.m.wikipedia.org/wiki/Khmer_Empire

For **the 1890s** (Neptune conjunct Pluto c.1892) through World War I in 1914 (Uranus opposite Pluto c.1901, Uranus opposite Neptune c.1908) as the start of the age we live in, see:

Kenneth Clark, Civilization, Harper and Row, 1969, p.344, said that by 1910 a new era had started even before World War I, and we are still living in that era.

William Langer, ed. and Richard Pipes, The Expansion of Empire to Europe in the Modern World, American Heritage Publishing, Harper and Row, 1968, p. 639: The years from 1890 to 1910 saw a cultural revolution in one of history's most creative periods, during which the principles of modern thought and arts were formulated. *Modern Thought*, Ibid., pp.638-657.

Oron J. Hale, The Great Illusion 1900-1914, Harper and Row, 1971, p.110, said that between 1895 and 1914 one era ended and a new one began.

https://en.wikipedia.org/wiki/Contemporary_history#Modern_era

If you make a count of all the inventions listed in the World Almanac, 2018, on pp. 289-91, you'll find that the vast majority were made between the mid-1880s and the 1910s.

c.1892:

Symbolism in literature, George Heard Hamilton, 19th and 20th Century Art, Prentice Hall and Harry M. Abrams, Inc. 1970, p.119. Post-impressionism, a similar movement, Ibid., pp.119-120. Cezanne's work decisive for 20th century painting, Ibid., p.123. Seurat an architect of 20th century vision in art, Ibid.

Achievements of the Post-Impressionists are necessary to know in order to understand 20th Century art-- Helen Gardner, Horst De La Croix and Richard Tansey, Art Through the Ages, Harcourt, Brace and World, 1970, p. 674. This is still the best textbook on art history I've seen, and it's timelines helped me see the correlations to the cycle of civilization.

Steps to World War I: Germany broke secret alliance with Russia, 1890; German Schlieffen Plan developed to attack France if Russia attacks Germany or Austria, 1892; Franco-Russian alliance, Jan. 1894; Arms race followed leading to World War I. Gordon A Craig, Europe, 1815-1914, Dryden Press, 1972, pp.426-27. On the Schlieffen Plan also see William Langer, ed., Richard Pipes, op.cit., pp.590-593.

See also: discovery of Pluto, above. Regarding the 1890s, see also Meece, Horoscope for the New Millennium, Llewellyn, 1997, pp.38-39, pp.203-206.

The Golden Ages
(golden ages may date from about 50 years before the listed date, or from the listed date and perhaps 50 to 100 years after; the timing of the sextile following the conjunction of Neptune and Pluto, and the subsequent aspects of these planets with Uranus, may affect the timing and stimulate the upsurge of the golden age)

c.2950 BC

Sumerian timeline: https://www.ancient.eu/timeline/sumer/ Uruk now had 80,000 people, the first big city.

c.2460 BC

First Dynasty of Ur, and Lagash: https://en.wikipedia.org/wiki/First_Dynasty_of_Ur

Old Kingdom art as classic, and never surpassed; survived 3000 years; examples given in the text from c.2600 BC and c.2500 BC-- Helen Gardner, Horst De La Croix and Richard Tansey, Art Through the Ages, Harcourt, Brace and World, 1970, pp.73-75.

c.1960 BC

Babylon rose to greatness after 2000 BC. King Hammurabi wrote first legal code in the world: https://www.nationalgeographic.com/archaeology-and-history/magazine/2017/01-02/babylon-mesopotamia-ancient-city-iraq/

Rock tombs of Egypt, c.1800: Helen Gardner, Horst De La Croix and Richard Tansey, Art Through the Ages, Harcourt, Brace and World, 1970, p.75.

c.1470 BC

New Palace of period in Crete began between 1600 and 1500 BC; according to the authors it was the Golden Age of Crete and the first great western civilization, with unsurpassed and precocious achievement in the arts-- Gardner, De La Croix and Tansey, op.cit., p.95.

Royal temple tomb for Queen Hatshepsut, c.1500 BC; Temple of Amen-Re, Karnak, c.1530-1300; Amarna period of Sun worship. c.1350: Gardner, De La Croix and Tansey, op.cit., pp.78-89. Also see: https://en.wikipedia.org/wiki/Eighteenth_Dynasty_of_Egypt

Conquests of Thutmose III created Egyptian Empire, 1468 BC, Stewart Easton, A Brief History of the Western World, Barnes & Noble, 1966, p.11.

c.970 BC

King David, c.1000 BC https://en.wikipedia.org/wiki/David; Solomon's reign circa 970 to 931 BCE
https://en.wikipedia.org/wiki/Solomon

c.470 BC

The Buddha is believed to have founded Buddhism near Benares India around 528 BCE when he gave his first sermon, "The Setting in Motion of the Wheel of Dharma", at nearby Sarnath: https://en.wikipedia.org/wiki/Varanasi

The Greeks defeated the Persians by 479 BC, stimulating the Greeks to do unprecedented things and enter their golden age: Will Durant, The Story of Civilization: The Life of Greece, Simon & Schuster, 1939, p.242.

Greek democratic constitution established 509 BC, p.57; Roman Republic begun, 508 BC: Stewart Easton, A Brief History of the Western World, Barnes & Noble, 1966, pp.41, 401.

Cyrus the Great became ruler of Persia; 538 BC, conquered Mesopotamia and allowed Jews to return to Jerusalem, where they rebuilt their temple (by c.515). Persia under Cyrus and Darius was the largest empire yet in history. It was well governed, and produced architecture and sculpture: Stewart Easton, op.cit., p.401. See also Durant, The Story of Civilization: Our Oriental Heritage, Simon & Schuster, 1935/1954, pp.352-363. Zarathustra or Zoroaster the later, prophet contemporary with Cyrus, brought religion of the light and the darkness to Persia and the world, Ibid., 378-379.

c.10 AD

Augustus reigned 27 BC to 14 AD; he achieved his goal to build a lasting government system, creating the Pax Romana for 2 centuries, Donald R. Dudley, The Civilization of Rome, Mentor Book, 1960, p.124. He marked his 10th anniversary with the saeculum ceremony, which according to occult knowledge was a 100-110 period of renewal. No-one had seen such a ceremony before; no-one would see it a second time. Ibid., p.130. Few periods in history can match the Age of Augustus for creative achievement; to this day a classical period in a nation's history is called its Augustan Age.-- Ibid., p.143.

Rise of Mahayana Buddhism 100-200 AD, Wm. Theodore De Bary, ed., op.cit.

Sun pyramid at Teotihuacan was built around 100 AD:
https://www.britannica.com/place/Pyramid-of-the-Sun

c.520 AD

Great age of architecture and mosaic at Ravenna under Theodoric and Justinian, 450-550 AD, Will Durant, The Story of Civilization: The Age of Faith, Simon & Schuster, 1950, p.2. Hagia Sophia, 532-537 AD, and other Byzantine art: Ibid., pp.128-135.

Ravenna, San Vitale, St. Sophia, from the 6th Century; the most majestic monuments of Byzantium, an immeasurable upward spring, and the summit of Christian art, according to Clive Bell, Art, Capricorn Books, 1913/1958, p.93. I picked up a used copy of this book while taking an art class at Mendocino; a real treasure find. He even used the words "the horoscope of humanity" in the text.

Buddhist golden age in China, 420-589 AD: The "artistic ardor" of this period is evident in museums around the world, and it created art in grottoes comparable to Christian art-- Goodrich, op.cit., p.101-103.

Golden Age of India in Gupta Empire, Hindu Renaissance, 320-480 AD:
http://indiansaga.com/history/golden_hinduism.html

The classical "Golden Age" of Hinduism (c. 320-650 CE), which coincides with the Gupta Empire:
https://en.wikipedia.org/wiki/History_of_Hinduism

c.1000

The Christian Church recovered in the 10th century from corruption, and organized a great monastic reform movement encouraged by the Ottonian rulers. By the early 11th century a cultural renewal was underway that would soon produce even greater monuments than those of ancient times.-- Gardner, De La Croix and Tansey, op.cit., p. 294-295.

Kiev reached its Golden Age as the center of the Kievan Rus' in the 10th–12th centuries:

https://en.wikipedia.org/wiki/History_of_Kiev

Sung Dynasty after 960 AD: an artistic renaissance flourished, L. Carrington Goodrich, A Short History of the Chinese People, Harper and Row, 1969, p.154.

South India in the 10th and 11th century AD under the imperial Chola Dynasty has been called a Golden Age. The period saw extensive achievements in architecture, literature, sculpture and bronze working, maritime conquests with extensive trade, and quasi-democratic reforms:

https://simple.wikipedia.org/wiki/Golden_Age_of_India

c.1500

Michelangelo, Raphael and Da Vinci: in this heroic golden moment humanity achieved a status it has hardly ever achieved; Kenneth Clark, Civilization, conclusion of Chapter 5, *The Hero as Artist*, c.1500, p.137. Northern humanist Renaissance, Erasmus, Durer. c.1490-1527, Ibid., pp. 142-157.

In the "High Renaissance" of 1495-1527, works were produced that instructed generations of future artists, Gardner, De La Croix and Tansey, op.cit., p.450. The most brilliant period of the Renaissance in Northern Europe corresponds almost exactly with the Italian High Renaissance. Ibid., p. 531.

Suleyman the Magnificent, sultan of Ottoman Empire 1520-1566, expanded the realm, and sponsored poets, architects, public works, and transformed his capitol city:

https://www.britannica.com/biography/Suleyman-the-Magnificent

Mughal India, Akbar the Great, 1556-1605, extended rule over most of India, took interest in all religions, made his court a center of culture:

https://www.britannica.com/biography/Akbar

c.1990

Widespread spiritual renewal, merging of spiritual paths, revival of esoteric traditions, emergence of holistic paradigms, nature mysticism, global mind, cyberspace, world wide web, deconstruction of old boundaries, metaphysical fiction, perestroika and fall of Berlin Wall, etc., Late 20th Century and turn of the Millennium, Richard Tarnas, Cosmos and Psyche, Viking Penguin Group, 2006, p.419ff.

Phases in the Cycle of Civilization
For other examples of the aspects and phases besides those mentioned in this book, see Horoscope for the New Millennium, end of Chapter 4. Dates listed for the aspects

arbitrarily assume a 10 degree orb. Exact years of the aspects are in the middle of the dates listed.

Waxing square of Neptune and Pluto, crisis:

(final exact square, May 18, 404 BC):
   The Peloponnesian War and the death of Socrates ended the golden age, c.404-399 BC, Will Durant, The Story of Civilization: The Life of Greece, Simon and Schuster, 1939, pp.451-455. The war drained Greece; serene idealism and balance replaced by greater cynicism and skepticism, Gardner, De La Croix and Tansey, op.cit., p.154.

(square c.1560s-1570s):
   Toleration was less after the Reformation; princes were the real victors. German cities and the Holy Roman Empire lost ground; commerce and culture weakened: Will Durant, The Story of Civilization: The Reformation, Simon and Schuster, 1957, *The Triumph of Protestantism: 1542-1555,* pp.456-57.
   Protestantism let loose bullies and destruction; wars of religion were used for political ambitions; Massacre of St. Bartholomew, mid-16th century wars of religion; Mannerism--Kenneth Clark, Civilization, Harper and Row, 1969, p.160.
   St. Bartholomew's Day massacre, August 1572: https://en.wikipedia.org/wiki/St._Bartholomew%27s_Day_massacre assassinations and mob violence against French Huguenot Protestants, killing thousands.
   The French Wars of Religion were a prolonged period of war and popular unrest between Roman Catholics and Huguenots (Reformed/Calvinist Protestants) in the Kingdom of France between 1562 and 1598. It is estimated that three million people perished in this period from violence, famine, or disease in what is considered the second deadliest religious war in European history: https://en.wikipedia.org/wiki/French_Wars_of_Religion

Waxing Trine, expansion, mobility

(trine c.106-125 AD, exact in c.114-115):
   Era of good government, expansion of the empire; best two emperors since Augustus and among all who followed them; Trajan, 98-117 AD; Hadrian, reformer and patron of the arts and architecture, 117-138: Donald R. Dudley, The Civilization of Rome, Mentor Book, 1960, p.172, 174.
   Trajan's column, 113 AD, often copied. p.208-210; The Pantheon, renowned and influential, built and perhaps designed by Hadrian, 118-125 AD: Gardner, De La Croix and Tansey, op.cit., p.218-219.
   Trajan and Hadrian, Will Durant, The Story of Civilization: Caesar and Christ, Simon & Schuster, 1944, p.408-422.

This was the peak and climax of the "Silver Age" in Rome. More broadly defined, the Golden Age extends from the start of Cicero's career in 63 BC to the death of Augustus in 14 AD, and the "Silver Age" extends from Tiberius reign starting in 14 AD to Hadrian's death in 138 AD. See: http://earlyworldhistory.blogspot.com/2012/02/roman-golden-and-silver-ages.html

See also Uranus conjunct Neptune, below.

(trine c.1093-1113 AD, exact around 1103):

Pope Urban called First Crusade in November 1095 in the most influential speech of the Middle Ages, Will Durant, The Story of Civilization: The Age of Faith, Simon & Schuster, 1950 p.613. The Crusade expanded commerce, Ibid., pp.586-592.

Round about the year 1100, an unthinkable leap forward, "like a Russian Spring," extraordinary energy. Durham Cathedral, the east end of Canterbury, Kenneth Clark, Civilization, Harper & Row, 1969, *The Great Thaw*, p. 33. Similar to the outburst of the Baroque: delighting and energetic, with swirling and twisting lines, as seen at Moissac portal (1115-1130 AD), Ibid., p.37-38. See also:
https://www.khanacademy.org/humanities/medieval-world/romanesque1/a/saint-pierre-moissac
Durham Cathedral begun 1093: https://www.khanacademy.org/humanities/medieval-world/romanesque1/v/durham-cathedral

(trine c.1587-1607, exact around 1597):

Baroque era started in c.1600, an age of expansion after the age of discovery, with powers colonizing and fighting across the globe; dynamic, colorful, extravagant, sensual, spacious style; Maderna's Santa Suzanna, 1597-1603; his Facade of St. Peter's 1607; Bernini's *David*, 1623, his Baldacchino for St. Peter's, 1624-33: Gardner, De La Croix and Tansey, Art Through the Ages, p.553-561. Rubens, 1610-1622, Ibid., p.577-580.

Baroque period: Elaborate, flamboyant, awe-inspiring:
https://mymodernmet.com/baroque-period/

Queen Elizabeth defeats Spanish Armada, 1588; establishes East India Company, 1600:
https://en.wikipedia.org/wiki/Elizabethan_era#Colonising_the_New_World

Greatest public plays of Shakespeare and Marlowe:
https://en.wikipedia.org/wiki/English_Renaissance_theatre#Timeline_of_English_Renaissance_playwrights

Opposition, climax

(opposition, c.340-320 BC, exact around 330):

Reign of Alexander 336-323 BC, Stewart Easton, A Brief History of the Western World, Barnes & Noble, 1966, p.47, 402.

Alexander the Great's conquests began Hellenistic era, mingling east and west, and completed trends since the archaic period in a new international, Greek-dominated culture,

Gardner, De La Croix and Tansey, Art Through the Ages, Harcourt, Brace and World, 1970, p.159.

Euclid, 325 BC to 270 BC: https://en.wikipedia.org/wiki/Euclid

(opposition, c.155-175 AD, exact around 165):

Ptolemy *c.* 100 CE-*c.* 170 CE, great astronomer, astrologer, mathematician, and geographer; created geocentric model of the universe: https://www.britannica.com/biography/Ptolemy

Reign of philosopher-king Marcus Aurelius, 161-180 AD; last effective emperor until late classical era, faced plague and a barbarian invasion of Dacia, Donald R. Dudley, The Civilization of Rome, p.177-78.

(opposition, c.1142-1162, exact around 1152):

Gothic cathedrals begun. St. Denis, 1135-1144: https://en.wikipedia.org/wiki/Basilica_of_Saint-Denis

Royal Abbey Church of St. Denis, the cradle of Gothic Art, designed by Abbot Suger, dedicated in 1144, Gardner, De La Croix and Tansey, op.cit., p.330-331.

Chartres Cathedral, built 1134-1160, Portions rebuilt 1194-1260, to which the common people contributed: https://en.wikipedia.org/wiki/Chartres_Cathedral

Chartres Cathedral, based on St. Denis but much larger, Clark, Civilization, pp.50-61.

Angkor Wat temple, first built 1113-1150: https://www.history.com/topics/landmarks/angkor-wat

See also Uranus conjunct Neptune, below.

(opposition, c.1636-1655, exact around 1645):

Reign of Louis XIV, 1643-1715; Europe became more cosmopolitan, Ragnhild Hatton, Europe in the Age of Louis XIV, Harcourt, Brace and World, 1969, p.7-8. Absolutist government restrained by reason. Many plagues and famines in colder climate, Ibid., p.67ff.

Moliere, 1622-1673, Racine 1639-1699, etc., Gardner, De La Croix and Tansey, op.cit., p.553. Greatest works by Poussin and Lorraine, 1640-1648, Ibid., p.594-98. The Louvre, 1667-70, Ibid., p.597. Borromini began building chapel of St. Ivo in Rome with dynamic curved, concave, convex and spiraling forms., Ibid., p.564-65. The Dutch masters, Ibid., pp.580-591. Velasquez, Las Meninas, 1656, Ibid., p.576.

Under Louis XIV of France the Ancien Régime reached an absolutist form of government: https://en.wikipedia.org/wiki/Ancien_R%C3%A9gime

Great temples: Taj Mahal, 1632-1653: https://en.wikipedia.org/wiki/Taj_Mahal. St. Paul's, 1669-1697: https://en.wikipedia.org/wiki/St_Paul%27s_Cathedral

Ching/Manchu Dynasty established, 1644, L. Carrington Goodrich, A Short History of the Chinese People, Harper & Row, 1951/1969, p.215.

See also Uranus conjunct Neptune, below.

Waning trine, distributive, leading to last glory

(trine, c.282-175 BC, close in 260s-250s, weak in 230s-210s, exact during 194-184 BC)
   Ashoka 273-232 BC. 262 BC, issues remarkable Buddhist edicts carved on pillars all over India; he made possible Buddhism in the rest of Asia and the world, Will Durant, The Story of Civilization: Our Oriental Heritage, Simon and Schuster, 1935/1954, p.446-450.

(trine, c.212-321 AD, close in 230s, still surprisingly strong in early 250s, weak and usually far out of orb 260s-270s, exact only during 301-309)
   Aurelian, 274 AD, restored empire under sun god, reforms of Diocletian, 284-305 AD, Donald R. Dudley, op.cit., pp.210-216. The blood of martyrs in the mid-3rd century and under Diocletian nourished Christianity's growth, and by 300 AD the Church was the greatest organization of the Empire, Constantine won battle of Mulvian Bridge 312, Toleration Edict of Milan 313, Ibid., p.213.
   Anarchy 235 AD to 270, hurts economy and the state; Will Durant, The Story of Civilization: Caesar and Christ, Simon and Schuster, 1944, pp.628. Aurelian restored empire under sun god, 274, Ibid., p.638. Diocletian, 284-305, oriental despot, ruled the economy and provided benefits to the poor, Ibid., p.640. Constantine's Christian vision and victory at Mulvian Bridge, Oct 27, 312, Ibid., p.654.
   Plotinus, philosopher: 204-270 https://www.iep.utm.edu/plotinus. See Durant, op.cit., pp.607-611.

(trine, exact c.800)
   Charlemagne crowned by the Pope, first Holy Roman Empire founded, Clark, op.cit., p.20.

(trine, c.1690-1798, exact during 1704-1741, and 1776-1786)
   The Enlightenment:
   Clark, op.cit., *The Smile of Reason:* belief in justice, tolerance, natural law; "not bad."-- p.245ff.
   Propaganda to advance reason, knowledge, human rights and freedom, opposed the Church, persuaded kings, William Langer, ed., J.H. Hexter, Western Civilization: The Struggle for Empire to Europe in the Modern World., Harper and Row, 1968, pp.185-211. Enlightened Despots, Ibid., pp.190-204.
   Enlightened Despots: https://www.britannica.com/topic/enlightened-despotism
   Rococo Art style: Watteau, 1712, Clark, op.cit., p.231-236. Bach and Handel, etc., Ibid., pp.224-231.

Waning square, last glory with dramatic events

(square, c.664-641 BC):

Ashurbanipal, reigned 668 to 627 BC:
https://www.britannica.com/biography/Ashurbanipal
(square, c.326-348 AD): Constantine, ruled 306-337, see above under trine, 212-321 AD.
(square, c.820-843): Charlesmagne ruled 768-814, Louis the Pious ruled 813-840:
https://en.wikipedia.org/wiki/Charlemagne   https://en.wikipedia.org/wiki/Louis_the_Pious
(square, c.1806-1829): Napoleon ruled 1799-1815: https://en.wikipedia.org/wiki/Napoleon
Will and Ariel Durant, The Story of Civilization: The Age of Napoleon, Simon & Schuster,
1975. p.159-236 etc.
Congress of Vienna 1814-1815 restored kings and created lasting balance of power:
 https://en.wikipedia.org/wiki/Congress_of_Vienna

Waning sextile, dissolution, invasion: what is mentioned specifically in the text are the
invasions, which continued into the start of the next cycle. References for the conjunctions
above should cover them. See below regarding Black Death.

Cycle of Revolution: Uranus-Pluto Cycle

   Uranus conjunct Pluto 441-433 BC: Peloponnesian War, 431 BC: Will Durant, The
Story of Civilization: The Life of Greece, Simon & Schuster, 1939, p.244, 440-441.
https://en.wikipedia.org/wiki/Peloponnesian_War
   Uranus conjunct Pluto 326-320 BC: Death of Alexander, break-up of his empire 323
BC, Stewart Easton, A Brief History of the Western World, Barnes and Noble, 1966, pp.47-
49.
   Uranus conjunct Pluto 73-66 BC: Slave Revolt of Spartacus, 73-71 BC, Donald R.
Dudley, The Civilization of Rome, Mentor Book, 1960, p.88-89.
   Uranus conjunct Pluto 324-332 AD: Constantinople founded 325-330 AD, Ibid.,
p.215-216.
   Uranus conjunct Pluto 1340-1347; also: waning Neptune-Pluto sextile, 1346-1357:
Black Death (bubonic plague) 1348-49, killed about 1/3 of Europe's people, especially in
the towns:
C. Warren Hollister, Medieval Europe, A Short History, John Wiley & Sons, 1968, p.321.
See also:
Stewart Easton, A Brief History of the Western World, Barnes & Noble, 1966, p.185-186,
1347-1350; Many lords could not hold their serfs afterward.
The 1340s: https://www.revolvy.com/page/1340s?cr=1   Mongol Empire falling apart,
source of Black Death; the humanist Petrarch wrote his greatest epic, was crowned poet
laureate, and was the major force for rediscovery of ancient literature in this period:
https://www.revolvy.com/page/Petrarch?cr=1
   Uranus conjunct Pluto 1452-1459: Fall of Constantinople, 1453, Stewart Easton,
op.cit., p.179, 403.
Gutenberg Bible, first printing, 1455, Kenneth Clark, Civilization, Harper & Row, 1969,
p.145. Wars of the Roses broke out, 1455, Stewart Easton, op.cit., p.168.

Uranus conjunct Pluto, 1594-1601: Galileo: In 1592-1610, he made significant discoveries about motion and astronomy and pioneered the telescope; his multiple interests included the study of astrology: https://en.wikipedia.org/wiki/Galileo_Galilei

Baroque style begun: see also above under waxing trine of Neptune and Pluto.

Uranus opposite Pluto, 1390-1399. Neptune conjunct Pluto 1399. Henry Bolingbroke overthrew Richard II, became King of England, 1399. Stewart Easton, op.cit., p.168.

Uranus opposite Pluto 1645-1652, Neptune opposite Pluto 1640s-1650s: Great Rebellion for parliamentary rule and a Puritan church, overthrew Charles I, 1641-1653, Will and Ariel Durant, The Story of Civilization: The Age of Reason Begins, Simon & Schuster, 1961, p.209-221.

Charles I beheaded, 1649, Will and Ariel Durant, The Story of Civilization: The Age of Louis XIV, Simon & Schuster, 1963, p.183. Puritan takeover; Levelers and diggers advocated for and demonstrated common ownership of land, Ibid., pp.183-191.

Fronde revolt in France for constitutional monarchy and tax reform, 1648-1653, Ibid., p.5-10.
See also: https://www.britannica.com/event/The-Fronde

*Uranus conjunct Pluto 1707-1714: (*First Great Revolution, c.1711-1848)
Arouet de Voltaire, exiled from his town, 1716: Will and Ariel Durant, The Story of Civilization: The Age of Voltaire, Simon & Schuster, 1965, p.34. Imprisoned in the Bastille for reciting an insulting verse about the king by another author, May 1717; released in 1718 and published his first play that year, a literary event. Ibid., p.35.

Newcomen steam engine invented in 1712; an instant success: William Langer, ed., J.H. Hexter, Western Civilization: The Struggle for Empire to Europe in the Modern World., Harper and Row, 1968. p.322, with illustration of the engine that resembles the symbol for Uranus. Rococo Art style: Watteau, 1712, Clark, op.cit., p.231-236. Bach and Handel, Ibid., pp.224-231.

See also waning trine, 1690-1798, above.

Uranus opposite Pluto 1789-1797
French Revolution, 1789-1815, repercussions felt in North and South America; Liberalism, democracy, socialism, nationalism and dictatorship: all launched on their modern careers.; a vastly different world emerged: William Langer, ed., Western Civilization: The Struggle for Empire to Europe in the Modern World., Harper and Row, 1968, p.251ff.

Excellent and thorough account of the Revolution: Will and Ariel Durant, The Story of Civilization: The Age of Napoleon, Simon & Schuster, 1975; pp.13-155. Louis XVI guillotined, Jan.1793, Leo Gershoy, The Era of the French Revolution, 1789-1799 Ten Years that Shook the World, Litton Educational Publishers, D. Van Norstrand Company, 1957. p.57. Nov.1792 the French offered assistance to all peoples seeking to recover their liberty, Ibid., p.57.

See also Discovery of Uranus, above.

*Uranus conjunct Pluto, 1847-1854: (*Second Great Revolution, c.1848/1850-1965)
George Fasel, Europe in Upheaval, The Revolutions of 1848, Rand McNally, 1970.
Craig, Europe 1815-1914, pp. 124-133.

Taiping Rebellion, 1850-1864: The goals of the Taipings were religious, nationalist, and political in nature; bloodiest civil war ever, largest conflict of the 19th century, and it sparked further rebellions, L. Carrington Goodrich, op.cit., p.224-225. See also: https://en.wikipedia.org/wiki/Taiping_Rebellion

Social consciousness and realism in art: Ford Maddox Brown, 1853; and "at the same time" Millet, and Courbet (*The Stonebreakers*, 1849)-- Kenneth Clark, Civilization, Harper and Row, 1969, p.337-338. *The Stonebreakers* also shown in Gardner, De La Croix and Tansey, op.cit., p.664.

Charles Dickens, Hard Times, 1854 https://en.wikipedia.org/wiki/Hard_Times_(novel) Social realism and criticism in Dickens' last great novels written between 1852 and 1865, and in works of other great novelists; Courbet's "Burial at Ornans" in 1850 prompted first use of the term "realism" to describe a style of painting: Gordon A Craig, Europe 1815-1914, Dryden Press 1972, p.149.

"Humanity divided after 1850":
After 1850 nationalism became ambitions to demonstrate national greatness, Craig, op.cit., p.152. Darwin's theory of the survival of species in the struggle for existence (1859) was applied to sociology, politics, economic activity and diplomacy, Ibid., p.145. Darwin's theory justified brutality, and Jacques Barzun reported that after 1870, the blood of parties, races, nations and classes was clamoured for; racism flourished after Gobineau's The Inequality of the Races (1853-1855): Langer/Pipes, op.cit., p.418-419.

The Convention at Seneca Falls New York launched the modern women's right's movement, July 19, 1848. Bailey, The American Pageant, p.344-345. https://en.wikipedia.org/wiki/Seneca_Falls_Convention

See also Discovery of Neptune, above.

Uranus opposite Pluto, 1898-1905:
1900 uprising in China, causing much destruction, was followed by the movement that created the Republic in 1912, L. Carrington Goodrich, A Short History of the Chinese People, Harper and Row, 1969, p.225.

Lenin defined his doctrine 1902, formed Bolsheviks 1903, William Langer, ed., Richard Pipes, Western Civilization: The Struggle for Empire to Europe in the Modern World., Harper and Row, 1968. pp.618-619. Soviet Union founded in 1917, Ibid., pp.623-627. Russian opposition groups furiously active 1899-1903 during factory shutdowns; revolution breaks out Jan.1905: Craig, op.cit., p.393. Between 1895 and 1905 shocks came to imperial ambitions in Italy, France, Great Britain, Russia and Germany, Ibid., pp.417-425. Opposition to the Boer War, and the publication of Hobson's Imperialism, inspired Lenin to declare imperialism as the highest stage of capitalism, Ibid., p.401; also see end of this article: https://www.encyclopedia.com/history/asia-and-africa/southern-african-history/boer-war Progressive Movement and Muckrakers in the USA, c.1901-1910: Bailey, The American Pageant, p.658-666.

Uranus square Pluto, 1928-1937: FDR's New Deal, Thomas A Bailey, The American Pageant, D.C. Heath and Company, 1956, pp.831-848.

Uranus conjunct Pluto, 1962-1970: (Third Great Revolution, c.1966-2103)
NOW (National Organization for Women) was established on June 30, 1966 in Washington, D.C., by people attending the Third National Conference of the Commission on the Status of Women: https://now.org/faq/when-and-how-was-now-founded/ (note: exact date of the conjunction)
Chinese Cultural Revolution launched May 1966, Red Guards formed: https://en.wikipedia.org/wiki/Cultural_Revolution
USA Anti-war Movement launched in 1965: William L. O'Neill, Coming Apart, An Informal History of America in the 1960s, Quadrangle/The New York Times Book Co., 1971, pp.141-146. By Oct/Nov 1969 the peace movement had created the largest peace movement events in history thus far, and the largest demonstration by this time in history in DC, Ibid., p.405. See also: https://en.wikipedia.org/wiki/National_Mobilization_Committee_to_End_the_War_in_Viet nam
Beginning of Black Power, June 1966, O'Neill, op.cit., p.173.
Save the Bay group began environmentalism, c.1961-65: https://youtu.be/408SHpeOt8o See also: https://en.wikipedia.org/wiki/Environmental_movement_in_the_United_States#Beginning _of_the_modern_movement
The Counter-Culture: O'Neill, op.cit., pp.233-271. Tom Wolfe, The Electric Kool-Aid Acid Test, Bantam Books, 1968. Theodore Roszak, The Making of a Counter Culture, Doubleday & Company, 1969.
David Caute, The Year of the Barricades: A Journey Through 1968, Harper and Row, 1988. This book has some good coverage of the various movements of the sixties worldwide, including:
Prague Spring, pp.105-207. French general strike, Ibid., pp.211-255.
Anti-war movement, April 1965: Vietnam Day committee, p.22-23; Nov.1966, Bertrand Russell and Jean-Paul Sartre organized the International War Crimes Tribunal, Ibid., pp.23-24. End of 1966: USA caught up in extraordinary debate over the war, Carman, Syrett, Wishy, A History of the American People Volume II, Alfred A. Knoff, 1967, p.801.
John Lennon, "Imagine" 1971 https://youtu.be/YkgkThdzX-8
See also discovery of Pluto-Charon, above.

Uranus square Pluto, 2007-2020:
Iran "green revolution" of 2009: see Saturn opp. Uranus 2008-2010 below.

Tunisia Revolution, Dec 17, 2010 to Jan 14, 2011:
https://en.wikipedia.org/wiki/Tunisian_Revolution
Arab Spring, 2011-2012: https://en.wikipedia.org/wiki/Arab_Spring
As the Recession deepened in Europe from mid-2010 through 2011, governments fell
"with dizzying speed" (as I predicted) in Britain, Ireland, southern Europe, the Middle East
and elsewhere: https://www.britannica.com/topic/euro-zone-debt-crisis
Occupy Wall Street protests in USA begin Sept.17, 2011:
https://en.wikipedia.org/wiki/Occupy_Wall_Street
Brazil protests, 2013: https://en.wikipedia.org/wiki/2013_protests_in_Brazil
Turkey protests, 2013: https://en.wikipedia.org/wiki/Gezi_Park_protests
Ukraine Revolution, 2014: https://en.wikipedia.org/wiki/2014_Ukrainian_revolution

Cultural Shifts: Uranus-Neptune Cycle

Peaks of cultural achievement

Uranus conjunct Neptune 409-399 BC: Socrates and Plato, Paul Friedlander, Plato, An Introduction, Princeton University Press, 1958, pp.3-5.

Uranus conjunct Neptune, 66-57 BC: Beginning of Roman Golden Age, c.63 BC: http://earlyworldhistory.blogspot.com/2012/02/roman-golden-and-silver-ages.html

Uranus conjunct Neptune, 106-115 AD: Trajan's Column (113 AD) and the Pantheon (118-25): Gardner, De La Croix, Tansey, Art Through the Ages, Harcourt, Brace and World, 1970, p.219, 210.

Uranus conjunct Neptune, 790-798: Carolingian Renaissance, c.787-814: Charlemagne created schools in the Charter of Modern Thought, issued in 787; his *Admonitio Generalis* was a manifesto for cultural revival (789): https://en.wikipedia.org/wiki/Carolingian_Renaissance

Uranus conjunct Neptune, 1132-1141, See also Neptune-Pluto opposition 1142-1162: Gothic cathedrals begun. St. Denis, 1135-1144: https://en.wikipedia.org/wiki/Basilica_of_Saint-Denis . Earlier Chartres Cathedral, 1134-1160: https://en.wikipedia.org/wiki/Chartres_Cathedral#Earlier_Cathedrals . Royal west portal of Chartres c.1145-1170: Gardner, op.cit., p.338. The faces of its sculpture reveal the spirit of the times 1144, when the faithful of all classes pulled carts of building supplies to the site in unity and devotion: Clark, Civilization, p.56-58. Angkor Wat, largest temple in the world, 1113-1150: https://www.history.com/topics/landmarks/angkor-wat

Uranus conjunct Neptune, 1303-1312: Giotto's paintings in the Arena Chapel, 1305. Gardner, De La Croix and Tansey, Art Through the Ages, Harcourt, Brace and World, 1970, p.385-393. Dante began Divine Comedy, 1308: https://en.wikipedia.org/wiki/Divine_Comedy

Uranus conjunct Neptune, 1474-1483: Lorenzo de Medici ruled Florence from 1469 to 1492; Lorenzo's court included artists such as Andrea del Verrocchio, Leonardo da Vinci,

Sandro Botticelli (*Birth of Venus*, 1480), Domenico Ghirlandaio and Michelangelo Buonarroti, who were instrumental in achieving the 15th-century Renaissance. Other artists from this time and place included Messina, Mantegna and Perugino. See: https://en.wikipedia.org/wiki/Lorenzo_de%27_Medici

Uranus conjunct Neptune, 1645-1655. See also Neptune-Pluto opposition, above. Great Baroque artists: Among those mentioned by wikipedia and shown in Gardner's Art Through the Ages who created works during this conjunction are Bernini, Velasquez, Rembrandt, Hals and Poussin.
Gardner, De La Croix and Tansey, op.cit., p.552ff;
https://en.wikipedia.org/wiki/Baroque_painting Louis XIV (reign started 1643) was the most lavish patron of literature in all history, especially between 1662-1667, Will and Ariel Durant, The Story of Civilization: The Age of Louis XIV, Simon & Schuster, 1963, p.129. His minister Mazarin founded Academy of Painting and Sculpture in 1648, Ibid., p.87.

Uranus conjunct Neptune, 1816-1826: Romanticism. Paintings from this period cited in Gardner, De La Croix and Tansey, Art Through the Ages, Harcourt, Brace and World, 1970: Gericault (1818-1823), Delacroix (1822, 1826), pp.645-651. Works by Friedrich (1819, 1821), Constable (1826), and poet John Keats (1819), and the painting of Lizst and fellow romantic composers gazing dreamily at a bust of Beethoven: William Langer, ed., Richard Pipes, Western Civilization From the Struggle for Empire to Europe in the Modern World, Harper & Row, 1968, pp.360-377. Beethoven composed his masterpiece the 9th Symphony in 1822-1824: see https://en.wikipedia.org/wiki/Symphony_No._9_(Beethoven) . Lord Byron wrote *Don Juan* 1818-1823: https://en.wikipedia.org/wiki/Don_Juan_(poem) . Shelley published *Prometheus Unbound* in 1820: https://en.wikipedia.org/wiki/Prometheus_Unbound_(Shelley) On Turner, see sea and landscapes, 1801-1844, here: https://en.wikipedia.org/wiki/J._M._W._Turner.

Uranus conjunct Neptune, 1987-1997: see above for golden ages, c.1990.

International Affairs and World Order

Uranus conj. Neptune 409-399 BC: Sparta defeated Athens in Peloponnesian War in 404 BC, but declined to destroy the city as its allies demanded, returning peace to Greece, Stewart Easton, op.cit., p.45.

Uranus conj. Neptune, 238-228 BC: Ashoka, 273-232 BC: Will Durant, The Story of Civilization: Our Oriental Heritage, Simon and Schuster, 1935/1954, p.446-450. Peace made in 241 BC in First Punic War, but Truce-less War continued to 238 when Rome captured Sardinia; Corsica and Sardinia became a Roman province, 227 BC: Donald Dudley, The Civilization of Rome, Mentor Books, 1960, p.46-47. C'hin Dynasty established first Chinese Empire, 221 BC, Goodrich, op.cit., p.31-36.

Uranus conj. Neptune, 66-57 BC: Julius Caesar, Pompey, and Crassus formed the first Roman triumvirate, 60 BC, after Pompey's campaign in the Near East, Stewart C. Easton, A Brief History of the Western World, Barnes and Noble, 1966, p.72-73.

Uranus conj. Neptune, 106-115 AD: Trajan established the Roman Empire's greatest extent of power, 106-117 AD; conquest of Dacia in 106, celebrated in Trajan's Column, 113 AD, Donald R. Dudley, The Civilization of Rome, Mentor Book, 1960, p.173-174.

Uranus conj. Neptune, 276-286 AD: Aurelian loses Dacia, restored empire under sun god (274); Diocletian (284-305) saved it as an Oriental monarchy with drastic authoritarian reforms: Dudley, The Civilization of Rome, p.210-212; Easton, A Brief History of the Western World, pp.94-96.

Uranus conj. Neptune, 448-456: Attila the Hun attacked Gaul, 451, defeated by Roman/Goth alliance; died in 453, ending threat of Asian domination in Europe; Venice founded: Dudley, op.cit., p.220.
Vandals sacked Rome, 455; Roman emperors became barbarian puppets, Easton, op.cit., p.97-99.

Uranus conj. Neptune, 619-627: Tang Dynasty founded 618, L. Carrington Goodrich, A Short History of the Chinese People, Harper & Row, 1969, pp.118-142.

Uranus conj. Neptune, 790-798: Charlemagne conquered Italy and Saxony from 774-800, crowned by Pope on Christmas Day 800, Easton, op.cit., p.118-120. Jayavarman II in 790 became king of Kambuja, and founded Khmer Empire in 802 in a great religious ceremony: https://en.m.wikipedia.org/wiki/Khmer_Empire

Uranus conj. Neptune, 961-969: Sung Dynasty established, 960, Goodrich, op.cit., pp.146-163. Otto the Great restores Holy Roman Empire. Crowned in 962, Otto installed a new pope and expanded his rule in Italy, 963, Will Durant, The Story of Civilization: The Age of Faith, Simon & Schuster, 1950, p.511-512.

Uranus conj. Neptune 1303-1312: French king Philip the Fair calls Estates General, 1302; humiliates Pope in 1303, new Pope Clement V moved to Avignon, 1305, Easton, op.cit., p.159, 170-171.

Uranus conj. Neptune, 1474-1483: Edward IV of York, absolute monarch from 1471, was accused of bigamy by Richard III, who thereby deposed Edward's son in 1483; Henry Tudor defeated Richard in 1485 and established a new dynasty, thus ending the Wars of the Roses: Easton, op.cit., p.168-169.

Uranus conj. Neptune, 1645-1655: Treaty of Westphalia in 1648 ended the last religious war that developed out of the Reformation (Thirty Years War); the French achieved hegemony under Louis XIV. Dynastic great-power wars with England and its allies followed later: Easton, op.cit., pp.227-229. Westphalian principles, especially the concept of sovereign states and a balance of power, became central to international law and to the prevailing world order: https://en.wikipedia.org/wiki/Peace_of_Westphalia

Uranus square Neptune, 1692-1703: Louis XIV attacked Germany in 1688, but his invasion of England in 1692 was repelled; he supported the Stewarts against William of Orange; after a "temporary truce" with the "Grand Alliance" in 1697, he fought it again over the Spanish throne, 1701 to 1713: Will and Ariel Durant, The Story of Civilization: The Age of Louis XIV, Simon & Schuster, 1963, pp.690-715.

Uranus opposite Neptune, 1730-1743: War of Austrian Succession, 1740-1748. Frederick the Great captured rich Silesia from Austria, but elsewhere the balance of power prevailed with no other changes, Will and Ariel Durant, The Story of Civilization: The Age of Voltaire, Simon & Schuster, 1965, pp.451-457.

Uranus square Neptune, 1778-1789: Britain against France and its allies over USA independence and in various global locales. France helped the USA win, but the cost plunged the nation toward revolution, Thomas A Bailey, The American Pageant, D.C. Heath and Company, 1956, p.116-121.

Uranus conj. Neptune, 1816-1826: The Great Revolution ended with Napoleon's defeat and the Congress of Vienna in 1815, which protected the balance of power and the right of kings over peoples and nations. But revolutions broke out all over southern Europe in 1820-21. They were suppressed, but Latin America was liberated: Gordon A Craig, Europe, 1815-1914, The Dryden Press, 1972, pp. 11-27. See also Easton, A Brief History of the Western World, Barnes & Noble, 1966, pp.331-333.

Uranus square Neptune, 1863-1874: German wars of unification, Craig, op.cit., pp.209-214, 234-238. Wars of "unification" in North and South America: USA civil war and radical reconstruction, 1861-1868, Bailey, op.cit., pp.416-439, 459-482; Paraguay vs. her neighbors, 1865-1870, Easton, op.cit., p.332.

Uranus opposite Neptune, 1901-1915: Austria annexed Bosnia in 1908, setting off the Bosnian Crisis of 1908 and the Balkan Wars of 1912-13; this plus the French-German Agadir Crisis of 1911 exploded into World War I after the Serbs assassinated the Austrian heir: Craig, op.cit., pp.435-447.

Uranus square Neptune, 1949-1960: USA-Soviet Cold War: 1947 through 1956, see Bailey, op.cit., 915-931, 939-943. U2 incident, 1960: O'Neill, Coming Apart, Quadrangle/New York Times, 1971, p.16. Berlin Crisis and Berlin Wall, 1961, Ibid., p.41-43. Cuba Crisis, 1962, Ibid., pp.69-71. Israeli War of Independence 1948 and Suez Crisis 1956 began Middle East conflicts embroiling the USA, Soviets and others: https://en.wikipedia.org/wiki/Timeline_of_the_Israeli%E2%80%93Palestinian_conflict

Uranus conj. Neptune, 1988-1998: liberal revolutions of 1989 and fall of the Berlin Wall ended the Cold War, Mandela released leading to the end of apartheid in South Africa, Richard Tarnas, Cosmos and Psyche, Viking, 2006, p.421. Soviet Union broke up in 1991; many new nations: https://en.wikipedia.org/wiki/Dissolution_of_the_Soviet_Union Breakup of Yugoslavia 1991-1992; new Balkan wars and nations: https://en.wikipedia.org/wiki/Breakup_of_Yugoslavia Oslo Accords provided path to Arab-Israeli peace in 1993, although deadlocked again after 2000: https://en.wikipedia.org/wiki/Oslo_Accords
After the Persian Gulf War in 1991, President Bush pronounced it a successful test of the Post-Cold War "New World Order" in which the powers could cooperate to enforce international law: https://en.wikipedia.org/wiki/New_world_order_(politics)#Gulf_War_and_Bush's_formulation

Uranus-Neptune and Revolutions

Uranus square Neptune, 1520-1532: Peasant revolt stimulated by Luther's Reformation and printing of the New Testament, c.1522-1526, Will Durant, <u>The Story of Civilization: The Reformation</u>, Simon & Schuster, 1957, pp.381-402.

Uranus square Neptune, 1778-1789: see above under international affairs

Uranus conj. Neptune, 1816-1826: see above under international affairs

Uranus square Neptune, 1863-1874: Paris Commune, March-May 1871. After defeat to Prussia, National Guard and workers lead republican cause, troops invade Paris, government buildings burn, brutal repression, Craig, <u>Europe: 1815-1914</u>, p.317-319.

Uranus opposite Neptune, 1901-1915: China, 1900-1912: see also Uranus opposite Pluto above. The Mexican Revolution began in 1910, ended dictatorship and created a constitutional republic: https://www.britannica.com/event/Mexican-Revolution

Uranus square Neptune, 1949-1960: Uprisings in Eastern Europe against Soviet domination: East Berlin, June 1953, Poznan Poland in Summer 1956, Hungary October 1956: Langer, ed., Pipes, <u>Western Civilization, The Struggle for Empire to Europe in the Modern World</u>, Harper & Row, p.816-817.
Iraq Revolution overthrew pro-western monarchy, July 14, 1958. Easton, <u>World Since 1918</u>, p.338-339.
Cuban Revolution, Jan.1959: Sarah Janssen, general editor, <u>World Almanac</u>, Infobase, 2018, p.666.
South Vietnamese Communist insurgency began in 1957: https://alphahistory.com/vietnamwar/viet-cong/

Uranus conj. Neptune, 1988-1998: Revolutions of 1989: https://en.wikipedia.org/wiki/Revolutions_of_1989 Philippine People Power revolt, 1986: https://en.wikipedia.org/wiki/People_Power_Revolution June 1987 uprising in South Korea and democratic reforms: https://en.wikipedia.org/wiki/June_Struggle Chile transition to democracy, 1987-1989: https://en.wikipedia.org/wiki/Chilean_transition_to_democracy
See also above under international affairs.

<u>The Age of Aquarius</u>
Charles A. Jayne, "Cycles" in <u>The Encyclopedia of Astrology</u>, by Nicholas DeVore, Philosophical Library, 1947.

<u>Other cycles</u>
William Strauss and Neil Howe, <u>The Fourth Turning: What the Cycles of History Tell Us About America's Next Rendezvous with Destiny</u>, Broadway Books, 1997.

The Valley of Transition
    The Mountain or Montagnards in the French Revolution, also known as Jacobins, sat on the high tier of seats on the Left in the convention hall, Leo Gershoy, The Era of the French Revolution 1789-1799, 1957, p.56.
    The Wizard of Oz: https://en.wikipedia.org/wiki/The_Wizard_of_Oz_(1939_film)
    1939 world's fair: https://en.wikipedia.org/wiki/1939_New_York_World%27s_Fair
    Dr. Martin Luther King Jr., "I've been to the mountaintop":
https://youtu.be/aL4FOvIf7G8
https://youtu.be/xZQdANyuh34
    Al Gore calls the year 2000 a mountaintop moment:
https://www.cbsnews.com/news/gore-mountaintop-moment/

References for Chapter 3: The Supporting Guideposts
(data on aspects from https://www.astro.com/swisseph/swepha_e.htm)

Saturn-Uranus
    Saturn conj. Uranus 1805: Napoleon I invaded Eastern Europe Dec.2, 1805, extending his 2004 legal code there, Will and Ariel Durant, The Story of Civilization: The Age of Napoleon, Simon & Schuster, 1975, p.204. Saturn 24Libra51 conj. Uranus 24Libra04.
    Saturn conj. Uranus 1851: Napoleon III took power, and thereupon expanded business credit methods and sponsored public works, Dec.1851, Gordon A. Craig, Europe, 1815-1914, The Dryden Press, 1972, p. 174-75. Saturn 28Aries conj. Uranus 1Taurus
    Saturn conj. Uranus 1942: USA enters World War II, Dec.1941: Saturn 23Taurus conj. Uranus 27Taurus. How World War Two empowered women:
https://www.history.com/news/how-world-war-ii-empowered-women Jet aircraft and ballistic missiles developed:
https://en.wikipedia.org/wiki/Technology_during_World_War_II#Weaponry Post-war democracy in Western Europe: https://study.com/academy/lesson/political-reconstruction-in-europe-after-wwii-history-impact-quiz.html
    Saturn conj. Uranus 1988: In December 1988, the Supreme Soviet approved formation of the Congress of People's Deputies of the Soviet Union as its new legislative body: https://en.wikipedia.org/wiki/Demokratizatsiya_(Soviet_Union) Saturn 4Capricorn conj. Uranus 1Capricorn.

    Saturn opp. Uranus 1829-1830: Jackson Democrats win USA presidency in "Revolution of 1828", Nov.1828, Thomas A. Bailey, The American Pageant, D.C Heath and Company, 1956, p.253. Saturn 4Leo opp. Uranus in 29Capricorn. Revolutions of 1830 restored constitutional monarchy to France and Belgium, March-Dec. 1830. March: French legislature demanded dismissal of reactionary King Charles X's ministry. July: Revolution overthrew Charles: Craig, op.cit., p.28-30, p.72-73. March 1830: Saturn 12 Leo opposite Uranus 9 Aquarius. July 1830: Saturn 18 Leo still opposite Uranus 9 Aquarius.

Saturn opp. Uranus 1875: Bosnia and Herzegovina rebelled against Turkish rule, August 1875; after the war that followed, the Congress of Berlin put Bosnia under Austrian rule instead: Craig, <u>op.cit.</u>, p.252-258. Bosnia is where the assassination happened that sparked World War I. Aug.1875: Saturn 22Aquarius opposite Uranus 16Leo; square Pluto 24Taurus.

Saturn opp. Uranus 1918-1919: Revolutions in Russia and Europe between late 1917 and early 1920: Bolshevik Revolution, Nov.7, 1917, Stewart Easton, <u>World Since 1918</u>, Barnes and Noble, 1966, p.39. Nov.1917, Saturn 14Leo opposite Uranus 20Aquarius. Arab revolt against Turks, 1917-18, Easton, <u>op.cit.</u>, p.131, 200. Polish Republic proclaimed, Nov.3 1918; war with Russia April 1920; Easton, <u>op.cit.</u>, p.8. Attempted communist revolutions in Germany, Jan.1919: https://en.wikipedia.org/wiki/Spartacist_uprising Jan.1919: Saturn 27Leo opposite Uranus 26 Aquarius.

United States: Congress proposes Prohibition, Dec.18, 1917: https://en.wikipedia.org/wiki/Eighteenth_Amendment_to_the_United_States_Constitution Saturn 14Leo opp. Uranus 21Aquarius. Ratified Jan.16, 1919, Saturn 27Leo opp. Uranus 26Aquarius. Great Steel strike, Sept.1919: http://www.ohiohistorycentral.org/w/Great_Steel_Strike_of_1919 Saturn 4Virgo opp Uranus 29Aquarius. President Wilson campaigns for League of Nations and collapses, Sept.1919; Versailles Treaty and League of Nations rejected by the Senate, March 19, 1920: Bailey, <u>The American Pageant.</u>, p.757-760. Saturn 7Virgo opp. Uranus 3Pisces.

Saturn opp. Uranus 1965-1966: In United States, "Black Sunday" in Selma AL, March 7, LBJ introduces voting rights act, March 17, 1965, William L. O'Neill, <u>Coming Apart, An Informal History of America in the 1960s</u>, Quadrangle/New York Times, 1971, p.169-170; https://en.wikipedia.org/wiki/Voting_Rights_Act_of_1965 Saturn 9Pisces opp. Uranus 12Virgo.

USA Anti-war Movement launched on March 24, 1965: William L. O'Neill, <u>op.cit.</u>, pp.141-146. Saturn 11Pisces opp. Uranus 12Virgo and Pluto 15Virgo. Pro-Western coup in Ghana, Feb.24, 1966: https://en.wikipedia.org/wiki/Lebanese_Civil_War#First_phase_1975%E2%80%9377 Saturn 18Pisces opposite Uranus 18Virgo and Pluto 17Virgo. Nigeria coup Jan.15, 1966; leads to civil war in 1967: https://en.wikipedia.org/wiki/1966_Nigerian_coup_d%27%C3%A9tat Saturn 14Pisces opposite Uranus 19Virgo and Pluto 18Virgo.

Saturn opp. Uranus 2008-2010 (see also Uranus sq. Pluto 2007-2020): Great Recession began in Sept.2008: https://www.thebalance.com/the-great-recession-of-2008-explanation-with-dates-4056832 Barack Obama elected first black president of USA, Nov.4, 2008, see: https://en.wikipedia.org/wiki/Tea_Party_movement#Commentaries_on_origin Nov.4, 2008: Saturn 19Virgo opp. Uranus 19Pisces, also just 2 days before Pluto entered Capricorn on Nov.6, 2008.

Tea Party Movement opposes Obama stimulus and Obamacare, c.Feb.2009, see: https://en.wikipedia.org/wiki/Tea_Party_movement#Health_care_bill Saturn 20Virgo opp.

Uranus 21Pisces. Iranians rebel in their "green revolution" over their election, June 2009 – Feb.2010: https://en.wikipedia.org/wiki/2009_Iranian_presidential_election_protests Saturn opp. Uranus started again in June 2009 and ended (for a while) in Dec.2009; exact in Sept.2009.

Greeks rebel against austerity, as debt crisis threatens Euro, May 5, 2010: https://www.britannica.com/topic/euro-zone-debt-crisis May 5, 2010: Saturn 28Virgo opp. Uranus 29Pisces, sq. Pluto 5 Capricorn.

Saturn square Uranus 1793-1794: Vendee revolt and civil war during French Revolution, March-Dec. 1793: https://en.wikipedia.org/wiki/War_in_the_Vend%C3%A9e July 1793: Saturn 14Taurus sq. Uranus 22Leo. Reign of Terror at peak, c.June 15-July 27, 1794, Gershoy, The Era of the French Revolution, Van Norstrand Co., 1957, p.67: exact T-square of Saturn 26Taurus, Uranus 26Leo and Pluto 26Aquarius, July 7.

Saturn square Uranus 1861: North American Civil War Began April 12, 1861, Bailey, The American Pageant, p.418: Saturn 3Virgo sq. Uranus 9Gemini.

Saturn square Uranus 1975: Lebanon civil war erupted Oct-Dec 1975: https://en.wikipedia.org/wiki/Lebanese_Civil_War#First_phase_1975%E2%80%9377 Oct 5, 1975: Saturn 1Leo sq. Uranus 1Scorpio.

Saturn-Neptune

Saturn conj. Neptune 1773: Committees of Correspondence organized, forerunner of first congress in 1774, Boston Tea Party Dec.16, 1773, British responded with repression, Thomas A. Bailey, The American Pageant, D.C. Heath and Company, 1956, p.95-97: Saturn 26Virgo conj. Neptune 21Virgo.

Saturn conj. Neptune 1809: Abraham Lincoln born Feb.12, 1809: https://www.astro.com/astro-databank/Lincoln,_Abraham Saturn 3Sagittarius conj. Neptune 7Sagittarius.

Saturn conj. Neptune 1846-1847: Fall of 1847, Marx writing Communist Manifesto (completed in Jan.1848), Craig, Europe 1815-1914, p.272: Saturn 6Pisces conj. Neptune 28Aquarius

Saturn conj. Neptune 1881-1882: Franklin D. Roosevelt born Jan.30, 1882, Ellen McCaffery, Graphic Astrology, Macoy Publishing Company, 1952, p.183: Saturn 6Taurus conj. Neptune 13Taurus.

Saturn conj. Neptune 1917: Bolshevik Revolution, Nov.7, 1917, Stewart Easton, World Since 1918, p.39. Saturn 14Leo conj. Neptune 7Leo. John K. Kennedy born May 29, 1917: Astarte, Astrology Made Easy, Wilshire Book Company, 1967, p.140-141: Saturn 27Cancer conj. Neptune 3Leo.

Saturn conj. Neptune 1953: Stalin died in March 1953, more liberal regime followed, William Langer, ed., Richard Pipes, Western Civilization: The Struggle for Empire to Europe in the Modern World, Harper & Row, 1968, p.811-812: Saturn 26Libra conj. Neptune 23Libra. CIA-backed coup deposed democratically-elected prime minister

Mosaddegh in Iran, August 19, 1953:
https://en.wikipedia.org/wiki/1953_Iranian_coup_d%27%C3%A9tat Saturn 23 Libra conj.
Neptune 22 Libra, square Uranus 21 Cancer. In 1953, Senator Joseph McCarthy began
hearings into Communist infiltration of the US army:
https://en.wikipedia.org/wiki/Army%E2%80%93McCarthy_hearings

   Saturn conj. Neptune 1989: Soviet Empire in Eastern Europe collapsed, Berlin Wall
fell Nov.9, 1989: https://www.history.com/topics/cold-war/fall-of-the-berlin-wall-video
Saturn 10Capricorn conj. Neptune 10Capricorn, also opp. Jupiter 10Cancer. Outbreak of
"velvet revolution" that overthrew Communist rule in Czechoslovakia, Nov.17, 1989:
https://en.wikipedia.org/wiki/Velvet_Revolution

   Saturn opp. Neptune 1792: French king overthrown August 10, 1792, etc., Gershoy,
The Era of the French Revolution, D. Van Norstrand Company, 1957, pp.47-49: Saturn
2Taurus opp. Neptune 27Libra. French king overthrown Aug.10, Francois Furet and Denis
Richet, French Revolution, The Macmillan Company, 1965/1970, p.143-144. Massacres
Sept.2-5, Ibid., p.156-159. Valmy and Goethe, Sept.20, Ibid., p.158-159. Year I of the
Republic declared Sept.22, Ibid., p.162: Sept.22, Saturn 1Taurus opp. Neptune 29Libra.
   Saturn opp. Neptune 1862: American War Between the States. Battle of Antietam
Sept.17, Bailey, op.cit., p.432: Saturn 26Virgo opp. Neptune 3Aries. Gettysburg, Ibid.,
p.437: Saturn 29Virgo opp. Neptune 6Aries.
   Saturn opp. Neptune 1936-1937: Spanish Civil War, outbreak July 17, 1936, Felix
Gilbert, The End of the European Era, 1890 to the Present, W.W. Norton and Company,
1970, p.259: Saturn 22Pisces opp. Neptune 15Virgo. C.I.O. sit-down strikes win General
Motors contract, late 1936, Bailey, op.cit., p.847: Saturn 16Pisces opp. Neptune 19Virgo.
   Saturn opp. Neptune 1971-1972: June 13, Pentagon Papers history of US-Vietnam
War leaked in order to end the war: https://en.wikipedia.org/wiki/Pentagon_Papers#Leak
Saturn 29Taurus opp. Neptune 1Sagittarius. White House "plumbers" forms to discredit
Daniel Ellsberg who leaked the Papers:
https://en.wikipedia.org/wiki/White_House_Plumbers Members of the Plumbers carried
out Watergate burglary against Democratic Party headquarters, June 17, 1972, resulting in
scandal: https://en.wikipedia.org/wiki/Watergate_scandal Saturn 12Gemini opp. Neptune 3
Sagittarius.
   Saturn opp. Neptune 2005-2007: Hurricane Katrina, Aug.25-29, World Almanac 2018
p.321; helped ignite concern over global warming. Al Gore released *An Inconvenient Truth*
in May, 2006; won Nobel Peace Prize 2007:
https://en.wikipedia.org/wiki/An_Inconvenient_Truth Academy Award:
https://youtu.be/JUVqUz8m2PQ

   Saturn square Neptune 1979: Islamic Revolution in Iran, Aug.1978-Jan 1979.
Theocracy established April 1979: https://en.wikipedia.org/wiki/Iranian_Revolution
Jan.1979: Saturn 14Virgo sq. Neptune 19Sagittarius. US hostages taken, Nov.4, 1979:
https://en.wikipedia.org/wiki/Iran_hostage_crisis Saturn 24Virgo sq. Neptune 19Sagittarius.

Jonestown cult suicide/massacre, Nov.18, 1978: https://www.history.com/topics/crime/jonestown World Almanac 2018, p.782. Saturn 13Virgo sq. Neptune 17Sagittarius.

Saturn square Neptune 1998: 1998 was the hottest year on record until 2016: https://www.sciencedaily.com/releases/2017/01/170104130257.htm Hurricane Mitch, second deadliest hurricane on record, c.Nov.1, 1998: World Almanac 2018, p.321, https://en.wikipedia.org/wiki/Hurricane_Mitch Saturn 29Aries sq. Neptune 29Capricorn. June 2016: Saturn 12Sagittarius sq. Neptune 12Pisces. Worldwatch says 1998 was record year for weather disasters. http://www.combusem.com/WWR.HTM

Saturn-Pluto

Saturn conj. Pluto 1914: Final crisis and outbreak of World War I, June 28-Aug.6, 1914, Stewart Easton, A Brief History of the Western World, Barnes and Noble, 1966, p.350-351. Aug.1: Saturn 28Gemini conj. Pluto 2 Cancer.

Saturn opp. Pluto 1931: Japan had designs on China in Jan.1915 (Saturn conj. Pluto), and started its conquest in Sept.1931 by invading Manchuria, Stewart Easton, World Since 1918, Barnes and Noble, 1966, pp. 185, 400: Saturn 17Capricorn opp. Pluto 22Cancer.

Saturn square Pluto 1939: Hitler's Germany invaded Poland, beginning World War Two, Easton, op.cit., p.219-220. Saturn 1Taurus sq. Pluto 2Leo.

Saturn conj. Pluto 1947-48: President Truman began containment policy against Soviet Union, March 12, 1947, Langer, ed., Richard Pipes, Western Civilization: The Struggle for Empire to Europe in the Western World, Harper & Row, 1968, p.804-805. Saturn 2Leo conj. Pluto 11Leo. Berlin Blockade, June 24, 1948 to May 1949, Felix Gilbert, The End of the European Era, 1890 to the Present, W.W. Norton Co., 1970, p.349-50. Saturn 19Leo conj. Pluto 13Leo. Israeli War of Independence against Arabs in Palestine, May 1948, Easton, World Since 1918, p.337, 403. Saturn 16Leo conj. Pluto 12Leo

Saturn square Pluto 1956: Suez Crisis. Egypt took over canal; Israelis, British and French attacked Egypt, Oct.1956, Stewart Easton, World Since 1918, p.337,403. Saturn 29Scorpio square Pluto 29Leo. Soviets invaded Hungary to quell revolution against them there, Nov.4, 1956: https://www.britannica.com/event/Hungarian-Revolution-1956 Saturn 3Sagittarius sq. Pluto 1Virgo.

Saturn opp. Pluto 1965-1966: USA bombed Vietnam, Feb 7, 1965, O'Neill, Coming Apart, p.131-138; Easton, World Since 1918, p.368-370. March 2, U.S. launched continuous bombing: https://www.history.com/topics/vietnam-war/vietnam-war-timeline#section_4 Marines land near Da Nang March 9: https://www.history.com/this-day-in-history/u-s-marines-land-at-da-nang   Saturn 9Pisces opp. Pluto 15Virgo. First US ground offensive, August 18, 1965: http://www.historyplace.com/unitedstates/vietnam/index-1965.html Saturn 16Pisces opp Pluto 15Virgo. April 28, 1965, US troops landed in Dominican Republic, O'Neill, op.cit., p.138-140: Saturn 14Pisces opp. Pluto 14Virgo.

Saturn square Pluto 1973: Yom Kippur Arab-Israeli War Oct.6-24, 1973. Janssen, ed., World Almanac 2018, p.789. Arab oil embargo caused energy crisis: https://en.wikipedia.org/wiki/1973_oil_crisis Saturn 5Cancer square Pluto 5Libra

Saturn conj. Pluto 1982: Israel invaded Lebanon, June 6, 1982, World Almanac 2018, p.789. Saturn 16Libra conj. Pluto 24Libra. US peacekeeping force sent to Lebanon, Aug.25, 1982: https://en.wikipedia.org/wiki/Multinational_Force_in_Lebanon Saturn 19Libra conj. Pluto 25Libra.

US marines and French soldiers massacred there Oct.23, 1983; hostages taken, World Almanac 2018, p.798. Saturn 6Scorpio conj. Pluto 29Libra.

Saturn square Pluto 1993: World Trade Center in New York bombed by Islamic terrorists, Feb.26, 1993: https://en.wikipedia.org/wiki/1993_World_Trade_Center_bombing Saturn 23Aquarius sq. Pluto 25Scorpio.

Saturn opp. Pluto 2001: Sept.11, 2001 attacks on World Trade Center Twin Towers and Pentagon, World Almanac 2018, p. 449; https://en.wikipedia.org/wiki/September_11_attacks Saturn 15Gemini opp. Pluto 13Sagittarius. US attacks Afghanistan Oct 7, World Almanac 2018, p.449. Saturn 15Gemini opp. Pluto 13 Sagittarius. Sagittarius "shoots his arrows" at the Gemini "Twins." US attacks Iraq, March 19, 2003: https://en.wikipedia.org/wiki/2003_invasion_of_Iraq Saturn 22Gemini opp. Pluto 20Sagittarius. Saturn conj. US Mars position.

Saturn sq. Pluto 2011: March 15, civil and proxy war began in Syria; also Libya, Yemen, Bahrain, World Almanac 2018, Syria, p.839; Libya p.799; Yemen p.851-52. March 15: Saturn 15Libra sq. Pluto 7Capricorn; got closer as Spring went on; in May: Saturn 11Libra sq. Pluto 7Capricorn. The aspect was over by the time ousted Libyan leader Qaddafi was killed in Oct.2011.

Saturn conj. Pluto 2019: June 2018, Erdogen won Turkish elections and consolidates power: https://time.com/5320864/recep-tayyip-erdogan-turkey-election-referendum/ Xi Jinping becomes president of China for life, March 2018: https://en.wikipedia.org/wiki/Xi_Jinping#Removal_of_term_limits Far right Bolsonaro wins Brazil elections late Oct.2018: https://www.bbc.com/news/world-latin-america-46013408   May 2019, reactionary Scott Morrison won Australia elections: https://www.cnn.com/2019/05/18/world/australia-election-scott-morrison-intl/index.html Reactionary Boris Johnson becomes Prime Minister of UK, July 24, 2019; pushes Brexit, suspends Parliament in late August: https://en.wikipedia.org/wiki/Boris_Johnson#Premiership March 2018: Saturn 8Capricorn, Pluto 21Capricorn. May 2019: Saturn 20Capricorn conj. Pluto 23Capricorn. More to come in 2020…..

<u>Jupiter-Uranus</u>

Jupiter conj. Uranus 1775: April 19, 1775, Battles of Lexington and Concord, the "shot heard round the world."-- Bailey, <u>The American Pageant</u>, p.98. https://www.history.com/topics/american-revolution/battles-of-lexington-and-concord Jupiter 22Taurus conj. Uranus 1Gemini. Battle of Bunker Hill, June 17, 1775; George III proclaims the colonies in rebellion: Bailey, <u>op.cit.</u>, p.105: Jupiter 5Gemini conj. Uranus 4Gemini.

Jupiter conj. Uranus 1789: June 17, National Assembly declared, Leo Gershoy, <u>The Era of the French Revolution</u>, p.31. Jupiter 1Leo conj. Uranus 3Leo. Fall of the Bastille July 14, 1789, new city governments, new militias, peasants storm manor houses; <u>Ibid.</u>, p.35: Jupiter 6Leo conj. Uranus 4Leo. August 4, old regime privileges renounced, Declaration of Rights Aug.27, <u>Ibid.</u>, p.36-37.

Jupiter conj. Uranus 1831: Massive unrest spurs British Great Reform Bill Oct 1831, passed in June 1832, Craig, <u>Europe, 1815-1914</u>, p.103. Oct.1831: Jupiter 12Aquarius conj. Uranus 11Aquarius.

Jupiter conj. Uranus 1844: May 1844, first telegraph message, Bailey, <u>op.cit.</u>, p.317. Jupiter 29Pisces conj. Uranus 5Aries. The invention is then rapidly accepted.

Jupiter conj. Uranus 1886: On May 1, 1886 half a million workers held strikes and rallies across the USA for an eight-hour day. At Haymarket Square in Chicago on May 4, a bomb thrown at police dispersing a big rally killed seven, and deadly gunfire ensued. Four "anarchists" were executed as scapegoats. International labor parties called a successful worldwide demonstration on May 1, 1890 partly in honor of the Haymarket martyrs, thus establishing International Workers' Day. According to Professor William J. Adelman, no single event influenced the history of labor more than the Haymarket Affair. https://en.wikipedia.org/wiki/Haymarket_affair May 4: Jupiter 27Virgo conj. Uranus 4Libra

Jupiter conj. Uranus 1900: Max Planck presented the thesis of quantum theory: Felix Gilbert, <u>The End of the European Era</u>, W.W. Norton, 1970, p.320-321. Freud discovers the power of the unconscious, <u>Ibid.</u>, p.317. Jupiter conj. Uranus in Sagittarius, all year.

Jupiter conj. Uranus 1927: Lindbergh's first so transatlantic flight on May 20 stirs huge mass enthusiasm and hero worship for Lucky Lindy, and boosts aviation, Frederick Lewis Allen, <u>Only Yesterday</u>, Harper & Row, 1931, p.180-181; Bailey, <u>op.cit.</u>, p.815-816: Jupiter in 27Pisces conj. Uranus in 2Aries. See also discovery of Pluto, above, regarding quantum theory.

Jupiter conj. Uranus 1968-1969: December 1968, first flight around the Moon by Apollo 8, Dec.21-25, 1968; first Moon landing, July 20, 1969, <u>World Almanac 2018</u>, p.327: Dec.1968, Jupiter 5Libra conj. Uranus 4Libra. July 20, 1969: Jupiter 1Libra conj. Uranus 1Libra. Woodstock Festival, Aug.15, 1969, O'Neill, <u>Coming Apart</u>, p.259-260. "No-one had ever seen such a large and ruly gathering before." Influenced by the be-ins and love-ins of the previous two years, it was the prototype for many more "Aquarian" festivals, communities, movements and gatherings of varying quality for decades to come, and it spread togetherness among youth across the land, especially in its era. Jupiter 5Libra conj. Uranus 2Libra.

Jupiter conj. Uranus 2011: Jan. 2011, Tunisia Revolution sparked the Arab Spring revolts. They were a big deal, but they only really went well in January and February while Jupiter was aligned with the ongoing Uranus square to Pluto; see above under that aspect for references. Jan 4: Jupiter conj. Uranus 27Pisces during solar eclipse that day.

Jupiter opp. Uranus 1962: John Glenn, Feb.20, made the first American orbital flight in space and became a hero like Charles Lindbergh in 1927 (see above). His flights and those of his fellow astronauts in the early sixties became as closely watched as Lindbergh's flight in his time, and helped stimulate the space program, O'Neill, op.cit., p.51-54: Jupiter 22 Aquarius opposite Uranus 28Leo.

Jupiter opp. Uranus, 1989: Revolution in Romania Dec.16-27, https://en.wikipedia.org/wiki/Romanian_Revolution Jupiter 6Cancer opp. Uranus 5Capricorn. See also Saturn conj. Neptune 1989.

Jupiter opp. Uranus 2017: In 2019, wikipedia listed the 2017 "Women's March" on March 21 in Washington and across the country to protest President Trump's inauguration as the largest demonstration in United States history, and it became an annual event. It was preceded by more-unruly protests on January 20, also in many places. https://en.wikipedia.org/wiki/List_of_protests_in_the_United_States_by_size https://en.wikipedia.org/wiki/2017_Women%27s_March Jupiter 23Libra opp. Uranus 21Aries.

Jupiter-Neptune

Jupiter conj. Neptune 1792: Marseillaise march July 14-29; King Louis XVI overthrown, Aug.10, 1792, inspired romantic movement, Kenneth Clark, Civilization, Harper and Row, 1969, p.296. The volunteers departed for Paris July 14, singing a new song that became the French National Anthem in 1795, https://en.wikipedia.org/wiki/1812_Overture#Anachronism_of_nationalist_motifs , which was the most "fortunate composition ever promulgated" according to Thomas Carlyle, The French Revolution, The Modern Library, 1837, p.444. July 14: Mars 13Libra conj. Jupiter 23Libra conj. Neptune 27Libra. Aug.10: Mars 28Libra conj. Jupiter 26Libra conj. Neptune 27Libra. "Strong to love" indeed: Clark, Ibid.

Jupiter conj. Neptune 1805: Napoleon went off to battle against the new Third Coalition completed on June 17, 1805: Jupiter 28Scorpio conj. Neptune 26Scorpio; on Sept.25 his new Grand Armee of 200,000 crossed the Rhine: https://en.wikipedia.org/wiki/Battle_of_Austerlitz#Preliminary_moves Every town on the way wished him well, Will and Ariel Durant, The Story of Civilization: The Age of Napoleon, Simon & Schuster, 1975, p.202-203. Sept.25: Jupiter 2Sagittarius conj. Neptune 26Scorpio. Battle of Austerlitz Dec.2: see Saturn conj. Uranus 1805 above. Mars joined

Neptune in Scorpio and then Jupiter in Sagittarius during the Battle of Ulm in October. "Sublime" indeed: Kenneth Clark, <u>Civilization</u>, p.307-308.

Jupiter conj. Neptune 1907: the Hague Conventions were among the first formal statements of the laws of war and war crimes in the body of secular international law. The first called by Tsar Nicholas II was held May-July 1899, as Saturn in Sagittarius opposed Neptune in Gemini. The Second Peace Conference called by Theodore Roosevelt was held from 15 June to 18 October 1907, and built on the first with more major powers involved: June 15:
https://en.wikipedia.org/wiki/Hague_Conventions_of_1899_and_1907#Hague_Convention _of_1899 Jupiter 16Cancer conj. Neptune 12Cancer.

Jupiter conj. Neptune 1920: League of Nations founded, January 1920, Easton, <u>World Since 1918</u>, p.402, 14-18. Jupiter 15Leo conj. Neptune 11Leo.

Jupiter conj. Neptune 1933: March 4, 1933, Franklin D. Roosevelt took office and began the Hundred Days reform congress, Bailey, <u>The American Pageant</u>, pp.834-846. The planets turn stationary-direct c. May 10-20, with Jupiter at 13 Virgo conj. Neptune at 7 Virgo and joined by Mars.

Jupiter conj. Neptune 1945: Establishment of the United Nations, Oct.24, 1945, Easton, op.cit., p.403, 249. October 24: Venus 6Libra conj. Jupiter 13Libra conj. Neptune 7Libra.

Jupiter conj. Neptune 1971: On July 15, 1971, President Richard Nixon spoke to the nation and announced he would visit Communist China, marking a turning point in American-Chinese relations:
https://www.politico.com/story/2016/07/nixon-announces-visit-to-communist-china-july-15-1971-225379
Jupiter 27Scorpio conj. Neptune 1 Sagittarius, opp. Saturn 3 Gemini.

Jupiter conj. Neptune 1984: Oct.1984, Bob Geldof decided to record a charity song with a new supergroup Band Aid, *Do They Know it's Christmas?*, after seeing reports of famine in Ethiopia: https://www.rollingstone.com/music/music-news/do-they-know-its-christmas-band-aid-1984-geldof-761428/ Jupiter at about 6Capricorn conj. Neptune 29Sagittarius. After they recorded the song in November Jupiter orbited on beyond the conjunction, but it became the best-selling single in the UK up to that time: https://en.wikipedia.org/wiki/Bob_Geldof#Band_Aid and the basis for the benefit concert Live Aid in July 1985, one of the biggest stage shows ever held.

Jupiter conj. Neptune 2009: Affordable Care Act. Since Jupiter was conj. Neptune continuously from March 2009 through February 2010, I thought that this "Obamacare" bill would pass. It took even longer, and passed by the skin of its teeth. New USA President Obama proposed February 2009 to work with Congress for healthcare reform. By July, House of Representatives committees approved the bills. From June to September the Senate developed its watered-down version. The House passed the Senate bill with a 219–212 vote on March 21, 2010:
https://en.wikipedia.org/wiki/Patient_Protection_and_Affordable_Care_Act#Healthcare_d ebate,_2008%E2%80%9310

Jupiter opp. Neptune 1964-65: Civil Rights Act of 1964 passed in June 19: https://en.wikipedia.org/wiki/Civil_Rights_Act_of_1964#Passage_in_the_Senate War on Poverty programs in August 1964, Medicare passed on July 27-30, 1965, https://www.senate.gov/artandhistory/history/minute/Medicare_Signed_Into_Law.htm , and other Great Society programs were passed in 1965 and 1966: Carman, Syrett, Wishy, A History of the American People Volume II, Alfred A Knopf, 1967, pp.793-797: June 19, 1964, Jupiter 15Taurus opp. Neptune 15Scorpio; in conjunction through April 1965.

Jupiter T-square Neptune and Mars, starting early May 1968: French student-worker strike, "greatest popular insurrection ever experienced by a capitalist democracy in peacetime," David Caute, The Year of the Barricades: A Journey Through 1968, pp.211-255. May 3: Mars 26Taurus, sq. Jupiter 26Leo, sq. Neptune 26Scorpio.

Jupiter opp. Neptune 1989: Soviet Empire in Eastern Europe collapsed; Berlin Wall fell Nov.9, 1989: https://www.history.com/topics/cold-war/fall-of-the-berlin-wall-video Jupiter 10Cancer opp. Neptune 10Capricorn, conj. Saturn 10Capricorn.

Jupiter opp. Neptune 2003: On February 15, 2003, protests across the world in more than 600 cities expressed opposition to the imminent Iraq War; social movement researchers have described the 15 February protest as "the largest protest event in human history"-- https://en.m.wikipedia.org/wiki/15_February_2003_anti-war_protests Jupiter 11Leo opp. Neptune 11Aquarius.

Jupiter-Pluto

Jupiter conj. Pluto 1918: accelerating toward the end of World War I, July 1918, Gilbert, End of the European Era, p.128-129. Second Battle of the Marne reversed last German Offensive, July 15-Aug.6: https://en.wikipedia.org/wiki/Second_Battle_of_the_Marne Jupiter 1Cancer conj. Pluto 5Cancer.

Jupiter conj. Pluto 1931: The Creditanstalt of Austria collapsed on May 11, sending shockwaves throughout Europe and quickly spreading the Great Depression, Gilbert, op.cit., p.209; https://en.wikipedia.org/wiki/Creditanstalt#First_Republic May 11: Jupiter 16Cancer conj. Pluto 19Cancer.

Jupiter conj. Pluto 1943: July 12-24, Battle of Kursk ends German offensives in Russia, enormous tank battle and casualties: https://www.history.com/topics/world-war-ii/battle-of-kursk#section_7 Jupiter 2Leo conj. Pluto 6Leo.

Jupiter conj. Pluto 1968-1969, also conj. Uranus: End of August, violent Democratic convention, protesters beaten, peace faction loses, Caute, The Year of the Barricades, p.294-323. Jupiter 14Virgo conj. Pluto 22Virgo. The conjunction was exact in October. During that Fall campaign, students continually heckled Democratic Party nominee Humphrey at almost every appearance, while American Independent Party candidate George Wallace insulted hippies and taunted the protesters who blocked Johnson's and

Humphrey's car by saying "If any anarchists lie down in front of my automobile, it will be the last automobile they ever lie down in front of"--.
https://www.theatlantic.com/ideas/archive/2018/06/incivility-vietnam-protests/563837/
https://en.wikipedia.org/wiki/George_Wallace_1968_presidential_campaign Some campus revolts, and People's Park rebellion at Berkeley, May 1969, Tarnas, Cosmos and Psyche, Viking, 2006, p.303. May 1969: Jupiter 26Virgo conj. Pluto 22Virgo.

Jupiter opp. Pluto 1975: accelerating toward the end of USA-Vietnam War, March 10 - April 30, 1975: https://en.wikipedia.org/wiki/1975_Spring_Offensive March 10: Jupiter 28Pisces opp. Pluto 8Libra. April 30: Jupiter 10Aries opp. Pluto 7Libra, sq. Saturn 14Cancer.

Jupiter conj. Pluto 2007: April 2007: New Century, a sub-prime mortgage investor trust, went bankrupt, spreading sub-prime crisis to banks around the world. October 9, 2007: The Dow Jones Industrial Average hit its peak closing price. Existing home sales began to decline. April: Jupiter conj. Pluto began, and was exact in Dec., but was over by Feb.2008. https://en.wikipedia.org/wiki/Financial_crisis_of_2007%E2%80%932008

Jupiter opp. Pluto 2013-2014: USA Syria Crisis over chemical weapons, August 2013, See World Almanac 2018, p.839. Islamic State (IS) captures Raqqa in Syria, and Fallujah and much of Anbar Province in Western Iraq, in January 2014, IS attacks and captures Eastern Syria territories April-June: https://en.wikipedia.org/wiki/Deir_ez-Zor_offensive_(April%E2%80%93July_2014) June 4, IS invaded Iraq and captured Mosul on June 10: https://en.wikipedia.org/wiki/Fall_of_Mosul
Revolution in Ukraine in Feb.2014 overthrew its Russian backed leader; Russia annexed Crimea in March, and civil war between Ukraine and Russian-backed rebels broke out that month in Eastern Ukraine: https://en.wikipedia.org/wiki/2014_Ukrainian_revolution
It's complicated! Jupiter opp. Pluto began in July 2013, exact in August. Jupiter retrograded back into opposition to Pluto starting in late November 2013, and back into its square to Uranus in December. c.Jan.10: Jupiter 15Cancer, Pluto 10Cancer, Uranus 9Aries, Mars 15Libra. Mars stationary-retrograde March 1, 27Libra. April 21: Jupiter 14Cancer, Pluto 14Capricorn, Uranus 14Aries, Mars 14Libra. Mars stationary-direct May 20, 9Libra. June 4: Jupiter 21Cancer opp. Pluto 13Capricorn, sq. Uranus 16Aries, sq. Mars 10Libra.

References for Chapter 12: Predicting Presidential Elections

Jupiter and Saturn

Presidents who died in office:
https://en.wikipedia.org/wiki/List_of_presidents_of_the_United_States_who_died_in_office

The Saturn Return

Saturn transits:

Michelson, Neil F. The American Ephemeris for the 20th Century. ACS Publications, 1983
Michelson, Neil F. The American Ephemeris for the 21st Century. ACS Publications, 1982
Rosicrucian Fellowship, Simplified Scientific Ephemeris, 1880s to 1990s
Stahlman and Gingerich, Solar and Planetary Longitudes for Years -2500 – 2000,
University of Wisconsin, 1963.
Swiss Ephemeris, provided by Astrodienst. https://www.astro.com/swisseph/swepha_e.htm

Historical references:

Thomas A Bailey, The American Pageant, D.C. Heath and Company, 1956, is a go-to
source for confirming the history of presidential administrations. I also refer to Carman,
Syrett and Wishy, A History of the American People, Volume II, Alfred A Knopf,
1952/1967. Later events can be referred to wikipedia and other websites. Page numbers
below refer to the Bailey work unless otherwise noted. References to Carman, Syrett and
Wishy are noted as CSW.

John Tyler's rocky term is described on pp.280-282.
Andrew Johnson's resisted radical Reconstruction, 468-482. Also see CSW pp. 29-34
Public unrest under Benjamin Harrison unseated him, p.591.
Grover Cleveland saddled with financial panic, and a revolt which he tried to repress,
pp.592-98.
McKinley's debacle in The Philippines is covered on pp. 623-628. Also CSW pp.294-
298.
Taft's sponsor Theodore Roosevelt rejected and ran against him. p.667, 679-680. Also
see CSW, pp.441-445.
Wilson's stroke while campaigning for the League of Nations, pp.757-760. CSW p.518.
Harding died under the strain of scandal, pp.784-785.
Coolidge declares he will not run in 1928. p. 804.
FDR died under strains of WWII, p.895, 898.
LBJ drops out of 1968 presidential race under the strains of the War in Vietnam and
protests against it. Speech announcing he won't run again: "Johnson, Lyndon B.," Vietnam
War Reference Library, Encyclopedia.com. https://www.history.com/news/lbj-exit-1968-
presidential-race
Richard Nixon: Pentagon Papers and Plumbers:
https://en.wikipedia.org/wiki/White_House_Plumbers
Richard Nixon: Watergate, resignation, and pardon by Ford:
https://en.wikipedia.org/wiki/Watergate_scandal
George W. Bush: Sept.11 attack by Al Qaeda: https://www.history.com/topics/21st-
century/9-11-attacks

George W. Bush: Attack on Iraq in 2003:
https://www.history.com/this-day-in-history/war-in-iraq-begins
George W. Bush mishandled Katrina: https://www.usnews.com/news/the-report/articles/2015/08/28/hurricane-katrina-was-the-beginning-of-the-end-for-george-w-bush
https://www.vanityfair.com/news/2015/08/hurricane-katrina-george-w-bush-new-orleans
George W. Bush: financial crash of 2008 and the Great Recession
https://en.wikipedia.org/wiki/Economic_policy_of_the_George_W._Bush_administration#Financial_crisis_and_Great_Recession

Connections to the USA Horoscope

Teddy Roosevelt's Big Stick: Bailey, The American Pageant, pp. 635-649

George H W Bush "overcome the Vietnam syndrome" and got us into wars again
https://thevietnamwar.info/vietnam-syndrome/

Thomas Jefferson quote: a little rebellion is a good thing every now and then:
from letter by Thomas Jefferson to James Madison, Paris, January 30, 1787
http://www.thisdayinquotes.com/2010/01/little-rebellion-now-and-then-is-good.html
Also: Bailey, The American Pageant, p.163.

Barack Obama tried to clean up the international mess left by George W. Bush. Some opinions that agree with mine on this:
https://www.salon.com/2014/06/16/sorry_george_w_bush_but_this_whole_mess_is_still_your_fault/ http://www.pbs.org/now/shows/503/bush-legacy.html

Obamacare: https://en.wikipedia.org/wiki/Patient_Protection_and_Affordable_Care_Act

Donald Trump promised to build a wall and make America great again through tough deal-making.
https://en.wikipedia.org/wiki/Make_America_Great_Again
76 of Donald Trump's many appealing campaign promises:
https://www.washingtonpost.com/news/post-politics/wp/2016/01/22/here-are-76-of-donald-trumps-many-campaign-promises/ including #1 to build a wall on the southern USA border and #45 to replace free trade with fair trade.
Trump is trying to fulfill his promise to be a deal maker around the world.
https://www.cnn.com/2019/05/11/politics/trump-deal-maker-image-2020-voters-base/index.html

List of Books Cited in this Appendix:

Frederick Lewis Allen, <u>Only Yesterday</u>, Harper & Row, 1931

Astarte, <u>Astrology Made Easy</u>, Wilshire Book Company, 1967

Thomas A Bailey, <u>The American Pageant</u>, D.C. Heath and Company, 1956

Don Beck, <u>Spiral Dynamics</u>, John Wiley and Sons Ltd., 2005

Clive Bell, <u>Art</u>, Capricorn Books, 1913/1958

Frtiz Brunhubner, <u>Pluto</u>, American Federation of Astrologers, 1934, 1966

Thomas Carlyle, <u>The French Revolution</u>, The Modern Library, 1837

Harry J. Carman, Harold C. Syrett, Bernard W. Wishy, <u>A History of the American People, Volume II</u>, Alfred A. Knopf, 1952/1967

David Caute, <u>The Year of the Barricades: A Journey Through 1968</u>, Harper and Row, 1988

Kenneth Clark, <u>Civilization</u>, Harper and Row, 1969

Gordon A. Craig, <u>Europe, 1815-1914</u>, The Dryden Press, 1972

Wm. Theodore De Bary, ed., <u>Sources of Indian Tradition Volume I</u>, Columbia University Press, 1958

Donald R. Dudley, <u>The Civilization of Rome</u>, Mentor Book, New American Library, 1960

Will Durant, <u>The Story of Civilization: Our Oriental Heritage</u>, Simon & Schuster, 1935/1954

Will Durant, <u>The Story of Civilization, The Life of Greece</u>, Simon and Schuster, 1939

Will Durant, <u>The Story of Civilization: Caesar and Christ</u>, Simon and Schuster, 1944

Will Durant, <u>The Story of Civilization, The Age of Faith</u>, Simon and Schuster, 1950

Will Durant, <u>The Story of Civilization: The Reformation</u>, Simon and Schuster, 1957

Will and Ariel Durant, <u>The Story of Civilization: The Age of Reason Begins</u>, Simon & Schuster, 1961

Will and Ariel Durant, <u>The Story of Civilization: The Age of Louis XIV</u>, Simon & Schuster, 1963

Will and Ariel Durant, <u>The Story of Civilization: The Age of Voltaire</u>, Simon & Schuster, 1965

Will and Ariel Durant, <u>The Story of Civilization, Rousseau and Revolution</u>, Simon and Schuster, 1967

Will and Ariel Durant, <u>The Story of Civilization: The Age of Napoleon</u>, Simon & Schuster, 1975

Stewart C. Easton, <u>A Brief History of the Western World</u>, Barnes & Noble, 1966

Stewart C. Easton, <u>World Since 1918</u>, Barnes and Noble, 1966

George Fasel, <u>Europe in Upheaval, The Revolutions of 1848</u>, Rand McNally, 1970

Paul Friedlander, <u>Plato, An Introduction</u>, Princeton University Press, 1958

Francois Furet and Denis Richet, <u>(The) French Revolution</u>, The Macmillan Company, 1965/1970

Helen Gardner, Horst De La Croix and Richard Tansey, <u>Art Through the Ages</u>, Harcourt, Brace and World, 1970

Leo Gershoy, The Era of the French Revolution, 1789-1799 Ten Years that Shook the World, Litton Educational Publishers, D. Van Norstrand Company, 1957

Felix Gilbert, The End of the European Era, 1890 to the Present, W.W. Norton and Company, 1970

L. Carrington Goodrich, A Short History of the Chinese People, Harper and Row, 1943/1969

John and Mary Gribben, Schrodinger's Kittens and the Search for Reality, Little Brown and Company, 1995

Oron J. Hale, The Great Illusion 1900-1914, Harper and Row, 1971

George Heard Hamilton, 19th and 20th Century Art, Prentice Hall and Harry M. Abrams, Inc. 1970

Ragnhild Hatton, Europe in the Age of Louis XIV, Harcourt, Brace and World, 1969

E,J Hobsbawm, The Age of Revolution 1789-1848, The New American Library, 1962

C. Warren Hollister, Medieval Europe, A Short History, John Wiley & Sons, 1968

Sarah Janssen, senior editor, The World Almanac and Book of Facts, Infobase, 2018

Charles A, Jayne Jr, "Cycles" in Encyclopedia of Astrology, Nicholas Devore, editor, Philosophical Library, 1947

William Langer, ed., J.H.Hexter, Richard Pipes, Western Civilization: The Struggle for Empire to Europe in the Modern World, Harper & Row, 1968

Joseph Machlis, The Enjoyment of Music, W.W. Norton & Co., 1963

Ellen McCaffery, Graphic Astrology, Macoy Publishing Company, 1952

Steve McIntosh, Integral Consciousness and the Future of Evolution, Paragon House, 2007

E. Alan Meece, Horoscope for the New Millennium, Llewellyn, 1997

Michelson, Neil F. The American Ephemeris for the 20th Century. ACS Publications, 1983

Michelson, Neil F. The American Ephemeris for the 21st Century. ACS Publications, 1982

William L. O'Neill, Coming Apart, An Informal History of America in the 1960s, Quadrangle/The New York Times Book Co., 1971

Rosicrucian Fellowship, Simplified Scientific Ephemeris, 1880s to 1990s

Theodore Roszak, The Making of a Counter Culture, Doubleday & Company, 1969

Martin Shapiro, ed. The Constitution of the United States, Appleton Century Crofts, Meredith Publishing Company, 1966

Charlene Spretnak, The Spiritual Dimension of Green Politics, Bear and Company, 1986

Stahlman and Gingerich, Solar and Planetary Longitudes for Years -2500 – 2000, University of Wisconsin, 1963.

William Strauss and Neil Howe, The Fourth Turning: What the Cycles of History Tell Us About America's Next Rendezvous with Destiny. New York: Broadway Books, 1997

J.L.Talmon, Romanticism and Revolt, Europe 1815-1848, Harcourt, Brace and World, 1970

Richard Tarnas, Cosmos and Psyche, Viking Penguin Group, 2006

Richard Tarnas, The Passion of the Western Mind, Ballantine Books, 1991

Tom Wolfe, The Electric Kool-Aid Acid Test, Bantam Books, 1968

Zim, Baker, Stars, Simon and Schuster, 1956

Glossary

A.D. Anno Domini, or year of our Lord, meaning the number of years since the presumed birth of Jesus, the most common way to designate a year in history. Nowadays C.E. for Common Era or Christian Era is the more commonly used abbreviation. B.C. for Before Christ refers to the years before Jesus. This is also written as B.C.E. for Before the Common Era or Christian Era.

Affliction. A square or opposition, aspects considered to be difficult or challenging.

Age. A long period of hundreds of years, defined by a 493-year conjunction cycle of Neptune and Pluto, a Triple Conjunction of the Transcendental Trinity lasting 3940 years, or one of twelve 2140 periods in the Precession of the Equinox Cycle (polar wobble). The New Age is an Age that is beginning soon or just underway.

Air signs. Social, intellectual, inventive, diplomatic, idealistic signs Gemini, Libra and Aquarius.

Angles. (1) The four most powerful points of the horoscope; the Ascendant, Midheaven, Descendant and Nadir. They are, respectively, the Eastern horizon (1st house cusp), the zenith or point overhead (10th house cusp), the Western horizon (7th house cusp) and the point below (4th house cusp). When planets are located on an angle at a particular place on Earth, they are most powerful at that location. (2) Aspects.

Angular. A planet on an angle, or in one of the angular houses: the 1st, 4th, 7th & 10th. These houses correspond in meaning with the cardinal signs.

Annular eclipse. A solar eclipse leaving a ring of sunlight because the Moon appears too small to block the Sun completely. It is almost as significant as a total eclipse.

Ascendant (A.C.). The Eastern horizon over which the planets and signs rise every day; the rising sign; cusp of the 1st house. In a chart the Ascendant represents the personality, mood, attitude or health of a person or people.

Aspects. Angles assumed by the planets in relation to one another. The most important aspects are the conjunction (0 degrees), opposition (180 degrees), square (90 degrees), trine (120 degrees) and sextile (60 degrees).

Asteroids. Planetary fragments found between the orbits of Mars and Jupiter. Some astrologers attribute meanings to the largest ones: Ceres, Pallas, Juno and Vesta.

Axis Age. The time in history after a triple conjunction of Uranus, Neptune and Pluto when a great awakening and transformation happens whose impact lasts for 4000 years.

B.C. Years Before Christ. Also commonly written as B.C.E. for Before the Common Era.

C.E. Year of the Christian Era that presumably began at Jesus' birth. Also known as A.D.

Cadent. The 3rd, 6th, 9th and 12th houses, whose meanings correspond to the mutable signs. They are especially concerned with travel, communication and adjustment.

Cardinal. Signs of leadership, assertion, initiative: Aries, Cancer, Libra and Capricorn.

Centaurs. A group of minor planets and small objects that orbit the Sun between the orbits of Jupiter and Neptune. Chiron was the first centaur to be discovered in 1977.

Chart. A horoscope cast for the exact time of an earthly or heavenly event. A complete chart includes houses as well as signs and aspects.

Chiron. A small planetoid or huge comet discovered in 1977 between the orbits of Saturn and Uranus. It represents "the wounded healer" and a bridge to the transcendent. The first of the centaurs to be known, many others of similar size were discovered in the early 1990s.

Conjunction, conjunct. Alignment, or 0-degree angle, between two or more planets, intensifying and focusing their power and beginning a new mutual cycle.

Constellations. Mythical pictures formed by our imagination out of the patterns of the stars in the sky. The constellations of the zodiac are not the signs, although they corresponded to them about 2000 years ago and have the same names.

Critical Degree. In this book, this refers to the degree in which a conjunction occurred that represented a dynamic transformation. A planet(s) or eclipse that returns to this degree, re-stimulates that ongoing process, and may indicate an event related to one at the time of the original conjunction.

Cusp. The border or boundary between two signs or houses.

Cycle. A recurring period between the same or similar events in the heavens or on Earth. It can be used to predict the return of a similar event.

Degree. 1/360th of the zodiac, approximately the motion of the Sun in one day. Each sign has 30 degrees, and each degree has a Sabian Symbol that describes its meaning.

Descendant (D.C.). The Western horizon where signs and planets set every day; the cusp of the 7th house. It rules relationships, war and diplomacy.

Direct (D) or (SD). A planet turns direct when it resumes forward motion after retrograding and appearing to turn stationary. When turning direct, a planet's energy is intensified and surges forth in outward expression.

Earth signs. Practical, worldly, cautious, constructive, consolidating signs Taurus, Virgo and Capricorn.

Eclipse. (1) A New Moon during which the Moon blocks the Sun's light. (2) A Full Moon during which the Earth blocks the Moon's light. Eclipses represent sudden change and can leave their mark on affairs for several years.

Elements. Basic four states of the natural and psychological world: Fire, Earth, Air and Water. Each sign is associated with one of the elements. Fire signs are vital and creative. Earth signs are practical and constructive. Air signs are social and mental. Water signs are emotional and intuitive. The fifth element is also referred to as Ether, Space or Spirit.

Ephemeris. A book which lists the zodiacal longitude of the planets and other information about their position and movement in the sky.

Equinox. The 2 times during the year when the days and nights are of equal length. The first day of spring is the Vernal Equinox (equal to the first degree, or beginning, of Aries). The first day of fall is the Autumn Equinox (equal to the first degree of Libra).

Eris. Discovered in 2003 as the Iraq War started, it is a "scattered disc" dwarf planet about the size of Pluto (without Charon) that astronomers used to bump Pluto into dwarf planet status along with it. It is considered a disruptive influence and may indicate connection to the galaxy. Being so distant and out of phase with other cycles and orbits, I don't consider it significant.

Factor. Any important aspect or other astrological indicator.

Figure. (1) a chart or horoscope. (2) a pattern of aspects among the planets.

Finger of God. A powerful symbol of creative adjustment. See yod.

Fire signs. Vital, enthusiastic, outgoing signs Aries, Leo and Sagittarius.

First Quarter. The Moon's waxing phase after the New Moon when half the Moon is visible. The waxing square between the Sun and Moon or two other planets in their mutual cycle.

Fixed. Representing stability, stubbornness, power and financial acumen, characteristic of the signs Taurus, Leo, Scorpio and Aquarius.

Full Moon. (1) The Moon seen in the sky as a full, perfect disc. The opposition between Sun and Moon; climax of the lunation cycle. (2) The analogous point in any mutual cycle between planets.

GMT. Greenwich Mean Time. The time zone of England's Greenwich Observatory at 0 degrees longitude; the time for which the positions of the planets are listed in the ephemeris. Now also called UT for Universal Time.

Gender. In astrology, the yin or yang polarity of a sign, similar to feminine and masculine. Yang or masculine signs are aspiring, outgoing and expressive, while yin or feminine signs are reflective, receptive and cautious. Fire and Air signs are yang, and Water and Earth signs are yin.

Grand Cross. 4 planets all squaring and opposing each other. It is a very powerful figure of maximum power, stability, control or conflict.

Grand Trine. 3 or more planets forming a mutual triangle. It is a very powerful, expansive, harmonious figure that tends to excess.

Hard aspect. Opposition, square, semi-square and sesqui-square.
Horoscope. A view of the hour; a map of the solar system as seen from the Earth at a particular time, from which events and persons on Earth can be interpreted.

Houses. 12 segments of space as seen from any particular place on Earth. The planets and signs pass through each house during each day as the Earth rotates on its axis. Each house represents a department of life or sphere of experience.

Inconjunct. A Quincunx, 150-degree aspect of incompatibility and adjustment. Sometimes the semi-sextile is also called an inconjunct.

Ingress. A planet entering a sign, usually referring to the equinox or solstice.

Kuiper Belt. A swarm of minor planets and small objects orbiting around the Sun beyond Neptune. Pluto is the largest member of this belt.

Lights. The Sun and Moon.

Last Quarter. The Moon's waning phase after the Full Moon when half the Moon is visible. The waning square between the Sun and Moon or two other planets in their mutual cycle.

Latitude. Position North or South of the Equator.

Longitude. (1) The point on Earth east or west of Greenwich, England. (2) The degree of the zodiac as measured from the vernal equinox, 0 degrees Aries.

Lunation cycle. The mutual cycle between the Sun and Moon, during which the Moon's light waxes and wanes through phases: New, Crescent, First Quarter, Waxing Gibbous, Full, Waning Gibbous, Last Quarter, Balsamic and back to New.

Midheaven (M.C.). The zenith of the horoscope, or point overhead; top of the chart; cusp of the 10th house. It represents status, career, ambition, the executive, the government. Abbreviated M.C. for the Latin term Medium Coeli or middle of the sky.

Modes. See Qualities.

Moon Nodes. The two intersections between the Earth's orbit around the Sun, and the Moon's orbit around the Earth. The North Node marks when the Sun moves above the Moon's orbit, and the South mode when it moves below it. They are also called the dragon's head and tail and are located opposite to each other. Eclipses happen when the Sun is within about 10 degrees of the Moon Nodes. The North Node indicates what is coming into being, and the South was has already been developed. The very-useful Draconic Zodiac is established by the North Node when it is considered as a 0 Aries point.

Mutable. Adaptable, flexible, distributive, dual, mental, "common" signs: Gemini, Virgo, Sagittarius and Pisces.

Mutual cycle. The moving, recurring relationship of two planets with each other, from one conjunction to the next.

Mutual reception. Two or more planets each in the sign ruled by the other, magnifying the significance of both planets.

Nadir (I.C.). Bottom of the horoscope wheel, or point below; cusp of the 4th house. It represents roots, home, land, the common people, farmers, weather, withdrawal from the world, rebellion against the government, spirituality, new beginnings and endings, the low point of fortune. Abbreviated I.C. or Imum Coeli, meaning bottom of the sky.

Natal. Of the nativity or birth; referring to the birth chart of a person or nation.

New Moon. (1) The Moon when totally dark and invisible. A conjunction between Sun and Moon, start of the lunation cycle. (2) The beginning of any mutual cycle between two planets.

Node. An intersection between orbits of the Sun, Moon and planets. The node between the Earth's orbit around the Sun, and the Moon's orbit around the Earth, is the most important node in astrology. See Moon Nodes above.

Opposition. Two or more planets on opposite sides of the Earth; a 180-degree angle. It is the powerful climax and half-way point in their mutual cycle, fulfilling what began at the conjunction. It represents clarity, schism, conflicts, polarities, revisions; it is a "Full Moon" between two planets.

Orb. The amount of inexactness allowed for an aspect to be considered in effect.

Orbit. One revolution of a planet around the Sun, or any revolution of one body around another.

Partial Eclipse. An eclipse in which the Sun or Moon's light is only partly blocked. It is not as significant as a total eclipse.

Period. A portion or era in time. It usually refers to a repeating cycle.

Phase. (1) An aspect, when a planet has reached a certain critical point in its mutual cycle with another, like the phases of the Moon in which its light waxes and wanes (see Lunation Cycle). (2) a stage in any cyclic or changing period.

Planets. The nine major bodies of the solar system, plus the Moon. Each planet represents a basic human drive. When a planet is located in a sign or house it activates the qualities of that sign or house. Some astrologers also include the four main asteroids and Chiron or other important members of the Centaur or Kuiper belts or other belts as "planets." The planets and their meanings in astrology are summarized at the beginning of Chapter 3. See table below.

Precession. (1) Backward movement of the Equinox through the constellations for about 25,700 years, divided into 12 Ages of about 2140 years, such as the Aquarian or Pisces Age. (2) Progressions of a chart backwards, equating one day before birth with one year before.

Progressions. A technique to interpret the past or future by equating one day after birth with one year of life, also called secondary progressions. One day can also be equated with one month.

Qualities. Modes of behavior and action: cardinal, fixed and mutable. Cardinal signs Aries, Cancer, Libra and Capricorn represent initiative. Fixed signs Taurus, Leo, Scorpio and Aquarius represent concentration of power. Mutable signs Gemini, Virgo, Sagittarius and Pisces represent adaptability.

Quincunx. A stressful or incompatible 150-degree angle between planets, requiring adjustments to be made.

Radical. Referring to the natal or birth chart.

Retrograde (R). After turning stationary, a retrograde planet appears to move backward through the zodiac as the Earth passes it, restraining its energy or turning it inward. It symbolizes events reversing their direction.

Return. Important milestone when the Sun or a planet returns to its original place in a horoscope.

Rising. A sign or planet on the Ascendant; coming over the horizon. In a horoscope it may signify increasing prominence or fortune.

Ruler. The planet associated with a sign or house because of its similar nature. The place where the ruler of a sign or house is will tell us more about what it means in a chart. The planet ruling the Ascendant is significant, often called the ruler of the chart.

Sabian Symbol. A mythical image that represents the meaning of each zodiacal degree.

Saeculum. Originally a 100-year cycle in Roman Times, authors Strauss and Howe define it as an 84-year cycle in American history of four turnings that are analogous to the seasons.

Semi-sextile. A 30-degree angle between planets, representing a developing trend.

Semi-square. A 45-degree angle between planets; an angle of friction about half as important as a square. It can represent constructive energy.

Sesqui-square. A 135-degree angle similar in effect to a semi-square.

Sextile. A 60-degree angle between planets considered harmonious, constructive, mentally stimulating and artistic in effect.

Sidereal. Astrologers who use the zodiac of constellations instead of signs are called sidereal astrologers. The sidereal zodiac has now shifted back almost one constellation from the tropical zodiac of signs based on the seasons. Sidereal time (S.T.) refers to the daily movement of stars (or signs) instead of the sun and is used to find the Ascendant and houses of the horoscope.

Signs. 30-degree segments of the zodiac measured from the vernal equinox. The Sun sign represents Earth's position in its yearly cycle around the Sun. The planets move "in" the signs as they move around the Sun as seen from the Earth. Each sign takes its meaning from its place on the cycle between one vernal equinox and the next. Signs are not constellations. See toward the end of Chapter 3 for information on the 12 signs, and see the table below.

Singleton. (1) One planet alone in at least half the sky relative to other planets, making that planet a powerful focal point. (2) Any other way in which one planet stands out in significance from the others.

Solstice. (1) Longest day of the year, and first day of Summer (equal to 0 degrees Cancer). (2) shortest day of the year, and first day of Winter (equal to 0 degrees Capricorn).

Square. A 90 degree or right angle between planets, bringing energy and conflict between the things they represent. A Quarter phase.

Stationary (S). A planet which appears to stand still as the Earth passes close to it in space, greatly magnifying its power and significance. After turning stationary, a planet moves backward (retrograde, R) or forward (direct, D).

Succedent. The 2nd, 5th, 8th and 11th houses, corresponding in meaning to the fixed signs. They are especially concerned with finances.

Stellium. Three or more planets in conjunction.

T-square. A planet squaring two others which are themselves in opposition, symbolizing maximum tension, energy and conflict.

Total eclipse. The most powerful kind of eclipse; light is completely blocked (see eclipse)

Transcendental Trinity. Uranus, Neptune and Pluto. See Chapter 2.

Transit. The current position of a planet. When it crosses another planet's original place in a horoscope, it affects everything connected with that planet in the chart.

Trine. A 120-degree angle between planets considered to be harmonious, invigorating, expansive, frivolous and/or visionary in effect.

Triple Conjunction (1) As used in this book, a conjunction among three planets. (2) A conjunction that happens three times because the faster planet goes retrograde soon after the first conjunction and makes a second conjunction, and then turns direct and makes a third.

Tropical. The zodiac based on the seasons, rather than constellations. At 0 degrees Cancer the Sun is directly overhead at the Tropic of Cancer; 0 degrees Capricorn, at the Tropic of Capricorn.

UT. Universal Time. An even more accurate version of GMT.

Water signs. Emotional, nurturing, intuitive, dissolving, transforming signs Cancer, Scorpio and Pisces.

Waxing and Waning. Increasing or decreasing in light or power, as in the phases of the Moon.

Yod. The "finger of God" pattern; a planet in quincunx to two others in sextile. It indicates adjustment through a creative outlet, adjustment through seeking of knowledge, and intuitive abilities through union of higher self and conscious mind.

Zodiac. (1) The path in space through which the planets and Earth orbit the Sun, and the 12 signs which describe this cyclic path. (2) The 12 constellations of the same name as the signs through which the planets pass as they orbit the Sun. The signs and the constellations are now about 25 degrees apart due to the precession of the equinoxes.

SYMBOL	SIGN	QUALITY	ELEMENT	GENDER	RULING PLANET(S)
♈	Aries	Cardinal	Fire	Masculine	Mars ♂
♉	Taurus	Fixed	Earth	Feminine	Venus ♀
♊	Gemini	Mutable	Air	Masculine	Mercury ☿
♋	Cancer	Cardinal	Water	Feminine	Moon ☽
♌	Leo	Fixed	Fire	Masculine	Sun ☉
♍	Virgo	Mutable	Earth	Feminine	Mercury ☿ / Chiron ⚷
♎	Libra	Cardinal	Air	Masculine	Venus ♀
♏	Scorpio	Fixed	Water	Feminine	Mars ♂ / Pluto ♇
♐	Sagittarius	Mutable	Fire	Masculine	Jupiter ♃
♑	Capricorn	Cardinal	Earth	Feminine	Saturn ♄
♒	Aquarius	Fixed	Air	Masculine	Saturn ♄ / Uranus ♅
♓	Pisces	Mutable	Water	Feminine	Jupiter ♃ / Neptune ♆

The North Moon Node's location is marked with ☊ or ☊
The South Node, at the opposite point, is marked with ☋

Made in the USA
Middletown, DE
03 February 2020

3R00197